THE GOVERNMENTS
OF THE
BRITISH EMPIRE

MACMILLAN AND CO., Limited
LONDON · BOMBAY · CALCUTTA · MADRAS
MELBOURNE

THE MACMILLAN COMPANY
NEW YORK · BOSTON · CHICAGO
DALLAS · ATLANTA · SAN FRANCISCO

THE MACMILLAN COMPANY
OF CANADA, LIMITED
TORONTO

THE GOVERNMENTS

OF THE

BRITISH EMPIRE

BY

ARTHUR BERRIEDALE KEITH

D.C.L., D.LITT., F.B.A.

OF THE INNER TEMPLE, BARRISTER-AT-LAW, AND ADVOCATE OF THE SCOTTISH
BAR ; REGIUS PROFESSOR OF SANSKRIT AND COMPARATIVE PHILOLOGY, AND
LECTURER ON THE CONSTITUTION OF THE BRITISH EMPIRE, AT THE UNIVERSITY
OF EDINBURGH ; FORMERLY ASSISTANT SECRETARY TO THE IMPERIAL CONFERENCE

MACMILLAN AND CO., LIMITED

ST. MARTIN'S STREET, LONDON

1936

PRINTED IN GREAT BRITAIN
BY R. & R. CLARK, LIMITED, EDINBURGH

PREFACE

SINCE this work was written certain matters of great importance have occurred which should be briefly recorded in their bearing on the statements made in this work.

The decisions of the Privy Council on June 6 in the cases of the *British Coal Corporation* v. *The King* and *Moore* v. *Attorney-General for the Irish Free State* accord the widest interpretation to the legislative authority given by the Statute of Westminster, 1931, to the Dominions. The former case establishes the right of the Canadian Parliament to abolish the appeal by special leave from Canadian Courts in criminal cases, on the ground that Section 2 of the statute authorises the Parliament to override the statutory power given to the Crown by the Judicial Committee Act, 1844, to admit appeals at discretion; that Section 3 enables the Parliament to give the abolition extra-territorial effect as regards action to be taken in England, and that the Parliament can validly deal with any royal prerogative connected with matters within its sphere of authority. The latter case is even more important. It establishes the validity of the abolition of the appeal from the Supreme Court of the Irish Free State, and on the widest grounds. It would have been open to the Court to rule that the power to abolish was consistent with the Treaty of 1921, because the Treaty gave the

State the position of Canada, and Canada had now the power to abolish, and that the treaty remained, as it was declared in 1922 by the Constituent Assembly to be, the supreme law of the Free State, a view asserted as recently as December 1934 by the Supreme Court of the Free State. But the Privy Council, following the rules of English law, ruled that the sole legal basis of the constitution was the British Act of 1922 approving it, and that since the Statute of Westminster that Act could be varied at will by the Free State, and the restrictions on constitutional change imposed could be repealed by a simple Act of the Irish Parliament. The Privy Council thus, so far as it can, emancipates the Free State Parliament from all legal fetters, a view which naturally must render it very difficult for the Supreme Court to insist on its interpretation of December last, though it is true that the Supreme Court is not bound by Privy Council decisions since the date of the abolition of the appeal.

The Privy Council decision is open to criticism in its assertion that the statute has empowered the Free State to abrogate the Treaty of 1921. Naturally this is terminologically inaccurate; the abrogation like the making of treaties is a matter of executive, not legislative, power. What is meant is that the Free State can, in its view, legally remove any provision of the treaty from the statute-book of the State in which it was inserted by the constitution. Thus the State could repeal the authority of Article 7 of the treaty under which British forces are lawfully in occupation of Irish territory. But, of course, that is quite irrelevant to the binding force inter-Imperially, or as the Free State holds internationally, of the treaty, which continues to exist, unless and until it is abrogated by the assent of the two Governments, parties to it, or it is formally repudiated by the Free State on the score that it was procured by force majeure or that relations have so changed since its conclusion that it has ceased to possess validity. But neither of these contentions would be legally convincing.

The judgments lend force to the view that the legislation of the Union of South Africa in 1934, conferring on the Governor-General power to exercise the external prerogatives of the Crown, including that of declaring neutrality, may be valid in strict law. They lend also a certain measure of support to General Hertzog's claim that it establishes the right of secession by unilateral declaration. In his policy speech on March 12, 1935, he stressed the absolute refusal of himself and his fellow Afrikaans-speaking citizens of the Union to co-operate with their English-speaking co-citizens on the basis of a freedom derived from "an integral and indivisible part of the British Empire". This negation of permanency of the British connection renders it difficult to arrange for the transfer of Basutoland, the Bechuanaland Protectorate, and Swaziland to Union control, especially as the power of disallowance of Union legislation has been abolished, and the safeguards inserted in the schedule to the South Africa Act, 1909, under which transfer was rendered possible, could not be made effective in the manner then contemplated. In the meantime transfer is delayed, in the hope that co-operation between the administrations of the Union and the territories may lead to ultimate acceptance by the natives of the desirability of transfer. In such an event it might be possible to safeguard their position by an agreement between the British and Union Governments and the tribal chiefs providing for inter-Imperial arbitration of difficulties.

The unfettered character of the executive was displayed by the conclusion of the accord with Germany on naval limitation without consulting prior to agreement Parliament, though that accord violates clauses of the Treaty of Versailles to which formal approval was accorded by Parliament in 1919, and by the remarkable offer to enable Ethiopia to buy off Italian attack by cession of territory in return for the transfer to it of a strip of land giving access to the sea. The episode was marked by confusion in governmental explanations, the Colonial Secretary having at first thought that British territory was involved, whereas the area in question is merely under British protection. It was also rather surprisingly indicated that it was not deemed necessary to obtain the royal assent prior to offering such a transfer. The matter having been dropped on the refusal of Italy to consider the project, the issues were not finally explored. It seems, however, clear (1) that His Majesty must be consulted before any suggestion of parting with territory under his protection is made to a foreign power; (2) that the transfer of rights of protection requires consultation with those affected by the proposed transfer; and (3) that, as protected territory is closely akin to British territory, the rule that Parliament should be asked to approve formally any transfer should be applied, so that the agreement to transfer should be made expressly dependent on approval by Parliament, as in the case of the cession of the Dindings.

The complexity and gravity of foreign relations, the whole validity of the League of Nations being challenged by the attitude of Italy towards Ethiopia, has resulted in the formal recognition of Mr Eden as Minister for League of Nations Affairs, though also ranking as minister without portfolio. The charge of foreign affairs is thus divided with the Secretary of State, an inexperienced minister being appointed to that office, but unity of action is secured by the superintendence of the Prime Minister and the control of the Cabinet, which takes an increasing interest in foreign affairs. Mr Eden's appointment rendered necessary some modification of the legislation dealing with re-election of ministers which authorised persons appointed ministers without portfolio to sit without re-election to the Commons, and at the same time authority was obtained for the presence in the Commons of a second Under-Secretary for Foreign Affairs, to aid him in his special task. The inclusion of two ministers without portfolio in the ministry of Mr Baldwin raised the number of the Cabinet to twenty-two, and the fixing of their salaries at £3000 emphasised the lack of system as regards ministerial salaries, which it is proposed to review. Moreover, Sir H. Samuel stressed the fact that, including private secretaries, the number of official posts in the Government was about ninety, a point of great importance as emphasising the control which the Cabinet exercises over the Commons through its power to reward the ambition of supporters who are completely loyal.

In connection with the formation of the Cabinet Mr Lansbury fell into a common error in thinking that reappointment was requisite in the case of ministers who are asked to remain in their posts. In fact, of course, the position is that all ministers are supposed to place their offices at the disposal of a new Prime Minister, but in law they still hold them until they formally surrender them in the appropriate mode, so that, if asked to remain in office in their old posts, they merely accept the request, without formal reappointment of any kind.

A further issue has been suggested by the determination of the Labour party in the constituency of the Speaker to contest his seat at the general election. The tradition that the Speaker should not be opposed is essentially bound up with the convention which requires from him absolute impartiality and non-intervention in political issues, and it is manifestly unfair that a member who cannot defend himself should be attacked. But it is true that a constituency loses by having as member one unable to act on its behalf in political issues, and it has been suggested that the Speaker, when elected, should be deemed to sit for a special constituency, remaining a member of the Commons so long as he is elected Speaker, while his former constituency is contested in the usual way on a vacancy occurring. It has been objected that the

Speaker would thus lose touch with his fellow-members, but the suggestion seems of dubious validity; as matters stand he already occupies a quite special position apart from all the other members.

The passing of the Government of India Act, 1935, indubitably marks the opening of a new chapter in Indian history. With all its limitations and grave dangers for India and the United Kingdom, it offers to India the possibility of responsible government in the provinces in a substantial degree quite different from the simulacrum of the Montagu-Chelmsford scheme. Much more doubtful is the effort to create a federation based on the intermingling of autocracy with the more conservative elements of British Indian political life. The most interesting change made in the House of Lords was that under which the Council of State was made as regards British India directly elected with 75 general seats, 6 for the scheduled castes, 6 for women, 49 for Muhammadans, and 4 for Sikhs. The electorate is to number about four or five times that— 25,000—for the present Council of State, and the qualifications will be high, as will be those for the upper houses in the Provinces. The demand of the Liberal party and others for direct election to the lower house, which the Government of India had favoured, is thus curiously countered. The upper chamber becomes decidedly more qualified to claim equality of rights with the lower, but at the expense of symmetry. Moreover, as direct election for the lower is clearly inevitable in due course, the desirable differentiation between the houses may be difficult to establish, as there will be strong resistance to any departure from direct election once introduced. The obvious risk is that India may be hampered in advance by the resistance of a completely reactionary upper chamber to the comparative democracy of the lower house. It must, however, be added that, despite efforts to extend the franchise, it has been found impossible to make any provision to secure that the interests of the poorer classes of the people shall be duly considered by the legislatures.

In view of the renewed insistence in the Free State on the desirability of republican status it may be added that there is considerable misunderstanding of the effect of a declaration of a republic, if made unilaterally, on the nationality of Free State citizens resident in the United Kingdom. It is clear that their nationality could not be affected by anything short of a British Act of Parliament, which alone could declare them aliens or oblige them to obtain permits to work in the United Kingdom, and it is inconceivable that persons who, though under Irish law citizens, desired to remain British subjects in the United Kingdom would be deprived of that status by a British Parliament. In the State itself Irish legislation has terminated the operation of the common and statute law of British nationality, but that has no effect to override British law outside the State; where the two collide British courts will clearly follow British law. It is possible, however, that it may be found practicable ultimately to arrive at a solution under which an Irish Republic would replace the Free State within the

British Commonwealth of Nations. So many radical changes have taken place that legal ingenuity ought to be able to dispose of such an issue, especially now that the Privy Council has definitely denied its right to hear appeals from the Free State.

It is most satisfactory to record that from July 1 Canada has given effect to the principle that the United Kingdom should be accorded most-favoured-nation treatment by extending to it and to the Union of South Africa the benefits of the duties given to France and Poland under her treaties. This action is entirely in accord with the consistent attitude of the British Government in refusing to extend to foreign countries benefits denied to parts of the Commonwealth; but it is interesting to note that in the House of Lords the Government successfully resisted an amendment to impose on India the obligation of giving to the United Kingdom such treatment. The anxiety of the British Government to further Dominion trade has been displayed in the generous arrangements made to assist Australia and New Zealand to maintain exports of meat products to the United Kingdom even at some risk of injury to British agriculture.

Critics of the "New Despotism" deplored by the Lord Chief Justice have learned with regret that the Government does not propose to take any general action on the recommendations of the Report on Ministers' Powers, and in fact in the current legislation on housing and prevention of ribbon development the ministry has conferred, despite protests in the Commons, most extensive authority on departments free from judicial control. Curiously enough, little notice has been taken of the most objectionable anomaly of all, the rule that the Postmaster-General pays compensation in respect of loss in the post of registered articles at his sole discretion, in complete disregard of the principle that no person should act as judge in his own cause,[1] and ignoring the natural tendency of the officials on whose advice he must act to disclaim the probability of losses due to their fellow-employees and to protect post-office funds. But far the most serious issue is the power given to deprive house owners of any substantial compensation for property on the decision of local or central executive authorities, whose zeal for public interests may blind them to the injustice of ignoring property rights.

Proof of the close control of expenditure is given by the discussion between the Public Accounts Committee and the Treasury regarding the date of repayment of the advance from the Civil Contingencies Fund to purchase the *Codex Sinaiticus*, the former holding that repayment should have been made in the year of the advance, the latter that repayment in the following year was proper and convenient. Apparently when repayment can be made in the year, it should be provided for in an estimate introduced before its close.

Some of the historical matter in this work is taken with minor changes from *The Constitution, Administration and Laws of the Empire*, written at the request of the late Sir Charles Lucas for a series on the Empire

---

[1] Recently affirmed in *Wingrove* v. *Morgan*, [1934] Ch. 423, 431. See also Anson, *The Crown* (ed. Keith), ii. 342.

which was issued contemporaneously with the Empire Exhibition of 1924. But in the main this is essentially a new work, so drastic have been the changes in the structure of the Empire in the last decade. In my former work, and in the preliminary preparation of this, I owed much to my late wife, and I have now to thank Messrs Macmillan & Co. for undertaking its publication, and Messrs R. & R. Clark for the care taken in printing it. For further discussion of controversial issues I may refer to my *Letters on Imperial Relations, Indian Reform, Constitutional and International Law,* 1916–1935.

A. BERRIEDALE KEITH

THE UNIVERSITY OF EDINBURGH,
July 27, 1935

P.S.—On the rising of Parliament it was announced that the list of those associated with the main Committee of Imperial Defence included the Lord President of the Council and the Home Secretary, a significant reminder of the latter's new responsibility for preparations to safeguard the civil population in case of air attack.

CONTENTS

PART I

THE FRAMEWORK OF THE IMPERIAL CONSTITUTION

CHAPTER I

CHAPTER II

CHAPTER III

PART II

THE GOVERNMENTS OF THE EMPIRE

CHAPTER I

CHAPTER II

CHAPTER III

CHAPTER IV

CHAPTER XI

TABLE OF CASES

PART I

THE FRAMEWORK OF THE IMPERIAL CONSTITUTION

B

CHAPTER I

THE NATURE AND SOURCES OF THE CONSTITUTIONAL LAW OF THE EMPIRE

1. *The Nature of Constitutional Law and Constitutional Conventions*

CONSTITUTIONAL law, as understood in the British Empire, includes all those rules which prescribe the distribution, or regulate the exercise, of the sovereign authority in the State, define the obligations of the subject towards the State, and lay down the rights which the State permits its subjects to assert even against itself. From this point of view the theory of sovereignty is largely a matter of indifference; the sovereign power for the constitutional lawyer is composed of those varied authorities by whom rights, that is, the capacity of one man to control the actions of another with the assent of the State, are created, and the acts or forbearances necessary for their maintenance enforced. Nor is the constitutional lawyer concerned with the problems of the limits of State interference and the theory of legislation, matters which properly appertain to the political philosopher. But he is directly concerned with the constitution of the executive government, the powers of the Crown, of ministers, and the Civil Service; the composition and authority of the legislature; the position of the judiciary; and the interrelation of these great branches of the administration of the State. All these authorities have rights against one another and against the general mass of the people, and the people in their turn have rights against the State. His task is not primarily historical, but he has constant need of history to explain the actual developments which he attempts to describe. Moreover, he must trespass in some measure into the realms of international law, for, though the rights of States among themselves are not within his sphere of interest, a vital element of the constitution of a State depends on the necessity of having an organisation to deal with other States, and the constitution must be so framed as to permit effect being given to the international obligations of the State.

This definition, it will be seen, leaves no room for an independent treatment of administrative law, which is merely an aspect of constitutional law, and its fundamental principles are therefore included in this work.

Complex as constitutional law always is, its complication is greatest by far in the case of the Empire, which has grown rather by hazard than by conscious purpose, developing in the process protean shapes of constitutional relations. The process has been rendered possible by the British willingness to compromise and reluctance to insist on strictly logical results. Lord John Russell, in 1839, proved conclusively that responsible government was impossible for any Colony, but proceeded in effect to concede all that the Colonies could then desire or assimilate. The Dominions grew into sister nations without legal change of status, and the Statute of Westminster, 1931, virtually gave formal sanction only to a *fait accompli*. When established categories fail to provide a due place for Indian progress, new ideas are evolved and made in some measure effective. The same political skill manifested itself at an earlier date in the sphere of the constitution of England itself, and its inheritance in the Dominions is attested in the creation of institutions so disparate, yet each so effective in its own way, as the federations of Canada and the Commonwealth of Australia and the semi-federal constitution of the Union of South Africa. Less ingenuity has perhaps been shown in the realm of municipal and local government, a topic which, though it falls essentially within the sphere of constitutional law, is yet of relatively minor importance, and hence will not receive treatment in this work.

The possibility of the development of so flexible and ingenious a network of relations has been in large measure due to the avoidance of undue legalism. The English constitution, which lies at the root of all the constitutionalism in the Empire, was a creature of gradual development, and, though under the Commonwealth Cromwell advocated the establishment of a rigid constitution, it happily escaped formal definition in any form of fundamental legislation which could not easily be altered. What was enacted in one session of Parliament might be repealed in the next, or by any subsequent Parliament by a simple Act, so that no Parliament could fetter the actions of its successor. The courts were thus exempted from the harassing duty of endeavouring to apply legal principles to the growth of the political organism, a process inimical to progress and tending to weaken the respect felt for the judiciary, which is inevitably in some measure thus involved in political conflicts. The principle of ministerial responsibility is one which could hardly be enacted in set terms without creating attempts to bring to bear on ministers the legal weapons of injunction and mandamus, and it would have been equally dangerous if any effort had been made at the outset of responsible government in the Colonies to lay down in precise terms the nature of the freedom conceded. The omission, which excites the petulant complaints of continental jurists, accustomed to written constitutions and precise definitions, was not accidental. So able a statesman as W. E. Gladstone, in his connection in 1845–6 with colonial affairs, would have been glad to see defined in precise form the subjects on which the Australian Colonies might legislate, unfettered by the Imperial power of intervention, but with a profound statesmanship the unwisdom of the task was finally admitted.

In the result, therefore, the constitutional law of the Empire falls into two different categories, *rules of law*, which are legally binding and which in many cases can be enforced by the law courts, and *conventions*, which in themselves are without legal force, and of which the law courts can take no notice. These conventions cover the most important of constitutional relations and determine the practical meaning of legal enactments. Save in the Irish Free State and the Union of South Africa, the power of the King on advice of the Imperial Government to disallow any Dominion Act is legally intact; constitutional custom has made it all but obsolete; similarly the right of the King to withhold assent from any Imperial Bill is unquestioned, though to exercise it would be revolutionary, and the Governor-General in a Dominion stands in a like position towards any Dominion Bill enacted by the Parliament. Rules that are conventional in the United Kingdom are sometimes formally included in the laws on which Dominion constitutions rest. The annual holding of a session of Parliament rests on usage in the former case, on law in the Dominions and India. The essential financial safe-guard that money votes can be proposed only on the authority of the Government, thus excluding private initiative, is conventional in the United Kingdom, statutory in the Dominions and India. That ministers of Cabinet rank must be members of Parliament is a customary rule in the United Kingdom; in some instances in the Dominions and in India a minister vacates office unless he is, or becomes within a limited period, a member of the legislature. On the other hand, save in the Irish Free State, the fundamental principle of responsible government, that the Crown or its repre-sentative acts on the advice of ministers possessing the support of the lower house of Parliament, is regularly a constitutional convention, without immediate legal sanction. In the United Kingdom and the Dominions alike, the relation and procedure of the two houses of Parliament is regulated in part by formal enactment, but in great measure depends on usage; no court would enquire into any practice such as the form of passing Bills in the United Kingdom.[1]

In binding force conventions differ largely; some are as rigidly observed as any law, while others are mere matters of common practice, as when, in the selection of a Dominion Cabinet in Canada, due regard is had to the claims of the provinces, and in special of the French element in Quebec, to have representation. The con-vention that a Prime Minister must be taken from the House of Commons dates from the passing over of Lord

---

[1] *Edinburgh and Dalkeith Ry. Co.* v. *Wauchope* (1842), 8 Cl. & F., at p. 723.

Curzon in 1923. Ultimately, no doubt, the binding force
of a convention may depend largely on the degree of
illegality in which he who violates a convention finds
himself almost inevitably involved. To ignore French
Canada in the personnel of a Dominion Cabinet might
be politically unwise, but the Prime Minister who did
so would not run any risk of illegality. But the British
Prime Minister who advised the Crown to refrain from
summoning Parliament for a year would find himself
without the means to enforce discipline in the army,
through the lapsing of the Army and Air Force (Annual)
Act, and, though much revenue would still be collected
under the authority of permanent Acts, for many
necessary forms of expenditure authority would be
wholly lacking. The courts, therefore, could at once
be invoked to bring the administration to a discreditable close. Though, therefore, a convention cannot be
directly enforced, its difference from a legal rule is not
absolute, and, on the other hand, it must be remembered
that there does not always exist machinery to enforce
the observance of formal constitutional laws. Neither
in the United Kingdom nor in the Dominions do the
courts claim authority to enforce the performance of
political acts proper; the remedies of injunction to prevent the doing of illegal acts and of mandamus to
compel the performance of legal duties, valuable and
important as they are, are not applicable to such
matters as the summoning and dismissal of the legislature, the formation or dismissal of ministries, and the
exercise by the Crown or by ministers of discretionary
authority.[1] Nor is there any ground for regretting this

---

[1] Cf. *Civilian War Claimants' Association* v. *R.*, [1932] A.C. 14; below,
Chap. VII., s. 4.

lack of judicial power; the courts have neither the means nor the proper qualifications to render effective their intervention in the executive acts of government, just as true legislative functions lie outside their capacity.

The difference between conventions and legal rules is not, as has at times erroneously been suggested, parallel with that between unwritten and written law. Conventions indeed are often unwritten, in the sense that they are not reduced to any formal shape, but this is no necessary part of their nature; the procedure of Parliament in dealing with Bills is formally regulated. Law is often written, but some of the most valuable principles of constitutional law exist only in the pronouncements of the courts, which in theory exist not to enact, but merely to declare the existence of, rules of law. The principle of British jurisprudence that the subject has a remedy, civil or criminal, against any tortious action of an official of the Crown rests on the unwritten law that the King can do no wrong, so that, if wrong is done by one of his officers, the latter cannot plead that he acted under the authority of the Crown. The most important rights of the subject, personal liberty, freedom of speech, of assembly, and of forming associations, and the right to follow such religious observances as he thinks fit, which form parts of the written constitution of the Irish Free State, are none the less legally valid in the United Kingdom because they are protected, not by direct enactment, but by the operation of rules of the common law. The formal inclusion of these rights in the Irish constitution marks a distinct breach with tradition; as lately as 1900 the Commonwealth of Australia constitution, and in 1909 that of the Union of South Africa, were content to leave these principles implicit, while the European practice generally has asserted the rights of the subject, but left them without effective means of enforcement against the State. It is significant that in practice the liberty of the subject has suffered severe infringement in the State under special legislation overriding the constitution, in special the Constitution (Amendment No. 17) Act, 1931.

2. *The Sources of Constitutional Law*

The conventions of the constitution have their source in political usage, which in its turn is dictated by manifold considerations of convenience and expediency, and ultimately stands in more or less close relation with positive legal rules. These rules themselves are either (1) enacted by the legislature or by subordinate authorities by virtue of delegated authority, written law; or (2) they are parts of that vast body of legal principles known as the common law, which lie implicit at the bottom of the life of the community, and are from time to time formally declared by the courts. The term "judge-made law" applied to the latter set of rules expresses a half truth; unquestionably in the Middle Ages the judges were virtually legislators, and were conscious of their creative rôle; even now it is impossible for judges in declaring the law on some abstruse topic not to perform work which is closely akin to that of the legislature, but their aim is in form different, for they are bound by the principles on which they act not to seek to create anything new, but to unfold a principle which is already contained in germ in more general

rules which have already received judicial acknowledgment.

It is the glory of English jurisprudence that the
common law of England lies at the root of the laws of
the greater part of the Empire, a result and reminder
of the fact that it was to English enterprise that colonial
expansion was mainly due. English settlers, it was
early ruled, wherever they went, carried with them the
principles of English law; even if they were largely
Scottish in origin, none the less in Nova Scotia their
common law must be English. It was, however, obvious
that the principles of the common law alone unmodified
by statute would be inadequate, and, in its application
to the Colonies, English lawyers held that the law
which came into being on the foundation of the Colony
included the common law in the narrower sense of that
term, the doctrines of equity, and the statute law as
then existing, subject, however, to the applicability of
such laws to the condition of the new Colony. The
definition of applicability is obviously difficult to frame;
must the law be applicable at the moment of the
foundation of the Colony,[1] or may it be judged[2] by its
suitability at the time when the question of its application arises? Or, as regards a statute, is not the criterion[3]
rather whether the English Act is one based on considerations of local policy, such as a statute affecting
mortmain, or an assertion of general principles? However these questions be decided, once the Colony has
come into being, no English Act can apply to it unless
it appears from its terms that it is intended to be a

[1] *Quan Yick* v. *Hinds* (1905), 2 C.L.R. 345, 356.
[2] *Cooper* v. *Stewart* (1889), 14 App. Cas. 286, *per* Lord Watson.
[3] *Att.-Gen.* v. *Stewart*, 2 Mer. 143, 160, *per* Sir W. Grant, M.R.

piece of Imperial legislation for the Colony, or unless it is made operative by a Colonial Act, in which event the Imperial Act has operation merely as a local Act, subject to change or repeal by the local legislature.

In some cases, however, the Crown became possessed by cession or conquest of territories already occupied by representatives of a civilised power, and in enjoyment of a code of law. The law of England admitted the absolute power of the Crown, so far as was consistent with the terms of cession, to alter the system of law prevailing, but it did not hold that the law was changed by the mere fact of conquest or cession, and, where the Crown refrained from action, the common law remained that prevailing before the British acquisition. Hence it is that old French law, the Coutume de Paris, underlies the law of Quebec and St. Lucia, and the French codes that of Mauritius and Seychelles, while Roman Dutch law has been recognised in Ceylon, the Cape of Good Hope, the Transvaal and Orange Free State, and extended to Natal and Southern Rhodesia, and until lately lingered on in British Guiana. In Trinidad the old Spanish law may still on occasion be referred to, though in all these cases modern enactments have largely remoulded the former basis of the law. From the point of view of constitutional law, however, these divergences from the normal rule are of minor importance. Whatever the local law may be, the fact of conquest or cession introduces automatically the English common law regarding the political rights of the Crown.[1] The cession of Quebec, for instance, introduced, despite the maintenance of the existing civil law, the sovereign authority of the English Crown unaffected by the

[1] Cf. *Ruding* v. *Smith* (1821), 2 Hagg. Con. 371, *per* Lord Stowell.

nature of the rights of the French Crown prior to Chapter I. cession. The local common law becomes of importance only as regards the minor rights of the Crown which are not essentially bound up with its sovereignty; thus it has been held that the priority in regard to payment of debts enjoyed by the Crown in England is not applicable in Quebec.[1] On the other hand, direct suit of the Crown is found in Ceylon as the analogy apparently of the position existing before its acquisition from the Dutch.[2]

Great as is the importance of the common law as forming the foundation of many most important constitutional principles, including the royal prerogative, and the authority of statute law; the machinery of legislation almost inevitably requires statutory regulation, and, though the executive authority of the Crown under the common law is large and important, many new powers have been conferred on the executive by statute to meet the new economic conditions and social developments, while in other cases existing powers have been regulated and defined. Judicial matters have long been the subject of express statutory regulation. The result of the intervention of the legislature has been that in the United Kingdom the prerogative of the Crown, that is to say, its rights at common law, has been entirely abolished as regards legislation proper; the laws of Great Britain, the Irish Free State, and Northern Ireland can be changed only by the authority of the legislature. Under many Acts the King in Council is authorised to make legal rules

---

[1] *Exchange Bank of Canada* v. *R.* (1886), 11 App. Cas. 157.

[2] This is uncertain; it may have developed spontaneously: *Hettihewage Siman Appu* v. *Queen's Advocate* (1884), 9 App. Cas. 571.

which have the force of a statute, but this power is statutory and does not rest on the prerogative. In judicial matters the power of the Crown to establish courts is strictly limited by statute. In the executive sphere alone are there still large tracts in which the prerogative remains unfettered. The sovereign rights of declaring war and making peace,[1] of appointing diplomatic agents and accrediting them to foreign courts, of receiving such representatives of foreign powers, of creating peers and conferring titles of honour, remain almost wholly matters of the prerogative, and the rule that these powers shall normally be exercised on the advice of ministers responsible to Parliament is a convention of the constitution only. The power of the Crown to summon and dissolve Parliament is another case of a fundamental prerogative right, which, however, is limited by the prescription that Parliament cannot endure for more than five years. In military, air, and naval matters the common law rights of the Crown and the duties of the subjects have largely been remoulded by legislation. A peculiarly delicate problem is presented by cases in which, without express limitation of the prerogative, legislation has dealt with a subject matter formerly left to the prerogative. The older rule, not formally renounced by the courts, held that nothing but express words would limit the prerogative, which, therefore, could still be relied on if the statute were inadequate; but the tendency of recent jurisprudence is shown by the decision of the House of Lords [2] that, where legislation is passed

---

[1] Objection has been taken to the use of prerogative to describe these powers, but usage justifies it: Keith, *Responsible Government* (1928), i. 93.

[2] *Att.-Gen.* v. *De Keyser's Royal Hotel*, [1920] A.C. 508.

providing for the taking of property for public purposes on payment of compensation, it must be held, even in the case of taking possession of hotel premises for governmental occupation in war, to supersede any prerogative right which formerly existed to take such property without obligation to pay for it. This decision is an interesting reminder of the triumph of democratic ideas since the days when the Crown lawyers under Charles I. maintained that the prerogative was something so holy and essential that it could not be overridden by any Act of Parliament.

In the rest of the Empire, with the slight limitation which has been noted in the case of territories where the English common law is not in force, the prerogative of the Crown is the same as in England, and is equally subject to limitation and modification by local legislation, in so far as it concerns local authority. But the prerogative also embraces certain rights which are obsolete in England, or inapplicable; thus in any settled territory the Crown has the right to create a constitution with a legislature on the English model with an elective lower house; once created, such a legislature alone can enact laws for that territory. In a conquered or ceded territory the Crown has absolute power to create any form of constitution it likes, but once it creates a constitution with a representative legislature,[1] that is, one in which there is a house one-half at least of whose members are elected, the power to change the constitution is lost, unless indeed it is expressly reserved to the Crown by the instrument creating the representative constitution.[2] The form of this preroga-

---

[1] Colonial Laws Validity Act, 1865, s. 1.
[2] *Campbell* v. *Hall* (1774), 1 Cowp. 204.

tive legislation is varied, Letters Patent under the Great Seal, Orders of the King in Council, or Charters of Justice, but in essence they all come to the same thing; they represent the formal expression of the will of the sovereign expressed with the approval of his Privy Council, the action being taken on the advice of the responsible minister, now the Secretary of State for the Colonies.

In addition to this prerogative legislation, there is the paramount legislative authority of the Imperial Parliament, on which rest the constitutions of the Dominions, with the exception of Newfoundland,[1] of India, and many of the Crown Colonies, while the constitution of the United Kingdom largely depends on this legislation. In the Irish Free State the constitution claims to rest on the will of the people of Ireland, but it was also sanctioned by Imperial Act. Of equal validity with Acts are Orders in Council and regulations made by ministers or other authorities under the express sanction of Acts. The practice has increased steadily of late to enunciate leading principles only in Acts, and to leave details to be prescribed by Order in Council, or by regulations, which are as effective as the Act itself if they do not exceed the authority conferred upon the authority concerned. The validity of an Imperial Act cannot be questioned in any court, but the validity of an Order in Council or regulation may be called in question on the ground that it is *ultra vires.*

In the Empire overseas the same distinction between Acts and Orders in Council, or regulations made under Acts exists, but the Acts of legislatures other than that

---

[1] An Imperial Act, the Newfoundland Act, 1933, has suspended for the moment the constitution; Keith, *Journ. Comp. Leg.* xvi. 25-39.

of the Imperial Parliament are liable to be questioned on the ground that on one ground or another they are *ultra vires*, and therefore are unconstitutional, for in the existing state of the Empire the Imperial Parliament alone possesses full sovereign power and absolute latitude of legislation.[1] But since the status of the Union Act, 1934, of the Union of South Africa that legislature claims undisputed authority to legislate for the Union.

---

[1] Thus in 1935 the power of Canada under the Statute of Westminster, 1931, ss. 2 and 3, to abolish in criminal causes appeal to the Privy Council was questioned in *British Coal Corporation* v. *The King*, [1935] A.C. 500. Similarly as regards the abolition of all appeals from the Irish Free State: *Moore* v. *Att.-Gen.* [1935] A.C. 484. See Preface.

CHAPTER II

THE CONSTITUTIONAL STRUCTURE OF THE EMPIRE

1. *The Component Parts of the Empire*

THE term British Empire has only recently received a formal legal definition and then only for certain specific purposes. It has long been familiar as a designation of all those territories which are subject to the executive authority of the British Crown; the sense in which the term is used in the Treaty of Peace with Germany of 1919 and the subsequent Treaties of Peace. In recent legislation it has been necessary to define the term in carrying out the doctrine of Imperial preference; thus in the Import Duties Act, 1932, the British Empire is defined to mean "His Majesty's dominions outside the United Kingdom, including all parts of India, territories under His Majesty's protection, territories in respect of which a mandate of the League of Nations is being exercised by the Government of a Dominion within the meaning of the Statute of Westminster, 1931, and any territory in respect of which a mandate of the League of Nations is being exercised by the Government of the United Kingdom". To complete the meaning of the British Empire in general, there must, of course, be added the United Kingdom itself. The definition would not include Egypt, for the protectorate over that country was terminated in 1922.

The expression British Commonwealth of Nations is of recent origin in a technical sense. It appears in the Treaty of 1921 with the Irish Free State as synonymous with British Empire, and when officially used in later documents, the terms are normally applicable to the same territories. But the expressions have differences in aspect; when British Commonwealth of Nations is employed, the tendency is to emphasise not the unity suggested by the term British Empire, but the fact that the Empire consists of a number of units which are declared by the Imperial Conference of 1926 to be autonomous communities within the British Empire, equal in status, in no way subordinate one to another in any aspect of their domestic or external affairs, though united by a common allegiance to the Crown and freely associated as members of the British Commonwealth of Nations. Units thus recognised as autonomous and equal in 1926 were: the United Kingdom with its dependencies; the Dominion of Canada; the Commonwealth of Australia with its dependencies; the Dominion of New Zealand with its dependencies; the Union of South Africa; the Irish Free State; and Newfoundland; but under the Newfoundland Act, 1933, Newfoundland has, for the time being, surrendered her autonomy and taken the position of a dependency of the United Kingdom.

India, on the other hand, has been assured that the ultimate goal of British policy is her attaining of dominion status, a fact foreshadowed in 1919, when there was accorded to India membership of the League of Nations on the same footing as the Dominions.

The Empire Commonwealth, therefore, can be divided as follows:

I.—(A) The United Kingdom of Great Britain and Northern Ireland, including England, of which Wales is an integral part in law, Scotland and Northern Ireland.

Northern Ireland possesses, for legal purposes, a Parliament and a Government responsible to it.

(B) The Dependencies of the United Kingdom.

1. Within the British Islands:

Isle of Man; Jersey and Guernsey (including Alderney and Sark).

These islands possess legislatures which are not wholly subject to control by the Imperial Government, but the executive government is under Imperial control.

2. Outside the British Islands:

(*a*) Southern Rhodesia, a Colony possessing a responsible government in nearly all internal matters, subject to certain restrictions in the interest of the native population, but in external matters controlled by the Imperial Government.

(*b*) Malta, a Colony which in matters strictly internal enjoys responsible government, but, in all questions of Imperial interest, is under Imperial government and control. The responsible government constitution, however, has been suspended since 1933.

(*c*) Ceylon, a Colony in which the executive government is carried on under the supreme control of the Governor by the Council of State, which also acts as the legislature and which thus in internal affairs has a limited form of responsible government, while in external affairs it is entirely controlled by the Imperial Government.

(*d*) Colonies in which the administration is carried on by public officers under the control of the Secretary of State for the Colonies:

(1) Colonies possessing an elected House of Assembly and nominated Legislative Council (a representative government): Bahamas; Barbados; Bermuda.

(2) Colonies possessing a partly elected Legislative Council, the constitution of which does not provide for an official majority: British Guiana; Cyprus. But the constitution of Cyprus has been suspended since 1931. For both Colonies the Crown can legislate by Order in Council.

(3) Colonies possessing a partly elected Legislative Council, the constitution of which provides for, or permits, an official majority: Mauritius; the Straits Settlements (Penang, Malacca, Singapore, and Labuan); Fiji; Jamaica; Leeward Islands (Antigua, Dominica, St. Christopher-Nevis, Montserrat, and the Virgin Islands); Grenada, St. Lucia, St. Vincent (known as the Windward Islands), Trinidad and Tobago; Sierra Leone; the Gold Coast; Nigeria; and Kenya Colony.

In all these Colonies, except the Leeward Islands, the Crown can legislate by Order in Council.

(4) Colonies possessing nominated Legislative Councils: British Honduras, Falkland Islands, Gambia, Hongkong, Seychelles.

In all these cases, save that of British Honduras, the Crown can legislate by Order in Council and there is a majority of officials on the Legislative Council.

(5) Colonies without Legislative Council, in which the Crown has the sole power of legislation, exercised through the Governor, or High Commissioner: Gibraltar; St. Helena; Basutoland; Ashanti; Gilbert and Ellice Islands.

In these Colonies the Crown has power to legislate by Order in Council.

Cyprus, which possessed, as above noted, a legislature with an elected majority (three Muhammadan and twelve Greek members) is now legislated for by the Governor alone.

All these Colonies, with the exception of Basutoland and the Gilbert and Ellice Islands, have Executive Councils to assist the Governor.

There are also a number of miscellaneous dependencies not regularly administered.

(c) Protectorates.

i. Protectorates in which the administration is carried on by public officers under the control of the Secretary of State for the Colonies:

(1) Protectorates possessing a partly elected Legislative Council, the constitution of which provides for an official majority.

Nigeria (which is part Protectorate and part Colony); Northern Rhodesia; Sierra Leone (part Colony, part Protectorate).

(2) Protectorates possessing nominated Legislative Councils: Nyasaland Protectorate; Uganda Protectorate.

(3) Protectorates without Legislative Councils: British Solomon Islands; Kenya Protectorate (legislated for by the Legislative Council of the Colony); Gambia Protectorate (legislated for by

the Legislative Council of Gambia); Northern Territories of the Gold Coast (legislated for by the Governor of the Gold Coast); Somaliland; Bechuanaland; Swaziland.

In all Protectorates the Crown has the power of legislating by Order in Council.

II. Protected States:

(1) States possessing internal autonomy, but in foreign affairs controlled by the British Government; British North Borneo; Sarawak.

(2) States whose internal administration also is controlled by the British Government: Federated Malay States; Unfederated Malay States; Brunei; Zanzibar; Tonga.

Egypt, formerly a protected State, is now independent, but only subject to certain special British interests which are reserved from Egyptian control. The United Kingdom retains full authority over the Anglo-Egyptian Sudan, which is in law held in condominium with Egypt.

The New Hebrides is administered under condominium with France.

(D) Mandated territories which are administered subject to the supervision of the League of Nations; Palestine (legislated for at present by the High Commissioner, assisted by an Advisory Council of officers); Tanganyika Territory, with nominated Legislative Council; Cameroons under British mandate, of which the northern parts are legislated for by the Governor of Nigeria, the southern parts by the Governor and Legislative Council of Nigeria; Togoland, under British mandate, legislated for by the Governor of the Gold

Coast; Transjordan, which has semi-autonomous administration.

II.—The Dominion of Canada.

Powers of legislation and government are divided between the federation and the Provinces, viz. Ontario, Quebec, Nova Scotia, New Brunswick, Prince Edward Island, Manitoba, British Columbia, Saskatchewan, and Alberta.

The federation controls directly the North-West Territories and the Yukon Territory, in the former of which there is a nominee, and in the latter an elective, Council with subordinate legislative powers.

III.—The Commonwealth of Australia.

Powers of legislation and government are divided between the Commonwealth and the States, viz., New South Wales, Victoria, Queensland, South Australia, Western Australia, and Tasmania.

The Commonwealth exercises direct control over the Northern Territory, and the site of the federal capital at Canberra.

Dependencies, not parts of the Commonwealth.

Papua, with a nominee Legislative Council; Norfolk Island; Australian Antarctic Territory.

Mandated Territories:

New Guinea; Nauru, under mandate to the British Empire.

IV.—The Dominion of New Zealand.

Dependencies of New Zealand:

The Cook Islands; Ross Dependency.

Mandated Territory:

Western Samoa.

V.—The Union of South Africa.

Subordinate legislative and executive authority is possessed by the Provinces, viz. the Cape of Good Hope, Natal, the Transvaal, and the Orange Free State.

Mandated Territory:

South-West Africa.

VI.—The Irish Free State.

VII.—Newfoundland (constitution in abeyance).

VIII.—India:

1. British India.
2. The Indian States.
3. British Burma.

2. *The Crown and the Executive*

Throughout the Empire the executive government in its higher branches is carried on in the name of the Crown through officers whose functions, whether derived from the prerogative or conferred by statute, are exercised, directly or indirectly, on behalf of the Crown. There is thus in the Crown a formal expression of Imperial unity, and allegiance to the Crown is a common tie between all British subjects in whatever part of the Empire they dwell. The value of this tie is immeasurably increased by the fact that the Crown is not an abstraction, but is manifested in the personality of the sovereign, supported by the members of the royal family. Of the highest importance in strengthening this link of Empire has been the recent activity of the Prince of Wales and other members of the royal family in visiting the Dominions and India; the extraordinary pressure of public affairs in Europe, affecting deeply

Dominion and Indian interests, has necessitated the continuous presence of the King himself at the seat of Imperial Government. It is doubtless almost impossible to exaggerate the importance of the personal element as a factor of cohesion within the Empire; the difficulty of preserving unity would be enormously increased if the United Kingdom were under a republican constitution. It was a true instinct which induced Sir John Macdonald to seek for the new Dominion of Canada the style of Kingdom, and it may be regretted that the fear of exciting American susceptibilities should have prevented the creation of so attractive a style.

The unity of the Crown is real,[1] especially in the realm of foreign relations, but it is a unity which presents aspects, and the Crown in respect to its different territories can be perfectly justly regarded as diverse.[2] Thus the Crown has rights in respect of the United Kingdom, and different rights in respect of Canada, while in Canada there are the aspects of the Crown represented by the Dominion and the Provinces. Similarly in Australia the States have distinct personalities alike from the Commonwealth and among themselves. Judicial cognisance is taken of these distinctions, as also of distinctions in the aspects of the Crown within the United Kingdom itself.

As the outcome of the long struggle between King and Parliament it is an essential doctrine of the law of the constitution that the King can do no wrong, and it is equally a fundamental principle that all official ac-

---

[1] This can be used to prevent the Crown having to pay a soldier twice: *Williams* v. *Howarth*, [1905] A.C. 551.

[2] Thus a claim against the Crown in respect of the Irish Free State cannot be pursued by Petition of Right in England: *Att.-Gen.* v. *Great Southern Ry. Co. of Ireland*, [1925] A.C. 754.

tions of the Crown, with very limited exceptions, must be based on the advice of some minister or official who is responsible in law for the legality of the action taken. Moreover, constitutional usage has established the principle that the executive must be subject to the control of the people, through their duly elected representatives. It would, indeed, have been absurd to object to the unfettered action of the King and to substitute for it the equally unfettered will of officials or ministers, and it is to judicial and quasi-judicial officers alone that exemption from immediate responsibility is extended. But it is also plain that no man can effectively serve two masters in the same capacity; to attempt to do so would merely lead him to violate his duty to one or more, probably both, and to render ineffective his responsibility.

From these considerations follows the essential principle throughout the Empire that all officers who act for the Crown must owe responsibility to some popularly elected body, and, if no such body exists locally, they must owe obedience to some authority which is directly responsible to such a legislature. In the United Kingdom ministers are responsible to Parliament, and all the official staffs under their control are thus immediately subject to Parliamentary control. In the Crown Colonies and Protectorates the officials are subject through the Governor to the will of Parliament, whose mandates are executed through the Secretary of State for the Colonies. In the States and the self-governing Colonies the Governor owes obedience to the Imperial Parliament, and has no responsibility to the local Parliament, which may disapprove his conduct but cannot remove him from office save by an appeal to the Imperial Government, which may or may not concur with the local view. Ministers, on the other hand, and official staffs owe no allegiance to the Imperial Parliament or obedience to the Secretary of State for the Colonies. The Governor has no right to issue orders of any sort to them; without their advice he is powerless to act, and has merely by constitutional usage a very limited sphere of power to refuse their advice, if he is prepared to fill their places, should they resign in consequence of his refusal, by other ministers. In India, during the transitional period, the rule is already clear that ministers are responsible solely to their legislatures, while officials in departments not under ministerial control still remain subject to responsibility to the Imperial Parliament and its agents. Officers, of course, may occupy two capacities, and in these be subject to responsibility to different legislatures, but obviously any long continuance of such an anomalous situation would be difficult.

The result of these conditions is that over the Crown Colony and Protectorate executives the Imperial Government holds complete control, however much it may on grounds of principle refrain from insisting on overruling the judgment of local authorities, especially when these are supported by the members of the local legislatures. The officials hold office at the pleasure of the Crown, and any attempt at disobedience can be visited with immediate dismissal. The precise degree of control actually exercised varies enormously, largely in proportion as the legislature is effectively representative of the wishes of the people. In a Colony like the Bahamas, with an absolutely independent legislature over which the Crown has no power of control, the executive power of the Crown is fettered by the fact that it cannot obtain legislation or funds at pleasure but must meet local views; in a territory like Gibraltar, on the other hand, without such a legislature the policy of the Imperial Government must prevail, but it is naturally largely motived by the desire, while preserving the safety of the fortress, to make the occupation as little irksome as possible to the people. In India again the influence of the Imperial Government is lent to the task of making the harmony between the legislatures and the Government, even in matters not placed under ministerial control, as effective as possible.

In the case of the self-governing Colonies and India efforts by the Governor to direct executive action are consistent only with a state when responsible government is yet imperfect, or when Imperial forces are required to preserve order, a condition signifying that local autonomy is temporarily ineffective. Even, however, in such instances colonial experience suggests that it is impossible effectively to assert the authority of the Governor, as was proved by the cases of Natal from 1893 to 1909, and of Western Australia from 1890 to 1897, when in theory the Governor was accorded special powers in respect of the aboriginal population. To exercise them effectively would have meant making ministers responsible to the Imperial and not the local Parliament for an important side of their activities, and the attempt in effect was never seriously made. Such control, in such cases, as does exist is exercised in the sphere of legislation, and through the medium of Imperial Acts to which ministers and officials must pay respect, as they are part of the law and cannot be ignored without fundamental repudiation of the Imperial relationship.

3. *The Supremacy of Imperial Legislation and the Statute of Westminster, 1931*

The foundation of the constitution of the Empire lies historically in the doctrine of the absolute validity throughout the Empire of any legislation by the Imperial Parliament whatever its subject matter. There is no such thing as an illegal act of the Imperial Parliament; its power of legislation is plenary, and its edicts must be enforced in every court of law throughout the British dominions, Possessions, and Protectorates, so far as they are made expressly applicable to these territories. The position was perfectly definitely set out in the Colonial Laws Validity Act, 1865, which did not impose any new restrictions on colonial legislation, but, by making precise the rules regarding the relations of Imperial and local legislation, relieved local legislatures from the risk of their legislation being denied validity on the ground of a supposed lack of conformity to the rules of English law generally.[1] A colonial law is void and inoperative if in any respect it is repugnant to the provisions of any Act of Parliament extending to the Colony, or to any order or regulation made under the authority of such an Act, but not otherwise. This is the negative side of the rule that every Imperial Act extending to a Colony is absolutely binding thereupon, and can be varied only either by the Imperial Parlia-

---

[1] Boothby, J., of South Australia, had compelled legislation by declaring void Australian Acts on inadequate grounds; Keith, *Responsible Government*, i. 310, 339, 350.

ment itself, or by the local legislature under express powers given by the Imperial Parliament. It is important to note also that the colonial law is not rendered totally invalid because of repugnancy; only such provisions as are repugnant are inoperative, so that an Act, which incidentally may contain an invalid clause, otherwise remains in full effect.

It is obvious that the frequent use of this paramount power of legislation would enormously lessen the area of colonial legislation, and that the Imperial Parliament is normally far from fitted to legislate on matters taking place within colonial limits. In 1834 the Assembly of Upper Canada and as early as 1839 the Secretary of State for the Colonies announced the principle that legislation for a Colony, which possessed a representative legislature, on a matter of internal concern was opposed to the principle of the constitution, and should only be resorted to in case of necessity, as when Parliament remedied the neglect of Jamaica to provide due prison accommodation. The growth of colonial self-government was accompanied by the steady diminution of Imperial legislation save in matters which could not effectively be dealt with by the colonies themselves, owing to the restrictions on their legislative authority. Thus the constitutions of the Colonies now Dominions, save Newfoundland, rest on Imperial Acts, without which neither Canada nor Australia could have federated nor South Africa been unified. Moreover, the territorial limitation of colonial legislation rendered it essential to pass Acts providing for the extradition of fugitive offenders, the removal of colonial prisoners, and the trial in the Colonies of offences committed beyond their territories. On this ground also, merchant shipping was long regarded as essentially a matter for Imperial regulation, but the Colonies were accorded full powers over ships registered therein or engaged in the coasting trade. On treaty grounds Imperial legislation was once usual, but the constitutional practice from 1911 required that any necessary legislation should be passed by the Dominions.[1] Even when the propriety of Imperial legislation was manifest, it was customary that its terms should be settled by consultation, such as evoked the British Nationality and Status of Aliens Acts of 1914, 1918, 1922, and 1933. These Acts are of special interest as indicating prior to 1931 the spheres of Imperial and Dominion powers; the definition of natural-born British subject was enacted for the whole Empire, but the arrangements for Imperial naturalisation were subject to acceptance of the legislation by the Dominions. Imperial legislation affecting the army and the navy and the air force is valid throughout the Empire and binds British troops outside it, but by constitutional usage Imperial troops are not stationed in the Dominions except by agreement.

Is the doctrine of the paramount character of Imperial legislation no longer applicable to the Dominions? As early as 1900 it was suggested that it was wrong to subject the Commonwealth of Australia to such a restriction, and the Free State constitution was in 1922 framed, though ineffectively,[2] with the aim of excluding legislative action for the Free State by the

---

[1] The Geneva Conventions Act, 1911, was passed for the whole of the British Dominions without consultation of the Dominions.

[2] See 13 Geo. V. c. 1, s. 4.

Imperial Parliament after the ratification of the Irish constitution.

It is, however, significant of the rapid development of the sense of autonomy in the Dominions that the Irish demand was shortly afterwards taken up by the Union of South Africa. On the coming into office in 1924 of the Government of General Hertzog it was made plain that his purpose was to establish the complete autonomy of the Union as a substitute for the republican status which he had formerly demanded. This attitude won, at the Imperial Conference of 1926, the co-operation of the Canadian Prime Minister, who had been converted to the importance of stressing the autonomy of the Dominions by the fact that, contrary to British usage, the Governor-General had asserted the right of refusing a dissolution of Parliament except at his personal discretion. The result therefore of the Conference was the determination to assert the status of the Dominions as one of equality with the United Kingdom. The United Kingdom and the Dominions were declared to be "autonomous communities within the British Empire, equal in status, in no way subordinate one to another in any aspect of their domestic or external affairs, though united by a common allegiance to the Crown and freely associated as members of the British Commonwealth of Nations", although it was pointed out that the principle of equality and similarity appropriate to status did not universally apply to function. The task of giving further definition to this principle was accorded to a Conference of experts which met in 1929. Their resolutions were formally approved at the Imperial Conference of 1930, which recommended that the new status should be given

D

effect so far as requisite by legislation of the Imperial Parliament, passed after submission to and approval by the Parliaments of the Dominions. This approval was duly accorded and the statute became law, as the Statute of Westminster, 1931.[1]

Under the statute no attempt is made to renounce the legislative supremacy of the United Kingdom Parliament, but by Section 4 it is provided that "No Act of Parliament of the United Kingdom passed after the commencement of this Act [December 11, 1931] shall extend, or be deemed to extend, to a Dominion as part of the law of that Dominion, unless it is expressly declared in that Act that that Dominion has requested and consented to the enactment thereof". In the case of Australia it is provided that the request and consent shall mean the request and consent of the Parliament and Government of the Commonwealth; in other cases the Government alone could act, but it may be taken as certain that the Imperial Parliament would not feel bound to legislate in any case without the assurance that its action would have the approval of the Dominion Parliament. In the case of the Union of South Africa the matter has been carried further, for it has been provided [2] that the Parliament of the Union shall be the sovereign legislative power in and over the Union, and no Act of Parliament of the United Kingdom shall extend to the Union as part of its law unless extended by an Act of the Union. It must be noted that the restriction of authority thus laid down as a constitutional principle, though it could

---

[1] Keith, *Speeches and Documents on the British Dominions, 1918–1931*, pp. 232-307.
[2] Status of the Union Act, 1934, s. 2.

not operate as a renunciation of legislative power, would be effective as a rule of interpretation. The suggestion made in the Irish Free State that a formal renunciation of legislative power should have been made as in the case of Ireland in 1783 was rejected; apart from the fact that it would have had no more binding effect than the present enactment, there were objections felt in Australia and New Zealand and Newfoundland to the surrender of Imperial legislative supremacy. It was felt also that such legislation might be a convenient method of carrying out for the whole Empire a common policy agreed to by the powers. Indeed so strong was this feeling that the Statute of Westminster was only approved by these Dominions, subject to the condition that none of its provisions should take effect therein unless and until they were adopted by the Parliament of the Dominion, and no such adoption has taken place.

It is to be noted that the new rule applies only to legislation which is intended to operate as part of the law of the Dominions. It has nothing to do with the power of the Imperial Parliament to make laws affecting the action of British subjects when outside the United Kingdom. The Imperial Parliament, normally, legislates for the United Kingdom or some portion thereof, but it can legislate [1] for any part of British territory and for British subjects anywhere. There are instances of such legislation as regards murder or manslaughter and bigamy; certain offences against the Foreign Enlistment Act, 1870, the Official Secrets Acts,

---

[1] As to legislation for subjects see *The Zollverein*, Swab. 96, *per* Dr. Lushington; *Cope* v. *Doherty*, 4 K. & J. 367; *Blain, Ex parte*, 12 Ch. D. 522, 526, 531; *Keegan* v. *Dawson*, [1934] I.R. 232.

1911–20, and the Explosive Substances Act, 1883, are punishable wherever committed, as also is perjury and forgery, committed out of England, in respect of proceedings to take place in England. Treason, wherever committed, is punishable in England. Moreover, the discipline of the military, air, and naval forces is appli cable wherever they are situated. Legislation of this kind may still be passed by the United Kingdom and made applicable to a Dominion. But clearly the position of an Imperial force in a Dominion would be impossible if that Dominion were not willing to afford the force the assistance of its courts and of its law, and this particular matter has been arranged between the United Kingdom and the Dominions by the enactment of legislation in Canada and the Union of South Africa on similar terms to that of the Visiting Forces (British Commonwealth) Act, 1933, of the Imperial Parliament.[1]

It is further provided by the Statute of Westminster (s. 2) as a necessary complement of Section 4 that the Colonial Laws Validity Act of 1865 shall no longer apply to Dominion laws made after December 11, 1931. A Dominion legislature may repeal or amend any Imperial Act or order, rule, or regulation made under such an Act, in so far as it is part of the law of the Dominion. The autonomy thus conceded is complete. But the statute of itself (ss. 7-9) makes the necessary reservations for the federal constitutions of Canada and the Commonwealth. Neither of these constitutions can be altered, save in accordance with their terms, and the new power which is extended also to the Provinces of Canada, though not to the States of Australia, does not

---

[1] Keith, *Journ. Comp. Leg.* xv. 255, 256.

empower either the Federation or the units in Canada or in Australia to make laws not already within their authority.

It is not customary to pass Imperial legislation for the Colonies under modern conditions except in cases where general legislation is obviously necessary, and in these cases it is usual to provide that the Act in question may be applied by Order in Council under the Foreign Jurisdiction Act, 1890, to territories in which the Crown has jurisdiction, a term which covers territories under mandate to the British Crown. A recent example is the Whaling Industry (Regulation) Act, 1934, enacted to give power to carry out the terms of a Convention for the Regulation of Whaling concluded at Geneva in 1931. The same Act provides for the extra-territorial application of legislation on this head which may be enacted by the Commonwealth of Australia and New Zealand, to which the Statute of Westminster has not yet been applied.

4. *The Limits of Dominion and Colonial Legislative Power*

The powers bestowed on colonial legislatures of every kind by the authority of the Crown under its prerogative, or by Parliament, are extremely wide and generous. In no case in the Colonies has the attempt, *prima facie* natural, been made to set up bodies with merely limited powers to deal with specific topics under delegation from the Imperial Parliament in the same manners as powers are conferred on municipal and other authorities in the United Kingdom. These latter bodies are subject to strict control by the courts in the exercise of this authority; a municipality may make a by-law, but the courts will scrutinise it to see (1) if it falls precisely within the scope of power given to municipalities, and (2) if it is a reasonable exercise of that power. It is different with the legislatures of the Empire; they are not delegates, who cannot pass on their authority to others, but within the limits of their power they are possessed of authority as plenary and ample as the Imperial Parliament, in the plenitude of its powers, possessed and could bestow.[1] A local legislature, therefore, in all that falls within its sphere— inevitably in the case of a federation, a strictly limited one—has full power and authority to decide how its powers shall be exercised; nay, it seems as if it may hand over its power to the electors to be exercised by initiative and referendum, thus denying itself the power to exercise its deliberative functions.[2]

But the legislation of a Colony is limited by one essential fact; the power to legislate is local, and the validity of the legislation stops at the territorial waters of the Colony, unless indeed some wider power is conferred by Imperial Act. Thus the Commonwealth laws under Section 5 of the Constitution Act, 1900, are in force on all British ships, other than men-of-war, whose first port of clearance and port of destination are in the Commonwealth, and all the Colonies may make laws regulating their own registered shipping wherever it is. Generally speaking, however, the limitation is effective; its existence hampered the creation of colonial navies and had to be removed in that express regard by

---

[1] *Hodge* v. *R.* (1883), 9 App. Cas. 117; Keith, *The Constitutional Law of the British Dominions*, p. 231.

[2] Cf. Keith, *Journ. Comp. Leg.* iv. 240 f.

Imperial legislation in 1911[1] before the Australian navy could be placed on an effective legal basis. The absence of the authority is sometimes obviously inconvenient; thus New Zealand cannot punish bigamy committed outside the Dominion[2] by a resident therein, and powers to deal with whaling outside territorial waters had to be given to Australia and New Zealand in 1934. The Imperial Parliament escapes this local limitation; the sphere of its legislation is limited only by considerations of international comity, and the power to make effective its laws. It is not surprising, therefore, if, with the development of air navigation, Canada should have definitely applied to the Imperial Parliament for an extension of her legislative authority.[3] The matter was not simple, since it was obvious that there would be much inconvenience in the existence of many competing legislative enactments, but it was clear that the Dominions required authority over their own citizens, even outside Dominion limits, when necessary for purposes of the peace, order, and good government of the Dominions, and over their own ships everywhere. There were obvious considerations of convenience which suggest leaving to the Imperial Parliament all legislation for, and control over, British subjects in territories in which, as in China or Ethiopia, the King exercises extra-territorial jurisdiction over British subjects.

After long discussion the matter was again taken up at the Imperial Conference of 1930 and all effort to

---

[1] The Naval Discipline (Dominion Naval Forces) Act, 1911. See also the Naval Discipline Act, 1922, s. 7.

[2] *R.* v. *Lander*, [1919] N.Z.L.R. 305; Keith, *The Constitutional Law of the British Dominions*, pp. 226-30.

[3] Cf. Keith, *Journ. Comp. Leg.* ii. 328 f.; iv. 234.

frame a due limitation of the power to be given to the Dominions was abandoned and, by Section 3 of the Statute of Westminster, it was declared and enacted that the Parliament of a Dominion had full power to make laws, having extra-territorial operation.[1] It must be assumed that in the courts outside the Dominion in which such legislation is passed, effect to that legislation will be given only in the same measure as it would be accorded to the legislation of a foreign State. The situation has in fact long existed as regards India, for the Indian legislature in 1869[2] was organised to legislate for Indian subjects anywhere outside India. It follows therefore that English courts will apply to British subjects the laws of the United Kingdom and will ignore the extra-territorial operation, for example, of Canadian laws; for instance, a Canadian Act if such were passed, rendering criminal acts done by Canadian nationals in England, if intended to contravene Canadian customs legislation, would not be enforced in English courts. Similarly, Canadian nationals in China remain subject only to the law which is laid down for British subjects in China, under the China Orders in Council.

A second limitation is probably inherent in colonial status. A colonial legislature is created for the purpose of legislating, and it may be held that it is not entitled of its own volition to extinguish itself; at any rate it was felt to be desirable when the representative legislature of Jamaica, as the result of the native rising of 1865, desired to surrender its powers, that the surrender should be approved by Imperial Act. Similarly, Im-

---

[1] *Croft* v. *Dunphy*, [1933] A.C. 156.
[2] 32 & 33 Vict. c. 98.

perial legislation authorised like surrenders in 1876, by Grenada and St. Vincent. Another application of the principle that a body created for one purpose cannot alter that purpose is seen in the doctrine which was applied in the case of the creation of the Canadian Federation in 1867, the Commonwealth of Australia in 1900, and the Union of South Africa in 1909, that colonial federation or union can be accomplished only by Imperial Act. It may be added that the territorial limitations of legislation would also have prevented effective colonial action. It may also be held that a colonial legislature could not legally enact that a declaration of war by the Crown was to be deemed null and void, though it might enact legislation mitigating the disabilities to which alien enemies would normally be subject. Such a legislature could not alter the rules of British nationality, but that is due to the fact of the paramountcy of Imperial legislation under the Colonial Laws Validity Act, 1865.

As regards the Dominions, in view of the repeal of the application to their laws of the Colonial Laws Validity Act, 1865, the question of the existence of any limitation of power is much more difficult of decision. The concrete issue, which has been freely discussed in the Union of South Africa and the Irish Free State, is the right of a legislature to enact the termination of the connection between the Dominion and the British Crown.[1] The achievement by the Dominions of a quasi international status in membership of the League of Nations led to the enunciation by the Nationalist party in the Union that a Union Act, assented to by the Crown, would be effective to bring about secession. It

[1] See Keith, *Letters on Imperial Relations, 1916–1935*, pp. 158-68.

was contended by General Smuts that the royal assent to such a Bill could not lawfully be accorded, and it is clear that, so long as the Governor-General was appointed on the recommendation of the British Government and held office during its pleasure, no such assent could have been given. Since then the decision of the Imperial Conference of 1930 has accorded to the local government the right of appointment and removal, and in the Union the Royal right to disallow Acts has in 1934 been formally abolished. It may therefore be conceded that an Act might be passed and assented to, providing for secession. On the other hand, it is pointed out that the right of secession has never been formally conceded by the Imperial Conference, and that, on the contrary, it is expressly stated in the preamble to the Statute of Westminster that—"Inasmuch as the Crown is the symbol of the free association of the members of the British Commonwealth of Nations, and as they are united by a common allegiance to the Crown, it would be in accord with the established constitutional position of all the members of the Commonwealth in relation to one another that any alteration in the law touching the succession to the throne, or the Royal style and titles shall hereafter require the assent as well of the Parliaments of all the Dominions as of the Parliament of the United Kingdom". But it must be noted that the enactment of the statute was approved by both houses of Parliament of the Dominion on the understanding that it did not derogate from the right of any Dominion to secede. As regards the Irish Free State, the claim to the right of secession is plainly in contradiction with the Treaty of 1921 and it can be contended for only on the assumption that the status stipulated for in 1921 is capable of extension, and that, if it is legitimate for the Union Parliament whose power is derived from the South Africa Act of 1909, which united the British colonies "under one Government in a legislative union under the Crown of the United Kingdom" to dissolve connection with the Crown, it is equally legitimate for the Free State to dissolve the connection which was forced upon it by threat of war. This argument is clearly without much cogency, because the treaty on both sides was the result of force, and it must be noted that Canada and the Commonwealth of Australia agree with New Zealand and Newfoundland in rejecting the existence of any right of secession. Moreover, the principle asserted in the preamble to the Statute of Westminster is in harmony with the terms of Article X. of the Covenant of the League of Nations, for the Dominions in accordance with the spirit of that Article, even accepting that it does not apply strictly to them, must be regarded as vitally interested in the territorial integrity of the Empire.

5. *The Constituent Powers of Dominion and Colonial Legislatures*

Though it is probable that a legislature whether Dominion or colonial may neither extinguish itself nor seek to erect itself into the legislature of an independent State, it has, nevertheless, in many cases, wide powers of constitutional change. Any doubt that might exist on this head was completely removed by the Colonial Laws Validity Act, 1865,[1] which pro-

---

[1] 28 & 29 Vict. c. 63, s. 5.

vided that any representative legislature, that is, one comprising a legislative body of which one-half are elected by inhabitants of the Colony, had full power to make laws respecting the constitution, powers, and procedure of the legislature, provided that any such law was passed in such manner and form as might from time to time be required by any Act of Parliament, letters patent, Order in Council, or colonial law for the time being in force in the Colony. The effect of this provision is to create a distinction of an interesting kind between the Imperial Parliament and a Dominion Parliament as regards its constituent powers; an Imperial Act can make any change in the constitution, but it cannot stereotype it if the Parliament decides to undo it; it cannot enact that a change shall be made only by an absolute majority of members or after a lapse of ten years, for it cannot curb its own sovereignty. But it can lay such injunctions on a colonial legislature, and by the Colonial Laws Validity Act a colonial legislature can successfully fetter its successor, by laying down some form to be followed in constitution-making.[1]

The existing restrictions on constitutional change differ greatly in various parts of the Empire. In Canada the provinces enjoy freedom in great measure, but only within the limited sphere of their own powers under the British North America Act; they cannot alter the division of powers between them and the Dominion, nor can they affect the office of Lieutenant-Governor as the executive link between them and the

---

[1] See *McCawley* v. *The King*, [1920] A.C. 691; Keith, *Journ. Comp. Leg.* ii. 330 f., xvi. 294 f.; *Att.-Gen. for New South Wales* v. *Trethowan*, [1932] A.C. 526; *Doyle* v. *Att.-Gen.*, [1934] A.C. 511.

Dominion. The Dominion, on the other hand, has extremely limited powers, because the federation was a
compact between the provinces, and it is held to be
illegitimate for the federal Parliament to change the
terms of that compact, unless with general assent from
the provinces. Imperial Acts were therefore necessary
in 1907 to alter the amounts of the provincial subsidies, in 1915 to readjust the representation of the
provinces in the Senate, in 1916 to extend the duration
of Parliament by a year, and in 1930 to confer on
certain provinces the right to their natural resources
and to readjust subsidies. The desire of the Dominion
to obtain wider constituent powers is natural, for new
economic conditions have antiquated arrangements
not unsuitable in 1867. But no agreement on the subject exists with the provinces, as Quebec fears that
any change might lessen the security for education, for
the equal treatment of the French language in federal
and provincial proceedings, and the position of the
Roman Catholic Church.

The Commonwealth of Australia has the widest constituent powers, to be exercised by absolute majorities
in both houses of Parliament, approved by a referendum of the electors, but one house may secure at the
discretion of the Governor-General, which, however,
would only be exercised as desired by ministers, a
referendum by passing a Bill for a change twice, an
interval of three months intervening. There arises,
however, the question whether any change abandon-
ing the federal character of the constitution is possible;
the answer would seem to be in the negative. The
States have full powers of constitutional change, but
within the limits of the federal constitution; Bills

effecting important alterations or dealing with the Governor's salary must be reserved unless approved in advance by the Imperial Government. Efforts to effect by referendum great changes in the relation of the States and the Commonwealth have so far been defeated at the polls, and the question of a revision of the constitution, which would probably involve Imperial legislation, is still unsolved. A demand for the right of secession by Western Australia was made in 1934-5 to the Imperial Parliament, but in vain.[1]

New Zealand originally had somewhat limited powers of constitutional change, but it is probable that since the Act of 1865 she has practically full authority in this regard, though any important constitutional change would probably be effected by a Bill reserved for the signification of the royal assent. The same position applies to Newfoundland, where the constitution—at present suspended—rests on the prerogative.

In the Union of South Africa under the South Africa Act, 1909, certain restrictions were imposed on constitutional change, but these were in part dependent on conditions which are now obsolete, and those alone still are effective which require that repeal or alteration of the provisions of Section 35 of the Act, which provides for the Cape Native Franchise, or of Section 137, which provides for the equality of the English and Dutch—now Afrikaans—languages, shall not be valid unless the Bill for such repeal or alteration is passed by both houses in joint session and

---

[1] Keith, *Letters on Imperial Relations, 1916–1935*, pp. 192-5, 344, 345. The Joint Committee of Parliament reported against even receiving the petition.

agreed to at the third reading by two-thirds of the total members of the houses. The same rule applies to the alteration of the Section (152) which prescribes this rule. The difficulty, however, arises that the Union Parliament is no longer subject to the restrictions of the Colonial Laws Validity Act and that therefore it may be held to be in the same position as the Imperial Parliament, so that these restrictions have no legal effect. However that may be, the Union Parliament which declined to recommend the safeguarding of these clauses by a clause in the Statute of Westminster expressed the opinion that despite the change of position the restrictions remain binding on Parliament, and probably it may be expected that they would be observed as a species of constitutional convention.

In the original constitution an effort was made to secure the position of the provinces by providing that Bills affecting the powers of the Councils should be reserved. The abolition of reservation deprives the provinces of this security, but it had already become unimportant. On the other hand, in view of the anxiety felt in the provinces, in 1934, the Act of 1909 was amended to provide that no alteration in provincial boundaries or abolition of any Council or abridgment of its power should be carried out except on the petition of the Council. It was admitted that the Act had no binding force except as an expression of what was deemed desirable as a constitutional doctrine.

In the case of the Irish Free State the constitution was enacted by Dáil Eireann sitting as a constituent body and in enacting the constitution it provided that a constitutional alteration must be consistent with the Treaty of 1921, and after eight years any alteration must be approved by referendum of the people. For eight years ordinary legislation would suffice. This period was extended to sixteen by the Constitution Amendment No. 16 in 1929. But, when it decided to remove from the constitution the oath required to be taken by the treaty, it was felt necessary to repeal the provision of the constitution imposing the obligation in constitutional alteration to respect the treaty. It must be doubted whether this alteration was valid and whether the oath was legally removed by the Constitution (Removal of Oath) Act, 1933.[1]

In the case of India under the Federal constitution power of change in any essentials is reserved to Parliament.

The legislatures in the Crown Colonies and Protectorates have as a rule no constituent powers, but those of the Colonies with representative legislatures have full legal powers of alteration, and such powers survive in some cases from a former representative position, as in British Honduras.

6. *Imperial Control of Dominion and Colonial Legislation*

The history of the development of the Imperial relations is a record of the gradual disuse of control of Dominion legislation by the Imperial Government, while the means of such control remained unrepealed and potentially available. The assent of the Governor

---

[1] Keith, *Letters on Imperial Relations, 1916–1935*, p. 157. Cf. *Moore* v. *Att.-Gen.*, [1935] A.C. 484.

is essential to the validity of any measure of the legis- lature; he may withhold it, or reserve a Bill for the signification of the royal pleasure, when, unless especially assented to by the Crown by Order in Council, it falls to the ground, while, even if the Governor assents, the Crown may disallow the Act. This process, as well as the refusal absolutely of assent by the Governor, may be deemed obsolete in the Dominions, but reservation is still possible, and in some cases Acts must be reserved, or the equivalent process of inserting a suspending clause delaying the operation of the Act until approved by the Crown is followed. The Imperial Conference of 1930 approved the abolition of disallowance and reservation if desired, but only the Union and the Free State have acted. The exercise of Dominion legislative powers, except in Canada, the Irish Free State, and the Union of South Africa,[1] under the Colonial Courts of Admiralty Act, 1890, and the Merchant Shipping Act, 1894, is still restricted, and, as has been seen, certain constitutional Acts must be reserved in certain cases under the express terms of the constitutions. Both in the Commonwealth and in the Union[2] legislation restricting the right of appeal to the Privy Council must be reserved. It is also within the power of the Crown to issue standing instructions to the Governors as to classes of Bills to be reserved, but this is not done normally in the case of the Dominions save that in the case of South Africa the Governor-General up to 1934 was bound to reserve all Bills abolishing the native vote in the Cape; in that year as in 1933 in the Irish Free State the power of reservation was repealed. But

[1] See Statute of Westminster, 1931, ss. 5, 6.
[2] This is the one case still admitted in the Union.

E

in the case of the States and under the suspended constitution of Newfoundland, Governors are required to
reserve, unless approved beforehand, Bills affecting
divorce, currency, treaty rights, or of an extraordinary
nature and importance to the prejudice of the royal
prerogative or the rights of persons outside the territory or the trade and shipping of the United Kingdom.
Other earlier restrictions have been abolished, such as
the prohibition of differential duties in Australia by
Acts of 1873 and 1895.

The purpose of these restrictions was rather to secure
full discussion between the Imperial and Dominion
Governments of any issue affecting Imperial relations
than to dictate policy. Reservation became exceedingly
rare, save under statute; but in 1906 an Australian
measure giving a preference to British goods, only if
imported on British ships, was reserved with the approval of Commonwealth ministers as contrary to
treaty rights, and an unexceptionable measure took its
place, and in 1910 a New Zealand Shipping Bill which
went clearly beyond the powers of the legislature was
reserved and abandoned. In the case of the Irish Free
State no right of disallowance was even conferred.

Similar rules as to reservation and disallowance exist
as regards the rest of the oversea territories, but the
fact that the Crown controls, in the great majority of
cases, the executive government, renders it easy to stop
legislation which is unacceptable, before it has reached
the stage of an Act. Nor is there any hesitation in disallowing measures which are held to be undesirable in
substance or form.

It would, of course, be a complete mistake to treat
these powers of control as having been used for selfish

interests of the United Kingdom. In the famous discussion, in 1859,[1] of the right of Canada to enact a protective tariff, thus departing wholly from the British ideal of free trade, the objections of the British Government, however incorrect, were at any rate not insincere; there was, it may be added, never any intention of actually disallowing the measure, and all that was done was to point out to the Colony the results of the course adopted. If at one time attempts of the Colonies to extend the sphere of divorce, and to relax the laws restricting the marriage of close relations or connections, were resisted, the true ground of opposition was the perfectly just one that divergence in these matters in the Empire would result, as it did, in cases in which persons legally husband and wife in one part were strangers in another.[2] The ineffective efforts of the Imperial Government to influence legislation in favour of the native races were not in any way discreditable. Great value, moreover, attached to the insistence with which direct racial discrimination as a means of preventing the immigration of coloured races was deprecated and prevented by the refusal to allow such Bills to pass into law. British diplomacy won from Japan the valuable admission that objection was felt mainly to the mode, rather than to the fact of exclusion, and the adoption of an education test brought about by the energetic intervention of Mr Chamberlain at the Colonial Conference of 1897, solved for some twenty years a problem which presents fundamental difficulties. The use of the Imperial authority to prevent

---

[1] Keith, *Speeches and Documents on British Colonial Policy*, ii. 1 ff.

[2] Divergence in divorce legislation even in Australia has been found inconvenient. Cf. Dicey and Keith, *Conflict of Laws* (5th ed.), pp. 926 ff.

until 1873 the possibility of differential tariffs in Australia was doubtless in some degree inconsistent, since it contradicted the sanction for special favours granted *inter se* by the Canadian provinces before federation, but the fact that no use was made of the relaxation of the restriction is significant of the hypothetical character of the grievance. The control over Dominion legislation as in the case of Newfoundland's feuds with France and the United States to prevent infractions of treaties was obviously one wholly to be commended. Nothing could have been more unsatisfactory than that the Imperial Government should have permitted the violation of conventional obligations, which would have given rise to heavy claims for damage done from aggrieved States as well as possibilities of reprisals.

The unwillingness of the Imperial Government to disallow legislation of a self-governing unit was remarkably exhibited in 1920 in regard to legislation of the State of Queensland, where a Labour majority, by swamping the nominee Legislative Council, succeeded in passing legislation which was hotly denounced as confiscatory in character, by investors in land both within and without the State. Petitions for disallowance presented to the Crown received a negative answer, although the legislation was clearly of a decidedly unusual character and created so much dissatisfaction in financial circles in London as to preclude the possibility of the successful flotation of a loan on the London market, which was only reopened later on reparation being made. This was followed in the next year, 1921, by the abolition of the Legislative Council, reducing the legislature to a single chamber, contrary to Australian practice, but this measure also was, in 1922, allowed to have effect, though it was duly reserved by the Governor, and strong petitions were addressed to the Crown against the grant of the royal sanction.[1] It may therefore be regarded now as dubious if the Crown will ever disallow or refuse assent to legislation not contrary to treaty rights or patently *ultra vires*, unless perhaps in the case of a measure impairing the security of loans which have been admitted to rank as trustee securities in the United Kingdom, for it is one of the conditions[2] on which admission to this position is granted that the borrowing Government should record its opinion that any legislation violating the security should properly be disallowed.

7. *The Judicial Power*

No less fundamental than the supremacy of the legislation in the British constitution, are the right and duty of the judiciary to interpret and secure the impartial application of the principles of law enacted by Parliament, and the absence of any system of according special privileges in judicial matters to the executive government. The courts do not exist to compel the

[1] The same legislature in 1922 also passed an Act, which was neither reserved nor disallowed, allowing proxy voting for members incapacitated by illness, a device to secure the majority of the Government. But its actions were approved by the electors at the General Election of 1923, and its policy persisted until in 1929 the electorate revolted against the cost involved in the reckless expenditure.

[2] Prescribed by the Treasury under 63 & 64 Vict. c. 62, s. 2. It was reaffirmed in 1934 by all the Dominions except the Union of South Africa, which in lieu engaged not to pass legislation of such a kind without British concurrence and to alter any legislation to concur with British requests on this score; Colonial Stock Act, 1934: Keith, *Journ. Comp. Leg.* xvi. 293 f.

performance by the executive of their duties, and the right to deliver declaratory judgments or to issue orders for acts to be done by mandamus or to restrain executive actions by injunction or prohibition is limited to those cases in which the legislature has evidently contemplated that course by placing upon an executive department some direct obligation to the public, which entitles the individual or the public generally to have some act done or prevented for their immediate benefit. On the other hand, the legality of the acts of the executive as opposed to their wisdom is nearly always subject to the scrutiny of the courts, and both in the United Kingdom and the Dominions the passage of Indemnity Acts after the war is a striking reminder of the fact that, whatever the needs of the country, the violation of normal rights must be validated by legislative action. The passing of such Acts is not, as sometimes asserted, an invasion of the sphere of the judiciary; it is a recognition that laws are inevitably broken during war or rebellion or serious disorder, and that it is necessary to save the judiciary from the duty of punishing or penalising acts which, though illegal, were necessary in the interest of the State.

To enable the judiciary to be impartial adjudicators between the governmental agencies and the people, and to relieve them from governmental pressure, the British constitution since 1701 has asserted the principle that the highest judicial officers shall be appointed under statutory authority[1] and shall normally hold office during good behaviour, and that the only

---

[1] The rule has been applied to a Dominion: *Buckley* v. *Edwards*, [1892] A.C. 387.

normal means of removing them shall be the act of the Crown on the passing of addresses by both houses of Parliament, while criticism of their action as judges is permitted only on formal motions.[1] In the Dominions also the rule in effect obtains, though historical accident sometimes assigns the power of removal to the Crown on addresses from the houses, in which event the intervention of the Imperial Government might be necessitated, and sometimes to the Governor. In the former case in the Dominions the Crown would act without exercising discretion, but a more difficult case might arise in a State.

In the case of the Crown Colonies and Protectorates the tenure of the highest judicial officers, in whatever form expressed, now usually during pleasure, is none the less subject to the general principle that it is so important that judicial independence should be preserved that, whatever the rights of the Crown as to removal, they should be exercised only on the most serious consideration, preferably and normally on reference to the Privy Council, which is always rich in trained lawyers, members of the Judicial Committee, and experienced administrators, from among whom a committee can be formed admirably suited to advise the Crown whether a judge has so offended against the principles of this office as to render his retention undesirable. Cases of removal have been few, and in every instance they have been clearly inevitable and essential.

---

[1] The reduction of judicial salaries by statutory Order in Council in 1931 was attacked as affecting the security of the judges, but the government stressed the national emergency and their respect for the judiciary.

In the federal constitution of India removal depends on the approval of the Committee.

The executive government must, of course, retain a certain liberty of action regarding the appointments of lower grades of judicial officers, but the power of the superior courts to control and override the actions of the lower courts affords on the whole an adequate protection against the intervention of the administration in the judicial sphere. In India supervision is largely assigned to the High Courts.

A special duty rests on the judges of the part of the Empire other than the United Kingdom, because they have to deal with the enactments of legislatures of limited and defined powers, and therefore must consider from time to time the question of the constitutionality in a legal aspect of legislation enacted in due form by the legislature. A Commonwealth Act, for instance, may be invalid because it purports to regulate matters beyond the territorial limits of the Dominion; or because it is repugnant to an Imperial Act applicable to the Commonwealth, the example *par excellence* of such repugnancy being that the Act trenches on the reserved sphere of State legislation as marked out by the Commonwealth Constitution Act, 1900. The federal constitutions, in special, raise remarkable difficulties of this kind, for in the case of the unitary Dominions the restrictions on their legislative authority comparatively seldom come into prominence.

8. *Appeals to the Privy Council*

From the outset of colonial development it was recognised that the subject had a right to appeal to the

King in Council [1] to remedy defects of justice done to him in oversea courts, and this prerogative right of the Crown to hear appeals from any colonial court was given statutory validity by the Judicial Committee Act, 1844,[2] which, save when expressly modified by subsequent Imperial legislation, applies to the whole of the Empire, except the United Kingdom. No limitation has ever been placed on appeals from Canada by Imperial Act, and thus in theory appeals may be permitted by the Judicial Committee of the Privy Council to be brought from any Canadian court. In practice, however, appeals are allowed only from the highest courts in the provinces, and from the Supreme Court and Exchequer Courts of the Dominion, and, if a litigant prefers to appeal from a provincial decision to the Supreme Court and not to the Judicial Committee, permission is normally refused to carry the case from the Supreme Court. Under this system the Judicial Committee has decided a very large number of Canadian cases, and especially cases involving the interpretation of the Canadian constitution. In the case of the Commonwealth, on the other hand, it was desired to retain the right to decide constitutional cases involving the rights of the States and the Commonwealth *inter se*, and this was finally accepted in the Commonwealth of Australia Constitution (s. 74) in 1900, after the Imperial Government had declined to concede any wider extension of exemption from the appeal. It was, however, still possible to hear appeals on every class of case, including constitutional

---

[1] Apparently this is in substitution for the older appeal to the King in Parliament gradually found insufficient during the intermission under the Tudors of Parliamentary sessions. [2] 7 & 8 Vict. c. 69.

issues, from the State Supreme Courts, and thus to have constitutional issues decided by the Judicial Committee. A conflict of decisions[1] thus arose on the liability of federal salaries to State taxation, and the High Court declined to follow the views of the Judicial Committee as regards appeals on matters on which an appeal did not lie from the High Court itself. The difficulty was conveniently solved by Commonwealth legislation in 1907, which deprived the Supreme Courts of the power of deciding constitutional issues of this kind, so that appeals from them to the Judicial Committee could no longer arise and the High Court became sole arbiter of constitutional questions of the rights of the Commonwealth and the States. Provision, indeed, exists for allowing an appeal in such cases from the High Court with the assent of that body, but, though the power to allow appeals was once in 1913 exercised, it has been laid down that leave will normally be refused. The decision is of interest, for the interpretation of the Commonwealth constitution has been very different from that of the Canadian constitution, largely as the result of the difference of court. On all other matters appeals are allowed freely enough from both the Commonwealth and the State courts.

In the case of the Union of South Africa the appeal, under Section 105 of the South Africa Act, 1909, is restricted to cases decided in the Appellate Division of the Supreme Court of South Africa, and permission to appeal is not freely granted. In the Irish Free State constitution the Union model was adopted, and there

---

[1] *Webb* v. *Outrim*, [1907] A.C. 81; *Baxter* v. *Taxation Commrs.* (*N.S. Wales*) (1907), 4 C.L.R. 1087.

was an appeal only from the Supreme Court of the
State, but that court was given appellate jurisdiction
from all the decisions of the High Court, and the High
Court had jurisdiction in all cases where the validity
of the constitution was called into question, thus assuring to the Privy Council the power of deciding ultimately every constitutional issue where either party
desired to have its decision. In the rest of the Empire
the appeal is unfettered, save, of course, by the discretion of the Judicial Committee.

Appeals may come to the Judicial Committee in one
or other of two forms: either they are brought as of
right, without special permission from the Committee
because the amount involved or the interests in
question fall under categories prescribed by Order in
Council, or local Act, as suitable for appeals; or they
are brought on the score of special leave granted by
the Judicial Committee or by the colonial court on its
behalf; special leave is necessary for any appeal from
the Supreme Courts of Canada, or the Union, or the
High Court of the Commonwealth.

On constitutional issues it is often obviously desirable to have a decision without the inconvenience and
complication of a concrete case; in the United Kingdom reference may be made under the Judicial Committee Act, 1833, Section 4, to the Privy Council,[1] and
in Canada frequent employment is made of the right
of referring matters to the provincial or the Supreme
Courts for advisory judgments, from which appeals
can be taken to the Judicial Committee. That body,

[1] The Labrador boundary issue was thus decided (1927), 43 T.L.R.
289; so the question of the composition of the Irish Boundary Tribunal
in 1924, *Parl. Pap.* Cmd. 2214; Keith, *The Constitutional Law of the
British Dominions*, p. 275.

however, though it has on occasion given valuable replies, is opposed to the principle of such appeals, nor does it deem itself in any degree bound by its opinions on abstract issues. By an extension of this principle, power is given by the Government of Ireland Act, 1920, to the Governor or Secretary of State to refer to the Judicial Committee the issue of the validity of any Act of Northern Ireland, and the decision of the Council in such a case is made binding on all courts. Normally, appeals from Northern Ireland lie to the House of Lords, as in England and Scotland.

The decisions of the Judicial Committee are binding on all courts of the Empire outside the United Kingdom in matters in *pari materia*, but English courts follow the Court of Appeal if it differs from the Privy Council. But the Committee is not absolutely bound by its own decisions, which are given in accordance with the voice of the majority without intimation of dissent, nor is it bound by the decisions of the House of Lords on United Kingdom appeals. Divergence of view between the two courts is rare, but not unknown.

To the appeal, as to the existence of every apparent limitation on Dominion autonomy, exception has often been taken in recent years in the Dominions. It is argued [1] that it is undignified for Canada to go outside its bounds for judicial capacity or impartiality; that ignorance of local conditions causes errors in the decisions of the Privy Council; that the process is expensive and dilatory, giving unfair advantages to rich corporations over poor suitors; and that the exist-

---

[1] W. E. Raney, *Canadian Nationality* (1920); contrast A. Robinson, *Appeals to the Privy Council in Constitutional Cases* (1921); L. A. Taschereau, *Canadian Annual Review*, 1921, p. 642; Keith, *The Constitutional Law of the British Dominions*, pp. 269-74.

ence of the appeal tends to lower the status and depress the merits of the Dominion courts. It is admitted that the legal profession on the whole approve the appeal, but this attitude is discounted on the score that it is a source of professional gain, and also gives Canadian counsel the profitable and interesting duty of visiting England to take part in appeals. On the other hand, stress is laid on the impartiality and dignity of the court; on its Imperial outlook; on its value as a link of Empire; and on its functions in securing uniformity of interpretation of such matters as the prerogative and constitutional law generally, of the common law, and of statutes adopted in the Dominions from English law. The necessity of a single Appellate Court in prize matters was manifested clearly during the war.

Since 1900 a proposal has been at times considered for the creation of a truly Imperial Court of Appeal through the merger in one court of the functions of the House of Lords as the Supreme Court of Appeal from United Kingdom courts and those of the Judicial Committee which, in addition to oversea appeals, already hears appeals in ecclesiastical matters and in prize. The suggestion, though ventilated at Imperial Conferences, has never led to any concrete action, mainly owing to indifference both in the United Kingdom and in the Dominions. Instead a somewhat imperfect effort has been made to secure the service on the Judicial Committee from time to time of judges from the Dominions; the Committee includes the Lord Chancellor, the Lords of Appeal in Ordinary, and Privy Councillors who have held high judicial office in the United Kingdom or in the Dominions. Two paid judges with Indian experience sit on Indian appeals. The sporadic [1] presence of such judges is valuable, but in the absence of any provision for permanent representation the Judicial Committee remains in essence a court manned by Imperial judges. It must, however, be added that these judges are men of the highest capacity and standing, whose judgments normally command respect, though from time to time there is little doubt that they are led by ignorance of local conditions, or the application of English ideas to unfamiliar topics, into the commission of errors, a fate from which no court is wholly exempt. Their decisions, it is admitted, are always free from any political bias, such as might be alleged in delicate issues against Dominion judges. There are obvious advantages in allowing so difficult an issue as the marriage law of French Canada [2] to be decided by judges who cannot be accused of reflecting either the Catholicism of Quebec or the Protestantism of Ontario.

It must, however, be admitted that even in Canada doubt has been widely felt regarding the desirability of the appeal in cases where no constitutional issue is involved. It is in fact impossible to justify the delay and expense involved in taking to the Privy Council cases turning merely on private law. In the case of the unitary constitutions, arguments against the appeal can easily be adduced. In the Union of South Africa appeal has been permitted to remain on the assumption that it is very seldom likely to be used and probably only when some constitutional question arises.

---

[1] Fairly effective in the case of Canada, thanks to its comparative proximity and the generosity of its Government.

[2] *Despatie* v. *Tremblay*, [1921] A.C. 701. The same consideration applies to educational issues involving ecclesiastical strife as in Manitoba (1891–6) and Ontario (1918–20).

Considerable resentment was expressed when in 1934 the Privy Council dealt with an appeal of purely civil law, especially as the Judicial Committee has no special expertness in dealing with Roman Dutch law.[1]

In the Irish Free State the appeal from the outset was strongly objected to as a sign of subordination and it was inserted only under pressure from the British Government, which contended that the necessity of providing such an appeal was implicit in the Treaty of 1921, since Canada, the model for the status of the Free State, recognised the appeal. The argument ignored the fact that the appeal was vitally connected with the federal character of the constitution. In point of fact, however, the Free State, by legislation, nullified appeals in the two cases in which they were allowed where private rights were affected. In the remaining case, the issue of the interpretation of the right to compensation to Civil servants, granted by the treaty, the Free State accepted jurisdiction of the Committee but repudiated its interpretation. When, on reconsideration, an error of fact having been committed in the first judgment, the Committee reasserted the doctrine, the Free State refused to carry out its decision and the British Government had to agree to pay the extra sums awarded and to alter the treaty to obviate further claims. The passing of the Statute of Westminster was inevitably taken as justifying the abolition of the appeal, and the constitution was so amended in 1933.[2]

In the case of criminal appeals, special considera-

[1] *Pearl Assurance Co.* v. *Govt. of Union of South Africa*, [1934] A.C. 570.
[2] Keith, *Letters on Imperial Relations, 1916–1935*, pp. 145-7.

tions apply. There are strong reasons which render it most undesirable that such cases should be reviewed in England. On the other hand, in the smaller colonies the judges are inevitably subject to the risk of committing error which might have fatal consequences. Accordingly a rule has been established that the Judicial Committee does not act as a Court of Criminal Appeal. It will only interfere with the finding of the court below in a criminal case where injustice of a serious and substantial character has occurred, either by disregard of the proper forms of legal process, not merely of a technical character, or by a violation of principle, such as amounts to a denial of justice. Such appeals are accordingly admitted from time to time from the Crown Colonies, the Protectorates, and India, but not from the Dominions. In the case of Canada, advantage was taken of the Statute of Westminster to abolish the appeal in criminal cases, although that term is wide enough to cover cases which turn on the interpretation of the relative powers of the Federation and the provinces, and which in themselves may be of great constitutional interest.

9. *Inter-Imperial Arbitration*

The development of Dominion status involved inevitably the emergence of the question of devising some method of deciding disputes between portions of the Empire. So long as British supremacy was real, issues could be decided by the British Government, but by 1914 that state of affairs was outgrown. When, therefore, General Smuts illegally deported from the Union certain labour leaders, the British Government was embarrassed; had the men concerned been foreigners, the foreign State to which they belonged could have demanded arbitration over the legality of the expulsion, and, if the matter had been pressed, the British Government would have been obliged to demand arbitration, for which purpose the then obvious tribunal was the Judicial Committee of the Privy Council. In such a case, of course, it would have been constituted with full Dominion representation and its function would have been arbitral rather than judicial. A kindred case arose in 1920[1] over the repudiation by Queensland of certain obligations; in that case the persons in the United Kingdom whose property was seriously affected urged the Secretary of State to suggest arbitration, but without result. The lack of any arrangements for settlement was felt during the war period and the subsequent winding-up of the business transactions in which the British and Dominion Governments had been engaged. But it was only in 1929 that the matter took more definite shape, and the Imperial Conference of 1930 agreed on a rather vague plan. The essential defect of the project was that it was found impossible to secure agreement to compulsory arbitration even of justiciable disputes between Governments, the matter being left facultative, and thus likely to break down on the first occurrence of a serious difference. It was agreed that any tribunal should be constituted *ad hoc*, though such a form of arbitration is plainly most unsatisfactory. A tribunal should consist of five members, none to be chosen from outside the Commonwealth; each party should select one from parts of the Commonwealth other than those in dispute,

Chapter II.

[1] Keith, *Letters on Imperial Relations, 1916–1935*, pp. 271-7.

F

the nominee to be a distinguished jurist, and one without restriction from the Commonwealth; these four choose the chairman.

The first formal proposal for arbitration was made by the British Government in 1932 in respect of the withholding by the Free State Government of the payments in respect of land annuities which under Mr Cosgrave's régime had been regularly remitted to the British Treasury as a legal obligation. Mr de Valera declined to accept the proposal if it were insisted that the members must be limited to the Commonwealth, the view in the State favouring the appointment of a foreign chairman. The modification of the agreement of 1930 was naturally unacceptable to the British Government, which has consistently maintained that the relations of parts of the Empire are not governed by international law so as to render appropriate an international form of tribunal of any kind. It must, however, be added that the British Government in stressing its case insisted that the vital agreement in dispute was binding on the Free State without ratification on the analogy of international law, an attitude rather inconsistent with its insistence that inter-Imperial relations were not governed by international law.

10. *The Prerogative of Mercy*

The British constitution recognises fully and frankly the right of the executive to remit, in whole or part, sentences imposed by judges on any ground, though it is unusual for the executive to intervene in cases of penalties inflicted for contempt of court, since such action might tend to weaken the position of the judiciary. The review of penalties and punishments, which is thus carried out by the executive, is essentially distinct from judicial review by a superior court; it is not based on any question of superior judgment of matters of law, but on considerations which cannot effectively, or at all, be taken into account in judicial proceedings. It is one of the most essential of the royal prerogatives and, as appertaining necessarily to the executive government, it is possessed by the Lieutenant-Governors of Canada in respect of offences against provincial enactments, though these are not crimes in the strictest sense of the term. Moreover, it is very rare that it is in any way regulated by statute save in so far as it is necessary to enable the Crown to remit sums due to private persons (*e.g.* informers under penal statutes),[1] for it is a discretionary authority, which would lose rather than gain by any effort at precise definition.

The personal intervention of the Crown in this regard disappeared in the United Kingdom during the beginning of Queen Victoria's reign,[2] owing to the manifest unsuitability of such issues for a young girl to decide, and, though appeals are sent to the King, they are always referred to the Home Secretary. But it was natural and desirable that in the early days of colonial development the Governor should be invested with a personal responsibility, which enjoined on him the necessity in capital cases of deciding on his own personal view, although he was to receive the advice of ministers. It was only in 1878, on the revision of the instruments regarding the constitutional position of

[1] *Orpen* v. *New Empire, Ltd.* (1931), 48 T.L.R. 8.
[2] 7 Will. IV. and 1 Vict. c. 77.

the Governor-General of Canada, that the personal element as a general rule was eliminated for that Dominion, and the Governor-General expected to act on ministerial advice save when any Imperial interest might be affected by his action. Not until fourteen years later was the same rule extended to the Australian Colonies and New Zealand, as the result of the representations of New Zealand ministers that the issue was essentially one appertaining to internal government in which the Governor should have no formal share. In truth, the dangers of leaving the matter in ministerial hands, which in the early days of the Colonies were formidable, had gradually ceased to be of importance, and the old rule became indefensible. Yet in Newfoundland it was not until 1908 that the new practice came into operation, the Governor having previously been expected to act on his own decision; and even now under the instructions in force in the Union of South Africa the Governor-General has a personal responsibility in capital cases. In the Dominions generally, however, the Cabinet exercises the decision in capital cases, and, as in the United Kingdom, strong and effective resistance is offered to any attempt on the part of the legislature to intervene in the matter, which is obviously one of the most unsuitable topics with which a legislature can attempt to deal.

Imperial intervention is thus practically unknown; it is true that a petition to the Crown may be received from a criminal in an oversea territory, but, although the power to pardon is vested in the Crown, it is the invariable practice to refer the petitioner to the responsible government, nor is any pressure brought to bear on those governments. The practice of adopting banishment as a punishment for certain offences has, however, evoked the rule that such banishment must not apply to British subjects or naturalised residents of the territory concerned, a rule the propriety of which is obvious, seeing that the Imperial Government itself in its legislation takes power to expel aliens but not British subjects, and, since no other country would receive them, all banished British subjects would necessarily drift to the United Kingdom.

11. *The Honours Prerogative*

The prerogative of granting honorary distinctions of every kind, from memberships of the peerage down to minor distinctions, rests with the Crown, and this prerogative is one which is not delegated to Governors, but is exercised on the advice of the Imperial Government directly by the Crown. In the case of the United Kingdom itself there remains to the Crown a personal discretion in regard to the award of honours, the extent of which it is impossible exactly to define. The position is summed up in the following terms by the Royal Commission on Honours of 1922: "The King is the fountain of honour, and all grants are made by him, but in the selection of the recipients of the grants, as in other things, he is in use to act, not on his own initiative, but on the advice of his ministers. The minister responsible for advising is the Prime Minister, except in certain special cases, *e.g.* the Order of St. Michael and St. George, naval, military, and air force honours, Orders of the Star of India and of the Indian Empire, where the minister in charge tenders his advice direct. With these exceptions and that of the Royal Victorian Order, which is a private order and is bestowed by the King alone and upon his own selection,[1] no grant of honour is ever made by the King except upon the recommendation of the Prime Minister. Even in the case in which the King might wish that an order or a peerage should be given to a member of his own household, the recommendation would appear on the Prime Minister's list." This statement is possibly a little misleading in the emphasis of its distinctions; it must not be thought that the Secretary of State for the Colonies, or for India, is free at his unfettered discretion to exercise the right of recommending honours, or that the Prime Minister has no power of suggesting appointments to the orders normally reserved for control by the Secretaries of State. Similarly the highest awards for military, naval, and air service could not be made without the concurrence of the Prime Minister, while, as regards foreign services, the Secretary of State for Foreign Affairs has the same power of recommendation as has the Secretary of State for the Colonies, for matters falling within the sphere of his department, and the Permanent Secretary to the Treasury is consulted on honours for Civil servants of all departments. The King again may make suggestions for appointment to any order, and he has essentially the right to object to being asked to confer orders in excessive numbers, or on persons not of unquestioned reputation. This is, of course, especially the case in regard to the highest orders, such as the Garter, the Thistle, the Order of St. Patrick, the Companionship of Honour, and the

---

[1] So on the occasion of the Duke of Gloucester's visit to Australia and New Zealand in 1934–5. The King apparently may claim as requiring his personal initiation the Order of Merit: Lee, *King Edward VII.* ii. 98, 99.

Order of Merit, which must be regarded as involving the deliberate and intelligent approval of the Crown, which on the other hand cannot be expected to scrutinise recommendations for minor honours.

The necessities of the war induced the establishment of the Order of the British Empire, and the indiscriminate distribution of that honour has certainly diminished the value of orders generally; moreover, during the war, and after it, the care taken in making appointments to the various orders and to other distinctions was called somewhat vehemently into question by public opinion. The matter came to a head in the United Kingdom in the Parliamentary session of 1922, as the result of well-founded allegations that offers had been made by certain persons to men of some standing to secure them hereditary honours in return for contributions to political party funds. The Royal Commission,[1] which the Government was compelled, in view of the feeling of Parliament, to appoint, received evidence convincing them of the dangers of the position, and recommended as a means of preventing the abuse of the practice of granting honours for political services the establishment of a Committee of three Privy Councillors, selected from among persons not members of the Government for the duration of the ministry. To this body there should be submitted the name of any person on whom for political services an honour was to be bestowed, with a statement of the grounds for the proposal, an assurance from the Patronage Secretary that no payment to party funds was connected in any way with the suggestion, and the name of the person who originally suggested the

[1] *Parl. Pap.* Cmd. 1789.

grant of the honour. If the Committee reported against
the grant, and the Prime Minister still decided to
recommend it, the report of the Committee should
be laid before the King. The suggestion was accepted
by Mr Bonar Law as Prime Minister, and brought into
operation with regard to the list of political honours
at the beginning of 1923. Further in 1925 was passed
the Honours (Prevention of Abuses) Act, which has
checked some of the worst features of a disgraceful
system.[1]

In other cases the responsibility remains wholly
with the Prime Minister, subject to the duty imposed
on certain other persons of aiding him in his work.
Thus the recommendations for appointment to the
Order of the British Empire are dealt with by the
Secretary of State for Home Affairs, as a means of
focusing the various claims, while the numbers of
members to be appointed have been regulated so as to
check the excesses of the past. As regards Civil Service
honours, the Secretary to the Treasury has a responsibility to the Prime Minister for advice. A special
rule is laid down by the Commission regarding honours
for Imperial services. The right of the Prime Minister
to make recommendations of this kind is admitted,
but it is suggested that the Prime Minister should communicate his intention to the Secretary of State for
the Colonies in the case of any person domiciled, or
recently domiciled, in the oversea Dominions, so that
the Governor, and the Prime Minister in the case of
a territory possessing responsible government, may

---

[1] Cf. *Maundy Gregory, In re* (1934), 50 T.L.R. 492; money paid for an
honour cannot be recovered: *Parkinson* v. *College of Ambulance*, [1925]
2 K.B. 1.

be consulted before the recommendation is formally made. It is significant that the constitution of the Irish Free State expressly provides that no title of honour in respect of any service rendered in or in relation to the Irish Free State may be conferred on any citizen of the Irish Free State except with the approval, or upon the advice, of the Executive Council of the State. In the case of Northern Ireland it appears that the recommendation of the Prime Minister of that territory is similarly regarded as the proper ground on which appointments to honours should be made.

Chapter II.

There is no ground to suppose that honorary distinctions in general have become unpopular in the United Kingdom. It is true that Mr Henderson, as Labour representative on the Royal Commission on Honours, suggested that the cessation of the grant of honours for political services was the only effective remedy against the misuse of the grant of honours for party services, on the ground that, as the Committee of the Privy Council would be appointed from among supporters of the administration of the day, it was improbable that in practice the element of political contributions to party funds could be ignored in making selections; but in 1924 and 1929–31 Labour seemed to delight in such distinctions and in all the formalities of Court etiquette.

In the case of the Dominion of Canada the objection to the distribution of honours had come to a head long before the indiscretions of the Imperial Government in 1922 led to the effective protests of the two houses of Parliament. In the early days of Colonial Government there was certainly no objection to such honours being conferred. But the growth of democratic sentiments rendered their bestowal somewhat invidious, and, though Sir Wilfrid Laurier was induced in 1897 to accept the G.C.M.G., he did so with reluctance, and as time went on increasingly regretted his action. But the matter might not have emerged from obscurity except for the adoption of the ill-advised practice of conferring hereditary honours on Dominion residents, or persons like Lord Beaverbrook therein domiciled, and the introduction of the new British Empire Order, entailing the offer of a large number of distinctions for Canada. The matter was taken up keenly in the Dominion House of Commons, which enunciated, in 1918, the principle that no honour should be conferred on a British subject ordinarily resident in Canada, save on the recommendation of, or with the approval of, the Prime Minister of the Dominion; that no hereditary title should be conferred on such British subjects; and that steps should be taken to terminate the hereditary character of such hereditary honours as had already been conferred. Even this, however, failed to meet Canadian feeling, and in the following year, 1919, the further position was adopted that no title of honour should be conferred on any British subject domiciled or ordinarily resident in Canada, save such appellations as were of a professional or vocational character or which appertained to an office, and an earnest request was made for legislation to extinguish the hereditary effect of honours already granted. It is not surprising that it was impossible for the Imperial Government to introduce legislation to effect the latter result, since it was deeply indebted to one of the peers involved and legislation to change the hereditary character in any case of the peerage would raise difficulties with many sections of British opinion, including quarters whence party funds are largely derived. But the principle of not awarding honours to Canadians was adhered to, so long as Canada retained its view, while the principle is nominally accepted that no award of any honour to persons normally resident in the Dominions shall be made save with the assent of the Dominion Prime Minister. The rule, it must be admitted, has been gravely violated in practice in one or two cases, but it has been expressly admitted in principle. Nor, indeed, is it possible to reconcile any other rule with the principles of responsible government.

The award of medals and minor decorations also rests on the prerogative, but as regards these matters local legislation has been undertaken, and medals in the Dominion naval and military forces, where these exist, are granted in virtue of regulations made under these Acts. It would also be competent to create honorary distinctions locally,[1] but there is to such distinctions the objection that they would be valid only locally, and thus would compare unfavourably with the distinctions awarded by the Crown which are valid throughout the Empire, save in the improbable event of their being declared nugatory by legislation in any part of it. This is the ground which explains

[1] A suggestion made in January 1923, in the Union of South Africa. Even in Canada foreign orders are readily accepted: *Canadian Annual Review*, 1921, pp. 187 f. See House of Commons Debates, March 19, 1923. Quebec has an Order of Agricultural Merit. In 1933 Canada resumed recommendations for honours, Mr Bennett unconstitutionally arguing that he was not bound by the resolution of 1919, instead of obtaining its rescission. The issue will be revived if the Liberal party regains power.

why it is impossible to concede to any Dominion the right of unrestricted nomination for honours; as the awards are Imperial, the responsibility must be Imperial, and due recognition of Dominion rights is afforded by conceding to them the sole right of deciding what Dominion subjects shall be awarded such honours, as may properly be made available for the Dominions, having regard to the necessity of limiting the total numbers awarded in the Empire. This principle was expressly conceded by Canada in 1918, when it was contemplated that the right of the Imperial Government to fix the number of honorary distinctions to be awarded to Canada should be recognised, but the recipients should be selected by Canada.

It is by the Crown also that the rule is laid down under which members of the Executive Councils of the Dominions are entitled to the style of Honourable while they remain such members, a distinction enjoyed by Senators of Canada and the Union of South Africa, Legislative Councillors, except in the Canadian provinces, and by the Speakers of Lower Houses. The permanent retention of the prefix may be granted after three years' service as an Executive Councillor or a year as Premier; members of Legislative Councils and Senators may have it after ten years' service and Presidents and Speakers after three. Local use is permitted to members of the executives and legislatures of Crown Colonies. In India the establishment of a bicameral legislature resulted in the confining of the distinction to members of the Council of State; in the federation a like rule may apply.

As a mark of distinction, Governors-General and their wives are entitled to the style of Excellency in all circumstances; Governors and officers acting as Chapter II. such only while in the local area of the Government. In the case of Lieutenant-Governors the style of His Honour is accorded in the Canadian provinces, that of Honourable to Administrators in the Union of South Africa, while Imperial recognition of the style of Honourable has been granted to Dominion judges, both while in office and on retirement. Locally colonial judges are styled His Honour.

12. *The National Ensign*

The ensigns of the Empire are determined by the executive under sanction given by various Acts of Parliament, including the Acts for the Union of Scotland and Ireland.[1] The common flag of the Empire is the Union Flag, without any badge, which may be displayed by any British subject, and which is the Imperial flag proper. Without the addition of the badge of the Colony it is to be flown daily at the Government Houses throughout the British dominions. The red ensign without any modification is prescribed as the proper national flag for all vessels and boats belonging to British subjects, except in the case of His Majesty's ships and boats, and any other ships or boats which are permitted by warrant from the King or the Admiralty to bear other national flags. Under such authority armed vessels belonging to colonial governments carry the blue ensign with the colonial arms or badge embroidered in the fly and a pendant; when not armed, the blue ensign without a

[1] 6 Anne, c. 11, Art. i.; 39 & 40 Geo. III. c. 67, Art. i.; 57 & 58 Vict. c. 60, ss. 73, 745.

pendant; in the case of the Dominion forces of Australia and Canada, the agreement of 1911 provides
that the white ensign is to be hoisted at the stern as a
symbol of the authority of the Crown and the distinctive flag of the Dominion at the jack-staff. In the
case of the Dominions generally, merchant vessels
have received authority to bear the red ensign with
the Dominion badge, and in the Colonies generally,
ensigns with such a badge may be borne in addition to
the red ensign. On land the Dominion flag has been
adopted for the use of the Commonwealth military
forces; similarly, the Dominion flag is also the national
flag for all purposes in New Zealand under an Act of
1901, and in Newfoundland.

In the case of the Irish Free State, the determination
of the flag has been left to the State, which has decided,
perhaps inevitably, against any perpetuation of the
Union flag, and adopted a tricolour.[1] In the rest of the
Empire, except the Union of South Africa, there seems
to be a clear realisation of the value of the expression
of Imperial unity by the use of one flag, and the
defacement of the Union Jack by the badges of the
Dominions and Colonies seems admirably calculated to
secure the recognition of that diversity in unity which
is the essential feature of the Empire.[2]

---

[1] Ships belonging to British subjects (including citizens of the Free
State) can only carry flags on the principle of the Merchant Shipping
Act, 1894, s. 73, which Irish legislation could not prior to the Statute
of Westminster, 1931, override. The matter now can be dealt with at
discretion, and legislation is contemplated.

[2] An Imperial stamp has been suggested, but the project has failed
to materialise. The arms adopted by Dominions are approved by the
King, *e.g.* the new arms of Canada (November 21, 1921). Coinage designs
are decided locally in those cases where, as in Canada, Imperial coinages are not in exclusive use; such coinages may be made by Imperial
legislation valid throughout the Empire, and there are branches of the

In the case of the Union of South Africa, after much
political strife, in 1927 a compromise was achieved, under which the Union has two flags, the Union Jack to denote the association of the Union with the other members of the British Commonwealth of Nations, and the National flag, whose design is three horizontal stripes, orange, white, and blue; the three flags, Union Jack, the old Free State flag, and the Transvaal Vierkleur, occupying the central stripe. Both flags are flown from the houses of Parliament, the principal Government buildings of the capitals of the Union and the provinces, at seaports and at Government offices overseas.[1]

13. *The Channels of Inter-Imperial Communication*

The equality of status between the United Kingdom and the Dominions is marked by the rule that the Prime Ministers of the units are entitled to communicate direct with one another, and that the use of the Dominions Office as a channel of communication is facultative. On the other hand, it is plain that either the Prime Minister himself must have a department on the lines of the Dominions Office, or the less important part of work affecting Dominion relations must be undertaken by some subordinate minister. There are, therefore, grounds of convenience for the existence

Royal Mint in Australia and South Africa, regulated under the Imperial Act by Dominion legislation; the Ottawa branch in 1931 fell under Dominion legislative control only.

Distinctive local coinages, superseding the use of British silver, which has in consequence been withdrawn on generous terms by the Royal Mint, have been set up in the Irish Free State, the Commonwealth of Australia and New Zealand (1935) under local legislation.

[1] Cf. Keith, *Letters on Imperial Relations, 1916–1935*, pp. 73, 74; Union Nationality and Flags Act, No. 40 of 1927, ch. ii.

of the Secretaryship of State for Dominion Affairs, though when first created it was held together with the Colonial Secretaryship, and even since the two offices were separated in 1930 the departments as regards all but the higher posts are liable to interchange in point of staff. This rule is clearly a historic survival without justification; there is more point in the suggestion of Mr Fisher at the Imperial Conference of 1911 that the Dominions should be placed in the sphere of the Foreign Office. An essential part of the work of the Foreign Office is securing that through the Dominions Office the Dominions are kept in close touch with the development of foreign relations in all regards.

The Dominions Office, however, has functions of its own to perform. The Secretary of State is bound to keep in touch with the Dominions in all aspects of their development; he has to keep them in touch with developments of British affairs outside the sphere of foreign relations, and be the channel of communication in issues such as those of ceremonial and honours of all kinds. But the existence of this minister does not interfere with direct communications between any of his governments and the King. The Irish Free State in 1931 and the Union of South Africa in 1934 have secured the royal approval of their own seals, and deal direct with the Crown, and any other Dominion may do so at pleasure; thus the appointment of the Governor-General of Canada in 1930 and 1935 alike was arranged without British mediation.

Normally, however, communications between the Dominions and the United Kingdom deal with matters not personal to the King, and the channels of communication are in the main two. In the first place the

Departments in the Dominions concerned with external affairs can communicate direct with the Dominions Office; in the second place communications can pass through the High Commissioners for the Dominions in London, and the High Commissioners or officers acting for them whom the British Government has appointed to Canada (1928), and to the Union of South Africa and the Commonwealth of Australia in 1930–31. The presence of these officers as of liaison officers in the Foreign Office or in the Dominions affords an opportunity for close personal touch which is of high value. New Zealand—and Newfoundland when autonomous—adhered to the use of the Governor-General as the channel of communication, a procedure which has the advantage of securing for the office of Governor-General a man of much higher political capacity than is possible under the system which ascribes to the Governor-General mainly ceremonial functions, or the fostering of Dominion dramatic or aesthetic tastes. In the case of the Union the High Commissioner takes charge of British relations with Basutoland, Swaziland, and the Bechuanaland Protectorate.

Relations with the Australian States pass through the Governors or the Agents-General of the States in London. But long practice renders it usual for political communications to pass through the Governors, and the Governors in any case are fully informed of any matters brought to the notice of the Dominions Secretary by the Agents-General. Their sphere lies rather in the region of commerce and finance.

Southern Rhodesia, though not a Dominion, being controlled by the British Government in external affairs and supervised in respect of native issues through the High Commissioner in South Africa, is in communication with the Dominions Office, and is represented in London by a High Commissioner. Newfoundland for the time being communicates through the Governor, and the High Commissionership in London is in abeyance.

The Dominions Office is of the usual type of the office of a Secretary of State. There is a Parliamentary Under-Secretary, a Permanent Under-Secretary, and two Assistant Under-Secretaries; it is divided into four Departments, and shares a Legal Adviser with the Colonial Office. Part of it is the Oversea Settlement Department, subordinate to a Committee presided over by the Parliamentary Under-Secretary as Chairman; which contains representatives of the British Government, the Dominions, States, and Provinces, and five private members. It is charged with licensing of passage brokers and agents and of emigration societies, and the dissemination of information and advice on accommodation and health on board ship. The Empire Settlement Act, 1922, has been administered under its advice, and its annual reports have been supplemented by special enquiries into emigration policy.

The promotion of commercial relations is the task of the Empire Division of the Department of Overseas Trade. It is represented in the Dominions and India by fifteen Trade Commissioners, and there are Commissioners in Kenya, Trinidad and Jamaica, and Singapore.

Canada has entrusted to the Prime Minister as Secretary of State for External Affairs since 1912 the conduct of her external relations, whether with the

United Kingdom or the foreign States or other Dominions. The International Joint Commission for the settlement of boundary waters disputes with the United States, though an independent tribunal, works in close connection with the Department. The High Commissioner in London, established in 1880, has of late assumed greater importance as a channel of communication with the Dominions Office; subordinate to him is the Canadian Air Liaison Officer. Some provinces maintain Agents-General—Ontario, Quebec, and British Columbia in special; their functions are commercial, and in political matters they have no access to the British Government, as the provinces are themselves cut off from direct contact with the Crown.

In Australia the Prime Minister takes direct charge of relations with other parts of the Empire, and relations with foreign States are deliberately conducted through British agencies,[1] a suggestion of Japan in favour of diplomatic appointments being declined in 1934. Touch with foreign affairs is maintained especially through the External Affairs Officer in London attached to the High Commissioner's office, who is in close communication with the Dominions and the Foreign Offices. The responsible department for external affairs in the Commonwealth is at present dissociated from the office of Prime Minister, but works in close relation. The High Commissioner is increasingly employed as a means of personal touch with the British Government, but does not form the normal channel of communication on political issues.

[1] For an occasional direct exchange of relations see the Belgium agreement, November 19, 1934 (Minister of Trade and Consul-General at Canberra).

In New Zealand the Prime Minister normally acts as Minister of External Affairs, and communications pass through the Governor-General, the Dominions Office, Foreign Office, etc., as formerly, no change having been made in view of the attainment of Dominion status, save in the case of League of Nations affairs, in which New Zealand acts direct, and occasionally in commercial relations as in negotiations with Japan in 1928 and Belgium in 1933. The High Commissioner is not a normal channel of political intercourse.

In the Union the Prime Minister is also Minister for External Affairs, and the Union is widely represented in foreign countries. The High Commissioner in London is aided by a Political Secretary in touch with the External Affairs Department in South Africa. As in the case of Australia and New Zealand, the Prime Minister undertakes responsibility for the mandated territory of the Dominion.

The Irish Free State has a Department of External Affairs, which is not controlled by the President of the Executive Council directly, and a High Commissioner in London, who is very freely used for negotiations with the British Government as in the case of the agreement of 1935 regarding exchange of concessions as to coal and cattle imports.

For the Colonies, Protectorates, and other dependencies the British Government is represented by the Secretary of State for the Colonies. All political matters are dealt with through the Governor or other head of the local government, and only in commercial and financial matters is action taken by the Crown Agents for the Colonies.

Indian government is in a process of transition, and the full development of Dominion status has not yet been attained. The Indian Government in external relations normally must act through the India Office and the Foreign Office. Only in minor issues respecting supply of information may it deal direct with the League of Nations. It has, however, a wider right of communication direct with the British Dominions, and since 1927 has been represented in the Union of South Africa by a High Commissioner charged with matters affecting the relations to the Union Government of the Indian population. It is also customary to choose officers of Indian experience for such posts as British Minister to Afghanistan or Nepal or even Tibet, and India supplies the consular officers in Afghanistan, Persia, Arabia, and Kashgar. Through the Governor-General, Indian contact with foreign issues is close and constant, and this contact will remain unaffected by the change of constitution, though in increasing degree the Governor-General will aim at securing the co-operation of the federal ministry and legislature in Indian foreign relations. The High Commissioner is not entrusted with political functions, nor normally with commercial negotiations. But at the Ottawa Conference of 1932 the Indian delegation was based on India House, and communicated with the Government through the High Commissioner. This procedure was chosen to emphasise the self-determination of India in commercial matters.

CHAPTER III

1. *The Unity of the Empire in International Law*

Chapter
III.

THE growth in population and power of the Dominions and of India, which was manifested so remarkably in the late war, has necessarily raised in a difficult form the question of the unity of the British Empire in the eyes of international law. No such issue could arise so long as the oversea possessions of the Crown were politically undeveloped, and only too glad to allow the whole burden, and therefore the control, of foreign affairs to rest in the hands of the United Kingdom. In international affairs the Imperial Government was responsible to foreign powers, and accordingly its voice was decisive in these matters; Australia and New Zealand might complain of opportunities of acquisition lost in New Guinea, the New Hebrides, or Samoa, Newfoundland of French or American encroachments, and the Cape of the German occupation of South-West Africa, but these complaints were matters concerning the internal relations of the Empire alone. In the many disputes which arose between the United States and Canada, the Government of the United States from time to time made it plain that the quarrel lay between the Imperial Government and the United States, and that, whatever the autonomy of the Dominion in internal affairs, for international purposes the Imperial Government was solely responsible.

To what extent has this position been changed by the war? Has the British Empire been divided up as the outcome of the conflict into a group of States: the United Kingdom, the Irish Free State, Canada, Australia, New Zealand, South Africa, and India, each with its dependencies, which collectively constitute the Empire, but each of which has a distinct existence as a unit of international law? For this, of course, there is the classical parallel of the long period (1714–1837) when Hanover was ruled by British kings but each State was a distinct international unit. To achieve such a result, however, it would be necessary both that the Governments concerned should aim at this goal and that foreign States should recognise the result as reached. Neither of these requisites has been in general fulfilled in this case, except in the limited and special degree implied in the Covenant of the League of Nations. The Covenant, however, makes no definite attempt to give its members the full status of units of international law; it contemplates the admission to membership of any fully self-governing Colony which can give effective guarantees of its sincere intention to observe its international obligations; it assumes thus that a territory can be a Colony, that is, not an independent State, be fully self-governing, and possess international obligations, which *prima facie* cannot attach at all to a Colony as such, seeing that an international obligation normally and properly must be incumbent on an international person and not on a dependency. No light is thus thrown on the real position of the Dominions and India in international law beyond the sphere covered by the Covenant of the League.

The position, accordingly, can best be gauged by references to cases unaffected by membership of the League. It was at one time claimed that the proceedings in connection with the signature of the Peace Treaties of 1919 were conclusive evidence that the Dominions and India enjoy the same international position as the lesser European and American powers, and the claim is supported by the undeniable fact that, at the instance of the British Government, the Peace Conference agreed to permit representation at Plenary Conferences to delegates of the Dominions and India, and that the treaties of peace were signed not only by the British delegates proper, but also by the Dominion and Indian representatives. But the argument is inconclusive. The Dominions and India, though allowed the right of expressing their views separately in respect of their special interests, were still primarily represented by the British delegation, which was formally styled the British Empire delegation, and on which the Dominions and India were able to secure representation from time to time by the use of the panel system. Similarly the treaties were signed for the British Empire as a whole, though by representatives of different portions, and not separately for each part of the Empire. Moreover, it is essential to remember that the representatives of the Crown were all appointed on the formal recommendation of the Imperial Government to the Crown. The various Dominion Governments and the Government of India approved their acting as representatives of these territories and gave them authority so to act, but their international competence was derived not from these powers, but from the formal Full Powers issued to them under the royal

sign-manual and the counter-signature of the Secretary of State for Foreign Affairs. Not less decisive is
the fact that, contemporaneously with the signature of
the Peace Treaty of Versailles, a tripartite agreement
was entered into by the Crown with the United States
and France to secure aid to the latter power in the
event of aggression from Germany. The treaty was
signed only by Mr D. Lloyd George and Mr A. J.
Balfour, and by no Dominion or Indian representative,
but it expressly provided that "the present Treaty
shall impose no obligation upon any of the Dominions
of the British Empire unless, and until, it is approved
by the Parliament of the Dominion concerned". The
conclusion is plain; the signatures of the British representatives were sufficient to bind the whole of the
Empire, and it was, therefore, necessary to exempt
the Dominions from its operation by expressly providing for their case.[1]

The same doctrine of the continuance of Imperial
unity for purposes of international law is clearly expressed in the outcome of the negotiations which took
place between the Imperial and Canadian Governments in 1919–20 on the question of the diplomatic
representation of Canada at Washington. Had Canada
attained the status of an international unit, it would
have been a matter of course that arrangements should
have been made direct between Washington and
Ottawa for an exchange of diplomatists. But no such
conclusion was drawn from the facts of the negotiation
of the peace treaties by either party. The net result of

---

[1] Similarly the renewals of arbitration treaties for the Empire were
signed by the Secretary of State for Foreign Affairs alone, *e.g.* with
Denmark, May 1, 1922 (*Parl. Pap.* Cmd. 1744).

the negotiations, as announced in the Imperial House of Commons by Mr Bonar Law on May 10, 1920, was agreement that the King "on the advice of his Canadian ministers, shall appoint a Minister Plenipotentiary who will have charge of Canadian affairs, and will be at all times the ordinary channel of communication with the United States Government in matters of purely Canadian concern, acting upon instructions[1] from, and reporting direct to the Canadian Government. In the absence of the Ambassador the Canadian Minister will take charge of the whole Embassy, and of the representation of Imperial as well as Canadian interests. He will be accredited by His Majesty to the President with the necessary powers for the purpose. This new arrangement will not denote any departure, either on the part of the British Government or of the Canadian Government, from the principle of the diplomatic unity of the British Empire." The Minister Plenipotentiary, it will be noted, was to be granted powers by the Crown, in accordance, of course, with the wishes of the Dominion Government, but on the formal recommendation of the Imperial Government through the Secretary of State for Foreign Affairs. He would, therefore, have spoken even on purely Canadian matters not as the mere representative of Canada, but as the representative of the Empire specially selected on grounds of knowledge to deal with a special branch of Imperial interests, and therefore deriving his instructions from that Government within the Empire which was immediately concerned.[2] Even

---

[1] See below, Chap. IV. s. 1.

[2] Compare Mr A. Meighen's doctrine at the Imperial Conference of 1921 that Canada's views on her relations with the United States should prevail in every case (*Canadian Annual Review*, 1921, p. 78).

so, it was seriously doubted in Canada how far such an appointment was likely to be effective, and, despite the agreement of 1920, the appointment was deliberately left in abeyance both by the then Government and its successor, though it was approved by Mr Mackenzie King's Administration.

Equally suggestive was the procedure adopted at the Washington Conference which culminated in the important agreements regarding limitation of naval armaments and replacing by a broader convention the Anglo-Japanese alliance of 1911. At the Imperial Conference of 1921, agreement was reached that the British Government should represent the whole Empire at Washington. In view, however, of the vital importance of the subjects to be considered at the Conference on Disarmament, it was felt to be very desirable that the Dominions should be represented by their Prime Ministers; but this proved impossible, and other nominees attended as representatives of Canada, Australia, New Zealand, and India, South Africa adhering to the original arrangement. The treaties were signed, as in the case of the peace treaties for the whole Empire, by the British, Dominion, and Indian delegates, the latter signing expressly for the Dominions and India respectively. The delegates were all given full powers by the King, under the countersignature of the Secretary of State for Foreign Affairs; in the eyes of the other powers and in their own view they formed a single Imperial delegation, representing the whole of the Empire.[1]

The conclusion to be derived was that the Empire remained a unit of international law, which could be

[1] *Parl. Pap.* Cmd. 1627.

bound by treaties entered into by any plenipotentiaries duly accredited by the Crown on the advice of
the Imperial Government. From the point of view of
international law the composition of the delegation,
which treated regarding the conclusion of treaties and
signed the agreements arrived at, was a matter of
indifference; these were purely internal matters, vital
from the Imperial point of view, but negligible in
international relations. Similarly the ratification of
the peace treaties and the Washington agreements
was an act of the Crown on the advice of the Imperial
Government; the fact that this advice was tendered
only after the Dominion and Indian Governments had
concurred and had obtained the approval of their Parliaments was a matter of fundamental constitutional
importance; but it lay outside the purview of international law. The Government of the United States
issued but a single invitation to the Imperial Government to be represented at the Washington Conference,
and explained, with perfect propriety, when complaints appeared in the press regarding the omission
of an invitation to the Dominions, that it was impossible for the Government to go beyond the established channels of communication, though Dominion
representatives among the Imperial delegation would
be made welcome.[1]

This unity, however, was shortly challenged in

[1] For a different view of these proceedings, see General Smuts's speech
in the South Africa House of Assembly, July 18, 1922. The essential
points against his opinion are (1) the Imperial appointment of the
Dominion delegates, and (2) the necessity of the Empire acting as a
whole. The United States would clearly not have accepted any derogation
from either principle. See Mr Massey's speech in the New Zealand House
of Representatives, August 18, 1922; Sir John Salmond, *New Zealand
Official Year-Book*, 1923, pp. 629-31; Keith, *Journ. Comp. Leg.* v. 161 ff.

Canada, as a result of the conclusion of a treaty with the United States in 1923 regarding the halibut fisheries. The treaty was negotiated by the British Ambassador at Washington in accordance with the wishes of the Canadian Government. The question then arose whether the Ambassador should sign, together with the Canadian Minister of Marine and Fisheries. The Canadian Government insisted that the treaty affected only Canadian British subjects and the Canadian Government, and should be signed for by Canadian representatives alone. Eventually this view was accepted by the British Government; the interpretation placed on the treaty by Canada was adopted by the United States, and the treaty was ratified by the King advised by the Foreign Secretary at the request of the Canadian Government. The propriety of the proceedings was affirmed by the Imperial Conference of 1923, which established the principle that a treaty ought to be specially signed for a part of the Empire to which it is specially applied. There next arose a crucial issue, owing to pressure of events and French objections to Dominion participation in the peace negotiations with Turkey. The Treaty of Lausanne was negotiated without any Dominion delegations being invited, though the Dominions were informed of the general progress of negotiations. When, therefore, Canada was asked to approve ratification, Mr Mackenzie King declined to ask his Parliament to accept any responsibility for the treaty.[1] He did not deny the power of His Majesty without Canadian advice to conclude or ratify the treaty as a matter of

---

[1] Keith, *Speeches and Documents on the British Dominions, 1918–1931*, pp. 322–41.

international law, but he denied that Canada could be bound, actively, to take measures arising out of any treaty which had not been signed by her delegates and ratified at her express request. The treaty was accordingly ratified by the King for the whole of his dominions, but it was recognised that the position was wholly unsatisfactory. Under the terms of the treaty the British Government might have to take action to secure the régime prescribed for the Straits, and for that purpose to go to war. Canada would be involved in such a war, but would be under no moral obligation to render support therein. At the Imperial Conference of 1926,[1] therefore, Canada joined the Union and the Irish Free State in demanding a more precise definition of the international position. It was therefore, in amplification of the resolutions of 1923, made clear that no Dominion could be bound by any treaty which was not signed by delegates empowered to act for it, and any treaty to bind a Dominion must be ratified at its request.

Further, approval was accorded to the principle of the representation of the Dominions by their own Ministers at foreign courts. This principle had been claimed as operative by the Irish Free State on the strength of the grant to it by the Treaty of 1921 of the same status as Canada. Accordingly in 1924 the British Government obtained the appointment to Washington of an Irish Minister Plenipotentiary. This appointment involved a distinct departure from the plan envisaged in 1920. It was no longer possible to contemplate the Irish Minister taking the place of the

[1] Keith, *Speeches and Documents on the British Dominions, 1918–1931*, pp. 380 ff.

Ambassador when on leave of absence and thus working in the closest connection with the British Embassy. When the principle was recommended for adoption in 1926 this idea was not revived even for Canada, but the United States Government now reciprocated by appointing Ministers to Canada and the Irish Free State.

Despite these important decisions of the Conference of 1926 which might be deemed to emphasise the distinct personalities of each Dominion and the emphasis laid, in the definition of Dominion status quoted above, on the equality of the Dominions with the United Kingdom in respect of external affairs, the Conference also enunciated a doctrine which asserted an underlying unity, which negatived the view that the Empire had been dissolved into a number of distinct international units. The Irish Free State[1] in 1924 made use of its admission to the League of Nations, which had been secured by the British Government, to register with the League Secretary the Treaty of 1921. The British Government insisted that since the Covenant of the League of Nations came into force it had consistently taken the view that neither the Covenant nor any conventions concluded under the auspices of the League were intended to govern the relations *inter se* of various parts of the British Commonwealth, so that the provisions of Article XVIII. of the Covenant were not applicable to the Treaty of 1921. The Free State dissented, but the Imperial Conference of 1926 apparently concurred with the Imperial Government, for it pointed out that the Legal Committee of the Arms Traffic Conference in 1925 had laid it down that the terms of League conventions must not

[1] *Ibid.* pp. 347, 348.

be regarded as regulating *inter se* the rights and obligations of various territories, subject to the same
sovereign. It was recommended that in any case where
the terms of conventions were to be made applicable
between parts of the Commonwealth, this should be
expressly indicated and such conventions should preferably not take the form of treaties between heads of
States.

The issue, however, has again been raised. The
Irish Free State in accepting the Optional clause of
the Statute of the Permanent Court of International
Justice declined to concur with the rest of the Commonwealth in excluding from the operation of its acceptance questions arising between itself and another
part of the Commonwealth, and though the Union of
South Africa excluded such disputes from its acceptance, it asserted that it did so, not on the ground that
the Permanent Court was not a legitimate tribunal
to deal with inter-Imperial disputes, but because it
thought that such disputes could be dealt with better
by another procedure. The Irish Free State repeated
this view when it accepted the General Act of 1928
for the pacific settlement of international disputes,
which the Union has failed so far to accept.[1]

The distinct character of the Dominion, however,
has been unquestionably increased since the decision
of the Irish Free State in 1931, followed by the Union
in 1934, to act in foreign affairs in direct communication with the King, without employing the formal
mediation of the Dominions or the Foreign Office. In
the case of the Union, independence has been further
stressed by the enactment of the Status of the Union

[1] Keith, *op. cit.* pp. 410 f., 435 f.

Act, 1934, under which the authority of the King with regard to external affairs may be exercised by the Governor-General. This is a striking innovation, for it has never been the practice for the King to delegate to the Governor-General his prerogative in respect of external affairs, such as the making of war or peace, the declaration of neutrality, and the conclusion of treaties.

On the other hand, it remains true that all foreign relations are conducted in the name of the King, and it is the view of the British Government, communicated to foreign powers, when arrangements are made for the separate diplomatic representation of the Dominions, that the arrangements proposed do not denote any departure from the principle of the diplomatic unity of the Empire, that is to say, the principle of consultative co-operation amongst all His Majesty's representatives, as amongst His Majesty's Governments themselves, in matters of common concern. Moreover, it is important to note that the parallel of Hanover is by no means wholly applicable, though naturally it is cited by those authorities in the Irish Free State and the Union who claim that these territories are sovereign International States. The Hanoverians, under the régime enforced in 1714 to 1837, were indeed regarded by English law as British subjects, but British subjects do not appear to have been regarded as Hanoverians. The Crown of Hanover was not indissolubly linked with that of the United Kingdom, but each was held on a separate tenure, and their separation was from the first inevitable so soon as the British crown passed to a woman. In the case of the Dominions there is no diversity in the

H

tenure of the crown, and the Dominions have never been wholly separate kingdoms.

The same issue, of course, presents itself in the form of the question whether a Dominion may remain neutral in a British war. A Royal Commission in Victoria in 1870 suggested the neutralisation of the Colonies on the Belgian model, but the idea had no success.[1] In 1899 the possibility of the neutrality of the Cape of Good Hope in the war with the Boer Republics was canvassed by the Cape Ministry but dismissed as a chimaera. In 1911 the same idea was disowned by General Botha, and the Union Government threw itself whole-heartedly into the Great War, declining any suggestion of remaining neutral as regards German South-West Africa. General Hertzog, however, has consistently asserted that the status of the Union involves the right to remain neutral and the passing of the Status of the Union Act and the Royal Executive Function and Seals Act in 1934 accords a certain speciousness to this claim, because in strict law the way has been left open for the issue by the Governor-General of a proclamation of neutrality. It must, however, be noted that the claim of General Hertzog is hard to reconcile with the obligation to protect, as regard land defences, the British Naval base at Simonstown, which was undertaken in 1921 by the Union, when the War Department lands were handed over, free of cost, to the Union Government.[2] It would clearly be inconsistent with the obligation of true neutrality for the Union to make good this

---

[1] Keith, *Responsible Government*, ii. 868 f.
[2] Keith, *Letters on Imperial Relations, 1916–1935*, pp. 166, 167; *Morning Post*, April 12, 1935.

undertaking, while to fail to do so would be a grave breach of faith. This consideration and the common allegiance to the Crown of the Union and the United Kingdom differentiate the case entirely from the position of Spain towards Gibraltar with which it has been repeatedly compared by General Hertzog.

In the case of the Irish Free State, the State is under obligation by the Treaty of 1921 to afford in peace certain harbour and other facilities for the purpose of coastal and other defence, and in time of war such further facilities as the British Government may require. As Mr de Valera has admitted, the carrying out of this obligation would be inconsistent with the duty of international neutrality, and on this and other grounds he has demanded abrogation of these obligations.

It must be added that no other Dominion claims the right of neutrality, nor does any other Dominion apparently adopt the view that the Commonwealth consists of distinct international units.

There is singularly little evidence as to the views held on the subject by foreign Governments. But what evidence there is, is unfavourable to the view that the Dominions are distinct international units. The question presented itself when it was proposed in 1929 in connection with the revision of the Statute of the Permanent Court of International Justice to ascribe to any Dominion the right of having a judge of its own appointed to the court, if the Dominion were involved in a dispute, despite the fact that there is a British judge on the tribunal. It was not felt desirable to include this provision in the revised Statute and, though the decision not to make the change was ascribed to technical grounds, it is probable that it was motived in part at least by reluctance to recognise the separate individuality of the Dominions.

2. *The Empire and the League of Nations*

The unity of the Empire, preserved, as we have seen, generally in diplomatic relations, is largely lost in the part assigned to it in the League of Nations. Under the Covenant, while the British Empire is a member of the League, the same position is assigned to the four great Dominions and to India, while, on the final completion of its constitutional arrangements, the Irish Free State claimed a like position, and in 1923 received similar treatment. Each of the members of the League is entitled to one vote in the Assembly of the League, and to be represented at Assembly meetings by three delegates. The British Empire, as one of the principal allied and associated powers, is entitled to permanent membership of the Council of the League, but the Dominions and India are admitted to be qualified for election to the places on the Council to be filled by the choice of Assembly from time to time. It is singularly characteristic that as early as 1927 Canada achieved membership, followed in 1930 by the Irish Free State and in 1933 by the Commonwealth.

There are obvious difficulties in applying to the Dominions and India the full terms of the Covenant. If applied, the various parts of the Empire would guarantee under Article X. the territorial integrity and existing political independence of one another, while, if any part of the Empire should enter into war

contrary to its duties under Articles XII., XIII., or
XV. of the Covenant, the other parts would be bound
to apply to it measures of commercial, and even of
naval and military constraint, on the ground that it
had committed an act of war against the other members of the League. There is, it is clear, an element of
absurdity in such a result; it assumes the power of
the Dominions to go to war separately which runs
counter to the fact that this is a right not yet claimed
formally by the Dominions, and one which cannot be
deduced from mere membership of the League of
Nations. Moreover, it is plausible to argue that the
reference in Article X. to existing political independence is enough to show that the relations of parts of
the British Empire are not within the scope of the
article, for in no sense could the Dominions, and still
less India, be asserted to possess independence, as contrasted with autonomy. In any case the special arrangements within the British Empire can probably
be brought within the spirit of Article XXI. of the
Covenant, which provides that "nothing in this
Covenant shall be deemed to affect the validity of
international engagements, such as treaties of arbitration or regional understandings, like the Monroe
Doctrine, for securing the maintenance of peace".
If the special relations of the parts of the Empire
are to be treated as international in the eyes of the
Covenant, then they may be regarded as falling under
this head. It may, however, be candidly admitted that
the terms of the Covenant in this as in other matters
are lacking in precision.

It might have been expected that the various parts
of the Empire would have adopted the plan of com-

bining in their action on the League Assembly, with
a view to make their point of view as effective as
possible. In point of fact no such result has been
achieved; instead the Dominions have shown themselves anxious to develop their individuality and to
impress their distinctive standpoints on the Assembly.
There is a vital distinction between the position of
their representatives at League Assembly meetings
and that which they held at the Peace Conference. At
the latter the separate representation of the Dominions
and India was intended to secure them some measure
of independence in representing their special interests
in the peace settlement, but the essential authority
rested with the British Empire delegation, on which
the Dominions were from time to time formally represented, and the policy of which was determined after
the fullest discussion by the whole body of representatives of the Empire. When a vote was to be taken,
the only voice was that of the British Empire delegation, on which ultimately the views of the British
Government necessarily prevailed, although in practice the result arrived at was the outcome of mutual
accommodation of opinions. In the Assembly the
Dominions and India do not look to the British
Empire delegation to express the views of the Empire
as a whole, and the policy of that delegation is not
decided by the representatives of the whole of the
Empire. Definite conflicts of view between the British
Empire delegation and the Dominion delegations have
taken place. At the first Assembly meeting in 1920,
Canada voted for the admission of Armenia to membership, and raised the most effective protest against
the suggestion that it fell within the scope of the

functions of the League to consider such issues as the due distribution of raw materials among those powers which required them for their industries, and reminded the representatives of European powers of the fact, commonplace to British minds but still strange to others, that the policy of the Dominions is not determined by the United Kingdom in any matter affecting their internal economy. This view, which was naturally effectively supported by the other Dominions, could not be shared by the British Empire delegation, since in the Council assent had been given to the principle that the topic was one suited for examination on behalf of the League. In the following Assembly, South Africa headed the revolt against the proposal adopted by the British Empire delegation that Albania should be refused admission to the League in view of her undefined frontiers and dubious international position, and by skilled management secured the final withdrawal of opposition to the application. The Assembly of 1922 was marked by the strong and effective defence by New Zealand of her rights and position in regard to the mandate over Samoa. The Commonwealth of Australia in 1921 refrained from formal concurrence in the admission of Austria to membership of the League on the ground that, if the question should in future be raised of the allocation to Germany, when admitted into the League, of a colonial mandate, Austria would almost certainly support the German claims. Most striking of all, however, has been the activity of Canada with a view to the revision of Article X. of the Covenant with its guarantee of the territorial integrity and political independence of the members of the League. Such a burden, it is urged, is unduly onerous on minor States with other claims on their resources, and should be assumed only by the great powers, a contention which has not so far obtained the general concurrence necessary for a change in the Covenant of the League. An interpretative explanation of the Article finally failed owing to the objections of Persia. In 1929 Canada stood out as a champion of minorities.

The distinctive position of the Dominions and India in the League is manifested formally by the fact that the representatives of the Dominions and India are not diplomatically accredited by the King on the advice of the Secretary of State for Foreign Affairs, but act simply under the appointment of their Governments, although like all other representatives they enjoy, while acting in this capacity, diplomatic immunities. The Governments also correspond direct with the League Secretariat, while they in diplomatic negotiations,[1] unless they are specially represented at a foreign court, must act through the Imperial Government or its diplomatic representatives. Canada, the Irish Free State, and the Union of South Africa keep representatives at Geneva. Ratifications of Conventions are effected by the Governor-General in Council, not the King.

The possibility of inconvenience resulting from divergent views in the League Assembly is minimised by the limited powers of the League, and the general rule that decisions must be unanimous to take effect.

[1] Thus in 1922 the Franco-Canadian agreement regarding trade was arranged through the Imperial Government by Canadian ministers, and New Zealand has emphatically repudiated the possession of a sovereign status. Cf. Sir F. Bell, Legislative Council Debates, February 9, 1923. Hence it has not adopted the Statute of Westminster.

Moreover, what may be lost by divergence of view is perhaps more than made good by the spontaneity of expression of Dominion and Indian aspirations which the system permits. Of special interest is the fact that disputes between different parts of the Empire can thus be brought to the cognisance of the League, and the influence of a wider public opinion brought to bear on them. Thus in 1922, in the Assembly discussion of the rights of minorities the representative of India pressed on the South African delegation the moral obligation of that Government to secure effectively the rights of the Indian minority in the Union, and a general assurance was given on behalf of South Africa that she would act in conformity with the spirit of the discussion, though the principles affecting the protection of minorities are not legally binding on the Union. The same issue will doubtless be raised again.

The independent position attained by the Dominions and India on the League is repeated in the organisation of the Permanent Court of International Justice. Whereas on the Arbitral Tribunal of the Hague the Empire was represented as a single unit, the Dominions and India are given perfectly distinct places in respect of the tribunal, and each is authorised to constitute a body of members empowered to nominate four members, not more than two being nationals of the Dominion concerned, for consideration by the Council and Assembly of the League in the task of choosing the judges of the court. Canada defined her nationals for this purpose by the Canadian Nationals Definition Act, 1921, so as to obviate any contention that every British subject is a Canadian national, and Sir Robert Borden, one of her nominees, was a serious candidate for election as a judge of the Court. Union and Irish Free State nationals have also been defined.

We have seen above that inter-Imperial disputes are not subject to the jurisdiction of the tribunal and that it has not been decided if a Dominion before the tribunal could claim the presence of a Dominion judge, despite the fact that there is a British judge on that body.

The provision of the League Covenant which secures a distinct vote for each Dominion and India was severely criticised in the United States, where it formed one of the grounds successfully alleged against the ratification of the Treaty of Versailles. The Convention on Air Navigation [1] sought to effect a compromise in this regard, for, while it gave the status of States to the Dominions and India, it allotted to them and to the British Empire only one representative each on the International Commission for Air Navigation, which is part of the organisation of the League, as opposed to two representatives each for the United States, France, Italy, and Japan, and provided that the total voting power of the Empire was not to exceed that of any one of these powers. The mode in which the voting power of the Empire was to be distributed was not touched on in the convention, which obviously derogated from the position of the Dominions and India as secured in the Covenant of the League. In 1933 the anomaly was finally removed.

---

[1] *Parl. Pap.* Cmd. 266, 1609, 4423; Keith, *Letters on Imperial Relations, 1916–1935*, pp. 13, 14.

3. *The Forms and Agencies of International Intercourse*

Apart from the special case of the Dominions, the rule is still absolute that the conduct of all relations with foreign States, which are intended to be capable of recognition under, and enforcement by the sanctions of, international law, rests entirely with the Crown, acting on the responsibility of the Imperial Government, whose advice is tendered by the Secretary of State for Foreign Affairs. There are, of course, necessarily many relations of a business character into which departments of the Imperial Government, and even Dominion, or other overseas Governments may enter, but these relations are not regarded as treaty relations, and, if intended to have such value, they must, even if negotiated informally, be reduced to treaty form. Of such an informal character were the trade arrangements made by Canadian ministers in 1910–11 with Belgium, Holland, Italy, and the United States; on the other hand, the trade arrangements in 1922–3 of Canada with France and Italy were expressed in full treaty form.[1]

The duty of conducting the foreign relations of the Empire is discharged under the supervision of the Cabinet and the Prime Minister [2] by the Secretary of State for Foreign Affairs with the aid of a Parliamentary Under-Secretary of State,[3] and a large staff.

[1] The agreement of South Africa with Mozambique (Cmd. 1888) was not a treaty proper, the description in the print being inaccurate. Nor is the accord of 1934 of Australia and Belgium (Cmd. 4812).

[2] Cf. Queen Victoria's insistence on Lord John Russell's supervision of Lord Palmerston in 1851 (Walpole, *Lord J. Russell*, ii. 173); Mr MacDonald's control of Mr Henderson in 1929–31.

[3] In 1934–5 he was aided in League of Nations matters especially by Mr Eden as Lord Privy Seal. See Preface.

At foreign courts the King is represented by diplomatists of varying ranks, Ambassadors in the case of the most important States or those on which for some special ground the King desires to confer a special degree of consideration; envoys and ministers plenipotentiary, or ministers resident, all of whom are accredited to the sovereign of the country to which they are sent, while in the case of minor powers *chargés d'affaires* are accredited to the foreign minister only. The reception of these envoys is a matter for the foreign Government, whose approval is normally obtained in advance of the formal appointment, in order to obviate friction of any kind. Their appointment is formally notified by means of letters of credence which invite the aid of the person to whom they are addressed in securing the carrying out by the envoy of his duties. For the purpose of concluding and signing treaties full powers under the Great Seal are always issued, on the authority of a sign manual warrant countersigned by the King. Similar full powers are granted to diplomatists sent to international conferences, no letters of credence being considered requisite in their case, as their function is limited to a definite purpose, and does not include any general duty of representation. The duty of a diplomat includes the supply to the Secretary of State of all political information which may be of interest, and the making of representations to the Government with which he deals on any matters affecting British interests, either under instructions from the Secretary of State, or, in minor cases of complaints of British residents, on his own initiative. To facilitate the performance of his duties he is normally entitled to important immunities, both criminal and civil, from the jurisdiction of the foreign State in which he resides.[1]

In cases of important legations the head of the mission, in addition to the secretary of legation and other members of his staff, may be aided by naval, military, or air attachés, charged with the special duty of preparing reports on these topics for the use of the Imperial Government. The collection of commercial information is partly dealt with by the commercial diplomatic service, but is largely the work of Consuls, who are charged also with miscellaneous functions in the interests of British subjects visiting or resident in the States whither they are sent, such as issuing or affixing a visa to passports, authenticating documents, births, marriages, and deaths, and in the case of seaport towns, receiving reports from merchant vessels and investigating complaints. A Consul has normally no diplomatic status or jurisdiction, but there is an important exception in the case of those countries in which the Crown exercises extra-territorial jurisdiction over British subjects and protected persons, and in which, therefore, Consular courts exist. Posts of lesser importance are filled by Vice-Consuls and Consular agents. Consuls are appointed by commission, and all Consular officers require the assent of the Government of the country in which they are to act before they can exercise their functions. They enjoy some measure of immunity in regard to the inviolability of their papers and exemption from demands inconsistent with their effective conduct of their duties. In recent years the effectiveness of the commercial activities of the Consular service has been increased by the abandonment

[1] Wheaton, *International Law* (ed. Keith), i. 453-70.

of the employment of other than British subjects in Consular duties, and by the extension and development of the appointment of more highly qualified officers to legations, while more effective use of the information obtained has been made through the activities of the Overseas Trade Department.

The Imperial Government is charged with the decision as to the reception of diplomatic representatives from foreign States, and it issues *exequaturs*, empowering Consular officers from foreign countries to carry on their duties. In the case of Consular officers to act in a Dominion an *exequatur* or other recognition was formerly not accorded save after consultation with the Dominion, if the nominee of the foreign Government was not a *consul de carrière*, but a local resident, to whose appointment there might accordingly be some objection on local grounds. Since 1926 *exequaturs* for such officers have been countersigned by Dominion ministers. To diplomats in the United Kingdom a very extensive criminal and civil immunity is granted, partly under the common law, partly under a statute (7 Anne, c. 12) passed in consequence of the detention on civil process of the envoy of Russia.

The communication between Governments by means of the diplomatists accredited to the Courts, may be supplemented by discussions between the ministries, in which the Secretary of State for Foreign Affairs normally takes part, and of which in any event he must be kept fully informed. Inevitably, however, the conduct of foreign affairs is a matter in which the Prime Minister normally takes a deep interest, and often, as during the late war and the Premiership of Mr Lloyd George and Mr Ramsay MacDonald, an active part in negotiations may be taken by him personally. An outcome of the war was the holding of frequent meetings between the representatives of the principal allied powers, and the relegation of minor issues to a Council of their Ambassadors at Paris. More normal are international conferences to discuss special issues, but the creation of the League of Nations has resulted in such conferences falling under the sphere of the League operations. The Foreign Secretary normally attends important meetings of the League Council and Assembly, and often travels, as in April 1935, to foreign courts.

The Dominions, as already mentioned, are entitled to be represented by their own ministers in foreign States. It is of course necessary that the agreement of the foreign States should be obtained for that purpose and this step is taken by the British Government. Subsequent appointments, of course, are carried out in the usual way, letters of recall of the minister and of credence for his successor being sent by His Majesty, on the advice of the Dominion concerned. As already noted, in the Irish Free State and the Union, the Dominion seal is employed. Foreign States, as a rule reciprocate representation, but this is not usually the case where a Dominion minister is accredited to two powers, but resides mainly at the capital of the more important State. At present Canada exchanges representation with the United States, France, and Japan. The Irish Free State exchanges representation with the United States, the Holy See, France, and Germany. The Minister to France is also accredited to Belgium. The Union of South Africa exchanges representation with the Netherlands, Italy, the United States, and

Germany, as well as France. The Minister at Paris is accredited also to Lisbon, and that at Berlin to Stockholm. In their action these ministers act solely under the instructions of their Government, but they cooperate freely among themselves, so as to decide what matters fall within the sphere of each mission. Occasionally joint action in the form of representation has been taken by the Canadian and British representatives at Washington, but normally, as in the well-known case of the *I'm Alone* in 1929, the cooperation takes the form of informal conversations. In that case, which involved the sinking of a Canadian ship, the Canadian claim against the United States was ultimately presented by Canada only and settled in 1934 by an arbitral award, though it rested on a British treaty of 1924 regarding the regulation of the Liquor Traffic, by which certain derogations from the usual rule of international law were stipulated.

The Dominions have, in the main, contented themselves without establishing separate Consuls. Dominion nationals, as British subjects, are freely entitled to make use of the services of British Consuls, though some difficulty has been raised in the case of the Irish Free State, and the situation is rendered more obscure by the claim of the Irish Free State Government that under its Nationality legislation in 1935, Irish citizens are not British nationals. As, however, it is claimed that they are entitled to the advantages of their status as connected with the British Commonwealth, it would seem that they may still expect aid from British Consuls; in any case they might seek such aid on the score that under British law they are still British subjects. The Irish Free State, however, has established a Consul-General at New York and at Paris and a Consul at Boston, and the Union of South Africa maintains a Consul-General at Lourenço Marques and a Consul at Hamburg.

In treaty negotiation the same principles apply to the Dominion ministers as apply to British representatives. In the Union the privileges of foreign representatives have been recognised by legislation based on the English model, the Diplomatic Immunities Acts No. 9 of 1932 [1] and No. 19 of 1934.

Agreements with foreign powers, whether general international conventions or special agreements, may be signed by the representatives of the Crown without reserve, or merely *ad referendum*, but in all normal instances they must be ratified by the Crown to become binding. Where delay would be inconvenient or dangerous, it may be agreed that the arrangement shall go into force pending ratification, but as a rule the operation of any treaty is in abeyance until it is ratified. The authority of the Crown to make, and to ratify on the advice of ministers, any treaty whatever, is undoubted, and by ratification the treaty attains full international validity, and becomes binding in international law. But this principle is affected vitally by the fact that it is not possible for the Crown by the making of a treaty to alter the law of the land,[2] and that, accordingly, if the treaty requires any change in the law, as for instance, the reduction of customs duties, the passing of legislation is essential in order to carry out the treaty obligation. It should be noted

---

[1] Cf. Keith, *Journ. Comp. Leg.* xv. 257.

[2] Cf. *Walker* v. *Baird*, [1892] A.C. 491; Keith, *Journ. Comp. Leg.* xii. 106.

I

that the assent of Parliament is not necessary to the validity of the treaty, as it is under many Continental countries, and as regards the Senate in the United States, but for practical purposes the difference is not of high importance. It is further clear that, if legislation is necessary for any change in the law, it is desirable in even a higher degree that Parliament should approve a treaty dealing with important political interests, and that in both cases it is unwise to ratify until Parliament has approved formally the terms embodied in the treaty. The step has accordingly sometimes been taken, first, in the case of the treaty regulating the cession to Germany of Heligoland in 1890, of making the treaty expressly subject to Parliamentary approval. The plan has been criticised as an abnegation on the part of the executive of a responsibility which ministers should be willing to assume on behalf of the Crown, but there really seems no objection even in theory to the frank recognition by ministers that they must act subject to the approval of Parliament. The insertion of such a clause acts as deliberate notice to the other party to the convention that the signature on behalf of the Crown binds only the Crown to endeavour to secure ratification, and does not mean that ratification will certainly be accorded. Hence the Irish Treaty of 1921 stipulated Parliamentary approval, as did the agreement of 1925 modifying its terms, and territorial cessions to Italy in 1926 and to Perak in 1934 were thus approved.

When a treaty of any kind affects a Dominion, or India, it follows that ratification should not be expressed unless adequate provision exists for carrying it into effect, and the legislature has expressed its approval. The ratification, however, is now made on the request of the Government affected, which is responsible for securing any necessary legislation.

4. *British Nationality and Alienage*

British nationality[1] is essentially bound up with the relation of the subject to the sovereign, and is, therefore, primarily a matter for regulation by the Imperial Parliament. Equally clearly it is a matter which vitally affects the Empire at large, and accordingly, since the development of the autonomy of the Dominions, the principle has been recognised and acted on in the Imperial legislation of 1914, 1918, 1922, and 1933 that any changes in the law of nationality should be made with the concurrence of the Dominions. The result is that there is a definition by Imperial Act of the character of a natural-born British subject; arrangements exist under Imperial and concurrent Dominion legislation for the grant of naturalisation, either in the United Kingdom or overseas, which will be valid throughout the Empire, and under local legislation naturalisation may be conferred which has merely validity within the territory under the control of the legislature. All these classes of British subjects are accorded protection in foreign countries by British diplomatic officials without regard to the exact quality of their British nationality. In all cases it is possible that a double nationality may exist, and that in the foreign State, the nationality of which is incumbent on

---

[1] See A. V. Dicey and A. B. Keith, *Conflict of Laws* (1932), chap. ii.; 12 Geo. V. c. 44; 23 & 24 Geo. V. c. 49; Cmd. 1987, pp. 21, 22; 1988. App. VI.

the British subject, the British nationality may be re-fused recognition as a ground of protection. This is a result inevitable in view of the fact that there is no recognised principle of international law regulating the classes of persons over which a country may claim rights, and, in fact, nationality in the British Empire and the United States is founded on the doctrine of local birth, and not as now generally in European countries on descent. The matter is complicated by the recent adoption of the principle that descent as well as local birth should be a ground of obtaining British nationality.

The primary rule is that every person born within the British dominions is a natural-born British subject, whatever his ancestry, insignificant exceptions being children of a diplomatic agent, or of an alien enemy born during the hostile occupation of British territory. Birth anywhere on a British ship confers the same status, but not birth on a foreign ship if merely within British territorial waters. Even if born out of the British dominions the son or daughter of a British father is a natural-born British subject, provided that his father was born either in some part of the British dominions, or in a place where the Crown exercises extra-territorial jurisdiction, as in China; or was natural-ised; or became a British subject by reason of annexa-tion of territory, as in the case of the annexation of the Transvaal; or was in the service of the Crown abroad at the time of the child's birth. There remains the case of the child of a British subject whose father was born in a foreign country and does not fall under any of the exceptional categories enumerated. Prior to the Act of 1914, British nationality was accorded by statute to the grandson of a natural-born British subject, but by that act this privilege was withdrawn, so that the son of a British father born abroad, if himself born abroad, was an alien. The harshness of such a provision was revealed by the war, where the most remarkable loyalty was displayed by communities of British origin settled in foreign countries, and the Act of 1922, carrying out a resolution of the Imperial Conference of 1921, provides that the child of a British subject may obtain British nationality if his birth is registered within a year at a British consulate, and if within a year after attaining the age of twenty-one he declares his desire to retain British nationality and at the same time renounces, where this is permissible under the laws of his country of origin, his allegiance to that country if any exists.

British nationality may also be obtained by annexation of territory to the Crown, when, subject to treaty arrangements, persons resident on the ceded territory normally become British subjects.[1] On the marriage to a British subject an alien woman takes the nationality of her husband, and retains it even after the dissolution of the marriage by death or divorce. But the woman does not acquire British nationality on the naturalisation of her husband except on her application. Any person who is not under twenty-one years of age may obtain naturalisation at the discretion of the Government on satisfying certain conditions, including as a rule five years' residence in the British dominions, the last year in the territory in which the application is made, or service under the Crown, the possession of a

---

[1] Recent cases are those of the South African Republic, the Orange Free State, and in 1914 Cyprus. See Keith, *State Succession*, ch. vi.

good character, knowledge of English or other official language in those cases where more than one is recognised, and intention to reside in the British dominions or serve the Crown abroad. Minor children may be included, at the discretion of the government, in the parent's certificate of naturalisation.

British nationality, thus acquired by naturalisation, gives the person acquiring it the full status of a natural-born British subject throughout the Empire, but this fact does not, of course, prevent any part of the Empire limiting the rights, political or otherwise, of any British subject. But, in addition to Imperial naturalisation of this sort, it is possible for any part of the Empire to confer a limited naturalisation which will have no effect outside the limits of the territory in which it is granted [1] other than securing British protection in foreign countries.

The loss of British nationality follows on the now rare case of cession of territory, unless as in the Dindings Agreement in 1934 it is otherwise provided; on a British subject voluntarily becoming naturalised in any foreign country; and on the making of a declaration of alienage, which is permitted to any child born in the British dominions, but possessed of double nationality, within a year after attaining the age of twenty-one, and to persons born out of the British dominions, but having double nationality, at any time. A minor child who obtained British nationality through the inclusion of his name in his parent's certificate may similarly disclaim British nationality within a year after attaining his majority. A woman loses British nationality on marrying an alien, if by

[1] *Markwald* v. *Att.-Gen.*, [1920] 1 Ch. 348.

marriage she becomes a citizen of her husband's State; but in the event of the State of which her husband is a national being at war with the British Crown she may be permitted to resume her nationality as British, and, if a woman marries a British subject and he subsequently abandons British nationality, she is entitled to declare her decision to retain that nationality, and retains it in any case if she does not automatically obtain her husband's new nationality. For fraud or misrepresentation in obtaining a certificate of naturalisation or certain forms of misconduct the certificate may be revoked.

An alien is granted by the Imperial Act of 1914, re-enacting the legislation of 1870, full rights of acquisition and disposal of personal property anywhere, and of real property in the United Kingdom, but these rights do not extend to the possession of any municipal or Parliamentary franchise or to ownership of a British ship. As a result of the war, various other disabilities, in the main temporary, were imposed on aliens, being subjects of States which during the war were enemies, and the general rule was laid down that no alien should be a member of the Civil Service.

The development of Dominion autonomy inevitably raises the issue how far each Dominion has nationals of its own, connected with it more intimately than ordinary British subjects. The question arose first in the case of immigration restriction Acts, as the problem necessarily arose what British subjects could properly be excluded. In the Commonwealth it was ruled by the High Court that the Parliament had no power to exclude natives of Australia who had gone on temporary visits abroad, since they were in no sense immigrants, and the Commonwealth power related to them only. The principle is obviously one of equity, and has tacitly been adopted in practice by the Dominions. Canada explicitly defined, in the Immigration Act, 1910, who are Canadian citizens for the purposes of laws restricting immigration, and in the Canadian Nationals Definition Act, 1921, she defined Canadian nationals, for purposes connected with the question of eligibility of persons for nomination for membership of the Permanent Court of International Justice. The term now includes every Canadian citizen within the meaning of the Immigration Act; the wife of any such citizen; and any person born out of Canada whose father was a Canadian national at the time of that person's birth, or would have been a Canadian national if the status had then existed. Canadian nationality may be renounced by any person born out of Canada who is a Canadian national under the Act, and also by any person born in Canada if at birth or during his minority he became a national of the United Kingdom, or a Dominion, as well as a Canadian national. The legislation is not altogether free from difficulty, but it was made abundantly clear in the House of Commons that there is no question of affecting the primary position of every Canadian national as a British subject.

The Irish Free State constitution conferred citizenship, and with it political rights, only on persons domiciled in the Free State on December 6, 1922, who were born there, or one of whose parents was born there, or who had been ordinarily resident for seven years.[1]

[1] The other two categories of persons were normally British subjects, but not the last category save within the limits of the Free State itself.

There was a vital distinction between this provision and that of the Canadian legislation, for Canada did not refuse political rights to British subjects because they have not attained Canadian nationality as defined in the Act.

The definition was clearly imperfect and it had therefore to be extended by the Irish Nationality and Citizenship Act of 1935. This measure follows in the main the principle of the British Nationality legislation of 1914–33, both as regards the definition of natural-born citizens and the grant of naturalisation. The treatment of women differs slightly. Marriage is denied any effect, automatically, on citizenship. But a citizen married to an alien, continuously resident outside the Free State and intending to reside outside, loses citizenship unless he or she lodges a declaration electing to retain such citizenship. Facilities are similarly given for naturalisation to aliens married to citizens. Provision is made for the grant by convention of mutual citizenship rights between the Free State and other countries, and without such convention the Executive Council may confer on citizens of any country, which confers rights on Irish citizens, rights in the Free State, similar to those enjoyed by Irish citizens in that country.[1] But this power does not apply to such political or economic rights as are specially reserved for Irish citizens.

What is more important is that the Irish legislation abolishes within the Free State the British Commonwealth Statute Law of Nationality and claims for Irish citizens both within and without the Free State

[1] See Aliens Act, 1935; Aliens (Exemption) Order, 1935, which confers a status corresponding to that already in force on British subjects.

national status as such citizens only. It is clear that this legislation is ineffective to deprive such persons of their status as British subjects in other British territories or in foreign countries, though a foreign State may, if it thinks fit, recognise Irish citizens as entitled only to the protection of Irish Legations.

In the Union of South Africa,[1] Union nationality is conferred on persons born therein; British subjects who have lawfully entered the Union and who have been domiciled therein for two years at least, while so domiciled; naturalised British subjects, after three years' continuous domicile; persons born outside the Union, whose fathers were nationals at the time of the child's birth, or would have been nationals if the Act had been in force, and the wives of Union nationals. There are, as in the case of Canada, provisions for the renunciation of Union nationality, by persons who are nationals of other parts of the Empire.

[1] Union Nationality and Flags Act, 1927. Union nationality has been accorded to ex-burghers who left the republics on annexation and so were not deemed to have become British subjects by Act No. 14 of 1932. Presumably they are not British subjects in English law.

CHAPTER IV

IMPERIAL CO-OPERATION IN FOREIGN AFFAIRS AND
DEFENCE

1. *Co-operation in Commercial Negotiations*

IT was inevitable and natural that in the early days
of colonial development the Imperial Government
should include the British Possessions in the conventions negotiated for the United Kingdom, but this
condition of affairs inevitably ceased to be applicable
when the abandonment in 1846 and the following years
of the policy of protection inaugurated a fresh era in
British commercial policy. The Imperial Government
was not slow to realise that the loss of the preference
formerly enjoyed by Canada in the home markets was
a serious matter to the young community, it abrogated
in 1849 the navigation laws which fettered Colonial
use of foreign shipping, and it was thanks to extremely
effective diplomacy on the part of Lord Elgin in
Canadian interests that a reciprocity treaty was negotiated with the United States in 1854, under which
Canada made rapid strides in economic development.
The termination of that treaty, through the discovery
by the United States that the bargain was too good a
one for Canada, resulted in several efforts in which the
United Kingdom strongly supported Canadian wishes
to secure a fresh treaty; but the steps taken proved
unavailing. The co-operation of British diplomats and

Canadian ministers was, however, continued, and Sir John Macdonald played a great part in the negotiation of the important Treaty of Washington of 1871, which settled many outstanding issues, both commercial and political, with the United States. The Imperial Government also showed itself anxious to aid Canada to obtain closer commercial relations with Cuba, Brazil, and Mexico, but enquiries, in 1866, of these Governments elicited no result. In 1879 a further effort was made to secure a special treaty with Spain, and Sir A. Galt, as representative of Canada, was associated, but in a subordinate capacity, with the British Ambassador at Madrid in the negotiations, which proved unavailing. The attempt was renewed in 1884, when the new High Commissioner for Canada, Sir Charles Tupper, attained the right of negotiating as a plenipotentiary in conjunction with the British representative at Madrid. The plan failed of fruition, as Spain did not care to negotiate, but the right of Dominion statesmen to take part as plenipotentiaries in the negotiations of special conventions was recognised again in 1887, when Sir Charles Tupper was associated with Mr J. Chamberlain, and Sir L. Sackville West, the British Minister at Washington, in abortive commercial negotiations in regard to the fisheries. A still more striking but informal episode took place in 1890; the Premier of Newfoundland succeeded in effecting an agreement with the United States Secretary of State, but strong exception was taken by Canada to the terms of the arrangements as certain to prejudice the efforts of Canada to secure agreement on the issue of the fisheries with the United States, and this effort at treaty negotiation went no further, the Imperial Government declining to convert the project into a treaty.[1] But in 1893, Sir Charles Tupper was successful, with the aid of a British diplomat, in securing a treaty with France regarding trade with Canada.

In the meantime a movement in favour of the conclusion of special arrangements with foreign powers on trade questions had been on foot in Australia, and the whole question was raised prominently at a largely attended Conference at Ottawa in 1894. The representations of the Colonial Governments received sympathetic consideration and the principles governing the matter were laid down by the Secretary of State for the Colonies in a despatch[2] of June 28, 1895. "A foreign power", Lord Ripon pointed out, "can only be approached through Her Majesty's representative, and any agreement entered into with it affecting any part of Her Majesty's dominions is an agreement between Her Majesty and the sovereign of the foreign State; and it is to Her Majesty's Government that the foreign State would apply in case of any question arising under it." Any arrangement regarding trade relations between a Colony and a foreign power must be concluded between the Crown and that State, and not between the State and the Colony, for the concession of the treaty power to the Colonies—as had been suggested in Australia as early as 1870—would at once break up the Empire, a result which neither the United Kingdom nor the Colonies desired. The negotiations would be carried on by Her Majesty's representative at the foreign court, with the aid as a plenipotentiary or in a subordinate capacity of a colonial delegate. The treaty would be signed by the plenipotentiaries, after the

---

[1] *Parl. Pap.* C. 6303.   [2] *Parl. Pap.* C. 7824, pp. 16 ff

preliminary approval of its terms by the Imperial and Colonial Governments, and would fall to be ratified by the Crown on the advice of the Imperial Government. In advising the Crown that Government would act on the representations of the Colonial Government, and it would be necessary before ratification could take place that any alteration in local legislation required should be carried through the legislature, so as to ensure that the obligations undertaken by the Crown in the treaty were certain of immediate fulfilment. At the same time the conditions on which such ratification must depend were indicated: (1) No treaty could be approved unless any concession made to a foreign power under it were immediately extended to every foreign power entitled to most favoured nation treatment in the Colony under existing treaties. (2) Further, any concession so made must be extended unconditionally to the whole of the British possessions, and (3) no concession must be accepted from a foreign Government which would prejudice the interests of other parts of the Empire. The first of these conditions was, of course, no addition to colonial obligations, while the other two asserted the fundamental principle that the different parts of the Empire should consider one another's interests as superior to the advantage to be derived for one part by concessions to a foreign power.

The decision of 1895 was accompanied by the passing of legislation to remove the last fetter on the freedom of legislation of the Australian Colonies in tariff matters imposed in 1842, and relaxed in part in 1873. There remained, however, one difficulty respecting the freedom of the Colonies to enact their own tariffs. Under the Treaties of 1865 and 1862 with Germany and

Belgium it was impossible for the Colonies to accord preferential treatment to British goods imported into them, since these conventions secured Germany and Belgium national treatment in regard to imports. The Liberal Government in 1895 was unwilling to risk disputes with these powers by denouncing the treaties, and it was not until after the subject had again been raised at the Colonial Conference of 1897, that steps were taken in 1898 to bring the treaties to an end, and Canada was able to grant an effective British preference, which no foreign power could share. Negotiations for foreign treaties in the interests of the Dominion hung fire until 1907, when Canadian ministers secured a fresh convention with France to supersede that of 1893. On the occasion of this negotiation Sir Edward Grey reiterated the principles announced in 1895, subject only to the modification that it was not thought necessary that the British representative at Paris should take an active part in the negotiations, which were conducted direct between the Canadian ministers and the French Government. The agreement reached, however, was signed by the British representative along with the Canadian ministers under the authority of full powers issued for the purpose, and signature was only authorised after careful scrutiny had satisfied the Imperial Government that the principles of 1895 had been fully adhered to. The change in the manner of negotiation was then claimed, erroneously, as a great advance in the freedom of Dominion negotiation; in point of fact, the actual course adopted had been foreshadowed in the case of Sir Charles Tupper's projected negotiation with Spain in 1884, and had been followed in principle in 1893. The actual Treaty of 1907 proved unsatisfactory to the French Parliament and was modified by a supplementary agreement of 1909, concluded in the same way, before it became acceptable. Changed circumstances during the war rendered the treaty unsuitable to the existing circumstances, and its operation was terminated by the wish of Canada in 1920. In 1921, however, a modified form of agreement was negotiated and signed,[1] as in 1907 and 1909. The question of the propriety of this mode of procedure in view of the new status of Canada, as a member of the League of Nations, was raised in the Dominion Parliament, but the Government had no hesitation in defending its action, and in 1922 a more comprehensive arrangement was similarly negotiated, and signed by the British Ambassador at Paris and two Canadian ministers.

It is important to note that in the legislation which was passed by the Canadian Parliament in order to give effect to the convention of December 15, 1922, full regard was had to the principles which were laid down by Lord Ripon in 1895 as essential if the Empire were to remain a unity, although these rules no longer had binding power. It was expressly provided that the advantages granted to France and to French possessions by the convention in matters of trade should be accorded to the United Kingdom in respect of its commerce with Canada for so long as the concessions remained in force with regard to France and her possessions. It was further provided that similar advantages should be enjoyed by the products of any British possession in respect of its commerce with Canada if that possession granted to Canada the benefit of the most favourable

---

[1] See *Parl. Pap.* Cmd. 1514. This has since been superseded.

customs tariff which it might accord to any foreign
State. The last provision was not, therefore, absolute in
its terms, but it effectively secured all that was aimed
at in Lord Ripon's conditions. The actual terms of the
convention further showed that care had been taken
not to make concessions to France which would be
likely, despite equality of treatment, to injure British
trade, while the concessions obtained from France were
obviously legitimate. In this case, of course, the special
nature of the trade rendered this possible; in any
further development of reciprocal trade relations with
the United States, which is always before the eyes of a
Dominion Government, equality of treatment, on geographical grounds, must result in an effective preference
in many respects to the United States over the United
Kingdom. But that is rooted on natural advantages
which it would be useless as well as idle to ignore,
though for the time being American feeling is opposed
to reciprocity on any substantial scale.

As already mentioned, in 1923 the discussion of the
Halibut Fisheries Treaty between Canada and the
United States resulted in the bringing before the Imperial Conference of that year of the question of treaty
negotiations. As a result of the rules laid down by the
Conference, any Dominion can negotiate through the
British Government, or where it maintains its own
diplomatic representative, by their instrumentality
any commercial treaty which it desires. In doing so
it is under an obligation, though not one with any
legal sanction, to keep other units of the Empire
informed, and the principles which were laid down
in 1895, though not binding, are clearly such as to
deserve the fullest consideration. Moreover, since the

K

doctrine of Imperial Preference was asserted during the war and given effect by the United Kingdom in the Finance Act of 1919, the general principle prevails that preferences to units of the Empire should, where possible, be given. It has been almost the invariable practice to make it clear in any treaties with foreign powers that inter-Imperial preferences are not affected by most-favoured-nation clauses in treaties; even the Irish Free State, in its commercial treaties negotiated freely by its own representatives, has adopted this principle. Considerable regret was felt in the Empire when in its Treaty of 1928 with Germany, the Union of South Africa pledged herself to extend to Germany any further British preference. In 1932 at the Ottawa Conference the principle that Imperial Agreements were not affected by most-favoured-nation clauses in treaties was laid down, and the Union of South Africa gave effect to the principle by securing release from the stipulations of the treaty with Germany.

When negotiations are conducted through British instrumentalities, inevitably it would be possible for objections to be raised more easily than is the case when the negotiations are conducted through Dominion representatives. Even in those cases in which, under the authority of the Imperial Conference of 1930, Dominion Governments deal direct with British representatives in foreign countries, these representatives must report to the Foreign Secretary their action. But it appears to be a convention that no greater advantage of this position shall be taken by the British Government, and that Governments which use British agencies shall be treated precisely as are those Governments which act direct. The latter, of course, are under

the obligation to inform the other units of the Commonwealth of their negotiations; thus the British
Government was given the opportunity to criticise the
German Treaty of 1928, though the Union Government then was unable to accept its suggestions. It is
obvious that the exchange of information is of high
importance, for the parts of the Empire are often
closely allied in interest. Canada and Newfoundland
have, in the past, been rivals for the favours of the
United States; the interests of Australia and New
Zealand do not always coincide; and the relations
between the Union and Portugal, as set out in the
Union-Mozambique Convention of 1934, are of substantial importance to the United Kingdom, in respect
of its African territories as well as to Southern Rhodesia.
Moreover, the British alliance with Portugal causes the
United Kingdom to be interested in all matters affecting that State.

The British Government in its own commercial
negotiations adopts the policy of endeavouring, as far
as practicable, to obtain from foreign powers the right
to secure the application of treaties to British Colonies,
Protectorates, and Mandated Territories. Moreover,
unless objections are raised by any Dominion, it
endeavours to secure the right of acceptance for the
Dominion, and, if the foreign power consents, the
principle that Dominion products shall enjoy in the
foreign country most-favoured-nation treatment, so
long as the Dominion accords such treatment to exports from that country. This concession is naturally
one which all foreign States are not willing to grant.

It is further the practice of the United Kingdom to
claim that the concessions which it obtains in these

treaties for British subjects as regards such matters as the right of entry, residence, carrying on business or professions, exemption from various obligations and other privileges, apply also to British subjects connected with the Dominions, even when the Dominion has refused to accede to the treaty in question. This claim has usually been acquiesced in by foreign countries, but with the growth of separate Dominion nationalities, its assertion becomes more and more difficult, and in its latest treaties with France, Canada has adopted the plan of having, in addition to a treaty definitely commercial, a general treaty covering those rights of subjects, which hitherto would have been claimed for Canadians simply as British subjects.[1] The Irish Free State, in the same manner, has negotiated conventions which provide for Irish nationals, or citizens, privileges similar to those which in British treaties are claimed for British subjects.

Under modern practice, the right to accede to treaties for Colonies or for Dominions to accede is accompanied by the right of withdrawal, without prejudice to the validity of the treaty in general. The earlier practice was to conclude for the whole Empire; by 1880 it was recognised that the Colonies ought not to be included without their consent, and in 1882, for the first time, the self-governing Colonies were given the right of adherence at their discretion. The rule was later extended to all Colonies, and from 1899 the right of separate withdrawal, generally, was asked for. Further, in deference to recommendations of the Colonial Conference of 1902 and 1907 and the Imperial Conference of 1911, the power to withdraw from

[1] Keith, *Journ. Comp. Leg.* xvi. 138.

earlier treaties concluded without limitation of date, was obtained for the Dominions.

In the case of India, control over treaty-making is still retained by the British Government, and under the new constitution external relations remain under the full control of the Governor-General. But by a convention, the conclusion of treaties with foreign powers is subject to the approval of the Indian legislature, and it is clear that only in very abnormal circumstances would the British Government be prepared to secure through the legislative powers of the Governor-General the giving of effect to a treaty rejected by the Indian legislature.

Apart from formal treaties, inter-governmental accords are recognised—formally by the Imperial Conference of 1923—as legitimate. But there are, in point of fact, inconveniences in proceeding in this manner, which were seen in Canada in 1910–11. In the former year informal negotiations between Canadian officials and the German Consul-General resulted in Germany deciding to abandon the tariff differentiation against Canada, which she had enforced in retaliation for the denunciation in 1897–8 of the Treaty of 1865, in order to permit of the British preference given by Canada. The hostility of Germany had evoked Canadian retaliation in the shape of a surtax on German imports; under the new understanding, which was quite informal, this was dropped while Germany admitted Canadian goods on the same terms as those accorded to British goods generally. The success of this arrangement led to informal negotiations resulting in concessions to Italy, Belgium, and Holland, and to the far more important effort to secure a reciprocity arrangement with the United States. This resulted in the signature of an agreement in 1911, which was to be carried out by legislation on either side, but was not to be treated as a diplomatic engagement, thus obviating the intervention, on the one hand, of the treaty rights of the United States Senate, and on the other hand, of the control of the Imperial Government. Although Canadian ministers had endeavoured to observe faithfully the substance of the rules laid down in 1895 and 1907, it was doubtful whether the treaty might not result as the President expected in the United States acquiring an undue political influence in Canada; the Bill to give effect to the arrangement was successfully obstructed in the House of Commons, and ultimately the Premier dissolved Parliament, to be decisively defeated, largely owing to the feeling that the interests of the Empire as a whole had been insufficiently considered, a position which could hardly have arisen had the agreement taken normal treaty form.

2. *Co-operation in Political Affairs before the War*

(a) Foreign Policy

From the earliest period of responsible government the Imperial Government recognised the necessity and propriety of taking no step in regard to issues affecting the Colonies without full consultation with the Governments of the territories concerned. Soon after the grant of responsible government to Newfoundland in 1856, a formal assurance was conveyed to the ministry that no change in the treaty burdens affecting Newfoundland, in relation either to France or to the United

States, would be agreed to without the discussion of the issues with the Colonial administration. Similarly in 1865–70 an elaborate interchange of views between Canada and the United Kingdom took place during the period of troubled relations which followed on the refusal of the United States to continue the policy of reciprocity, and the revival in an acute form of the controversy over American fishery rights on the Canadian coast, complicated by the resentment felt in the United States towards the British attitude in the war of secession, the *Alabama* claims, and Canadian counter-claims in respect of the Fenian invasion of Canada from American territory. The difficulty of envisaging such issues from a broad point of view is revealed by the complaints made by Sir John Macdonald, who represented Canada in the negotiation of the Treaty of Washington, 1871, of the failure of his British colleagues to press Canadian interests. The British delegates realised very keenly the strength of anti-British feeling in the United States, and the complete inability of the United Kingdom to give effective aid to the Dominion in the event of hostilities. Moreover, if they were unable to press Canadian interests as far as Sir John Macdonald desired, they effected a settlement of the fisheries question which the United States thought very disadvantageous to herself, and they consented to a settlement of the *Alabama* episode, which was certain to involve Britain in heavy payments, and which went far beyond the code then recognised at international law.

Nor can the United Kingdom justly be blamed for the loss to Germany of South-West Africa in 1884, for the prime responsibility for a misfortune—since happily remedied—lay with the dilatoriness of the Government of the Cape of Good Hope, including Cecil Rhodes, which refused until too late to give the assurance as to expenses of administration which the Imperial Government very naturally made the condition of consent to annexation. The almost contemporaneous dispute with Queensland, over the attempt of the former in 1883 to annex the island of New Guinea, reveals the impossibility of expecting a colonial Government, remote from Europe, to appreciate the gravity of the breach with France over the occupation of Egypt, and the determined efforts of Germany to secure a colonial empire, which rendered insistence on the whole extent of the colonial demands out of the question.[1] Equally unjust, if natural, were the reproaches addressed by Mr Seddon to Mr Chamberlain in 1899, when the cession of British claims in respect of Samoa was enforced by Germany through the medium of a menace of hostility if her demands were not conceded, at the moment when the British forces in South Africa had suffered a series of disasters equally unexpected and humiliating. Similarly the representations of Australia and New Zealand, at the Colonial Conference of 1907, in regard to the failure of Britain to secure full sovereignty over the New Hebrides, ignored the fact that Britain never had the means sufficient for wholesale acquisitions of territory, and that her failures are far less noteworthy than her successes in securing lands. Newfoundland at the same Conference protested vehemently against the conduct of the negotiations with the United States regarding the rights of American fishermen in the Newfoundland fisheries, and refused absolutely to accept the pro-

[1] Cf. Keith, *The Belgian Congo and the Berlin Act* (1919).

posals of the Imperial Government for a *modus vivendi* pending the reference of the dispute to arbitration. It became, therefore, necessary for the Imperial Government to proceed to the extreme step of suspending the operation of Newfoundland legislation against American rights or pretended rights, by the issue of an Order in Council under an Imperial Act of 1819, passed in order to empower the carrying out of the Treaty of 1818 with the United States, under which extensive rights in Newfoundland were conceded. It is significant of the unwisdom of the Newfoundland attitude that none of the other Dominions supported the attitude of that Government.[1] By the prudent decision of the Imperial Government a grave state of friction with the United States was obviated, and the reference of the question to arbitration resulted in a settlement advantageous for Newfoundland. On the other hand, persistence in the Newfoundland policy of seeking to enforce her authority on American vessels in the Newfoundland fishery must have meant a serious rupture with the United States, all the more inexcusable since there was agreement to refer the question to arbitration, and it was obviously essential to come to a reasonable compromise for the period pending the decision of the arbitral court.

While there has never been any doubt as to the necessity of consulting the Dominions on matters specially affecting their interests, the idea of taking those Governments into the councils of the Empire on general political questions is of quite modern growth. It was natural enough that this should be so. The colonists in the early period of the development of the territories

[1] Cf. Keith, *Speech and Documents on British Colonial Policy*, ii. 167-81.

were most anxious to be free from any connection with high policy which they could not hope seriously to modify. This spirit found its fullest expression in the proposal emanating from a Royal Commission in Victoria in 1870, which suggested that the Colonies should be given the power of making treaties so as to be able to arrange their own commercial relations, and be secured by international negotiations the status of neutrality, while remaining under the British Crown. The idea was prompted in part by the fact that the case of the neutrality of Belgium was held to encourage belief in the inviolability of such neutrality in war; it proved far from acceptable generally in Australia and nothing came of it. But the spirit of aloofness to foreign affairs, not immediately affecting the Colonies, remained. It showed itself in the failure to realise the complexity of international relations, evinced in the impatient denunciations of every action of the Imperial Government which did not accord precisely with colonial interests. In more mature judgments, such as that of Sir Wilfrid Laurier, it took the form of resolute insistence on the attainment of autonomy in all internal affairs and rigorous abstention from any general interference in foreign relations, an attitude which he manifested consistently at the Colonial Conferences of 1897 and 1902. The position was not unnatural, for Mr Chamberlain's efforts at these meetings were rather concentrated on the necessity of the rendering of support by the Colonies to the Imperial Government in arranging for Empire defence, the burden of which he considered too great for the United Kingdom to bear alone, than on the possibility of securing the Colonies an effective voice in foreign affairs. The two positions were each natural and defensible: Mr Chamberlain, in effect, contended that it was not just that the United Kingdom should alone defray the cost of defence of the Empire, a proposition not in itself answerable; Sir W. Laurier met the demand by the arguments, first, that it was impossible to expect the Colonies to accept taxation for defence other than local, when over foreign policy in general they neither had, nor could effectively be given, any real control, since, even if federation were practicable, the voices of the Colonies would be over-ridden by weight of numbers; second, that the resources of Canada were far better expended, even from the point of view of Imperial defence, on building up the Dominion, and equipping it with its great trans-continental railways.

The passage of time, bringing with it growth of population, greater accumulated wealth, increase of communications, and a higher standard of education in political issues, resulted in the appearance of a demand in the Dominions for a share in Imperial policy. This was voiced insistently at the Imperial Conference of 1911 by the Commonwealth of Australia, where much feeling had been excited by the conclusion of the Declaration of London as the result of the labours of a Conference summoned under a decision of the Hague Conference of 1907. It is significant of the change of attitude that the Dominions had shown no interest in the Hague Conference of 1907, and that it was the propaganda in the United Kingdom against what was asserted to be a dangerous surrender of sea power by the Declaration that raised fears in the Commonwealth regarding the position of her trade and general security in any future war. The Imperial Government made no attempt to justify the policy of not consulting the Dominions in these matters; it pointed out that, in failing to do so, it had simply followed precedent, and suggested the creation of a new rule for the future, under which the Dominions should be consulted when preparations were being made to issue instructions to the British delegates at future Hague Conferences, and that, when draft conventions had been provisionally agreed to at these Conferences, they should be circulated to the Dominions for any observations these Governments might desire to offer before final signature. The same procedure, when time and opportunity and subject matter permitted, was to be followed as regards other conventions affecting Dominion interests. It is, however, important to note that Sir W. Laurier expressly dissented from any attempt to make it a rule that the Dominions must be consulted on international issues not immediately affecting them, on the broad ground that, if such consultation took place, the Dominions became involved in the necessity of supporting the action decided upon, at any rate if they concurred in it.

The change of Government which took place in Canada at the close of 1911 resulted in a fresh effort to promote Imperial co-operation in foreign affairs. Contemporaneously with the Imperial Conference of 1911, a meeting of Dominion ministers had taken place at the Committee of Imperial Defence at which Sir E. Grey made a full disclosure of the situation of European politics, with special reference to the growing danger of friction between Germany and France, and the meeting in view of the European situation decided unanimously to support the renewal of the alliance with

Japan, which on its merits was not popular in Australia or Canada. The same information then accorded to Sir W. Laurier had now to be given to his successor, Mr Borden, and, as the outcome of discussions with him, the Imperial Government suggested to the Dominions that each should be represented in London by a resident minister of the Dominion Cabinet, who would attend meetings of the Committee of Imperial Defence, when matters interesting the Dominions were under consideration, and should be in free and full communication with British ministers, so as to be kept properly informed on all matters of British and foreign policy, although, of course, the final control of such policy must rest with the Imperial Cabinet. The proposal was intended at once to strengthen the preparations of the Empire for defence, and to secure that, while the Dominions could not control foreign policy, every important step should be taken with their knowledge, so that any representations which they deemed it desirable to make, could be brought effectively by an officer of Cabinet rank before the Imperial Government. The suggestion, however, was coldly received in the Dominions generally, being treated as premature, and it was not until 1914 that even Canada on Lord Strathcona's death carried it into effect to the extent of appointing a Cabinet minister to act as High Commissioner, in lieu of filling that office on a purely official basis.

It is characteristic of the general tendency in the Dominions and the United Kingdom alike during this period that a formal suggestion of Imperial Federation, put forward by Sir Joseph Ward at the Imperial Conference of 1911, received scant shift from the Conference, though it is fair to say that the scheme was presented to the Conference in an unexpected form, and that both its presentation and discussion showed evidence of insufficient preparation or appreciation of the issues involved. It was made clear, however, by all the Dominions save New Zealand, that no surrender of their autonomy was possible even for the sake of securing a formal, as opposed to a real, voice in determining foreign policy.

(b) Defence

The state of feeling during the early years of colonial existence, and the material conditions prevailing, rendered any idea of preparation for co-operation in Imperial defence out of the question. On the contrary, Imperial forces were for a time maintained side by side with local militia, governed by colonial Acts, in order to protect the Colonies from internal risks, arising from local elements of danger as well as from external attack. The difficulty of such an arrangement became early obvious in New Zealand, where the Maoris were formidable antagonists of the young Colony. There was disagreement in 1862–70 between the officer commanding the forces and the local Governments as to the plan of campaign and the measures to be adopted; the Imperial Government did not concur in the views of ministers, and pointed out that it was impossible for them to accept the position that the Imperial Exchequer was to defray the cost of, and the War Office to provide, troops to be used at the sole discretion of the local Government. The local Government naturally enough could not see its way to accommodate its native policy to the views of the Imperial Government, with the inevitable result of the recall of the Imperial forces, leaving New Zealand to provide for its local defence. The Imperial Government, however, acting in accordance with a resolution of the House of Commons of 1862, raised in all cases the question of payment by the local Government for troops provided in instances where local defence alone was likely to fall to their lot; the Colonies, both on financial and general political grounds, realised that it was unwise to retain troops on the condition of payment, and the Imperial troops were rapidly withdrawn, being left only in stations of Imperial as opposed to local consequence, at Halifax and Esquimalt in Canada, and in South Africa, where there was not only need for a naval base, but the Imperial Government was responsible for peace and order in large native areas. Thus it resulted that, while Imperial troops were available in 1870 for the suppression of the Red River rebellion, in 1885 the troubles in the north-west were dealt with by Canadian forces only.

In these circumstances it was not to be expected that regular military aid from the Colonies to the Empire should be arranged for, though Canadian voyageurs served on the expedition up the Nile during the abortive attempt to meet the Dervish advance in the Sudan, and New South Wales sent a contingent. The need of the Empire in the South African War (1899–1902), however, resulted in large bodies of volunteers from Australia, New Zealand, and Canada, where the Governments assumed responsibility for arrangements for raising the men, and of course, the Cape and Natal local forces and volunteers lent their aid to their own defence against attack from the Boer republics and rebellion within their boundaries. The experience thus gained showed many inconveniences from the point of view of efficiency in improvising co-operation between the Imperial and local forces, but both at the Colonial Conferences of 1902 and 1907 it was recognised to be impossible to devise any system securing military aid to the Imperial forces in the event of a war. As the outcome of the latter Conference, however, an Imperial General Staff was organised at the War Office early in 1909; its position and functions were considered fully at the Naval and Military Conference of 1909, and the Imperial Conference of 1911. It was recognised that there could be no idea of subordinating in any way Dominion forces to Imperial control, but that there was much to be gained by standardising military matters, as far as possible, in respect of formation of units, patterns of weapons, training, and methods of transport, so that, while each Dominion force would be perfectly autonomous, it would be possible effectively to merge the whole, if in the event of war the Dominions so desired, into a homogeneous Imperial army. There was planned the attachment of Dominion officers to the Imperial General Staff in the United Kingdom, and the loan of British officers to the Dominions, with a view to the establishment there of branches of the Imperial General Staff, charged with the duty of corresponding with that body in order to concert plans of Imperial defence. During the Conference of 1911 the importance of the Committee of Imperial Defence was emphasised. This body, revived through the interest of Mr Balfour as Prime Minister, primarily to consider defence matters in the United Kingdom from a broader point

of view than the War Office or the Admiralty, was
shown to be admirably suited as a means by which
representatives of the Dominions could discuss with
the Imperial Government matters of general importance of defence, and the suggestion was made that in
each Dominion a Defence Committee should be set up
charged with the duty of considering the defence of the
Dominion as a whole, and in relation to Imperial
defence. Though little use was actually made of the
arrangement under which a Dominion representative
was to be invited to meetings when matters affecting
Dominion defence were concerned, the Committee with
the Overseas Defence Committee working under its
aegis concentrated its attention on defence problems,
and produced a valuable *War Book*, containing detailed arrangements to be acted on in the event of
war, which was adopted by Canada as a model for a
similar production for use in that Dominion.

The question of naval defence from the outset had a
more Imperial aspect, since the primary function of
the British navy was to defend the British possessions
against the possibility of attack, and any contribution
to local defence was of immediate concern as aiding in
reducing the burdens imposed on the navy. As early
as 1865 an Imperial Act [1] authorised the maintenance
by the Colonies of local forces for coast and harbour
defence, and some small use was made of its provisions in Australia. A more important step was taken
in 1887 when, as the outcome of the Colonial Conference of that year, an agreement was made under
which a stronger squadron was placed on the Aus-

[1] 28 & 29 Vict. c. 14. This Act was re-enacted with some improvements
as the Colonial Naval Defence Act, 1931 (21 Geo. V. c. 9).

tralasian station on consideration of a contribution of £126,000 a year to the extra cost involved beyond what was deemed desirable on Imperial grounds. The agreement was renewed and extended at the Conference of 1902, the contributions being increased to £200,000 for the Commonwealth, which had now succeeded to the obligations of the former colonies, and £40,000 by New Zealand. But Australian feeling naturally enough resented the payment of charges without control, and Mr Deakin adumbrated a scheme under which the subsidy should be dropped and Australia undertake the maintenance of a local flotilla for her own defence, a scheme which was regarded coldly by the Admiralty on the score of ineffectiveness in war and inconvenience in peace through division of control. The European crisis, which was the subject of anxious speeches by ministers in the House of Commons in 1909, resulted in the offer by New Zealand to present one or, if need be, two Dreadnoughts to the Empire.[1] and this was followed by offers of action by the States of New South Wales and Victoria, if the Commonwealth, then under the Labour Government of Mr Fisher, should fail to act. The Commonwealth Government, however, proposed to establish a local navy, under its control in peace, but falling automatically under Imperial control in time of war. A coalition between its opponents, the parties of Mr Deakin and Mr George Reid, ejected it from office and procured the offer of a Dreadnought. The whole subject was discussed at a Naval and Military Conference at London, with the result that a scheme was evolved for the creation of a Pacific fleet of three units,

---

[1] This took material shape in H.M.S. *New Zealand*.

East Indies, China, and Australian, the last to be supplied and controlled by Australia, the first by the British Admiralty, which was also to control the China unit, though the New Zealand contribution was to be employed in providing part of the fleet. It was also agreed that Canada should make a beginning of fleet construction, on the same principle as Australia. The case of South Africa, where the Cape and Natal were making monetary contributions of £85,000 a year, was allowed to stand over in view of the formation of the Union.

There remained to be settled the delicate question of harmonising the existence of independent Australian and Canadian units with the international unity of the Empire, and the necessity for co-operation in time of war. This issue was adjusted at the Imperial Conference of 1911. It was agreed that in time of peace Dominion forces should be under the sole control of the Dominion Governments, but care was to be taken to secure similarity of training and discipline with the Imperial navy. Definite areas were marked out as the Canadian and Australian stations within whose limits the movements of the fleets would normally be confined. If any foreign ports were to be visited, the concurrence of the Imperial Government must be first obtained, so that the necessary diplomatic notification of the intended visit could be given to the foreign power concerned. While at a foreign port a report of the ship's proceedings was to be forwarded to the Commander-in-Chief on the station, or the Admiralty, and any instructions as to international relations given by the Imperial Government were to be obeyed, the Dominion Government also being informed. Arrangements might be made for joint exercises with the Imperial fleet, the senior officer taking command of the whole fleet, but not interfering save when necessary in matters of internal economy. The officers of the various fleets were to be ranked by seniority, and the necessary personnel to start the new fleets was to be provided by the Admiralty, which would also afford facilities for training. In time of war it was contemplated but not made essential that the Dominion fleets would fall under complete Imperial control.

Australia persevered in the projected fleet creation, and New Zealand, after the overthrow of the Liberal Government in 1912, decided to aim at a local flotilla, while consenting that the Admiralty should retain in European waters the vessel presented by her as the outcome of the Conference of 1909, in view of the menacing position of European politics. In Canada a legal foundation for the creation of a separate fleet was made in 1910, but little progress was made with the project even after the doubt which soon presented itself as to the power of the Dominion Parliament to regulate events taking place beyond its territorial waters was solved by the Naval Discipline (Dominion Naval Forces) Act, 1911, of the Imperial Parliament.[1] The change of government and the impression of the seriousness of the naval position made upon Mr Borden on his visit in 1912 to England, resulted in his making instead proposals of an immediate grant of thirty-five million

[1] Under this Act full arrangements have been made by Orders in Council, August 12, 1913, June 28 and July 16, 1920, to regulate the relations of Dominion and British forces, and Canada has received all naval lands and dockyards under 9 Edw. VII. c. 18. Since 1935 British personnel may be required by the Admiralty to serve on Dominion ships.

dollars to the British Government for the construction of Dreadnoughts, a proposal frustrated by the refusal of the Senate, on which the Liberals had a majority, to accept the Act proposed for this purpose. The Dominion Government, for its part, was not prepared to proceed with a local fleet, so that no progress in this regard was made before the war.

3. *Imperial Co-operation during the War*

The decision of the Imperial Government to enter upon the war was taken on its own responsibility under circumstances of so pressing a nature as to render consultation with the Dominions impossible.[1] But the Dominion Governments had, before war was seen to be inevitable, intimated their recognition of the probable conflict and their loyal determination to afford full support of the Empire; indeed in Australia, at least, there was some popular feeling of doubt lest the Imperial Government would fail to realise the necessity of resisting aggression. Moreover, once the die was cast, the Dominions hastened to express their readiness to afford aid. It was, in fact, obvious that with constitutional relations such as they were, it was impossible to find any fault with the attitude of the Imperial Government, whose scheme of 1912, for the appointment of resident ministers, if accepted, would have secured the Dominions both fuller and earlier touch with the developments of the European situation, without fundamentally altering the position of the Dominions.

The extraordinary danger to the Empire revealed by

[1] See Keith, *War Government of the Dominions* (1921).

the strength of the German attack in Europe, supplemented by the decision of Turkey to effect the overthrow of British power in the East, led to remarkable
sacrifices by the Dominions. Their naval forces, of
value and importance in the case of Australia, were
placed immediately under the control of the Admiralty,
and steps were promptly taken to raise large bodies of
troops to serve under the command of the British
commanders in the field. It was early recognised that
any attempt to assert independent control of these
forces would be fatal to effective action, and the disadvantages in war of divergences from the standard
military equipment of the British army were revealed
in the defects of the Ross rifle, which had been adopted
in Canada as the service weapon. On the other hand,
as the numbers of the Dominion troops grew, due
recognition was accorded to their national character;
the Canadian forces, when they achieved the dimensions of an army corps, were retained in that formation,
and their commander was a Canadian officer whose
opinion weighed admittedly more seriously with the
British Commander-in-Chief than did that of the
average corps commander on the score of the nationality of his forces. The Canadian Government also felt
itself entitled to intervene against a use of the troops
deemed inadvisable, as when the idea was mooted in
1917 of sending to Italy reinforcements amounting to
less than a corps, a step which, applied to the Canadians,
would have broken up their homogeneity. Similarly,
while the Australian troops were under the control
of British commanders, their immediate leaders were
Australian officers, and in most matters of internal
economy they were free to act as they thought best.

The result of this measure of autonomy within the British forces as a whole was unquestionably satis- factory in producing more effective results than any effort to secure more uniformity could have been.

The services of the Dominion troops had the special value in the later period of the war that the men were almost wholly volunteers; it is true that in 1916 New Zealand, and in the following years Canada and New- foundland, adopted compulsory service as was done in the United Kingdom, excluding Ireland, in 1916, but very little was done by Canada to make conscription effective until the armistice was almost at hand. In the Commonwealth the political blunder was made of sub- mitting the question of compulsory service to a refer- endum, which twice failed to elicit a favourable re- sponse. The result was practically inevitable, since the electorate included a large number of women who could hardly be expected to rise to the difficult and invidious position of imposing by their votes sacrifices on men from which they themselves would be exempt, while bitterness on political issues between the Coalition Government, formed to carry on during the war, and the Labour Party led to many supporters of the latter voting against the proposals, rather because they sought thus to embarrass the administration than because of any conviction against the principle of conscription. In South Africa conscription was, of course, rendered impossible by the acute division of feeling between the English-speaking population and a section of the Dutch, which led to a rebellion immediately after the Union Government had decided in 1914, in deference to the suggestion of the Imperial Government, to in- vade German South-West Africa. The rebellion was put down, not without considerable difficulty and loss of life, by the exertions of General Botha, largely with the support of the loyal Dutch population, and the collapse of the insurrection was followed by a brilliant campaign to reduce German South-West Africa. Both volunteers and a General were lent by the Union for operations in East Africa, while the German possessions in the Pacific were reduced by military expeditions in 1914 from the Commonwealth and New Zealand under the protection of the Australian fleet unit, which had been handed over to Admiralty control.

It was, of course, inevitable that the bulk of the burden of the war, both in expenditure of money and in men, should fall on the United Kingdom as most immediately and vitally concerned in success, and the Dominion Governments concurred readily in the opinion of the Imperial Government, expressed early in the course of hostilities, that the Imperial Conference meeting, which would normally have fallen in 1915, should be postponed, an assurance being given that it was the intention to consult the Dominion Governments, preferably personally, before any peace settlement was arrived at. They consented also that any territorial acquisitions made by their forces during hostilities should be held at the disposal of the Empire in the event of peace. The prolongation of the war, however, made it obvious that consultation was essential, and the fall of Mr Asquith's administration was immediately followed by the issue of an invitation to the Dominions and to India to be represented at discussions with the Imperial Government regarding the conduct of the war and the possible terms of peace. These meetings in 1917, and 1918, were organised in two forms: one set, styled the Imperial War Cabinet, meeting under the chairmanship of the Imperial Prime Minister, dealt with the fundamental questions of the war; the other, presided over by the Secretary of State for the Colonies, concerned itself with minor war issues and such matters not immediately concerning the war as required discussion even during hostilities; the proceedings of the former body were secret, those of the latter had largely the same character. Great importance attached to the position of India which, on the score that it did not enjoy responsible government, was excluded, somewhat unwisely, from the Imperial Conference of 1911; realisation of the great importance of the resources of India for war purposes resulted in the extension to her of an invitation to be represented not only by the Secretary of State, but also by representatives of the Indian Government and the Native States.

The Imperial War Cabinet was doubtless in a sense misnamed, for it was, if a cabinet at all, only one in the applied signification of a cabinet of governments, as it was styled by Sir R. Borden. Unlike a true cabinet, as understood in the British Empire, it owed no common responsibility, but consisted of members who represented and were answerable for their actions to different Parliaments. There was, and could be, no Prime Minister to act as head; the British Premier presided only as *primus inter pares*, by the courtesy due to the greatest partner in the Empire. It was impossible to take majority decisions; whatever the views of the greater part of those present might be, each Government remained unfettered, if it disagreed with the common purpose adopted by the rest of the Conference.

The War Cabinet had no executive officers to carry out its resolutions, even when they were unanimous; each Government had to give its own orders. To say, therefore, that an executive for the Empire, even in war only, had been created is erroneous. But there was a very real value in the device; the Dominions had willingly handed over to the Imperial Government control of their military and naval forces, and it was all to the good that the whole Empire should meet in Council to discuss the aims for which these forces were being employed, and the uses to which they were being put. In the last resort, of course, the decision lay with the Imperial Government, but that Government had every reason to secure that its policy won the hearty approval of the other portions of the Empire. Nor can it be seriously doubted that the Dominion representatives, speaking in a position of absolute freedom, possessed far greater influence than they could ever have exerted merely as minority members of a federal legislature or executive.[1]

The co-operation thus attained was continued in 1919 in the shape of the British Empire Peace Delegation taken as a whole. The separate representation secured to the Dominions and to India, in just recognition of their vast services to the cause of liberty throughout the world, was doubtless less important in practice than the opportunity afforded to them to discuss British policy, and to secure that it should be determined in such a sense as would best meet Dominion and Indian needs, for India had a special

[1] This fact refuted Mr A. Fisher's argument (*The Times*, January 31, 1916), that the then existing position gave the elector in the United Kingdom more power in foreign affairs than a Dominion Prime Minister. See Mr Hughes's declaration, Commonwealth *Debates*, 1923, p. 1779.

interest in modifying the terms offered to Turkey, in view of the strong pro-Turkish feelings of her Moslem population, whose religious convictions outweighed their sense of the treachery of Turkey to the allies, and the appalling losses inflicted on them by her action in preventing effective relations with Russia and Rumania during the crisis of the war. The peace terms secured for the Dominions mandates over the territories annexed, and membership of the League of Nations, as well as rights of indemnity and full authority to deal with the property of enemy nationals within their territory. The signature of their delegates to the Peace Treaties and the various other conventions concluded with the new States and the lesser allies, if not essential in any way to the validity of the treaties, was a graceful assertion of the constitutional propriety of their formal participation in these arrangements, even when their interest in them was remote. Similarly the British ratification of the arrangements was withheld in order to allow of the Governments consulting their Parliaments and receiving formal approval before steps formally to ratify were taken. There was, of course, no legal obligation on the Dominion Governments to obtain Parliamentary sanction before they requested ratification, but the growing tendency to ask formal Parliamentary sanction was shown by the action of the Canadian Government in thus obtaining approval in 1922 for the acceptance of the amendments to the Covenant of the League of Nations adopted in 1921, although none of these in itself required any legislation or Parliamentary approval to make it effective.

It might have been expected that the co-operation

for war purposes would have resulted in the closer unity in structure of the Empire, and in the United Kingdom an energetic campaign, promoted by the "Round Table" group of political thinkers, was conducted in order to secure the adoption of some form of Imperial federation, as the only proper means by which the Dominions would be enabled to share in the control of foreign policy. The argument, however, that the humblest voter in the United Kingdom had more power in moulding Imperial policy than the Prime Ministers of the Dominions was proved palpably false by the proceedings of the War Cabinets of 1917 and 1918, while a marked disinclination was manifested by all the Governments to touch on the subject during the war. The Imperial War Conference of 1917 recorded the view that the readjustment of the constitutional relations of the Empire was too important and intricate a subject to be dealt with during the war, and that it should form the subject of a special Imperial Conference to be summoned as soon as possible after hostilities. They deemed it, however, their duty to place on record their view "that any such readjustment, while thoroughly preserving all existing powers of self-government and complete control of domestic affairs, should be based on a full recognition of the Dominions as autonomous nations of an Imperial Commonwealth, and of India as an important portion of the same, should recognise the right of the Dominions and India to an adequate voice in foreign policy and in foreign relations, and should provide effective arrangements for continuous consultation in all important matters of common Imperial concern, and for such necessary concerted action, founded on consultation, as the several Governments may determine".

To this the Imperial War Cabinet, on July 20, 1918, added the principle that the Prime Ministers of the Dominions, as members of the War Cabinet, should have the right of direct communication with the British Prime Minister on all such matters as they deemed of sufficient consequence, instead of communicating through the Governor-General, and the Secretary of State for the Colonies, and that in the interval between plenary cabinet meetings they might be represented by ministers resident in, or visiting, London.

4. *Imperial Co-operation in Foreign Affairs and Defence since 1919*

(*a*) Foreign Affairs

The Constitutional Conference proved impracticable in 1919, owing to the pressure of other business, and reconstruction both in the Dominions and at home prevented any meeting of the ministers of the Empire in 1920. A meeting, however, was convened in 1921, partly at the urgent representations of the Prime Minister of the Commonwealth, partly because of the necessity of devising some common policy for the Empire in regard to the matter of the Anglo-Japanese alliance. The situation in this regard was obscure,[1] for the Covenant of the League of Nations imposed on the members of the League the necessity of revising any agreements, to which they were already parties, with a view to their being brought into harmony with

[1] Keith, *Letters on Imperial Relations, 1916–1935*, pp. 315, 316.

the terms of the Covenant. In accordance with this provision, in July 1921, the British and Japanese Governments notified the League of their intention to carry out this principle with regard to the Anglo-Japanese Treaty of 1911, and it was open to argument, though this was afterwards decided in the negative by the Law Officers of the Imperial Government, that this notification amounted to a formal denunciation of the Treaty of 1911. Apart, however, from this point there was the essential question of principle to be decided; was the alliance to be continued, or was it to be abandoned? The dominant motive in the matter was, inevitably, the feeling of Canada that the alliance, as indicating the possibility of hostility to the United States, should be terminated. It was admitted that the terms of clause 4 of the treaty itself were clear enough to obviate the chance of the Empire being involved in war with the United States on behalf of Japan, since that clause provided that, if either party to the alliance concluded a treaty of general arbitration with a third power, nothing in the alliance would entail upon that party an obligation to go to war with the power with which it had made the treaty of arbitration, and there was no possible doubt that the Peace Commission Treaty of September 15, 1914, between the British Crown and the United States was such an arbitration treaty as was contemplated in the pact of alliance. None the less, Canadian opinion, moved by United States feeling, disliked any alliance which might even be regarded as implying that Britain favoured Japan rather than the United States. In Australia and New Zealand there was every anxiety to maintain the closest relations of friendship with the United States, and popular opinion was in full sympathy with the feeling against Japanese immigration into territories occupied by Europeans. But these Governments had to face the facts of their geographical proximity to Japan, and the close relations which the war had induced, involving the participation of the Japanese navy in the essential work of keeping the seas safe, both against German raiders and interference with the transport of the Australasian forces and products to Europe. If the alliance were terminated then Australasia would be confronted with the possibility of a hostile Japan, even if it were assured of the sympathy of the United States and the protection of the United Kingdom. It was felt, therefore, that the treaty should be continued in operation, subject to such modification as would make it absolutely clear that the alliance involved no conceivable risk of hostile relations with the United States. The Union of South Africa, not immediately concerned with Japanese immigration possibilities, was prepared to regard the question from a broad Imperial point of view, while the British Government, keenly sensible to the enormous advantages derived during the war from Japanese friendship and aid, was wholly unwilling to abandon the convention out and out.

The Imperial Conference thus convened had no difficulty in disposing of the issue of an Imperial constitution.[1] It hastily and effectively repudiated the

[1] The merits of this decision were insisted on by Mr Lloyd George in the House of Commons, August 18, 1921, but a protest was offered by Sir R. Borden in his lecture at Toronto University, October 7, 1921. In the Canadian House of Commons, on February 1, 1923, Mr Mackenzie King insisted that the Dominion Parliament must retain the right to decide the issue of taking part in any war, negativing the possibility of any unity of control. Cf. the *Debates* for March 26, 1923.

proposal of 1917, and decided that it would not encourage the summoning of any constitutional convention. All the parts of the Empire, it seemed, desired
autonomy, and all wanted to co-operate, but it was
impossible effectively to arrange any method of
securing any formal improvement of relationships. It
was understood that the Prime Ministers had the right
of direct access to the British Prime Minister, that
they should be informed of all important matters of
foreign policy, and that they should be consulted as
far as distance allowed. Stress was laid on the difficulties which distance made in annual conferences;
the airship was not developed enough to render the
journey from Australia swift, telegrams were not an
ideal mode of discussion. In short, the conditions
announced as indispensable to any constitutional readjustment in 1917 really precluded any readjustment at all, at any rate of a formal kind. If full
autonomy is to be preserved, there can be no central
body with any executive powers; the final right of deciding on all matters of foreign policy must rest with
the Imperial Government, subject to the obligation on
that Government to make its policy acceptable, as far
as possible, to all the Dominion Governments, and to
India, and to the right of the Dominions to refuse to
participate in the action taken. The difficulty of this
idea is obvious; no better example can be imagined
than the impossibility of meeting the views both of
Australasia and of India, as to the policy to be adopted
towards Turkey, as was strikingly shown in September
1922, when Australia [1] and New Zealand, in response
to the appeal of the British Prime Minister, were pre-

---

[1] See Commonwealth *Debates*, 1922, pp. 2347 ff., 2395 ff.

pared to send troops to preserve the freedom of the Straits, while India was equally insistent on urging Britain to concede Turkish demands *en bloc*, and Canada declined to express any view, unless full information could be given to Parliament and its decision taken.

It followed inevitably from the attitude of the Dominions that no attempt has been made even to adopt the suggestion of the Imperial Government in 1912, renewed by the Imperial War Cabinet in 1918, that each Dominion should be represented in London by a resident minister of cabinet rank, whose duty it would be to keep the Dominion Government in effective touch with Imperial and foreign policy, even the experiment made by Canada for a time after 1914 having been abandoned and the office of High Commissioner filled up in the ordinary manner. On the other hand, the supply of weekly reports on foreign affairs as well as generous telegraphic notifications to Dominion Premiers by the British Premier has continued, though apparently not with complete effectiveness since one ground for the hesitation of Canada to give in September 1922 the assurances of aid asked for was the absence of adequate information regarding the issues involved. In truth, however, it is clear that by the means at present employed, Dominion Governments cannot either be adequately acquainted with foreign policy generally or effectively consulted, except on a few special issues.

Such an issue was the Japanese alliance, which formed the topic of full investigation at the Imperial Conference, and resulted in the decision to seek to extend the scope of the arrangement so that any idea

M

of hostility to the United States could be dismissed. This project was greatly furthered by the policy of the United States, which resulted in the summoning by that Government of a conference at Washington, which attained, on January 6, 1922, far-reaching and most important conclusions. A treaty was concluded between the United States, the British Empire, France, Italy, and Japan, for the limitation of armaments, allotting a maximum capital ship tonnage of 525,000 tons to the United States and the British Empire, 175,000 to France and Italy, and 315,000 to Japan. A further treaty forbade the use of submarines as commerce destroyers, and the use of poisonous gases or liquids in war. The United States, the Empire, France, and Japan agreed on December 13, 1921, to the substitution for the Anglo-Japanese Alliance of 1911, of an agreement as between themselves to respect their rights as to their insular possessions and dominions in the Pacific Ocean. In the event of any controversy arising as regards these rights, which diplomacy could not dispose of, and which was likely to affect the harmonious accord existing between the powers, it should be referred to a joint conference of all four powers for consideration and adjustment. The powers also agreed to consult together in the event of aggression by other powers infringing the *status quo*, and to include the mandated islands within the purview of the treaty, while assurances were given by all four powers to the Portuguese and Dutch Governments of their intention to respect the possessions of these powers in the Pacific, despite the fact that they were not asked to take part in the treaty. At the same time a large number of important arrangements regarding China were agreed to between the five great powers, China, Belgium, Holland, and Portugal.

In the disarmament discussions internationally the British Empire delegation formed a single unit, with but one voice, and, though the delegates concerted their policy in common, the final decision inevitably rested with the British delegation. It is obvious that such a condition of affairs raises great possibilities of friction; the position would be equally embarrassing if the Imperial Government persisted in signing such a treaty in defiance of the wishes of a Dominion, and if the objections of a Dominion were to render it impossible to adopt a policy approved by the majority of the Governments of the Empire.

In other matters the Dominions necessarily played a more passive rôle; the question of reparations [1] was necessarily only handled in regard the apportionment of the hypothetical indemnity to be obtained from Germany. In these questions, as at the Genoa Conference of 1922, to which invitations to the Dominions and India were issued by the Italian Government, there was harmonious co-operation between the various parts of the Empire in attaining a common policy.

This spirit of compromise and co-operation was manifested to the full at the Imperial Conference of 1923,[2] which was marked by the attendance for the first time of representatives of the Irish Free State, the ministers of Education and External Affairs. The subject of foreign affairs occupied the prolonged attention

---

[1] The shares of the 22 per cent of the Empire were fixed at Canada and Australia 4·35 each, New Zealand 1·75, India 1·20, South Africa 0·60, Newfoundland 0·10.

[2] Keith, *Speeches and Documents on the British Dominions, 1918–1931*, pp. 315 ff.

of the Conference, and an important departure from previous practice was made in the immediate publication of the portions of the address of the Secretary of State for Foreign Affairs dealing with reparations and the Turkish settlement. A full discussion of the foreign situation resulted in the adoption by common consent of a line of policy. While the Conference was in session, the offer of the President of the United States to assist in an investigation of the possibility of German reparation payments was heartily welcomed by that body, though the project at first failed to materialise, owing to French objections. The Conference recorded its opinion that in the event of failure in this regard, the British Government should consider very carefully the summoning itself of a Conference to examine the financial and economic situation in its widest aspect, and on its initiative strong representations were addressed to the allied Governments against any policy likely to break up the unity of the German State as inconsistent with the Treaty of Peace, and incompatible with the discharge by Germany of her obligations. The Conference also approved the Turkish policy of the British Government and its action as to Egypt, while it recorded its satisfaction with developments regarding the Pacific as the outcome of the Washington Conference, its assurance that British and Japanese relations would be as sincere and cordial as under the former alliance, and its sympathy with Japan in her grave disaster. The policy of the Empire delegates to the League of Nations, especially in regard to the critical issue between Greece and Italy, arising from the hostile action of the latter towards the former at Corfu in defiance of the League Covenant, was cordially approved, and there was full accord that the League should be given the unabated support of all the members of the League, as a valuable instrument of international peace, and as the sole available organ for the harmonious regulation of many international affairs. With significant insistence the Conference added to the record of its deliberations a reminder that it had no executive power and that its conclusions were necessarily subject to the action of the Governments and Parliaments of the various portions of the Empire, and it expressed its trust that its deliberations would meet with their approval. This is a most significant admission that foreign policy is now a matter which ought to form the subject of consideration not merely, as in the past, by the Imperial Parliament, but also by the Parliaments of the Dominions.

The Conference further carefully considered the complex issue of the negotiation, signature, and ratification of treaties, to which, as has been seen, especial attention had been drawn by the controversy over the Pacific halibut treaty of Canada with the United States. The result of their deliberations contained nothing essentially new, but it recognised clearly the distinction between treaties proper, concluded between heads of States and signed by plenipotentiaries, holding full powers from these heads, and agreements between Governments, usually of a technical or administrative nature, concluded by representatives of these Governments,[1] not acting under full powers granted by heads of States, and not ratified by such heads, though sub-

---

[1] Such negotiations were carried out in November and December 1923, between the Canadian and the United States Governments as to measures to facilitate the enforcement of prohibition.

jected in some cases to confirmation by the Governments concerned. The propriety of these agreements
was expressly admitted, but it was recommended that,
before entering on such negotiations, any Government
should consider whether the interest of any other part
of the Empire might be affected, with a view to enabling
the Government of such a part to express its opinions
on the proposed negotiation.

As regards the negotiation of treaties, the Conference
held that it was desirable that no treaty should be
negotiated by any of the Governments of the Empire
without due consideration of its possible effect on other
parts of the Empire, or, if circumstances so demanded,
on the Empire as a whole. Before negotiations were
opened with the intention of concluding a treaty, steps
should be taken to ensure that any of the other
Governments of the Empire likely to be interested
were informed, so that any such Government, which
considered that its interests would be affected, might
express its views, or, if its interests were intimately
involved, might participate in the negotiations. In such
a case of participation in negotiations, the Governments should exchange views in the fullest manner
before and during the negotiations, and in cases of
International Conferences, where a British Empire
delegation acted, containing representatives of the
Dominions and India, this body should be used for the
purpose of such discussions. In every case steps should
be taken to keep those Governments which were not
participating in the negotiations informed of any points
arising, which might affect their interests.

As regards signature, it was agreed that bilateral
treaties imposing obligations on one part of the Empire

only should be signed by representatives of the Government of that part, acting under full powers indicating the part of the Empire in respect of which the obligations were to be undertaken, care being taken in the preamble and text of the treaty to make its scope clear. Where a bilateral treaty imposed obligations on more than one part of the Empire, the treaty should be signed by one or more plenipotentiaries on behalf of all the Governments concerned. In the case of treaties negotiated at International Conferences, the existing practice, of signature by plenipotentiaries on behalf of all the Governments of the Empire represented at the Conference, should be continued, and the full powers issued should be in the forms employed at Paris and Washington, that is, without local restriction for the British representatives, and with local specification for those of the Dominions and India.

As regards ratification the Conference approved the maintenance of the existing practice, which, to obviate error, was expressly defined. Under it the ratification of treaties imposing obligations on one part of the Empire is effected at the instance of the Government of that part, while, if more parts than one are affected, ratification is expressed only after consultation between the Governments of the parts concerned, each Government having the duty of deciding whether Parliamentary approval or legislation is required before the desire for, or concurrence in, ratification is intimated.

The arrangements for treaty negotiations laid down in 1923 were reconsidered in 1926,[1] and were modified in detail. It was insisted that the duty of notification of

[1] Keith, *Speeches and Documents on the British Dominions, 1918–1931*, pp. 380 ff.

the intention to negotiate ought to be fully respected; the Governments receiving notification should intimate their views or be deemed to assent, but no Government should take action involving other Governments in active obligations without obtaining their definite assent. It is admitted that in some cases—not specified —ratification should take place for the whole Empire; it might be assumed that a Dominion which had not objected, or which did not require that a treaty to be ratified on its behalf must be signed by the plenipotentiary appointed for that purpose, would concur in the ratification. No such instance appears to have occurred. It was further agreed to drop the practice of concluding treaties in the name of the British Empire, thus obscuring the distinction between Great Britain and Northern Ireland with the Colonies and Protectorates and the Dominions and India. Henceforth treaties should be concluded in the name of the King and the parts for which they were signed should be expressly signified. The former practice, therefore, under which British plenipotentiaries signed without specification has been definitely abandoned, and the full powers issued to plenipotentiaries show clearly for what part of the Empire they are to sign. Treaties also normally cover mandated territories. It was agreed that to avoid confusion in treaties concluded under the auspices of the League of Nations, which required a specified number of ratifications for coming into effect, each member of the League should count as a unit. The views of the Conference on these topics were, at their request, duly intimated to the League of Nations by the Foreign Secretary in 1927. As regards political Conferences, it was pointed out that three methods of representation were possible: (1) The use of a common plenipotentiary to whom full powers should be issued on the advice of all parts of the Empire participating. (2) A single British Empire delegation composed of separate representatives of the parts participating, as at Washington in 1921. (3) Separate delegations representing each part of the Empire. In fact, this form of procedure has been uniformly adopted since, subject to the observation that any Dominion may choose the representative of the United Kingdom or another part of the Empire as its representative. In the same way when treaties are concluded generally in countries where the Dominions are not represented, it is the practice for the British minister to sign separately for those Dominions which desire to accept the treaty.

The Conference further approved the co-operation in political relations of the parts of the Empire and urged the adoption of this system as between the Dominion ministers at foreign courts, whose appointment it contemplated, and the British ambassadors. It also approved the rule that *exequaturs* of foreign consuls in the Dominions should be countersigned by Dominion ministers. The Conference also discussed the question of arbitration in international disputes and agreed not to take separate action, for the time being, regarding the acceptance of the optional clause of the Statute of the Permanent Court of International Justice. At the same time it indicated in the fairest manner the refusal of the Dominions to take responsibility for the Locarno Pacts, under which the Dominions had been expressly exempted from obligation together with India, unless their Governments should accept liability. New Zealand had proposed to do so, but the Dominions contented themselves with congratulating the British Government on its share in this contribution towards international peace.

The necessity of unity in certain international matters was impressed on the Dominions in the negotiations which resulted in the conclusion of the Paris Treaty for the renunciation of war as an instrument of national policy. The British Government made it clear that it could not act otherwise than jointly and simultaneously with the Dominion Governments and the Government of India. Even in this case, however, complete unanimity could not be achieved, for the United Kingdom made it clear that its signature was subject to the reservation that it must regard attack on certain regions (doubtless Egypt and Iraq) as involving the right of British self-defence. Canada intimated that this was not regarded as a formal reservation, and the Irish Free State insisted that its own acceptance was entirely without reservation. In the same way the Irish Free State accepted absolutely the compulsory jurisdiction of the Permanent Court of International Justice, while the United Kingdom and the other Dominions excepted disputes with other members of the British Commonwealth. On the other hand, the necessity of regarding the Commonwealth as a unity for matters of naval limitation was accepted even by the Irish Free State in the Treaty of London of 1930 for the doctrine of the limitation of naval armaments; but the Free State, at the earliest opportunity, in 1931, refused to agree with the other parts of the Empire as to excepting inter-Imperial disputes from acceptance of the General Act of 1928 for the pacific settlement of international disputes.

The Imperial Conference of 1930 [1] added nothing of importance to the system of co-operation with regard to international affairs. It stressed the principle already operative and pointed out that communication of intentions should apply to all aspects of foreign affairs and not merely to treaty negotiation. It also stressed the advantage from this point of view of the interchange of information between diplomatic representatives of the several parts of the Empire in foreign countries, and it insisted on the doctrine that Governments must be assumed to concur in policies of other Governments if they did not make use of the opportunity afforded them to point out objections.

Chapter IV.

It was also agreed that Dominion Governments, in matters not of general and political concern, might communicate direct with His Majesty's representatives in foreign countries. This action would be appropriate in respect of commercial treaties affecting exclusively a Dominion Government, invitations to non-political conferences, and requests for information of a technical or scientific character. In other matters Dominion Governments might communicate direct but should at the same time send the necessary request for action to the British Government, whose instructions the British representative would normally await before acting.

The Conference also expressed its approval of the system of strengthening the means of contact between the British and Dominion Governments by the appointment to Dominion capitals of High Commissioners for the United Kingdom, corresponding to

[1] Keith, *Speeches and Documents on the British Dominions, 1918-1931*, pp. 427 ff.

the High Commissioners for the Dominions in London. This step was a logical sequel of the decision of the Imperial Conference of 1926, that the Governors-General should cease to act as representatives of the British Government; in 1928 a High Commissioner had thus been appointed to Canada, and similar steps were taken, or resolved upon in 1930-31, as regards the Union and Australia. In New Zealand the Governor-General still acts as intermediary.

Inevitably the Dominions have taken little active share in the important foreign questions turning on disarmament and security which have continuously occupied the attention of the European powers since 1932. They have been kept continuously informed and the tentative arrangements achieved for the settlement of the reparations issue were approved by them, while the British Government has waived all claim for repayment of war loans or of interest, an offer refused only by the Union, whose gold resources have enabled the Government to discharge its debt. It has been made clear in New Zealand and Australia that they must follow British policy in these European issues, and South Africa has expressed sympathy with the efforts of the United Kingdom to promote peace. More active assistance it has been impossible for them to accord.

(b) Defence

The unity of the Empire in military and naval matters was, inevitably, brought to a close as soon as possible after the conclusion of the war, when the Dominion troops were hastily demobilised and returned to their homes, and it was no longer necessary to maintain the Dominion naval forces under British control. The question of naval defence, however, was an essential problem for the consideration of the Imperial Conference of 1921, in view of the recent decision of the United States to enter upon a policy of naval construction, which would rapidly place that power at the head of all the naval powers in the world. The Conference, however, only reached a negative conclusion; it recognised the necessity of co-operation among the various portions of the Empire to provide such naval defence as might prove essential for security, and it held that equality with the naval strength of any other power was the minimum standard for that purpose, but it held that the method and expense of such co-operation were matters for the final determination of the several Parliaments concerned, and that any recommendation thereon should be deferred until after the then imminent conference on disarmament. The Conference decided that it was unnecessary to make any recommendations regarding military matters in view of the change in the position of the world brought about by the Peace Treaties and the policy of disarmament inaugurated by these conventions.

The effect of the Washington Conference was naturally to diminish the inducement to the Dominions to adopt any policy of naval development. The result was most marked in the case of Canada, partly as the sequel of the change of Government, as the outcome of the general election of December 1921. The new administration decided to merge into a Ministry of National Defence the whole of military, naval, and air defence arrangements, and also the Royal Canadian Mounted Police. At the same time drastic economies of every kind were effected, including the putting out of commission of the small Canadian naval force, consisting of a cruiser, two destroyers, and two submarines, presented as a free gift by the Imperial Government, and the reduction to 1,500,000 dollars of the appropriation for naval services. In the Commonwealth also the expenditure on naval services was very largely reduced, and the fleet in commission diminished, while the *Australia*, the one capital ship of the Dominions, was scrapped under the terms of the Treaty of Washington. New Zealand, however, expressed its appreciation of its duty to share in the burden of Imperial naval defence, but pressure of financial difficulties prevented the development of any steps to this end until 1923. In South Africa strong exception had been consistently taken by the Nationalist Party to the continuation of the payment of a subsidy of £85,000 to the Imperial Government, though the payment was successfully defended by the administration, which laid stress on the fact that the cost of any naval defence for South Africa, on her own account, would far exceed the resources available, and that the payment served as a recognition of the protection afforded by the Admiralty, however inadequate it might be in amount. The contribution, as a result of the discussions of 1921, was in 1922 dropped in favour of local expenditure on naval defence.

The Imperial Government, on the other hand, has accepted the obligation of continuing to afford protection to the Empire as a whole, including the Dominions, and of safeguarding the trade routes of the world for British trade. While the far-reaching scheme for a great Far-Eastern Fleet, in whose formation

Australia, New Zealand, India, Canada, and South Africa should have in various degrees assisted, proposed by Admiral of the Fleet Viscount Jellicoe during his visit to the Dominions in 1919, has been generally treated as superseded by the results of the Washington Conference of 1921, the Imperial Government announced, in 1923, its determination to adopt one item of the plan, which is a necessary preliminary to the formation of the fleet, namely, the construction of a great naval base at Singapore, at a total cost ultimately of some £10,000,000. The decision was expressly stated not to be based on any existing needs, but to contemplate possibilities of difficulty in years to come. The value of the decision to Australia and New Zealand was obviously very great, and the Dominion Government, in June 1923, announced that it would increase its naval expenditure to £200,000 a year, of which one-half would be paid to the Imperial Government as a contribution in aid of the expenditure on Singapore.

The whole issue of defence was considered in detail at the Imperial Conference of 1923,[1] the Lord President of the Council, as Chairman of the Committee of Imperial Defence, initiating a discussion in which the Admiralty, War and Air ministries gave full information. The conclusions, however, arrived at were not of substantial novelty, though they embodied in a convenient shape the outstanding principles of Imperial defence. The Conference recognised the elementary fact that provision must be made for the defence of the territories and trade of the Empire, and that it was for

Chapter IV.

[1] Keith, *Speeches and Documents on the British Dominions, 1918–1931*, pp. 396, 397.

the Governments and Parliaments of the Empire to decide the nature and extent of any action to be taken. Subject to this, it was agreed that the primary responsibility rested on each portion of the Empire represented at the Conference to provide for its local defence. More vaguely, and without any apportionment of responsibility, the Conference recognised the necessity for adequate provision to safeguard the maritime communications of the several parts of the Empire and the routes and waterways along and through which their armed forces and trade passed, and for the provision of naval bases and facilities for repair and fuel, so as to ensure the mobility of the fleet. It also asserted the desirability of the development of the air forces of the several countries of the Empire upon such lines as would make it possible by means of the adoption, so far as practicable, of a common system of organisation and training, and the use of uniform manuals, patterns of arms, equipment, and stores, for the several parts of the Empire to co-operate with the least possible delay and the greatest efficiency. It also reaffirmed the principle of the minimum standard of naval strength accepted at Washington, equality with the naval strength of any foreign power; but, while deeply convinced of the paramount importance of providing for the safety and integrity of all parts of the Empire, it expressed the earnest desire for the further limitation of armaments, and urged that no opportunity should be lost of pressing this proposal.

Desirous of undertaking a proportionate share of the burden of defence, the British Government, recognising the difficulties facing the Dominions, proceeded with the establishment of the proposed naval base at Singapore and with the reorganisation of the machinery for planning defence, in the shape of the creation of a Chiefs of Staff Sub-Committee of the Imperial Defence Committee and the establishment of an Imperial Defence College. Contributions were received towards the cost of the Singapore base from the Federated Malay States, the Straits Settlements, and Hongkong. At the Imperial Conference of 1926[1] full information on defence was given to the Dominion Governments, but the only outcome of the discussions was the reaffirmation of the principles of 1923, the approval by Australia, New Zealand, and India (Canada and South Africa adopting a somewhat marked reticence) of the construction of the Singapore base, and a resolution in favour of the necessity for creating and maintaining an adequate chain of air bases and refuelling stations. The Conference also urged the adoption of a system of mutual interchange of individual officers and of complete air units, and it noted the decision of the Government of India to create a Royal Indian Navy and urged the free use of the new Imperial Defence College in London for the education of officers in the broadest aspects of strategy. It also reaffirmed the principle laid down by the Imperial Defence Committee on May 30, 1911, that it was desirable that representatives of the Dominions should attend the Committee of Imperial Defence and that Defence Committees should be established in each Dominion. The greatest stress, however, was laid by the Dominions on the importance of the limitation of armaments, nor has there been exhibited on the part of the Dominions much sign of

Chapter
IV.

[1] Keith, *op. cit.* pp. 392 ff.

N

appreciation of the gravity of the European situation. Canadian defence has been allowed to lapse, save in so far as it is required for the maintainance of internal order. The Union of South Africa has concentrated on the development of the air power so as to be in a position to prevent any outbreak of native disorder. The Irish Free State has equally restricted its defence preparations and has made no serious effort to make use of the authority given by the Treaty of 1921, to raise at its discretion with the United Kingdom the question of its undertaking the burden of its own defence by sea. The Commonwealth and New Zealand have abandoned compulsory military service, but since 1934 especially there has been visible in both Dominions an increased realisation of the dangers of the situation in the Far East, with the result that a new interest has been shown in the development of naval forces.[1]

It is, however, significant that the one important achievement of the consultation of the Dominion representatives on May 23, 1935, on the occasion of the King's Silver Jubilee celebrations, was the assurance given for the Irish Free State and the Union as well as Australia and New Zealand that they endorsed British policy, and the declaration authorised by Mr de Valera that the Free State would not, despite its differences with the United Kingdom, permit use of its territory by a power hostile to the latter. The Canadian Premier had left before the meeting was held, and no active obligation of aid was undertaken by any Dominion, though exchange of information and consultation were once more approved.

[1] See below, Part II. Ch. IV. s. 8.

CHAPTER V

IMPERIAL CO-OPERATION IN DOMESTIC AFFAIRS

1. *The Imperial Conference*

ABSORBED in local affairs and anxious only to be freed from Imperial intervention, Colonial Governments in the early years of self-government neither desired nor contemplated any attempt to form closer relations with the Imperial Government. The movement for Imperial federation, which succeeded the period when ultimate secession was regarded on all hands as probable, and by many treated as desirable, failed to excite any real popular sentiment in the Colonies; as in the revival of the idea in 1916, it was, and remained, the expression of a narrow circle of political opinion, which appreciated the importance of co-operation in matters of defence and foreign affairs, and could see no method of effecting this result save by the development of a formal federation. It required, therefore, some courage in 1886 to issue invitations for representatives of the Colonies, including both those enjoying and those without self-government, to attend discussions on matters of common interest contemporaneously with the celebration of Queen Victoria's Jubilee. The experiment was interesting and successful, partly because all idea of Imperial Federation was ruled out as unacceptable, and ten years later, for the celebration of the Queen's Diamond Jubilee, the Premiers of the self-governing

Colonies were gathered together and engaged in confidential discussions with the Secretary of State for the Colonies, and other Imperial ministers. In 1894 Canada assembled at Ottawa a Conference which suggested Imperial preference and paved the way for the creation of the Pacific cable. The coronation of King Edward VII. in 1902 afforded the occasion for a further meeting of Premiers, at which the principle of future conferences was generally welcomed. The idea of creating some permanent advisory body to keep alive the relations established at these conferences was entertained by Mr A. Lyttelton, but the suggestion of any Imperial Council, however small its functions, caused dubiety in Canada, and, when the Conservative Government of the United Kingdom resigned office in 1905, the project was not homologated by their successors in office. The Colonial Conference of 1907, however, if it did nothing in the way of creating a new organisation for the conduct of Imperial affairs, was noteworthy for the effort of the Dominions to induce the Imperial Government, which had been returned to power on a policy of free trade, to adopt the idea of Imperial Preference, which had been inaugurated in 1897–8 by the generosity of the Dominion of Canada. The attempt necessarily failed, but the Conference served a valuable purpose by stressing the fact that the advance of the Empire depended as much on material co-operation as on changes of governmental organisation. The Conference also marked an interesting epoch in the history of the Empire, for it changed its style to Imperial Conference, and bestowed on the self-governing Colonies the title of Dominions, as a complimentary acknowledgment of their higher status. On the other hand, the exclusion from the Conference of India, on the score of its lack of responsible government, was an error which had to be undone during the war. While establishing the principle of the holding of conferences every four years, under the presidency of the Prime Minister of the United Kingdom in lieu of the Secretary of State for the Colonies, the valuable suggestion was also made that matters of less importance should form the subject of subsidiary conferences of governmental representatives.

Curiously enough, the exact form of Imperial Conference contemplated by the constitution of 1907, met only in 1911; in 1915 war prevented its being summoned, and the Imperial War Conferences, which were held simultaneously with the War Cabinets of 1917 and 1918, were especially concerned in war issues, and their proceedings were largely aimed at results which, with the termination of the war, rapidly became antiquated. No conference was held in 1919 or 1920, and the Conference of 1921 was officially denied the title of Imperial Conference, although in point of fact ministers so described it officially in Parliament, and though in effect it corresponded with the Conferences of 1907 and 1911, save in the extreme secrecy of its proceedings. Its most essential work, however, was certainly the negation of the idea of the renovation of the texture of the Imperial constitution, which the War Conference of 1917 had appointed for a special conference to be held on the close of the war, and thus the method of conference was once more asserted to be that method of co-operation which alone is suited to the present condition of feeling in the Empire.

The permission to hold subsidiary conferences, on

the other hand, proved of wide value and importance. Thus in 1910 the vexed question of copyright, on which once the Prime Ministers of Canada waged war on the Colonial Office on the issue of constitutional right, was amicably settled in a Copyright Conference, though more than a decade was to elapse before Canada carried out its part of the agreement then achieved.

The greatest achievement, from the Dominion point of view, was doubtless the reversal during the war of the refusal of the Imperial Government to consider favourably the question of a preference to the Dominions, and the carrying out of this change of view at the first tariff revision after the war.[1] It is true that the preference was then confined rigorously to duties existing before the war and those imposed during hostilities for revenue purposes, and that food and raw materials were excluded from its operation. But the principle was conceded, and if its value to the Dominions was not very great, it was of real importance to India in its incidence on tea. Of other measures not the least important was that of the promotion of effective shipping communications at reasonable rates, which is one of the objects of the Imperial Shipping Committee, representative of the various Empire Governments, which was set up in 1921, and immediately set to work to investigate the thorny questions of shipping rebates in Australian and New Zealand trade.[2] In 1921 the Imperial Shipping Committee found it possible to effect agreement on the long-discussed and controversial

---

[1] The Finance Act, 1919 (9 & 10 Geo. V. c. 32); *House of Commons Papers*, Nos. 164, 165, 1919. Special assurances as to the continuance of preference for ten years were given to the West Indies in 1922; *Parl. Pap.* Cmd. 1683.

[2] *Parl. Pap.* Cmd. 1483, 1486, and 1564.

question of limitations on shipowners' liability in bills of lading and cognate matters,[1] and the Imperial Customs Conference discovered a large measure of agreement on the nature of the information to be required from the British exporter, who had in the past been needlessly harassed by the constant variations between the requirements of the different Dominion authorities on matters of no importance.[2] Agreement was also reached on the desirability and practicability of a patent right operative throughout the Empire, obviating separate applications in every jurisdiction.

A further outcome of the war was the renewed activity of the Imperial Government in the work of emigration. At the Imperial Conference of 1911 the view of that Government was that it was impossible and undesirable to encourage actively emigration from the United Kingdom, as the annual emigration without such encouragement absorbed practically the whole effectively available surplus, and in the case of Scotland was actually gradually reducing the agricultural population, which formed the foundation of the population, just as had long been the case in Ireland. The Dominions Royal Commission, a body established as the outcome of the Imperial Conference of 1911, recommended the proposal to aid emigration. At the close of the war the Imperial Government adopted the principle of providing free passages to the Dominions for men and women who had served in the war, with their dependents.[3] In 1921 the matter was considered first by a special conference, and the views of that body were endorsed by the Imperial

---

[1] Cmd. 1205.   [2] Cmd. 1231.
[3] *Parl. Pap.* Cd. 8672; see Cmd. 1134, 1580, and 1804.

Conference of that year. Effect to them is given by the Empire Settlement Act, 1922, which set aside £3,000,000 annually to be expended on promoting emigration by assisted passages and furthering schemes of land settlement and the training of emigrants.

The spirit of co-operation was seen also in two valuable proposals which became law in 1920 in the United Kingdom, followed by legislation in the Dominions and other oversea territories. The one [1] provided a fairly simple and effective means by which maintenance orders, obtained in the place where the deserted wife or family become a public charge, can be enforced through courts in other parts of the Empire without prohibitive expense or undue facilities for evasion. The other reform [2] provided for an extension in a modified but still useful form to the Empire as a whole, of the facilities which already existed for enforcing judgments obtained in the highest courts of the different parts of the United Kingdom.

The system of conference also proved its value in the final adjustment of the difficult issue respecting the admission of Canadian live cattle into the United Kingdom for purposes other than immediate slaughter. The exclusion of these cattle was clearly induced by false fears of disease among the cattle of Canada, but it was maintained stoutly through the interested efforts of English agriculture. A promise to remove the embargo given at the Imperial War Conference of 1917 was not implemented until the hands of the

---

[1] Maintenance Orders (Facilities for Enforcement) Act, 1920 (10 & 11 Geo. V. c. 33).

[2] Administration of Justice Act, 1920 (10 & 11 Geo. V. c. 81). Merged in part now in the Foreign Judgments (Reciprocal Enforcement) Act, 1933; S.R. & O. 1933, No. 1073.

Government were forced by agitation in the United Kingdom; the outstanding difficulties were disposed of in 1922, thus removing from the British Government the stigma of having failed to implement a promise made under stress of war conditions.[1]

The Imperial Economic Conference of 1923, held contemporaneously with the Imperial Conference of that year, marked a definite severance of the Conference into an economic and a political side. It arose from the decision of Mr Bonar Law as Prime Minister to summon an economic conference to concert measures with a view to relieve the mass of unemployment which manifested itself in Britain as the aftermath of the war, and its composition diverged from that of the Imperial Conference proper by including representatives of the non-self-governing parts of the Empire, while it met under the presidency of the President of the Board of Trade, and not of the British Prime Minister. Its most important achievement was the decision of the British Government to offer to increase largely the existing preferences on Empire imports, and to add to their number in respect of certain foodstuffs, while adhering to the decision to refuse to place taxes on fundamental articles of food. The Conference accepted also the principle of preference to Imperial goods and materials in all government contracts. It was agreed that the services of British Commercial Diplomatic officers in foreign countries should be placed at the disposal of the Dominions; that Trade Commissioners appointed by the Dominions should be placed at the service of other

[1] *Parl. Pap.* Cmd. 1722; Importation of Animals Act, 1922 (13 Geo. V. c. 5).

parts of the Empire; and that, where different parts of the Empire maintained representatives in the same place, there should be co-operation between them. The maintenance of the Imperial Shipping Committee responsible to the Governments represented at the Imperial Conference was approved, and the adoption of uniform legislation on bills of lading recommended. The question of wireless communications failed to attain settlement, owing to serious divergences of view as to the policy of private as opposed to public enterprise. In view of the importance of freedom for British shipping it was agreed to assert the principle of non-differentiation in all Empire ports against foreign shipping, on condition of reciprocity, subject to the possibility of combined action against any attempt in the future to discriminate against British shipping in any foreign country.

There was also agreement on the important principle of the desirability of promoting the mutual enforcement in the several parts of the Empire of judgments of courts and arbitration awards, and on the propriety of subjecting to the fiscal legislation of each part of the Empire governmental enterprises carried on there by other Governments, British or foreign, and of abolishing the exemption from jurisdiction of State-owned vessels engaged in trade, as opposed to governmental functions proper, but this still remains an ideal.

Great stress was laid throughout the discussions on the entire autonomy of the several Governments, and it was insisted that the scheme of Imperial preference did not represent any bargain between the parts of the Empire or treaty arrangement, each part being free to change its tariff policy at any time, while India wholly declined to accept preference as incompatible with her interest in free access to foreign markets.

The exact character of Imperial Conference resolutions was elucidated immediately after the Conference. Mr Baldwin's appeal to the electorate to accord a mandate for the preferential proposals of his Government resulted in his defeat and the new Government naturally was unable to carry into effect the proposals of Imperial Preference, though they were laid before Parliament in June 1924, when they were rejected by varying majorities. On the defeat of the Labour Government Mr Baldwin included in the Budget of 1925 the proposals of 1923, which involved no increase in duties, and made up the loss involved in the rejection of the other proposals by the establishment of an Empire Marketing Board. In this year also an Imperial Economic Committee was set up by general agreement which *inter alia* made recommendations regarding the administration of the sums available to facilitate the marketing of Empire foodstuffs. The Empire Marketing Board came into operation in 1926, a sum of £500,000 having been voted by Parliament.

The Imperial Conference of 1926 considered a large number of issues, including Imperial air communications, overseas settlement, research, forestry, the encouragement of Empire films, industrial standardisation, and the future of the Imperial Shipping Committee and the Imperial Economic Committee. In 1927 the Pacific Cable Board was reorganised and placed on a footing of complete equality for the Domnions.

In 1928 a Conference on Cable and Wireless Communications was held which led in 1929 to the creation of an Imperial Communications Advisory

Committee and the formation of a Communications Company to undertake control of the cables of the Pacific Cable Board, the West Indian cable and wireless system worked by the Board, and the Imperial Atlantic cable, and to lease the Post Office Beam services. In the same year the expert Committee, which dealt with constitutional questions referred to it by the Imperial Conference of 1926, drew up a draft agreement as to merchant shipping. This was signed on behalf of the Dominions and the United Kingdom on December 10, 1931, just prior to the royal assent to the Statute of Westminster.

The Imperial Conference of 1930 appointed a Committee on economic co-operation which dealt with the proposal to secure a fixed quota for Dominion wheat milled in the United Kingdom, and examined other questions relating to Import Boards, bulk purchase, and other schemes. Its most important recommendation was in favour of the holding of a further Conference to promote economic co-operation, and this Conference met at Ottawa in 1932.[1] After much difficulty contracts were agreed upon between the United Kingdom, the Dominions other than the Irish Free State, India, and Southern Rhodesia. These agreements contemplate the revision of the Dominion tariffs by Tariff Boards so as to permit competition on equitable terms with local manufactures, while, in return, exemption from duty on agricultural exports was assured to the Dominions, and special arrangements made to assist the Dominions successfully to market their meat products in the United Kingdom.

[1] *Parl. Pap.* Cmd. 4174. Cf. Keith, *Letters on Imperial Relations, 1916–1935*, pp. 112-15.

Terms were also included to promote trade between the Dominions and the Crown Colonies. The agreements in practice have proved somewhat disappointing to the United Kingdom. The agricultural industry has suffered from unrestricted Dominion imports [1] and British manufacturers have received comparatively little concession from Dominion Governments, reluctant to injure in any way the secondary industries of the Dominion. The conclusion of the agreements for a period of five years, to which exception was taken at the time by the Opposition in Canada [2] and Australia and by Sir H. Samuel in the United Kingdom, has turned out in practice to be of considerable disadvantage to the United Kingdom.

The Ottawa Conference saw also some progress in the grant of inter-Imperial preference by units of the Empire *inter se*. It has always been very difficult to secure the effective operation of preferences between the Dominions owing to the diverse interests involved. It has been comparatively easy for Canada to come to terms from time to time with the West Indian Colonies,[3] as their exports are not as a rule competitive with those of Canada. But until 1922 Australia had a reciprocity of preference only with the South Africa Customs Union which lasted from 1906 to 1926. With New Zealand she achieved agreement in 1922, but several changes have had to be made in 1926 and 1928 to

---

[1] Grave difficulties developed in April 1935 in adjusting meat exports from Australia and New Zealand in view of Argentine competition.

[2] Mr Mackenzie King, *Journ. Parl. Empire*, xiv. 68-75; Mr Beasley, 113, 114.

[3] See *Parl. Pap.* Cd. 6674; Cmd. 864; Agreement, July 6, 1925. At Ottawa, Canada secured agreements with the Union, Southern Rhodesia, and the Irish Free State.

avoid conflict, and equal trouble arose from time to time with Canada, with which an accord was reached first in 1925, to be widely altered in 1931. New Zealand, though anxious from 1903 on to extend preferential arrangements widely, has also found much difficulty in adjusting terms with Canada. The Union of South Africa, which at first was of easy access, became under General Hertzog anxious to confine preferences to cases where something like equivalent advantages could be reaped, and by this policy special agreements have been made at Ottawa with Canada and the Irish Free State. With Southern Rhodesia Union customs arrangements have been subjected to considerable strain, and a new accord is now pending.

It is characteristic of the recent agreements that they aim at enabling either party to point out to the other that in practice it is suffering disadvantage of a serious character from some provision in the compact; if the other party does not within a period of three months remedy the disadvantage, the clause impugned may be cancelled without affecting the rest of the agreement. No provision is made for arbitral decision of disputes, apparently because it is felt that each unit must reserve the right to decide for itself the carrying out of its obligations in such a vital question.

2. *The United Kingdom and the Colonies*

In imitation of the Imperial Conference, a Conference of Governors and other official representatives of dependencies not possessing responsible government met in 1927 under the style of " The Colonial Office Conference". It dealt with matters of general concern to the Colonies, the recruitment and training of colonial Civil servants, medical, agricultural, forestry, and transport questions, organisation of scientific research, education, cinematograph films, colonial trade agencies in London, civil air development, wireless communications and broadcasting, etc. A second Conference was held in 1930, a notable feature being that, in addition to the twenty-seven Governments represented, observers attended the meetings on behalf of India, the Union of South Africa, Southern Rhodesia, the South African High Commission territories, Sarawak, and North Borneo. Among the matters discussed were the colonial development fund, broadcasting, civil aviation, and mechanical transport, the organisation of colonial services as a whole in the light of the report of the Committee on the system of appointment in the Colonial Office and the colonial services, the organisation of the scientific services, including proposals for a unified agricultural service, labour questions, prison administration, and the treatment of juvenile offenders.

3. *The Agencies of Imperial Co-operation*

There must briefly be noted the main agencies of Imperial co-operation which have been established in part on the recommendations of the Imperial and the Colonial Office Conferences.

The *Imperial Economic Committee*, established in 1925, is authorised to investigate the marketing of foodstuffs, to undertake enquiries into the production and marketing of Empire raw materials, to prepare surveys of any branch of Empire trade and marketing, to facilitate conferences among those engaged in the particular industries in various parts of the Empire, and to report on any economic questions referred to it. On it are represented all the Dominions, India, and Southern Rhodesia, with two representatives for the Colonies and Protectorates. The Empire Marketing Board, set up in 1926, after accomplishing much useful work, has ceased to function; this was the outcome of the unwillingness of the Dominion Governments to contribute to its cost, after it had been decided that the British Government, having adopted the principle of granting preferences to the Dominions, could no longer bear the sole cost.

The *Imperial Shipping Committee*, established in 1920, derives its authority from the Governments represented at the Imperial Conference. It consists of 15 members, 9 Government nominees, 5 experienced in shipping and commerce, and 1 representative of civil aviation, under an independent chairman. Its authority extends to enquiries into complaints from interested persons with regard to ocean freights and the survey of facilities for maritime transport on Empire trade routes.

The *Imperial Communications Advisory Committee*, constituted in 1929, consists of 8 members, representing the United Kingdom, the five Dominions, India, and the Colonies and Protectorates. It is concerned with questions of policy regarding the institution of new services, the discontinuance of existing services, alteration in rates, and the distribution of traffic between alternative routes, and is charged with these responsibilities in connection with the activities of Imperial and International Communications, Ltd., the public utility company formed to co-ordinate the telegraphic services connecting the various parts of the Empire.

The Dominions are concerned, together with the Colonies and Protectorates and India, in the maintainance of the Imperial Institute of Entomology, established in 1913, and the Imperial Mycological Institute, founded at the recommendation of the Imperial War Conference of 1918 for the co-ordination of work on the diseases of plants caused by fungi. They are also interested, together with India and the Colonies, in the Executive Council of the Imperial Agricultural Bureaux and the Empire Forestry Conference and the Standing Committee on Empire Forestry. Certain of the Governments contribute to the Oversea Mechanical Transport Council and Directing Committee, established in 1928. All the Dominions and India have representation on the Board of Governors of the Imperial Institute, which since 1925 is controlled by the Parliamentary Secretary of the Department of Overseas Trade.

Of special colonial interest are the Colonial Advisory Medical Committee, established in its present form in 1931 ; the Colonial Survey Committee, constituted in 1905; the Advisory Committee on Education in the Colonies, constituted in 1928; the Colonial Research Committee, constituted in 1919; the Discovery Committee, established in 1923 for whaling research; and the African Liquor Control Committee, established in 1924. In 1929 the Colonial Development Advisory Committee was set up to advise on applications for assistance from the Colonial Development Fund, established by the Colonial Development

Act, 1929, under which grants are made to aid agriculture and industry in the Colonies and Protectorates. Currency questions are dealt with by the West African Currency Board, established in 1912; the East African Board, established in 1920; and the Palestine Currency Board, established in 1926. The Bureau of Hygiene and Tropical Diseases is maintained partly from Imperial funds and partly from Dominion, Colonial and Protectorate funds. The business requirements of the Colonies and Protectorates and their finance are controlled under the supervision of the Secretary of State for the Colonies by the Crown Agents for the Colonies in London. In addition, the Straits Settlement and the Federated Malay States maintain the Malayan Information Agency in London to advertise the productions and attractions of Malaya. A similar office exists since 1925 for Kenya, Uganda, Tanganyika Territory, Nyasaland, Zanzibar, Northern Rhodesia, and the Kenya-Uganda transport administration.

The Imperial College of Tropical Agriculture was incorporated by Royal Charter in 1921 to promote the study of tropical agriculture in suitable surroundings at St. Augustine, Trinidad, and to create a body of expert British agriculturists, versed in the knowledge of the cultivation of land in the Colonies, and of scientific advisers, acquainted with the means of combating pests and diseases.

The accounts of certain Colonies and Protectorates are audited on behalf of the Secretary of State by auditors and assistant auditors acting under the supervision of the Director of Colonial Audit, who is assisted in London by a central establishment connected with, but not forming part of, the Colonial Office. The auditors and assistant auditors, as well as the staff of the central office, form one department, the cost of which is defrayed by the Governments which make use of the services. Historically may be compared the Audit of Royal Revenues recorded of the American and West Indian Colonies in the seventeenth and eighteenth centuries.[1]

4. *The Dominions and India*

In the main, India occupies in the matter of Imperial co-operation precisely the same position as any of the Dominions, but there is one essential question which affects deeply the position of India in the scheme of the Empire, the issue of differential treatment based on race. The question which at present is acute as regards inter-Imperial relations only in regard to India, is one which must also arise in the future in accordance with the development of the civilisation of the negro population of South, West, and East Africa, and on its successful solution must depend the possibility of maintaining the Empire in its present dimensions, or its reduction to the territories inhabited by a white population, and minor colonial outposts which cannot expect to develop any independence of their own.

The acuteness of the problem as regards India is of recent growth, for the earlier controversies regarding immigration exclusion, based on colour considerations, which evoked discussions of some liveliness between the Imperial Government and the Colonies, concerned rather Chinese and Japanese immigration. But the

[1] Cf. G. A. Jacobsen, *William Blathwayt* (1932), pp. 150-85, 355-400.

Chapter
V.

emergence of a strong political feeling in India has necessarily resulted in the complete revision of the conception of the situation. India has rightly put an end to the system of the export of indentured Indian labour, which conferred great benefits on the West Indian Colonies, Mauritius, and Fiji, and Indians in these territories are now absolutely free settlers, thus removing a condition of affairs which was as damaging to Indian prestige as it was of dubious advantage to many of the labourers. On the other hand, the Dominions have closed effectively the door to any serious Indian immigration; the Commonwealth immigration legislation since 1901 has been based on an education test, which can be so manipulated as to exclude any person whose entry is not desired; Canada has attained the same result in diverse forms, especially by requiring that any immigrant must come by continuous journey from his place of origin and possess a considerable sum of money on arrival, or by simply closing immigration altogether in places where Indians can be expected to land. New Zealand, which at first used a language test, in 1920 adopted with complete success the regulation that an immigrant from any foreign place, or from a British possession, if a native of an aboriginal race, can only enter the Dominion on the strength of a permit from the Dominion Government applied for from his place of origin. In the case of South Africa since 1906 exclusion is directly effected. It would be idle to deny that in this wholesale exclusion policy there lies a deep wound to Indian material interests and to Indian national sentiment. There are large territories in the Dominions which are well suited for Indian settlement; in British Columbia, and in many parts of Australia, and in most of South Africa they could find homes and prosper. The resentment at exclusion is not diminished by the reflection that in Natal it was Indian labour which built up much of the prosperity of the province.

The problem, however, would be comparatively simple, were it confined only to the matter of exclusion, but it is aggravated by the treatment meted out in the Dominions to British Indians already legally settled there, and by attempts to penalise British ships trading with the Dominions on which lascar crews are carried. Thus since 1903 the Commonwealth has forbidden the grant of postal contracts to ships with such crews, and the effect of its merchant shipping legislation is to render it practically impossible to employ lascars on ships engaged in the coasting trade of the Commonwealth, a term which covers the oversea ship which takes up passengers and goods at any Australian port to carry them to the next. In 1910 New Zealand actually proposed to tax heavily any ships trading to New Zealand which employed lascars, but this proposal failed to take effect through the Imperial Government refusing to sanction the bill. The franchise was refused to Indians in Queensland and Western Australia, and also for Commonwealth elections as regards these States, and miscellaneous provisions in factory and agricultural and land Acts were aimed at differentiating against Indians, who for instance are more or less effectively excluded from the sugar and banana industries [1] in Queensland. In Canada the centre of trouble lies in British Columbia, where not only are Indians denied the franchise, with

---

[1] See the Banana Industry Preservation Act, 1921.

the result that for federal elections in that province they are also excluded, but every effort has been made to prevent them obtaining employment on mining and other works of varied kinds. That the prohibition has not been more extensive is largely due to the fact that the issue is complicated by the question of treatment of Japanese who have had treaty rights in Canada, which the Canadian Government has necessarily protected,[1] naturally with advantageous results for the Indians also. It is, however, in South Africa that the gravest ground for offence lies, for the large resident population there, mainly in Natal and the Transvaal, is definitely subjected to conditions of racial inferiority, and a steady effort is made to induce members of the Indian race to return to India to escape the difficulty of local circumstances, on condition that they shall never return to Africa. The difficulty of the position in South Africa must be conceded; the restrictions which shut out Asiatics from landholding in the Transvaal are inherited from the republic, and Boer opinion denies formally any possibility of equality in Church or State between the white and the coloured races, with whom the Indian is in effect classed. There is keen jealousy throughout the Union of the business activity and success of the petty traders whose rivals, many of them naturalised incomers from Eastern

---

[1] The legislation of the Dominion giving effect to the treaty with Japan, as applied to Canada in 1913, overrides provincial legislation of 1921 attempting to exclude Japanese from working under governmental timber licences: cf. *Att.-Gen. of British Columbia* v. *Att.-Gen. of Canada*, [1924] A.C. 203; Keith, *Journ. Comp. Leg.* v. 280 f. The question of further restriction was discussed in the Commons on May 8, 1922, but inconclusively. Since then by an informal accord with Japan fresh immigration is restricted to 150 a year. See also Angus, *Canadian Bar Review,* ix. 1 ff.

Europe, wage war on them, with the aid of the legis- lature, by securing control of the right of licensing petty traders for municipal bodies on which the Indians have, of course, no representation. The denial of the Parliamentary franchise in the Transvaal and in effect in Natal renders it impossible for the Indians to secure effective spokesmen of their own in Parliament, and led to the adoption, under the aegis of Mahatma Gandhi, of tactics of passive resistance which gave great trouble both to the Union and to the British and Indian Governments, until it was brought to a close for the time being by concessions made by the Union Parliament in Acts of 1913 and 1914. These measures while preventing immigration provided means for the recognition of monogamic Indian marriages and the introduction of the wives and offspring of such marriages into the Union by persons lawfully domiciled in the Union.

The grant of a new status to India, as the results of her services in the war, necessarily revived the issue in an acute form, and both in 1917 and 1918 the Imperial War Conferences had the matter under close consideration. The solution adopted was that of reciprocity, as a matter of courtesy and justice, although it was obvious that the working of such reciprocity would in the main leave the issues unaffected in substance. It was agreed that each part of the Empire should enjoy complete control of the composition of its own population by means of restriction of immigration from any other community, but British subjects domiciled in any part of the Empire should be admitted into other parts for purposes of visits for pleasure or commerce, or for educational purposes, as

opposed to permanent residence or temporary residence for labour purposes. India, therefore, was entitled to subject persons from any overseas territory
to the same conditions as were applied in that territory
to persons from India. Visits for temporary purposes
were to be arranged on the basis of passports granted
by the country of domicile and approved by an officer
there on behalf of the country to be visited, a suggestion based on an effective agreement as to temporary visits arranged between the governments of the
Commonwealth and India in 1904. It was also agreed
that Indians lawfully domiciled in the Dominions
should have the right of introducing one wife and her
children, if certified by the Government of India to be
lawfully married under Indian laws, a recommendation which was aimed at Canadian conditions, and to
which Canada proceeded to give effect.

India naturally was not satisfied by this measure of
concession, and feeling was also aroused there by the
departure of the Imperial Government [1] from the old
rule of non-discrimination between members of the
British race in the case of Kenya, where special areas
of land in the highlands were reserved exclusively for
Europeans, an unfair system of segregation in trading
areas was enforced, and the Indians were placed in a
wholly inferior political position to the white population, being denied electoral rights or effective representation in the legislature. In 1921 the question was
debated at the Imperial Conference with the result
that, while the right to control immigration was once
more reaffirmed, it was recognised that there was an
incongruity between the position of India as an equal

---

[1] See *Parl. Pap.* Cmd. 1311, 1922. Lord Elgin was largely responsible.

member of the British Empire and the existence of disabilities upon British Indians lawfully domiciled in some other part of the Empire. The Conference accordingly expressed the opinion that in the interests of the solidarity of the British Commonwealth it was desirable that the rights of such Indians to citizenship should be recognised. Unfortunately, however, the representatives of South Africa were unable to accept this resolution in view of the exceptional circumstances of the greater part of the Union, and the Indians' representatives felt bound to place on record their profound concern at the position of Indians in South Africa, and their hope that by direct negotiations some way might yet be found to a satisfactory solution of the position there.

The Conference resulted in the decision of the Indian Government to despatch on a mission to the Dominions, Mr Srinivasa Sastri, in order that by personal discussion and expressions of view in public he might awaken Dominion opinion to the creation of a new régime in India, and explain the implications of the change in its bearing on relations with the Dominions. His mission, which concluded in 1922, was marked by some success in the form of educating public opinion and achieved definite promises of amendments of acts, both in Australia and in Canada, where the Government undertook to consider granting the federal franchise in British Columbia as in the rest of the Dominion to Indians. Unfortunately he was unsuccessful in obtaining any real change of opinion in British Columbia, where the Government was unable to consider relaxation of its anti-Indian legislation, until popular opinion should be sufficiently educated

Chapter
V.

to appreciate the necessity for an alteration in the policy of hostility even to domiciled Indians. In the case of Kenya the question proved to be extremely complicated by reason of the existence of pledges to the European population rashly given by Lord Elgin in the early days of settlement, when the Indian question had not arisen in an acute form, and above all by the consideration that in that territory the prime duty of the Government ought to be to safeguard the interests of the natives against undue encroachment, both by the European and the Indian immigrants. But it was not contended that the existing situation in 1922 was in harmony with the essential principles of Imperial co-operation, and a change of Governor was arranged to facilitate a solution.

The decision arrived at by the Imperial Government in July 1923, after full discussion with the various interests involved, negatived the proposal that an attempt should be made to place European and Indian electors on the same footing with a single electoral roll.[1] On the contrary, it adopted the principle that the European electors should return eleven members and retain manhood suffrage, while the Indians should be given five members with a wide franchise, one elected member being similarly conceded to the Arab community. The same principle was to be adopted when electoral institutions were introduced into municipalities. It was determined also to maintain the reservation of the highlands for European settlement, and that immigration must be supervised with a view to secure the native African from

[1] On the other hand communal representation has been refused, on convincing grounds, to the Indian communities in the West Indies.

undue competition in subordinate mechanical and clerical work and in petty trade, that is, in effect from Indian competition. The only substantial concession made to Indian views was the abandonment of the attempt at segregation, either for residential or trade purposes, the impracticability of which was in fact patent. The decision was inevitably regarded in India as a complete victory for the European section of the population, although stress was laid by the Imperial Government on the view that the interests of the African natives must be paramount, and on the retention of control of the legislature in the hands of an official majority. Despite repeated reconsideration the issue has remained unsettled, the European community retaining its unfair predominance of legislative power, and in 1935 India bitterly protested against further reservation of lands.

In the Union of South Africa, which Mr Sastri did not visit, the question was not materially changed in aspect by the resolutions of 1918 or 1921. The temper of the people was sufficiently shown by the legislation of 1919, when the Transvaal Asiatics (Land and Trading) Act of the Union Parliament effectively put an end to the practice of securing the holding of land in the Transvaal by Asiatics, which was forbidden by the old Act of 1885 of the Republic, through the medium of the creation of companies which, though composed of Asiatics, were as juristic persons not Asiatics, and therefore were exempt from the operation of the law. At the same time effective steps were taken to complete the operation of the Gold and Township Laws of the Transvaal, under which the trading by Indians in gold areas and townships, that is, the most profitable places for trade, is prohibited, and thus a promising source of livelihood, for which they are naturally fitted, is withheld from Indians. For Indians also the inter-provincial barriers of freedom of movement are retained, and they are denied access to the Orange Free State. The action of Natal in 1921–4, in seeking to deprive Indians of even the municipal franchise, is striking evidence of the refusal of the people of the Union to accept any sentiment of Imperial co-operation in this regard.

The same spirit animates the report of the Asiatics Enquiry Commission of 1920–21. Not only does it decline to recommend any relaxation in the restrictions affecting Indian landholding and residence in gold areas for trade, but it makes further suggestion that in Natal fresh restrictions should be imposed, under which the right of Asiatics to acquire and hold land for farming and agricultural purposes outside townships should be confined to the coast area, while a system of voluntary residential and trading segregation of Asiatics in townships is advocated together with efforts to secure the voluntary repatriation of Asiatics from the Union. The proposals were naturally strongly resented in India, and the Union Government in January 1923 intimated that it was not prepared to legislate during the current session in accordance with the recommendations of the Commission.

The grave importance of the issue from the Imperial point of view was made apparent during the Imperial Conference of 1923, when the Indian representatives urged that steps should be taken to carry into effect the principle of equality for domiciled Indians adopted at the Conference of 1921, and suggested the appointment of Committees by the British and Dominion Governments to examine in co-operation with a Committee appointed by the Government of India the modes of making effective that resolution. The Canadian Prime Minister admitted that it would be difficult to secure legislation conferring the federal franchise on Indians in British Columbia[1] generally, though it was already given to such Indians as had served in the war, while the Prime Minister of the Commonwealth promised to consider legislation[2] to carry out in spirit the resolution of 1921, and the Prime Minister of New Zealand welcomed the proposed visit of a Committee from India. General Smuts, on the other hand, declined wholly to agree, and denounced the resolution of 1921 as unwise. He insisted that disabilities were imposed on Indians not on racial, but on economic grounds, and he held out no hope of any political or other concessions to Indians in the Union. The representatives of Newfoundland, and of the Irish Free State, on the other hand, approved heartily of the Indian desire for full equality of status, and the Imperial Government accepted the proposal of a Committee, although insisting that the Kenya decision could not be reopened. A strong protest against the attitude of General Smuts was made by Sir Tej Bahadur Sapru, who insisted that the attitude of South Africa was fatal to Imperial unity, and intimated that it would probably be necessary for India to treat the question as one of international law, and bring it before the League of Nations as an issue of the rights

[1] The provincial legislature on November 28, 1923, passed a resolution of protest against any concession, and it is still withheld.

[2] Old-age pensions and the franchise were the outstanding questions; both points have been conceded.

of minorities to fair treatment. He also insisted that the people of India could never accept as final the Kenya decision.

In 1924 relations between India and the Union were further strained by the determination of General Smuts to provide for the segregation of Indians for purposes of residence and trade, especially in urban areas. On the fall of General Smuts from power, the idea was sponsored by General Hertzog. Indian representations and the visit of an Indian delegation to the Union and of a Union Parliamentary delegation to India resulted in a Conference at Capetown which ended on January 11, 1927, with agreement on certain principles. It was recognised that the Union was justified in seeking to maintain Western standards of life, and that Indians of Union domicile who desired to maintain such standards should be helped to do so. Other Indians might be aided to emigrate to India or other places where Western standards were not required; they would then after three years lose the right to return; within that period they must refund the cost of their emigration. The Indian Government would look after such emigrants on their arrival in India. The entry of wives and minor children of domiciled Indians would be governed by the rules laid down by the Imperial War Conference of 1918. In view of this scheme the plan of reservation of areas would be dropped, and at the request of the Union Government an agent of the Indian Government would reside in the Union to secure effective co-operation between the Governments.

In 1932 the issue was again discussed as contemplated in the agreement of 1927. It was then found that the possibilities of emigration to India were, in view of

economic and climatic conditions in that country, practically exhausted, especially as 80 per cent of the Indian
population in the Union was born there. The possibility
of finding another outlet was envisaged, but so far
nothing effective has emerged from such investigation.

Naturally the feeling in India regarding Dominion
treatment of Indians has grown deeper and wider with
the development of the sense of Indian nationality and
the claim of Dominion status. It was proposed by the
British Government in 1933[1] to permit India to exclude
Dominion British subjects from immigration, but to
forbid discrimination against them if lawfully resident.
This proposal was entirely inconsistent with the status
of India, and was disapproved by the Joint Select
Committee which examined the governmental proposals, and was very wisely dropped from the Government of India Act as passed. The Indian Government
is thus left free to deal with any part of the Empire
except the United Kingdom without being fettered,
and it is indeed difficult to understand how Sir S. Hoare
adopted a proposal so unfair to India and so inconsistent with the Imperial Conference resolutions of
1917 and 1918.

[1] Keith, *Letters on Imperial Relations, 1916–1935*, pp. 226, 227.

CHAPTER VI

THE GOVERNMENT OF NATIVE RACES

1. *Imperial Control of Native Races*

Chapter VI.

In the main the task of the Imperial Government in regard to native races is of a simpler character than that of the Dominions, in so far as the problem is not raised of the rival claims of white and coloured populations to dominate the territories. It is a significant reminder of this fact that the chief difficulties now to be faced by the Imperial Government are precisely in cases where, as in the Dominions, white settlers are able to stand the climatic conditions and to increase in numbers by natural growth. The complexity of the Indian problem would have been inextricable, had India permitted of true European settlement, and had a large European community grown up accustomed to political domination over the rest of the people.

For the tropical portions of the Empire in general, the rôle of the Imperial Government must be that of a protector, who ensures the existence of conditions and circumstances of peace and order, calculated to promote the development of the native race or races inhabiting the territory. In West and East Africa, for instance, it would be idle to ignore the necessity of a European Government to permit of any chance of the development of civilisation. The melancholy history of Liberia illustrates acutely enough the difficulties facing the growth of negro States even under comparatively favourable circumstances. The same lesson can be read from the history of the Zulus, or the Bechuanas, or Basutos, or the Swazis in the south. Through a variety of circumstance, of which political incapacity must be reckoned an important factor, these races failed to develop any organisation of substantial value as an instrument of civilisation. It is essential to remember that the great achievement of the Zulus was to build up a military force with vast potentialities for destruction, and the subjugation of rival tribes, but without any conception of the creation of a body-politic.

It is obvious that, while it is the prime duty of the Imperial Government to secure peace and order by the suppression of tribal warfare and of domestic slavery,[1] of the slave trade and slave raiding, it is essential that the administration of native territories should be conducted on the basis of enabling the natives to learn to rule themselves. This is doubtless a conception which at times has not been clearly realised by British administrators, who have aimed, as formerly in India, rather at developing the maximum of efficiency in the administration regardless of the fact that this process has only a limited sphere of validity. The financial burden imposed by an administration through imported officers is a grave burden; it renders it necessary to impose taxation, which in itself may be light, but which none the less presses heavily on natives with scanty means, and it does little or nothing to develop the power of the natives

---

[1] Thanks to Lady Simon's observations and public exposure, in 1927 domestic slavery still lingering in the Sierra Leone Protectorate was definitely declared illegal and similar legislation was passed for the other Protectorates. On slavery in the Sudan see *Parl. Pap.* Cmd. 2650, 2872.

for self-government. On the contrary, it tends to injure the moral character of the people by robbing them of the power of self-direction; the chiefs lose their utility and sink to the rank of minor servants of the Government, who perform their work without much capacity or interest. The native system of tribal life is interfered with, and nothing effective is supplied in its place. It is an easy step to the further policy of putting compulsion on the native to work for private European employers, a project once favoured by the administration in East Africa, and for a time even viewed with some measure of approval by Lord Milner, as Secretary of State for the Colonies. Happily his policy in this regard was effectively repudiated by Mr Churchill, and the idea of turning the native population into a piece of machinery for the profit of immigrant white settlers has been officially and emphatically repudiated by the Duke of Devonshire, Lord Passfield, and the Joint Select Committee of Parliament on Closer Union in East Africa.[1] Instead, it is now more clearly recognised that the native is by no means so lazy as his detractors make him out to be; that his disinclination to work, when it exists, is largely the outcome of communal customs which have abstracted much of his energies for work for the benefit of his chiefs; and that there is no insuperable difficulty in securing his active co-operation in development of local resources by the process of assuring him personal gains from his labour. The enormous extension of the production of cocoa in the Gold Coast is a classical and most remarkable example of the energy

[1] Cf. *Parl. Pap.* Cmd. 2387, 2904, 3234, 3573, 3574; *H.C. Pap.* 184, 1931.

of the native when he is allowed to work on his own
land in his own way for his personal profit, and incidentally, of course, for the profit of the State whose
taxes are largely based on his capacity to earn and
purchase imported goods, as well as pay more direct
taxation. It is possible, of course, to point to wasteful
and inefficient modes of cultivation adopted, but it
would be idle to imagine that any system of compulsion could have produced more satisfactory results on
the Gold Coast, and the experience of the Belgian
Congo under forced labour [1] is a painful reminder of
the dangers of leaving human life at the mercy of
exploitation by commercial interests.

For communities such as those of West Africa
policy cannot be simple, for circumstances are wholly
diverse. There exists, for instance, on the coast in the
Gold Coast, Sierra Leone, and Lagos a population
which has acquired a tincture of European ideas, and
adopted European dress and in some measure social
habits; such a community must be educated to self-
government as a distant goal through participation
in municipal government on an elective basis leading
to the adoption of election as the method of selecting
the members of the legislatures, which thus will gain
gradually fuller control over the executive, while the
executive should more and more completely be recruited from among the ranks of educated natives,
whose employment incidentally must result in large
economies in the cost of administration.

Inland, however, in West Africa there are the regions
governed as protectorates, in which exist the descendants of ancient native kingdoms such as those founded

[1] Cf. Keith, *The Belgian Congo and the Berlin Act* (1919).

in Northern Nigeria by the Fulani at the expense of
the Haussa population. These Muhammadan States
were a burden to the country, in that they waged
war on one another, and raided for slaves far and near,
but they had acquired a tincture of Muhammadan
law, and were not unfamiliar with conceptions of
administration and a regular judiciary. To replace
these potential instruments of government by British
officials would have been a suicidal policy, and successive administrators of Nigeria must be accorded
the credit of having aimed at indirect rule through the
native chiefs, rehabilitating the older form of administration, ridding it of its arbitrary and barbarous character, and making it a reasonably efficient method of
government, and at any rate something more work-
able than a European administration. The Emirs and
their subordinates are thus converted into instruments
of government, deriving their authority from governmental recognition, and carrying on their administration subject to the general laws enacted for the territory by the Governor. A form of direct taxation based
on the native system purified of its abuses, is in force;
the chiefs collect the taxes, a fixed share of which is
retained by the Native Treasuries from which are paid
the salaries of the native officers.[1] Supervision over their
executive authority is exercised by the residents and
their subordinates, and the judicial activities of the
Kadis and Emirs, while left intact so as to secure the
adoption of Muhammadan and native law in regard
to civil rights, is curtailed so as to prevent any serious
injustice in the administration of criminal law. To
European officers certain classes of crimes are en-

[1] See Lord Lugard, *The Dual Mandate in British Tropical Africa.*

trusted for punishment, especially such as are not offences against native law, or as are barbarously punished by that law. There is no doubt the possibility of injustice and oppression by native courts, but on the whole the system of supervision is adequate to prevent the occurrence of very grave evils, and no other practical system has even been suggested.

In other regions of Nigeria the effects of tribal wars and slave raids left no semblance of effective authority among the pagan tribes, and it has been necessary laboriously to seek to build up a framework of government on the basis of Native Councils, a task of the utmost difficulty, but the only means of securing any practical results of value.

The case of Nigeria is typical of African problems generally. The development of native administrative capacity remains the essential problem to which only a gradual, and as yet often slight, progress has been made. It is accompanied as a matter of course by constant regard for native law; the laws of England, including the statutes of general application, are doubtless in force in West Africa, while Indian legislation, based on that law, prevails in East Africa, but these facts are subject to the rule that native law, so far as it is not contrary to the elementary principles of equity and natural justice, is administered in cases, whatever the court before which they are brought, where the sole parties are natives.[1] Where one party is a native and the other a European, or native living as such, more difficult questions arise, since it might be as unjust to apply unadulterated native law to the European as to apply English or Indian law to the

[1] Cf. *Idewu Inasa* v. *Sakariyawo Oshodi*, [1934] A.C. 99.

native, and the Courts have to be guided largely by their own discretion. For such difficulties there is of course, ample precedent in the history of British relations with the much more advanced and elaborate civilisation of India.

It is clear that legislation and administration for such communities cannot appropriately or wisely be entrusted to any persons who are not under effective Imperial control. To create a legislature in which Europeans occupying private positions were given a preponderating power would be most unjust, since they could hardly do other than legislate predominantly in their own interest, even if they had the necessary knowledge to understand native interests, which is normally not the case. Hence, at an early date, power was given to the Crown by Acts now consolidated in the British Settlements Act, 1887, to legislate for British territories in West Africa, even if not acquired by cession or conquest, by Order in Council, and to create dependent legislatures in these possessions. Over the Protectorates in East and West Africa similar legislative authority, but less restricted, is possessed under the Foreign Jurisdiction Act, 1890; Kenya is apparently regarded as ceded and so subject to the Crown's prerogative of legislation.

In the case of the Kenya Colony the Imperial Government is faced with the difficulty of a resident white population, which may find a permanent home on the highlands, and a large native population, combined with a very considerable body of Indian immigrants, who have deserved well of the country by reason of the services rendered by workers from India in the building of the railway to Uganda, which could never have been carried out without their labour. It is impossible to avoid the conclusion that in the interests of the native population restrictions on immigration both of Europeans and Indians are essential. The policy of the European residents, who have disproportionate power on the legislature,[1] is inevitably directed at securing native labour at low rates, for which purpose various efforts at compulsion have been mooted,[2] while the growth of the Indian community can hardly be expected to tend to the benefit of the natives, to whom they are no more akin than Europeans, and on whom their influence is alleged to be often detrimental. In Uganda the ruler of Buganda governs with the advice of the Governor and a Council which has also judicial functions.

The necessity and the value of Imperial supervision is obvious in regard to the fundamental issue of land ownership; if local legislatures were relieved from Imperial control, it would be impossible to expect the adoption of sufficiently generous measures in native interests. Both in East and in West Africa, in point of fact, the fullest recognition has in the main been accorded to the fundamental principle that British political sovereignty or protection does not mean the confiscation of native land interests. The legislation of Northern Nigeria, which has sometimes been treated as deviating from this rule, is, on the contrary, a complete affirmation of it; in a closely settled territory there is no room for any policy save of frank and immediate

---

[1] The legislature includes the Governor, 11 *ex officio* members, 9 nominated officials, 11 elected European and 5 elected Indian members, with an elected Arab member and 2 nominated members to represent native interests.

[2] Compare *Parl. Pap.* Cmd. 873, 1509, 2464.

recognition of native land rights under native law; in Northern Nigeria wars and raids had created a position in which *de facto* large areas of land had no just owner, and the Protectorate legislation recognised this fact by claiming such lands for the Crown, but only as a trustee for native rights. In West Africa no case has arisen of disregard of native land interests for the sake of Europeans; instead, great care has been taken of late years to prevent imprudent grants of such rights by the natives themselves, a most beneficial series of legislative interventions. In East Africa the settlement of the Kenya Colony has been attended by the assigning of native reserves definitely delimited, and there has been some complaint that the marking out of these reserves is an unjust deprivation of the natives. The answer, to some extent valid, is that there was more land than could properly be used by the natives, and that tribal wars had ousted, or reduced to an inferior status, the original proprietors, so that claims to ownership rested merely on rights of conquest, not made good by effective possession. Further difficulties arising from gold discoveries were to some degree met by the recommendations of the Land Commission of 1933.[1] The problem, however, remains, whether it was wise policy to seek to establish a European resident community in a limited area of a native territory, thus inevitably creating a difficult racial problem.

In the Western Pacific, in the Gilbert and Ellice Islands Colony, there may be found the same principle

---

[1] See *Parl. Pap.* Cmd. 4556, and for the Government's decision Cmd. 4580. The Archbishop of Canterbury has shown just concern for the rights of the native.

of government through local chiefs, or more often native magistrates, aided by councils, who under the supervision of a small British staff effectively carry on and raise the necessary revenue for the cost of administration. There is a native code of law authorised by Colonial Ordinance. The Solomon Islands Protectorate presents the beginnings of a similar system, but the task is of more difficulty owing to the lack of civilisation among the tribes. In Fiji the preservation of the native forms of government and native rights over land, which are recognised in the widest sense, has to be combined with the government of a large resident British Indian population, and a steadily growing European population in close touch with Australasian sentiment. To concede an independent legislature would obviously be impossible with due regard to the interests of the natives by whom the islands were ceded to the Crown, but the legislature includes six elected Europeans, three elected Indians, and three natives, besides thirteen nominated officials. Their traditional system of village and district councils has been recognised and strengthened, while native affairs form the subject of triennial meetings between the Governor and the high chiefs and representatives of each province. A Native Regulation Board, consisting of the Governor and four officials with five native members, is charged with the duty of making regulations with regard to marriage and divorce, succession to property, the jurisdiction of civil and criminal native courts, and other matters relating to the well-being of the natives, these regulations attaining the force of law on submission to the Legislative Council.

In other parts of the Colonial Empire the problem of

government differs fundamentally in that there is now no possibility of using native institutions. The West Indian islands presented for the most part the difficulty of the existence of two strains in the population, one of European origin, one the descendants of African slaves, with, of course, the inevitable intermixture of races. Experience has in some degree shown that such communities have not, under modern conditions, economic strength sufficient to maintain themselves without external assistance, and that it is impossible to entrust full legislative power to either a section of the people, or the people as a whole, in the present state of development of these territories, some of which at one time enjoyed full representative government, but found that condition impossible when the foundation of their prosperity was destroyed by the abolition of slavery, and competition of beet sugar with their staple product. The presence of Indian immigrants in considerable numbers in such places as Trinidad and British Guiana is a further ground for Imperial control.

The eastern Colonies present complex problems. Ceylon naturally claims gradual advance through a stage of constitution analogous to that of India to the goal of self-government. In Mauritius the presence of an enormous population of Indian origin causes a position of delicacy as regards the French creole population, and necessitates an impartial control. In Hongkong and the Straits Settlements, Imperial control is obviously desirable, while in the Malay States is presented a classical example of administration through native agency with British advice.

South Africa also presents two classical instances of the preservation of native institutions in the case of

Basutoland and the Bechuanaland Protectorate, both governed by Resident Commissioners under the High Commissioner for Basutoland, the Bechuanaland Protectorate, and Swaziland, who alone legislates for the territories. The native institutions in either case are carefully preserved, subject to intervention both in executive and judicial matters to prevent injustice. Basutoland also boasts an advisory council of 100 members, ninety-five nominated by the chiefs, and five by the Government. Disputes between Europeans and natives are dealt with by European magistrates. Swaziland is shared between natives and Europeans, the latter having an elected Advisory Council to aid the Resident Commissioner.

2. *Dominion Control of Native Races*

The Dominion Governments, in a greater or less degree, have all been confronted with the task of dealing with bodies of aborigines situated within their central territories, and, save Canada and Newfoundland, with dependencies largely occupied by native races.

(1) In *Canada* the position was largely simplified by the comparatively small numbers of American Indians, and by their inability to combat the advance of civilisation. By careful treatment of Indian claims it was found possible for the agents of the British Government to acquire from them the necessary cessions of their lands on suitable terms of payment, and the responsibility for native relations throughout Canada was vested by the British North America Act, 1867, in the Dominion Parliament. The object of Canadian

policy has been to secure the development of Indians within the large reserves—nearly five million acres for little over 120,000 Indians—which have been set aside for Indian occupation, to provide facilities for education, and to train them with a view to their gradual complete emancipation from a status of inferiority and complete merger in the general population. Some objection has been taken to this policy by sections of Indian opinion; it has been claimed that the Indians are on a basis of alliance with the British Crown and that, save by agreement, no alteration can be made in their status; exception was on this ground taken to the inclusion of Indians in the Canadian legislation of 1917, imposing compulsory service, though there was no lack of anxiety to aid the Empire in the struggle, and the percentage of voluntary enlistments in the Canadian forces for the war was exceptionally high. The aims of the Government are set out effectively in the amendments of the Indian Act carried out in 1920. Provision was then made for the establishment of day schools and industrial or boarding schools, for the transport of children to these schools, and for allowing inspection of the schools by the chief and council of any band of Indians. Attendance at such schools may be made compulsory for Indians between seven and fifteen years of age. Moreover, the Governor in Council is authorised, on the report of the Superintendent-General of Indian Affairs, to enfranchise Indians, male and female, above the age of twenty-one, and to issue to them patents for their lands.[1] On such enfranchisement an Indian with

[1] In 1922 the Act was amended to make it necessary that the Indian should desire enfranchisement. The possibility of compulsion had aroused dissatisfaction among the Six Nation Indians, who claimed to be allies, not subjects, and the alteration conduced to restore harmony.

his wife and children becomes on a footing of equality with any other British subject in the Dominion. An Indian woman is also freed from disability by marrying a non-Indian. In the same year the franchise was specially conceded to every Indian who served overseas, although the franchise is normally denied to unenfranchised Indians.

Newfoundland has been fortunate in escaping difficulty as regards native rights. The aborigines there have become extinct, and those on the Labrador coast, which is included within the limits of the Dominion, are disappearing rapidly despite philanthropic efforts to save the race, a task for which the Dominion Government has no funds to spare.

(2) In the *Commonwealth of Australia* the aborigines have largely ceased to present a problem of serious concern through the diminution of their numbers. There are still apparently, including half-castes, some 60,000, mainly in the Northern Territory, in Queensland, and in Western Australia, and considerable sums are expended by the responsible Governments, State and Commonwealth, in providing for their relief when need drives them to approach mission stations and other sources of aid. In the Northern Territory their interests are secured in some degree by the fact that legislation is carried out by the Governor-General on the advice of the Commonwealth Ministry; but it is clear that contact with civilisation is fatal to the vitality of a race, never apparently numerous, but healthy enough in its normal condition. The Commonwealth

---

But in 1933 compulsory enfranchisement was again rendered possible, on a report as to fitness by a judge, an officer of the department, and a member of the band, but not contrary to any treaty rights.

further has, apart from its mandated territories in New Guinea, control of the British portion thereof, Papua with its large and uncivilised aboriginal population. The legislative authority for the territory may be exercised by Parliament, or normally by a local legislature of officials and nominees of the Government, and its legislative activities are closely supervised to secure native interests. The administration aims at using native instrumentalities in government, and has been successful in preserving native interests with scanty resources. A simple code of regulations is in force. Native land rights are fully recognised, and dealings between Europeans and natives in land are forbidden, sales of land being permitted only by the natives to the Government, which then makes such grants to Europeans as it deems fit. The native race is further protected from Indian or Japanese immigration and exploitation by the immigration restriction policy of the Commonwealth. The Commonwealth is responsible also for the government of the tiny Norfolk Island and its mixed population, in part descendants of the mutineers of H.M.S. *Bounty*.

(3) *New Zealand* alone of the Dominions has been in the position of having to deal with a warlike and intelligent native population which has made a real stand against the deterioration of European influences. The Maoris, though stationary as regards numbers of the population of full blood, have shown ability in many directions, and their interests have been greatly furthered by the provision for them of four elective seats, confined to Maori electors, in the House of Representatives. The Maoris have stoutly maintained their rights to their lands, and, though from time to time

surrenders of surplus lands have been arranged, and certain lands were forfeited for rebellion, the land legislation of New Zealand has respected and safeguarded native rights from diminution by the errors of the Maoris themselves. Moreover, recently compensation has been granted for certain injustices done in the early days of settlement. Nor has effort been spared for the social and moral welfare of the race, which has produced politicians and administrators of far more than average accomplishment. If, as is possible, the ultimate fate of the full-blooded Maori is extinction, the race will nevertheless have left an abiding mark in the history of New Zealand, and have affected in sensible measure the population.

New Zealand, however, also controls, in addition to her mandated territory, the important islands known as the Cook group, which became her possession by annexation in 1901. The administration of these islands has been a happy adaptation of the native form of government, and now stands consolidated in the Cook Islands Acts of 1915 and 1921.[1] Islands Councils exist, consisting either in whole or part of official, elected or nominee members; the official members are generally European officers and Arikis, native chiefs; nominated members hold office during the pleasure of the Governor-General or for a fixed period, not exceeding five years. Women as well as men are eligible as electors and members of the Councils. The Councils have power to make laws for the good government of the islands, provided that the laws must not be

[1] Niue is placed under the administration of Western Samoa for convenience. The final control of the islands rests with the Minister for the Cook Islands.

repugnant to Acts of the New Zealand Parliament. The maximum penalties imposed under such laws must not exceed three months' imprisonment or a £50 fine, and no law may deal with customs duties; borrowing of money is prohibited, nor can a Council establish Courts of Justice or appropriate expenditure of revenue other than that raised under authority of their laws. These laws must be assented to by the Resident Commissioner or the Governor-General, and the latter may disallow within a year an ordinance assented to by the former. The laws are enforced through the High Court, which has all jurisdiction, civil or criminal, necessary for the administration of justice. Judges and Commissioners of the court are appointed by the Governor-General. A Commissioner may with some exceptions exercise the full powers of a judge, subject to appeal to a judge. Judgments in the High Court are subject to appeal to the Supreme Court of New Zealand, and judgments in civil cases are enforceable in the Dominion by that court. The manufacture and importation of intoxicating liquor are absolutely forbidden, even for European use, this arrangement being the condition on which, in 1921, the Island Councils accepted the proposal that a white representative elected by the white population should be added to these bodies, a change which could not be made without their consent, as the terms of annexation provided for the maintenance of the councils as they stood. As in the case of the Maoris of New Zealand proper, the essential aim of the administration is to preserve all that is sound in native custom, while directly or indirectly terminating pernicious practices.

(4) In *South Africa* the native question presents

difficulties of the most formidable character, for which no solution is even in sight. The mere fact that the native population, exclusive of mixed and other coloured populations, forms 67 per cent of the total population, places the question in a wholly different light from that found in the other Dominions. The standard of civilisation among these natives varies greatly, and an important factor in the problem is presented by the existence of very miscellaneous elements of mixed blood, while even in the reputed white population there is often some admixture of negro descent. Chapter
VI.

The political power of the natives of the Union is definitely limited. In the Cape no racial discrimination as such was permitted by the Imperial Government when representative government was granted in 1853. But the uneducated and uncivilised native was excluded from the franchise as the result of the individual property and educational qualifications requisite;[1] in Natal practically total exclusion was attained, and in the Transvaal and the Orange Free State the vote was never conceded. The Union of South Africa constitution, while retaining (s. 35) and safeguarding from hasty alteration the Cape native vote, excludes any native from membership of Parliament. It provides in their favour, however, the inadequate protection that four of the members nominated to the Senate by the Governor-General shall be selected by reason mainly of their thorough acquaintance, by reason of their official experience or otherwise, with the reasonable wants and wishes of the coloured races of South

[1] See Act No. 9 of 1892. In 1933 there were 35,781 non-European voters in the Cape, but only 316 in Natal.

Africa. A further safeguard against ill-considered local action is provided by the rule that the control and administration of native affairs throughout the Union are vested in the Governor-General in Council, who is authorised to exercise all the special powers possessed by the Governors of the Colonies before the union.

The actual control of administration is exercised through the Minister for Native Affairs and his department of State, under the direction of a permanent secretary. The Native Affairs Act, 1920, makes provision for the establishment of a Commission presided over by the Minister, whose functions and duties include the consideration of any matter relating to the general conduct of the administration, of the legislation in so far as it may affect the native population (other than matters of departmental administration), and the submission to the Minister of its recommendations on any such matter. If the Minister refuses to accept their recommendations, they can compel the consideration of the matter by the Governor-General in Council, and ultimately the laying of the papers before Parliament. The plan is based on the arrangements laid down in the schedule to the South Africa Act, 1909, regarding the administrative system to be applied to the native territories still retained under Imperial control, if they are transferred in due course to the Union, and its aim is to secure the adoption of a consistent and well-thought-out policy in native affairs, experience in the Colonies having shown that native policy was ever in a state of confusion and flux through changes in ministries and lack of continuous purpose. In practice its work is advisory, and its influence does not appear to have been great so far.

Further, the Governor- General is authorised to establish a native local council for areas where aboriginal
natives predominate, with power to provide for the
maintenance of roads, drains, dams and furrows,
water supply, suppression of stock diseases, destruction of noxious weeds, sanitation, hospitals, methods
of agriculture, and educational facilities, for which
purpose they may levy a rate of £1 annually on each
adult male. Rules may be made for the consultation of
the natives before the members of the councils are
nominated, and for their tenure of office and remuneration. A number of such bodies have on the advice of
the Commission been set up. Each council is presided
over by a permanent Civil servant. The Governor-
General may also on the advice of the Commission
summon an assembly of native chiefs, members of
native local councils, and prominent natives with
a view to ascertaining the sentiment of the native
population of the Union, a proposal based on the
powers given to the Governors of the Transvaal and
the Orange River Colony constitutions of 1906 and
1907, but not then acted upon. Use of this power was
made in 1922–7, but only in 1930 was it again resorted
to, presumably because the conference proved hostile
to the ministry's proposals in 1927 for the abolition of
the Cape native franchise.

The system of councils is one which has been in the
past best exemplified in the Transkeian territory, the
chief aboriginal area in the Cape. Under Proclamations
of 1930 and 1932 the United Transkeian Territories
General Council assists the Chief Magistrate of the
Territories by its advice; it consists of magistrates
and native members, who represent the 26 District

Councils, which are in effect executive committees of the General Council; these Councils consist of a magistrate and six councillors, two nominated, and the rest proposed by the local representatives of the ratepayers. Their functions are on the lines of those provided in the Act of 1920. There is an Executive Committee of the General Council which deals with certain matters affecting official staffs, scholarships, agricultural institutions, and public works. In the Glen Grey area there is a district council composed of a magistrate, with six nominated and six elected members, charged with the raising of a rate and its expenditure, dipping of cattle, roads, agriculture, irrigation, and public health. In the Orange Free State the Witzieshoek Reserve has a Board, constituted under an ordinance of 1907, of two Europeans and five nominated natives, with powers over roads, water supply, sanitation, and education, while the chief exercises civil jurisdiction, subject to appeal to the European Commandant, who alone deals with criminal cases. In certain town areas, including Cape Town, Port Elizabeth, Bloemfontein, the chief mining and industrial areas in the Transvaal, Durban, and Pietermaritzburg, natives are required to live in locations.[1]

Both as regards industry and land holding, insoluble questions present themselves. In the mines of the Transvaal native labour is essential if the industry is to be preserved, but white labour opinion insists on confining native workers to other than skilled labour, and this is supported by Transvaal regulations having the force of law. Political reasons also tell in favour of the

[1] See Natives (Urban Areas) Act, 1923, amended by No. 25 of 1930. The members resident may be limited.

contention of the white miners, since, if the natives were permitted to become skilled workers, their demand for political rights would be greatly strengthened. In the Cape education has been stimulated by missionary efforts, and has resulted in the establishment of a South African Native College, which aims at education of a University standard and opens its doors to natives and coloured persons, and Indians of both sexes, a factor which will render it increasingly difficult to maintain the Boer doctrine of refusing equality to the coloured races, though it accords admirably with Mr Rhodes's dogma of equal rights for every civilised person. The serious manifestations of industrial trouble of late years in the Transvaal are a symptom of the effect of unrest among the white miners on the native mind, and it is significant that in the grave events of 1922, in the Transvaal, a disquieting feature was shown in the savage attacks on peaceful natives made by the revolutionaries.

The question of native land rights is at least as complicated. In 1913 a preliminary step was taken in the Natives Land Act, 1913, which was intended to clear the way for a policy of reserving certain areas in the Union definitely for European occupation, and other areas for native occupation, the conception being that the natives should be encouraged to develop within these areas a civilisation peculiarly their own, not along mere European lines. The Act provided for the maintenance as far as possible of the *status quo* as regards land tenure by Europeans and natives respectively, and set up a Commission charged with the duty of recommending to Parliament what areas should be set aside for European, and what for native occupation.

The fatal difficulty, however, soon appeared when the Commission reported in 1916: the Government could not give the natives more land without annoying its supporters, and the issue remained unaltered in 1935.[1] The task proved extremely difficult, and the complication of the whole scheme led among other things to the passing of the legislation of 1920, for the creation of a Commission which might study at leisure and in detail the problems of racial segregation, native education, native taxation, native life in urban and industrial areas, and the native pass laws. The latter, which are of the most complex and harsh character, represent the devices of the Governments of Natal, the Transvaal, and the Orange Free State, for supervising and restricting the movements of natives, which are free only in the Cape, outside the Transkeian area. The necessity of amending these laws is patent and not denied, but unhappily nothing effective has yet been found practicable, thus perpetuating a grievance which is undoubtedly serious. A remedy in the more generous issue of exemptions from these laws has been too sparingly applied, and there is no doubt that abuses of power and injustice are only too easy under the existing condition of the law, which involves constant punishment of natives for purely technical offences.

The issue of segregation presents the fatal difficulty that, if it is to work at all, it must be complete, and

[1] The Joint Committee of Parliament (April 1935) recommended the passing of a Native Trust and Land Bill to secure additional lands for natives to be administered by a Trust; and of a Representation of Natives Bill to terminate the native vote in the Cape (saving the rights of natives already registered) and to substitute the election of four European senators by natives indirectly; to provide for the election similarly of two Cape Provincial Councillors, and to set up an advisory Natives Representative Council, part elective.

in that case the farmers of the Union would be reduced to cultivating with their own hands and European labour, which would probably not be economically possible, and which at any rate they are not prepared to try. Any partial form of segregation would obviously defeat the purpose of inducing the natives to develop their own civilisation, for it would mean a constant communication between the reserves and the non-native areas. Nor is it easy to see how the ideal of allowing the natives to develop on their own lines can be attained; the influence of European civilisation on the Bantu has been far too lengthy to have failed to destroy the vitality of native institutions; what is possible in Northern Nigeria is hardly practicable in the Cape or the Transvaal. An extremely disquieting fact was also revealed by the war, the efficiency of native troops when effectively trained, as experience against the German native levies in East Africa showed only too plainly. The Union Governmental policy excludes natives from military training, but it is idle to ignore the rising self-consciousness of the native or the difficulty, which must become steadily more obvious, of maintaining a policy of repression. The religious activity of the separatist Churches is a further sign of the aim of the native to attain for himself a status independent of European control and supervision. Unfortunately racial subordination is incompatible with the teachings of the New Testament, as the natives easily recognise.

Much resentment has been created among the natives by General Hertzog's proposal to abolish Cape franchise for natives, for the proposal in lieu, the granting of strictly limited representation of natives throughout the Union, is naturally regarded as un-satisfactory. Moreover, the Native Administration Act of 1927, though it contained some valuable provisions, including the recognition of native law throughout the Union, the establishment of special native civil courts, and the introduction of greater uniformity in administration, has tended to strengthen tribalism and to bear hardly on the urban and detribalised natives. Moreover, it has substituted for the rule of law of the supremacy of the courts a system of privileges held at official discretion, a sort of *droit administratif*. Further resentment has been caused by the total exclusion of natives from the Old-Age Pensions Act of 1928, and by the fact that the election of 1929 was for the first time in Union history fought on the issue of the "Native menace". Morcover, by the operation of the Women's Enfranchisement Act of 1930, from the operation of which all non-European women were excluded, the political power, slight as it was, of the native voter has been gradually reduced, so that they constitute less than 2 per cent of the total electorate. In the same year the Riotous Assemblies (Amendment) Act gave to the Minister of Justice powers almost unprecedented in a Parliamentary State in time of peace. In 1932 a further blow to native interests was struck by the Native Service Contract Act, which is intended to terminate the practice of "squatting" and to reduce all natives in European rural areas to the status of labour tenants, who, by legislation of 1926, have been placed for disciplinary purposes in the position of labourers, subject to penal measures in the case of breach of contract. In the same spirit the Labour Department, created in 1924, has ostentatiously disregarded the interests of native labour; the Industrial Conciliation Act excludes natives from its provisions for peaceful settlement of industrial disputes, and the governmental policy [1] has closed to natives employment on the railways, while the customs tariff has been used to compel manufacturers to prefer white to black labour. The result has been loss of earning power for the natives, the growth of anti-white prejudice, and the embitterment of race relations.

The coloured population in the Union stands in a somewhat different position. The colour bar operates against it as against the natives in the higher posts of the public services. Entry to any South African University is very difficult and most churches exclude coloured Christians no less than natives. General Hertzog's franchise proposal contemplated at first equal terms with Europeans for coloured voters [2] and the extension of the franchise for them in the Transvaal and Orange Free State, but when in 1930–31 adult suffrage was created in the Union, the new extension was not applied to coloured persons.

[1] See General Hertzog's Circular No. 5, October 31, 1924, which urges use of European labour in all Government services at the cost of native labour. Yet the Government is not paid for by Europeans only.

[2] The Joint Committee contemplates the grant to individual coloured persons of non-native status by the Governor-General in Council after a semi-judicial enquiry, subject to disallowance by Parliament.

CHAPTER VII

THE RULE OF LAW AND THE RIGHTS OF THE SUBJECT

1. *The Rule of Law*

THROUGHOUT the Empire the system of government is distinguished by the predominance of the rule of law. The most obvious side of this conception is afforded by the principles that no man can be made to suffer in person or property save through the action of the ordinary courts after a public trial by established legal rules, and that there is a definite body of well-known legal principles, excluding arbitrary executive action. The value of the principles was made obvious enough during the war when vast powers were necessarily conferred on the executive by statute, under which rights of individual liberty were severely curtailed both in the United Kingdom and in the oversea territories. Persons both British and alien were deprived legally but more or less arbitrarily of liberty on grounds of suspicion of enemy connections or inclinations, and the movements of aliens were severely restricted and supervised; the courts of the Empire [1]

[1] Keith, *War Government of the Dominions*, pp. 307 f. Discretionary action if authorised by law is legal and in one sense compatible with the rule of law, but the essential meaning of the rule excludes any wide executive arbitrariness, such as is permitted by the Union of South Africa Riotous Assemblies (Amendment) Act, 1930, which allows a minister to control the movement of any person whom he believes to be promoting feelings of hostility between Europeans and others.

recognised the validity of such powers under war conditions, but it is clear that a complete change would
be effected in the security of personal rights if executive
officers in time of peace were permitted the discretion
they exercised during the war, and which in foreign
countries they often exercise even in time of peace.

A further aspect of the rule of law is the fact that in the
main the law makes no discrimination between private
individuals and officials in regard to its enforcement.
It does not, save where statute has intervened, afford
any further protection to an official than to an ordinary person, and such statutory consideration is largely
justified by reasons of convenience, as in the case of
the requirement that actions against public authorities
should be brought within a reasonable limit of time.
But special courts are not constituted to deal with
cases in which officials are parties, nor in the ordinary
courts is any special code applied to the consideration
of such cases. There is no real exception to this in the
fact that, as will be shown later, under such Acts as
those dealing with health insurance various matters
interesting individuals are assigned for settlement
to quasi-judicial bodies constituted from executive
officers, for these matters do not touch on any fundamental rights and are manifestly unsuited for ordinary
judicial determination.

This absence of anything really corresponding to the
droit administratif of continental law has resulted in
the fact that the fundamental rights of the subject
are nothing more or less than principles evolved by the
law courts in the application of the general principles
of law to individual cases. To enact them formally has
accordingly been rare in British constitution-making,

and the fact that they are formally enacted in the Irish constitution is due to a deliberate following of Continental and American precedent. It is important to note that in the Free State, as often elsewhere, the enunciation of principles is not accompanied by any effective means of enforcing them, so that they possess no more validity than the same principles do in cases where they are implicit in the constitution.

2. *The Rights of the Subject*

(1) The right to personal freedom essentially rests on the fact that machinery exists under which any person not deprived of liberty by sentence of a judicial body can, if placed under restraint, assert his freedom and punish those who have illegally deprived him of it. Thus he can by setting the criminal law in motion secure punishment of the offender for assault and false imprisonment, and he can by bringing an action obtain damages to such extent as seems suitable to a jury interested in vindicating the rights of the individual. More important still, by the use of the writ of habeas corpus,[1] he, or his friends, can secure that whoever detains him shall be compelled to explain the grounds of his detention, so that if it be illegal he may be liberated by the court. The power has repeatedly been exercised to secure the vindication of liberty, to protect the subject against illegal proceedings under martial law, to deny to a husband the right to confine a wife, to restore children to parents, and to secure the

---

[1] This common law writ is reinforced by Acts of 1679 (dealing with confinement on criminal charges), and 1816 covering other cases. Application may be made to different judges, and no appeal lies if liberty is granted by the Court.

liberation of a man detained as a slave, and the de- claration that slavery was unlawful in England. Moreover, the principle applies to all the dominions of the Crown; the English courts have jurisdiction and indeed must issue the writ save as regards possessions where courts exist with authority to issue the writ and secure its execution,[1] and they would exercise it if necessary to prevent injustice. The extent of the value of the existence of the writ is shown by the necessity which has arisen, whenever political prisoners have been deported to any Colony, to secure local legislation to legalise their detention, so that they may not secure their discharge from custody on a habeas corpus. Moreover, so effective is the security for early trial or discharge in case of allegations of crime that, in time of civil disturbance, especially in Ireland, or in risk of war, it has been necessary to suspend the operation of the writ as regards persons suspected of treason or other grave offences against the security of the State. As, moreover, a mere suspension does not extinguish rights, though it delays remedies, it is necessary to indemnify by Act of Parliament, as in 1901 and 1920,[2] any illegal interference with personal liberty.

A striking example of the effective action of the courts was afforded in 1923, when a unanimous judgment of the Court of Appeal [3] procured the release from internment in the Irish Free State of a large

---

[1] The Habeas Corpus Act, 1862 (25 & 26 Vict. c. 20).

[2] The Indemnity Act, 1920 (10 & 11 Geo. V. c. 48).

[3] *Ex parte Art O'Brien*, [1923] 2 K.B. 361. The House of Lords decided, on May 14, that no appeal lay to them in such a case; *Secretary of State for Home Affairs* v. *O'Brien*, [1923] A.C. 603. An apparent attempt of the Government to alter the law *pendente lite* to legalise the detention was ruled irrelevant.

number of persons who had been arrested in Great Britain and deported to Ireland on the strength of a regulation made under the Restoration of Order in Ireland Act, 1920, and believed by the Law Officers of the Crown still to be valid despite the establishment of the Free State. The action of the ministry, which was motived by the desire to counter what was believed to be a conspiracy to aid the rebels in the Free State, was indemnified by Parliament, but full provision was at the same time made for the establishment of a tribunal to receive claims from persons thus wrongfully deported and interned, and to award them damages on the same principle as would be applicable in an action for false imprisonment. Moreover, the Government accepted in the House of Lords on June 6 a resolution moved by Viscount Grey to the effect that the House affirmed "the long-established principle of the constitution that the Executive should not, without the previous and special authority of Parliament, exercise the power of arrest without bringing to trial by due process of law".

(2) Freedom of speech or discussion is assured similarly merely by the rule that a man may say or write anything he pleases, subject to liability to punishment if he is guilty of sedition, that is, exciting disaffection against the Government, of blasphemy or indecency, or of libelling any person, and that whether he is guilty of any of these offences will be decided by a judge and jury,[1] or at any rate by a court of law. The extent to which freedom is thus attained obviously largely depends on public opinion, but it is not subject to direct

[1] On the jury as a safeguard to liberty stress is laid by Lord Tomlin, Royal Institution, April 5, 1935.

governmental control, and in practice in the United Kingdom and the Dominions a very wide liberty is enjoyed, particularly as regards attacks on the form of government, even in South Africa to the extent of permitting unchecked propaganda for a republic. Preliminary censorship of the press is essentially a war expedient, but in India and some Crown Colonies efforts have been made to cope with sections of the press believed to be seditious by requiring deposits of money, to be forfeited on conviction for sedition or otherwise, a proceeding of decidedly dubious value. The Union Riotous Assemblies (Amendment) Act, 1930, authorises prohibition of publication of documents deemed likely to excite hostility in the community.

In order to protect armed forces against subversive propaganda it was made criminal in 1797 to incite to mutiny, and a more convenient procedure for this purpose was devised by the Incitement to Disaffection Act, 1934. It is significant of the feeling in favour of the utmost freedom of discussion that the Bill excited bitter opposition in Parliament and was only carried, despite the enormous strength of the governmental majority, after drastic modifications had been made to prevent any possibility of abuse, especially of the limited powers of search for seditious literature permitted. The grant of search warrants has been confined to High Court judges, and the Attorney-General in Northern Ireland and the Director of Public Prosecutions in England must sanction proceedings.

(3) The right of public meeting again rests merely on the fact that a man commits no breach of the law if he gathers with others and engages in any discussion,

neither trespassing on private ground, violating local regulations of municipalities, nor obstructing the public streets.[1] If the purpose of the meeting is in any sense illegal, then the members taking part in it have no grievance if they are dispersed by authority. It may even be that a perfectly legal and orderly meeting may be broken up by the police without illegality,[2] if that be the only means of preventing a breach of the peace caused by opponents of the meeting without legal justification, though it is plain that the first duty of the authorities is to protect the meeting in the exercise of its legal freedom. Restrictions on the right, such as requiring previous consent of magistrates or other authorities, have been enacted from time to time, and some use of these powers to restrict meetings deemed politically dangerous has been made of late both in the Union of South Africa and in India, in either case with dubious results.

(4) Freedom of conscience and worship exists as the result generally of the absence of any established church, and where such churches exist in the restriction of the authority of these churches to those who are voluntarily members of them. In both parts of Ireland they are secured by express enactment, and similar provision for religious toleration is made in Malta, where the population is devoted to the Roman See. The misuse of episcopal power to determine elections, as in 1932 in Malta, has been met in Canada by insistence that use of these means may void an election.[3] The exclusion of persons from office on the score of

---

[1] *Beatty* v. *Gillbanks* (1882), 9 Q.B.D. 308.

[2] *Wise* v. *Dunning*, [1902] 1 K.B. 167.

[3] *Langevin* v. *Brassard* (1876), 1 S.C.R. 145; Keith, *Letters on Imperial Relations, 1916–1935*, pp. 292, 293, 294.

religious belief has been reduced to very narrow limits in the United Kingdom, and has been repeatedly repudiated in India.

None of these rights nor such other rights as those of bearing arms and possessing property are regarded as in any way fundamental constitutional principles in the great majority of British possessions. The right to expropriate property without compensation belongs to every Government to which the legislature accords it, save in Northern Ireland, and in India, and the carrying of arms is regularly, in the United Kingdom,[1] as well as in India, restricted by the requirement of official permission. The degree of private right must depend on the interest of the State, whose strength lies in the measure in which room can be found for the individuality of the subject in the unity of the political organism.

3. *Martial Law*

The rights of the subject would be ineffective if the executive government possessed normally any right of interference at discretion with these rights, and there are grave disadvantages in any legislation, such as in Continental countries often exists, authorising the Government to proclaim a state of siege in cases of emergency, and permitting wholesale disregard for the ordinary laws of the land. It is a far better safeguard for individual liberty and the security of property that, if circumstances require violations of normal right, express sanction should be given by Parliament; the vast powers wielded by the Government in the United Kingdom during the war, under regulations made under

---

[1] Firearms Act, 1920 (10 & 11 Geo. V. c. 43).

R

the Defence of the Realm Acts, would much better have been conferred in greater particularity, as need arose, by the legislature.[1] If Parliament is not in session, and in case of sudden emergency, it may often be found necessary to break the law frankly and to rely for legal sanction on an Act of Indemnity. This is essentially the position created by a declaration of martial law by the executive; legally it has no effect whatever in the absence of express statutory sanction, and it leaves the rights of all persons unaffected unless and until they are varied by statute. That is not, of course, to say that Acts done under the supposed authority of martial law are necessarily illegal. The common law of the several parts of the Empire, including the Roman Dutch law of the Union, recognises more or less distinctly the rule that in emergency private rights may be disregarded for the sake of the security of the State; it is no trespass to enter and use land without the owner's consent for military purposes, though compensation should be paid; it is not illegal to kill persons joining in insurrection, or to detain them in custody. But the limits of the power to ignore private rights in emergency are wholly vague and Acts of Indemnity are essential to avoid claims after the emergency has passed. Such Acts, it is clear, should cover all actions done in good faith, even if erroneous or foolish; it should, however, be made clear that malicious misuse of authority, to gratify private ends, is utterly excluded from indemnity, and complaint has on occasion been made of the extremely wide terms in which, in the Union of South

---

[1] Certain wide powers in grave emergencies are given to the Government by the Emergency Powers Act, 1920, but under conditions securing effective Parliamentary control; s. 1 (2). See p. 295 *post*.

Africa, indemnity in respect of the suppression of insurrection and riot has been conferred.[1] There is, it is clear,
a real danger in passing unlimited Acts of Indemnity;
on the next occasion of disorder evilly disposed men
may, under cover of aiding the Government, take the
opportunity of paying off old scores, confident that the
indemnity accorded will be wide enough to shield them
from punishment for their misdeeds.

Martial law has not been formally resorted to in the
United Kingdom since the Stuarts, but instances in
the Colonies and Dominions and in Ireland have not
been rare, and certain principles of law can safely be
deduced from the decisions of the courts. There is a
common law right of suppressing riot and insurrection,
but it is impossible to say whether we are to hold that
the right extends to authorising the Government to
carry out any Acts which it deems reasonably necessary
for the suppression of disorder, or whether the power
covers only such Acts as in the opinion of the court
before which a case comes were actually necessary.[2]
The courts, it is clear, ought not to interfere with the
action of military authorities *flagrante bello*;[3] it is not
proof that there is no state of war because the courts
are permitted to function by the military authorities
for some purposes and under certain conditions; it
would be different if all the courts were functioning as
usual. It is for the court to decide if there exists such
a state of circumstances as excludes its jurisdiction,

[1] The Imperial House of Commons drastically revised the Indemnity
Bill of 1923 (13 & 14 Geo. V. c. 12).

[2] See the discussion in *Law Quarterly Review*, xviii. 117 ff.; Dicey,
Law of the Constitution, Note X.

[3] *D. F. Marais, Ex parte*, [1902] A.C. 109; *Tilonko* v. *Att.-Gen. of
Natal*, [1907] A.C. 93.

bearing these principles in mind. If it holds that there is, no redress is possible, unless and until the state of things ceases.[1] Thereupon the courts may function freely and must judge causes brought before them,[2] unless, of course, they are prevented from doing so, or limited in doing so, by an Act of Indemnity.

The declaration of martial law overseas may serve useful purposes in placing it beyond doubt that the Government is being challenged and demands all the aid of its subjects. Moreover, it simplifies the taking of authority into the hands of the officer engaged in suppressing revolt. On the other hand the prolonged maintenance of martial law when peace had been or should have been restored, as a method of maintaining illegal action pending an Indemnity Act, as in Natal between 1906 and 1908, is a clear abuse of power.

Martial law, as here discussed, refers to steps of Government taken against rebels whether in time of peace or of war, when internal disturbances are greatly to be feared. The term is also used as in the Duke of Wellington's definition[3] to describe the system administered by a General who invades enemy territory, and must there enforce a system of law. It applies historically to the law employed[4] to maintain order in English forces when at war, whether within or without the realm, but that is more conveniently described as military law.

---

[1] *R.* v. *Allen,* [1921] 2 I.R. 241; *R. (Childers)* v. *Adj.-Gen. of Provisional Forces,* [1923] 1 I.R. 14.

[2] *Wright* v. *Fitzgerald* (1798), 27 St. Tr. 765; *Higgins* v. *Willis,* [1921] 2 I.R. 386.

[3] *Parl. Deb.* 3rd Series, cxv. 880.

[4] In the Court of the Earl Marshal and Constable.

4. *Remedies against the Crown*

English law recognises that the Crown can commit personally no wrong, but from an early date it provided means, now stereotyped by statute, by which a subject might, by petition of right, have a judicial decision as to any land or goods of his which, he claimed, had come without lawful ground into the possession of the Crown, and as to any contract entered into with the Crown which had not been fulfilled. But the Crown is not liable in tort for any wrong done by its officers, and it has been necessary, when it has been desired in the oversea possessions to give rights against the Crown in tort, to confer them by special enactment. In Scotland, and in a few Colonies, by practice, and in many others including Canada, the Commonwealth of Australia, and the Union of South Africa by legislation, suits directed to obtain damages in tort are entertained, and there seems no adequate ground for the maintenance of the English rule of governmental immunity, at least as regards commercial undertakings; a distinction in this respect is recognised in India.

In accordance with these principles no remedy is available against an official who contracts for the Crown, for he is not personally any party to the contract, but merely acts as the mouthpiece of the Crown. On the other hand, as the Crown can do no wrong, any wrong done is that of the officer, and no plea of the royal command or of State necessity[1] will be heard to justify a wrong. The person who actually commits the wrong is liable, and so also may be his superior if he ordered the committal of the wrong, as opposed to

[1] *Entick* v. *Carrington* (1765), 19 St. Tr. 1030.

giving an order which might have been carried out without breach of law.

There are few exceptions to this general principle. If an alien outside the realm suffers wrong at the hands of an officer of the Crown acting on authority, or having his action ratified *ex post facto* by the Government, he can successfully be met with the plea of "Act of State", which bars the investigation of his claim in any British Court,[1] the matter becoming one for diplomatic representations if redress is to be claimed. But, if the alien is on British territory, the plea is inadmissible,[2] and in any case it cannot be urged against a British subject or perhaps a person under British protection as regards an act done in a protectorate.[3] A soldier again, though he commit an illegal act, may be excused by the fact that he acted on the orders of his officer, provided that the order was not manifestly illegal, for he is under obligation to obey his officer, and cannot weigh the legality of any order closely, but the officer will be liable for the order given.[4]

In certain other cases the excuse of Act of State is effective. If the British Crown seizes hostile territory and annexes or otherwise deals with it, no action lies against it or its officers for what is done in regard to the seizure in question; thus if money is taken possession of, the ruler of the State or his officers cannot recover payment by legal action in a British court.[5] Secondly,

---

[1] *Buron* v. *Denman* (1848), 2 Ex. 167.

[2] *Johnstone* v. *Pedlar*, [1921] 2 A.C. 262.

[3] *Eshugbayi Eleko* v. *Nigeria Govt.*, [1931] A.C. 662; Keith, *Journ. Comp. Leg.* xiv. 118.

[4] As in Sheehy-Skeffington's Case (1916), Cd. 8376.

[5] *Rajah of Tanjore's Case* (1859), 13 Moo. P.C. 22; *Ex-Rajah of Coorg* v. *East India Co.* (1860), 29 Beav. 300.

the British Government does not accept liability for debts either in contract or in tort of a Government to which it succeeds through conquest or cession, to such an extent that it will allow legal action in its courts to claim rights.[1] These are matters to be dealt with by executive grace, not legal means. Thirdly, acts done against enemy invaders of British territory are not governed by principles of municipal law any more than are such acts as they do. To kill an invader or shoot a spy is not murder, nor does the invader commit murder, assuming, of course, that he is acting under the authority or his action is ratified by some foreign State. Great friction was long caused between the United Kingdom and the United States through the failure of the latter Government promptly to give effect to this doctrine in the case of Macleod, arrested in the United States and charged with complicity in the destruction of the *Caroline*,[2] though that destruction was accepted as an act of the British Crown by the Foreign Secretary.

Judges are exempt from liability for anything done or said by them in their judicial capacity, even if they are alleged to have acted maliciously, provided, of course, that they have acted within the limits of their jurisdiction which, of course, varies with the status of the judge or magistrate; the privilege, which is conceded for the purpose of ensuring the fearless execution of justice, cannot extend to acts done where no jurisdiction exists.[3] The principle applies to judges overseas[4] as much as to English judges, except, of course,

[1] *West Rand Central Gold Mining Co. Ltd.* v. *R.*, [1905] 2 K.B. 391.
[2] Wheaton, *International Law* (ed. Keith), i. 152.
[3] *Scott* v. *Stansfield* (1868), L.R. 3 Ex. 220.
[4] *Anderson* v. *Gorrie*, [1895] 1 Q.B. 668.

where special statutory provision exists. Special protection is also extended to military and naval officers who set in motion proceedings leading up to courts martial on subordinates, even if they act without adequate justification or maliciously.

The Lord-Lieutenant of Ireland[1] was held to be exempt from legal process of any kind in Ireland, and thus to have the same immunity as the King, but it is quite otherwise with the Governor of a Dominion or Colony, who possesses no immunity whatever from process, whether for private or public acts, even though he merely acts on the advice of his ministers. For wrong-doing in a Colony a Governor may be also punished criminally in England under Acts of 1699 and 1802 still unrepealed, though the necessity for such action is obsolete, while in India no proceedings lie in any court against a Governor-General or Governor for acts or omissions in office. A general power to punish in England persons guilty of oppression while in office in India will be obsolete under the new régime.

There are definite limits to the powers of the courts over the executive. The courts are not adapted to compel the performance by the executive of their duty to administer the law on behalf of the Crown, and they will issue a mandamus to compel action by a Government department in such cases only as are characterised by the definite imposition by Parliament, or the Crown, on a department of a specific obligation to the public as opposed to the Crown. Hence actions to recover money and applications for a mandamus against

---

[1] It may be presumed that the Governor-General of the Free State does not inherit this immunity, nor presumably the Governor of Northern Ireland, at least so far as he acts as a representative of that Government.

the Treasury[1] or Secretaries of State have failed, while departments such as the Board of Education or the Commissioners of Inland Revenue have been held subject to judicial control in certain respects. But the courts do not claim the right to compel the Crown to distribute moneys received under treaty with foreign powers an account of injuries inflicted on British subjects,[2] nor will they rule that the Crown is not entitled to charge sums for affording special protection to British shipowners against piratical attacks.[3]

The courts may issue declaratory judgments stating the position of individuals under the law, and, for instance, negating the duty of making returns demanded by a Government department without full authority,[4] but the procedure is of limited competence, and is not available to obtain a declaration that a subject is entitled to obtain sums of money from the Crown. In such instances procedure must be by petition of right.[5]

The courts, however, have power to issue prohibition or certiorari to restrain tribunals from acting in excess of jurisdiction, or to require a tribunal to send up for examination and, if proper, quashing an order which it has made. These writs, it has been held, may be issued to bodies which are not, strictly speaking, courts, but which, having legal authority to determine questions affecting the rights of subjects, and

---

[1] *R.* v. *Lords Commrs. of Treasury* (1872), L.R. 7 Q.B. 387; *R.* v. *Secretary of State for War*, [1891] 2 Q.B. 326.

[2] *Civilian War Claimants Assocn.* v. *R.*, [1932] A.C. 14.

[3] *China Navigation Co.* v. *Att.-Gen.*, [1932] 2 K.B. 197.

[4] *Dyson* v. *Att.-Gen.*, [1911] 1 K.B. 410.

[5] *Bombay and Persia Steam Nav. Co.* v. *Maclay*, [1920] 3 K.B., at p. 408.

having the duty to act judicially, act in excess of their legal authority. It was held that the Electricity Commissioners might be prohibited from proceeding with a proposed scheme to constitute a joint authority, although the scheme could have no effect unless approved by the Minister of Transport and by resolutions of both houses of Parliament.[1] But it has been held that certiorari does not lie to quash a provisional order made by a Secretary of State under the Local Government Act when that order is without effect until confirmed by Act of Parliament.[2] Certiorari, however, has been used to quash a determination of the Board of Education on a dispute between the local education authority and the managers of a non-provided school,[3] and to discuss the validity of a closing order in respect of a dwelling-house, confirmed by the Local Government Board,[4] and of an order of confirmation of a housing scheme under the Housing Act, 1925.[5] But it does not lie to quash the proceedings or order of a military tribunal acting under martial law and not claiming to have any legal status.[6]

The same powers are exercised by the courts overseas, subject to like limitations. Thus a mandamus will not lie to a Governor of a State of the Commonwealth even if he has a clear duty to perform if that duty be of a political character.[7]

[1] *R.* v. *Electricity Commrs.*, [1924] 1 K.B. 171.
[2] *R.* v. *Hastings Local Board* (1865), 6 B. & S. 401.
[3] *Board of Education* v. *Rice*, [1911] A.C. 179.
[4] *Local Government Board* v. *Arlidge*, [1915] A.C. 120.
[5] *Yaffé, Ex parte*, [1931] A.C. 494. The Housing Act, 1930, s. 11, provides a simpler procedure for such cases.
[6] *Clifford and O'Sullivan, In re*, [1921] 2 A.C. 570.
[7] *R.* v. *Governor of State of South Australia*, 4 C.L.R. 1497.

CHAPTER VIII

CHURCH AND STATE

1. *The Churches of the British Islands*

ENGLAND, excluding Wales, is possessed of a national Church closely related to it by legal ties. The Eliza-
bethan Act of Supremacy asserts the sovereignty of
the Crown over all persons and causes ecclesastical
and temporal, to the exclusion of any foreign power.
Further, by the Acts of Uniformity, the Articles of
Religion and the Book of Common Prayer are made
the binding rules of the faith of the Church, which
cannot be altered without the assent of Parliament.
Subject to these articles and the rubric, the Convocations may make canons binding on the clergy, but
in this action the Crown exercises complete control.
In the first place, the royal licence is necessary for
the meeting of Convocation in either province, and
secondly the canon enacted must be confirmed by the
Crown before it can take effect, while, if the laity are
to be affected, then Parliament must enact the canon
as part of the law of the land. As the two Convocations
are composed solely of ecclesiastical persons, bishops,
deans, proctors, one for each chapter, archdeacons,
and representatives of the diocesan clergy in the case
of Canterbury, or the archdeaconry in the case of
York, it is clear that neither body is well adapted to
deal with matters affecting the laity also, and there

Chapter
VIII.

251

was created, in 1919, a National Assembly of the Church of England, representative of all the sides of the Church.[1] It consists of two houses: the bishops, who are members of the upper houses of the Convocations, form one house, and clergy members of the lower houses of the Convocations and laity elected periodically by members of the Church form the other. Matters dealing with the doctrinal formulae, sacraments, or services of the Church must be discussed by each house separately, and finally voted on in the form approved by the bishops, and the Assembly may not define the doctrine of the Church on any matter of theology, and it cannot deal with any matter belonging to the bishops in right of their episcopal office. Any measure passed by the Assembly is submitted by its Legislative Committee[2] to an Ecclesiastical Committee of Parliament, fifteen members selected by the Lord Chancellor, and Speaker respectively from each house; that committee drafts a report on the nature and legal effect of the proposals, and gives its opinion on its expediency, especially in relation to the constitutional rights of all His Majesty's subjects; the report is sent to the Legislative Committee, and only if it so desires is the measure then presented with the report to Parliament; if then both houses resolve that it be presented to the Crown, it has effect on assent of an Act of Parliament, and may repeal or amend any Act referring to the Church other than the rule as to the procedure to be followed in Parliament on any

[1] The Church of England Assembly (Powers) Act, 1919 (9 & 10 Geo. V. c. 76); see also *H.C. Pap.* No. 102, 1919; No. 50, 1922.

[2] Neither prohibition nor certiorari may be issued by a court to control its action as it is not bound to act judicially: *R.* v. *Legislative Committee of Church Assembly*, [1928] 1 K.B. 411.

measure sent from the Assembly. The Church has thus acquired much freedom, but subject to some degree of supervision by Parliament, for in 1927–8 the Commons rejected proposed changes in the Prayer Book.

The jurisdiction of the Church, once largely secular and including to 1857 probate and administration, is now ecclesiastical in type, dealing with questions regarding church ornaments, erection of funeral memorials, and offences by clerical persons, who, by virtue of membership of the church hierarchy through ordination, are subject to exclusion from Parliamentary office. The most important functions of these courts, which are diocesan and provincial, are under the Public Worship Act, 1874, and the Church and Clergy Discipline Acts, 1840 and 1892, to deal with offences by clergymen against Church rules and morality; appeals lie to the Judicial Committee of the Privy Council which is aided in deciding them by such archbishops or bishops as are Privy Councillors summoned as assessors.[1] An ecclesiastical person may be punished by admonition, by suspension from the exercise of functions, and by deprivation of his preferment; if he defy the judgment he may be sentenced to imprisonment. But against excess of jurisdiction he is protected by the civil courts, which may by prohibition forbid the ecclesiastical courts to exceed their authority, or, if he is in prison, by habeas corpus investigate the legality of the order for his detention. The present system of protecting the public from inefficient or undesirable clergy is admittedly inadequate, although the Benefices (Ecclesiastical Duties) Measure, 1926, provides a method by which, after enquiry by

[1] *Wakeford* v. *Bishop of Lincoln*, [1921] 1 A.C. 821.

a Commission, action may be taken by a bishop, subject to appeal to the archbishop acting with a High Court judge.[1] A like court hears appeals from refusals by bishops to institute to benefices under the Benefices Act, 1898.[2]

The Crown has further extensive patronage; the archbishops, the bishops, and deans are appointed by the Crown on the recommendation of the Prime Minister, as also are some canons, while the bishop appoints others as well as archdeacons and rural deans. Presentations to benefices are also owned in considerable numbers by the Crown. Further, through the Ecclesiastical Commissioners, the State controls the administration of important Church estates in order to regulate the application of the income of the Church and secure the foundation of new livings. Tithes as Church property were not a State grant, but a customary donation, which has become stereotyped, and tithes are often owned by non-ecclesiastical persons. The Tithe Act, 1925, has conferred on Queen Anne's Bounty the duty of collecting and disbursing to those entitled the rent charges substituted for tithes.

The Church of England is now, under Acts of 1914 and 1919, disestablished in Wales, and a body with elaborate provision for its self-government has been substituted under Parliamentary authority.[3] In Ireland the Church of Ireland was disestablished by the Act of 1869, and now exists as a voluntary body with

---

[1] *Huntley* v. *Norwich (Bishop)*, [1931] P. 210.

[2] If the bishop refuses to obey an order to admit, the archbishop may be ordered to do so: *Notley* v. *Birmingham (Bishop)*, [1931] 1 Ch. 529.

[3] For its relation to the Church of England see *Clergy Orphan Corporation* v. *Christopher*, [1932] Ch. 267.

large powers of alteration of its constitution. The many other Churches of England and Wales and Ireland are all without State connection, treated in law as voluntary associations whose regulations are binding on the members *inter se* as matters of contract, and may be interpreted by the courts if any dispute arises as to property or other civil rights, *e.g.* tenure of office. Mere disputes as to doctrines, unconnected with civil rights, the courts do not attempt to decide.

The Act of Union with Scotland asserts, as a fundamental condition of union, the maintenance of Presbyterian Church government as the established religion, and incorporates the provisions of the settlement effected in 1690 and 1693, as to Church government. This system has a hierarchy beginning with the Kirk Session, consisting of the minister and elders; the presbytery, composed of the ministers and elders in equal number in its area, which the General Assembly determines, and exercising similar powers as regards ordination, induction, and supervision of ministers, to those exercised by the bishop in England; the Synod, consisting of all the members of the presbyteries in its limits; and the General Assembly, which is composed of a quarter of the ministers from each presbytery, and elders in equal numbers.

The General Assembly is the final Court of Appeal from the courts of the Church; no appeal lies from it to any civil court, nor does prohibition run against it. As a legislature it meets annually on a date fixed by the Moderator, at the close of the preceding year's meeting; it passes overtures which are sent down to the presbyteries and may, at its discretion, become law on their approval being accorded. No royal

sanction is required, but a reminder of the old controversies between Church and State now happily terminated is afforded by the High Commissioner appointed
by the King, who occupies a ceremonial position
at each Assembly. Dislike of interference with its
privileges is marked in the Church; the restoration of
patronage by Parliament in 1711, in flagrant breach
of the Act of Union, resulted, in 1843, through the
intervention of the courts to protect the rights of
patrons against the claims of the Assembly to disregard statute law,[1] in the secession of a powerful
minority to form the Free Church. Overtures for
reunion resulted in 1921[2] in legislation to give the
Church unquestioned power to determine, within very
wide limits, its own constitution in complete freedom
from the State, in order to facilitate the reunion of the
Church with the United Free Church, a body representing the amalgamation of the Free Church majority
and the United Presbyterian Church of Scotland. The
union took effect in 1929, but part of the United Free
Church has retained a separate existence. The other
Churches of Scotland are voluntary bodies, including
the Episcopal Church; they are subject to State intervention through the action of the courts in matters of
status and property; in the litigation arising from the
amalgamation of the Free Church and the United
Presbyterian Church, the House of Lords[3] finally held
that the amalgamation involved the loss of the Free
Church endowments, as the new Church did not comply
with the conditions affecting these endowments, and

[1] *Presbytery of Auchterarder* v. *Lord Kinnoull*, 6 Cl. & F. 646.

[2] 11 & 12 Geo. V. c. 29. Property questions were dealt with by 15 & 16
Geo. V. c. 33; 23 & 24 Geo. V. c. 44; 22 & 23 Geo. V. c. xxi.

[3] *Free Church of Scotland* v. *Lord Overtoun*, [1904] A.C. 515.

the intervention of Parliament was requisite to apportion, on a just basis, the property of the Free Church between those who had accepted the amalgamation and the minority who disputed it.

2. *The Church Overseas*

It was natural that in the light of the American Revolution it should have been thought possible and desirable to establish as a bond of loyalty in the remaining Colonies the official position of the Church of England, and that the Crown should have purported to confer by letters patent under the prerogative on bishops in the Colonies ecclesiastical jurisdiction. But the circumstances were adverse to this effort to create Established Churches; the Judicial Committee held, in certain cases in South Africa,[1] that the Crown has no right in Colonies with legislative institutions to confer coercive jurisdiction of any kind, so that it became clear that without legislation the Church of England could have in the Colonies no higher status than any voluntary Church. The doctrine of the Privy Council clearly applied properly only to cases in which the Crown had no power to legislate by the prerogative, and accordingly coercive jurisdiction might have been legally conferred in any Colony acquired by conquest or cession, in which no representative legislature had been created to deprive the Crown of the prerogative of legislation, but advantage was not taken of this fact. In Canada, where extraordinary pains had been taken in the Constitution Act of 1791 to secure the Church of England

---

[1] *Lord Bishop of Natal, In re* (1865), 3 Moo. P.C. (N.S.) 115; Keith, *The Constitutional Law of the British Dominions*, pp. 433, 434.

S

a position of favour and revenue, the advent of responsible government was followed in 1854 by the definite abandonment of the idea of establishment. In Canada, at present, the nearest approach to an Established Church is the position of the Roman Catholic Church in Quebec, though all its authority and power, including the levying of tithes on all Roman Catholics and the establishment of parishes, which the civil Government accepts, are such as could be recognised under the general principles of law as belonging to a voluntary Church. Similarly the Churches in Australia and New Zealand are wholly on a voluntary basis as regards State connection; in part their constitutions rest on contract, in part on local Acts. In South Africa, despite legislation for the Union of the Dutch Reformed Church in the four provinces by the Union Parliament, that Church is as little an Established Church as the Church of the Province of South Africa, the official title of the Church of England in South Africa. The relations of communion between these Churches and the Church of England are matters entirely of ecclesiastical concern, and are not within the purview or control of the State. As in England and Scotland, the courts concern themselves only with religious issues if they are necessarily involved in determining civil rights, such as the claim to ownership of trust property or the validity of tenure of office.[1]

In these autonomous Churches, whose chief contact with the Church of England is through the periodic Lambeth Conferences, in which branches of the Church

---

[1] Such questions arose freely in Canada as a result of the amalgamation of the Methodists, Congregationalists and Presbyterians in 1925. Cf. *St. Luke's, Saltsprings, Trustees* v. *Cameron*, [1930] A.C. 673.

in foreign countries take part, the consecration of bishops takes place without any intervention by the State. But the Church of England maintains closer relations with Colonies and other territories where no autonomous Churches exist, and bishops to act in these areas, without any coercive jurisdiction, are appointed from time to time. The only intervention of the Crown is the grant of licence under the sign-manual and signet to the archbishop to consecrate the proposed bishop for service in an oversea possession, or in foreign parts; the Colonial and the Foreign Secretaries countersign the warrants. The bishops thus appointed have episcopal status, but are merely members of voluntary associations for legal purposes.

In India, as often, there was an exception to this normal rule, for the Crown by statute of 1813 and 1833 had power to create certain bishoprics and to define and confer ecclesiastical jurisdiction. There was, however, no Established Church in India, though in the past considerable sums in the aggregate have been and still will be spent on the provision of religious establishments for the benefit of the civil and military European residents. In 1930, under the Indian Church Act, 1927, and the Indian Church Measure, 1927, an autonomous Indian Church in full communion with the Church of England was created. Under the new régime the Government will continue to provide ecclesiastical services of the Church of England and the Church of Scotland to troops and the Civil Services.

In the Crown Colonies such payments have become more and more limited in amount in the course of time, but, while the Colonial Office has never of late years encouraged religious endowments, it has left matters largely to local feeling, especially when the policy of small grants to various denominations on an equitable basis has been adopted, and when for any reason without endowment there might be lack of facilities for religious worship. Absolute toleration, of course, is the policy of the Crown, which consistently asserted this doctrine from its assumption of direct rule in India.

A difficulty of some seriousness arises in cases of protectorates where Muhammadan intolerance is opposed to Christian missions; in the Moslem States of Nigeria the Emirs have been permitted in effect to discourage or prohibit Christian propaganda, while no restriction exists on Muhammadan propaganda in British territory. But the apparent anomaly is explicable on the ground that insistence on toleration in the Emirates in this regard might involve riots and murders, which would necessitate the overthrow of the régime of ruling through the local authorities and impose excessive burdens on the State.

PART II

THE GOVERNMENTS OF THE EMPIRE

CHAPTER I

THE UNITED KINGDOM

1. *The Crown*

THE royal and Imperial crown is held under statutory enactments by the House of Windsor, descendants of the Princess Sophia, daughter of Elizabeth, Queen of Bohemia, and granddaughter of James I., who married the Elector of Hanover. These statutes [1] implicitly negatived the doctrine of divine right of hereditary succession and established the supremacy of the nation, for they excluded one line of kings and laid down conditions binding on all future sovereigns. To become a Roman Catholic, or marry one, involves forfeiture of the Crown; the people are absolved from their allegiance, and the next in the line if Protestant succeeds. Moreover, the sovereign must be in communion with the Church of England. The coronation ceremony retains traces of the Anglo-Saxon doctrine of approval of the King by the people, and the anointing is an ancient religious rite. The regency, in the event of the minority or incapacity of the sovereign, is also regulated by Parliament, which has further conferred on the Crown the right of refusing sanction to the marriage

[1] 1 Will. & Mary, st. 2, c. 3; 12 & 13 Will. III. c. 2. The Crown since Victoria's accession is granted for life a Civil List, now £470,000. The married younger sons receive £25,000 a year, the unmarried £10,000, Princess Mary £6000, but the Prince of Wales is provided for by the Duchy of Cornwall.

of any descendant of George II., save in the case of the issue of princesses married into foreign houses, though such descendants may marry at twenty-five, after giving twelve months' notice to the Privy Council, unless both houses of Parliament dissent. The eldest son is by birth Duke of Cornwall, and is created Prince of Wales and Earl of Chester by letters patent. The descent of the Crown is analogous to the rule of inheritance of land at common law, but of two or more daughters the eldest succeeds; thus after the Duke of York Princess Elizabeth is next in order of succession.

The person of the King and the sovereign power are protected by the law of treason, a term which covers anything done or designed to lead to the death, or bodily harm or restraint of the King, adhering to his enemies or levying war against him, while conspiracies to levy war or deprive the Crown of any part of its dominions, or to incite foreigners to invade the realm, are treason-felony, as is also force contemplated or applied to make the King change his counsels or intimidate either house of Parliament. An alien within the realm owes allegiance,[1] and can be guilty of treason no less than a subject, nor can a subject evade the penalties by seeking to assume foreign nationality.

The royal power is continuous despite the decease of the holder; neither Parliament nor officers of the Crown now vacate office on the death of the sovereign.

The extent of the royal authority has been continuously under modification and reduction from the vast powers of the Norman kings, who combined executive, legislative, and judicial functions, and were also under the feudal system the supreme holders of land. The

[1] *De Jager* v. *Att.-Gen. of Natal,* [1907] A.C. 326.

revolutionary settlement embodied in the Bill of Rights (1689), and the Act of Settlement (1701),[1] denied the Crown the right (1) to tax in any form, (2) to maintain a standing army, and (3) to suspend or grant dispensations from the operation of laws, while by securing the judges tenure during good behaviour, subject, however, to removal on addresses from both houses of Parliament, the Crown was deprived of the weapon which the Stuarts found so useful, the packing of the bench with servile instruments. It was also now impossible to tamper with Parliament by creating new boroughs, for the House of Commons was determined to preserve itself from control in this way. Further, Parliament was decided on compelling the King to have recourse to it; it granted him revenues for life, the Civil List, adequate only for the bare maintenance of the civil government; it legalised a standing army, but only annually, and provided for it by yearly grants. But the King might influence Parliament by bribery, in one form or another, of its members, and the Act of Settlement (1701) would have banished from the House of Commons every person holding office under the Crown. Had the proposal ever become effective, a non-Parliamentary executive would have resulted, but the error was recognised, and legislation, in 1707 and later, aimed at allowing only a certain number of political officers to be in the Commons, subject to the rule that acceptance by a member of the House even of these offices normally vacated the seat and made it necessary for him to seek re-election, thus securing the electors the opportunity of approving or rejecting the new minister. Through its control of these officers the Commons expected, rightly, to be able

[1] 12 & 13 Will. III. c. 2.

to control the executive actions of the Crown, and thus far more effectively to control administration than could be effected by any attempt directly to interfere with it.

The Crown, it is now clear, must in political matters normally act on the advice of ministers responsible to, and commanding a majority in, Parliament. The King has not since 1784 and 1807 attempted to dismiss a ministry, for the alleged dismissal of Lord Melbourne in 1834 has been shown by the actual correspondence to have been merely the acceptance by the King of a suggestion of resignation. The legal power is unquestioned, but its use would be as revolutionary as the refusal of assent to legislation which has been in abeyance since 1707. If ministers possessed a majority in the Commons when dismissed, a dissolution would be necessary if the new ministry were to be able to carry on, and the general election would become a contest between the Crown and the people, with results disastrous to the State and the monarchy alike. If ministers are in a minority in the Commons, the Crown can leave it to the House to force their resignation of office, and the reduction of the duration of Parliament to five years [1] assures the electorate control over their representatives. On one condition only could the power to dismiss properly be exercised, namely, that a ministry, with a majority in the Commons, but unpopular in the constituencies, insisted on legislation to extend the life of Parliament, thus overriding the electorate, or proposed without a mandate vitally to alter the constitution.

It might seem at first that the Crown should be free

---

[1] The Parliament Act, 1911 (1 & 2 Geo. V. c. 13), s. 7.

to refuse a dissolution to a defeated ministry, as is still
the rule in the Dominions, but there is no doubt that
such action would be unwise and, in view of invariable
usage since Victoria's reign, unconstitutional,[1] unless,
of course, a ministry after an unsuccessful dissolution
were to attempt to secure another. The electors are the
true sovereign authority, and ministers who advise
dissolutions are entitled to ask from them judgment on
their deeds. The one case, in fact, in which personal
selection can really take unfettered effect is when a
ministry resigns, and the Prime Minister tenders no
advice to the sovereign; as when in 1894 the Queen
sent for Lord Rosebery without asking Mr Gladstone's
advice, or in 1923 the King selected Mr Baldwin, Mr
Bonar Law having offered no opinion. Where such
advice has been tendered, it does not seem that it has
ever been neglected; so in 1922 Mr Bonar Law was
sent for on Mr Lloyd George's suggestion, in 1931 Mr
MacDonald was reappointed on his own advice, in 1935
Mr Baldwin on that of Mr MacDonald.

The King must have a ministry acceptable to
Parliament, and he must not act without its advice or
except as it advises. Nor can he take a direct part in
deciding the character of the advice to be tendered to
himself; since 1714, with rare exceptions,[2] no sovereign
has deliberated in the Cabinet. Anne interviewed
foreign ministers, but her successors accepted the

---

[1] Cf. Queen Victoria's *Letters*, iii. 289 ff.

[2] To consult members of the Opposition, as Queen Victoria was apt
to do, especially with Disraeli, or to investigate the possibility of over-
throwing a ministry (*e.g.* that of Lord Rosebery in 1894), is clearly unconstitutional. A Prime Minister, of course, will always agree to the
King's seeing Opposition leaders in crisis, as in 1909–10 over the controversy between the houses of Parliament. Cf. Anson, *The Crown* (ed.
Keith), i. 141 ff.

limitations of their position, and, in 1825, Canning made it absolutely clear to George IV. that he must be present as Foreign Secretary at any interview with a foreign minister. The intercourse of the Crown with foreign sovereigns is subject to the rule that for anything beyond social intercourse ministers are responsible, and the Crown must express their views. Victoria and Edward VII. were keenly interested in foreign affairs, and freely expressed their views to ministers, but they invariably accepted the decision of their advisers. In 1832 and 1911 alike, the sovereign agreed to create peers to overcome the resistance of the House of Lords to the will of the people expressed through the Commons, a supreme instance of acceptance of advice which it was painful to accept. The Crown, however, is entitled to receive full information on all matters of State, and to offer freely and unreservedly its views if it thinks desirable; Victoria intervened on several occasions, for example, as regards the disestablishment of the Irish Church in 1869 and redistribution of seats in 1884–5 with much effect, and opposed successfully Palmerston's projects of adventure in Europe. George V., in 1914, made energetic efforts to secure a settlement by consent of the Irish question by conference between the parties interested, though the plan failed to achieve success. In 1921 he promoted the Irish settlement, in 1931 secured the substitution of the National Government for the Labour Government. The experience and judgment of the sovereign are of clear value, especially when that sovereign has a personal knowledge of the Empire denied to the average minister.

The dependence of the action of the Crown on

ministers is expressed formally by the normal rule that no official action is performed except in such a manner as to make it clear that the Crown has acted on advice. Personal acts, such as opening Parliament and the handing of seals to Secretaries of State, or declaring the President of the Council, are done on ministerial advice, and the King's speech is prepared by the Cabinet, with, of course, the concurrence of the King. For all his actions, therefore, there is ministerial responsibility; the Crown is legally answerable to no court of law, but, as the Crown can do no wrong, any wrong done is not the action of the Crown, and the doer is answerable for it to the courts, and in matters above judicial intervention, such as high political acts, Parliament may punish through the process of impeachment as in Danby's case,[1] as well as by dismissal from office.

The forms in which the royal pleasure are expressed are numerous. The most formal are letters patent under the Great Seal of the Realm. They are used under modern practice for a variety of purposes, to authorise the opening of Parliament by Commissioners, and the assent to Bills; in these cases the document itself is signed by the King as well as sealed. The offices of the Lord High Admiral and the Treasurer are placed in commission by such instruments, corporate bodies created, offices such as judgeships conferred, peerages created, pardons granted to accomplices, licences to alter canons given. Constitutions for the Colonies or constituting the office of Governor-General in the Dominions take the form of letters patent. Instruments to negotiate treaties, full powers,

---

[1] (1679) 11 St. Tr. 599. He pleaded vainly the King's orders.

and instruments of ratification also pass the Great Seal; so also writs for the election of members of Parliament, addressed to the returning officers for counties and boroughs, and summoning peers. Proclamations calling attention to affairs of State of various kinds, dissolving or summoning Parliament, declaring war or neutrality or changes in currency, are also thus sealed.

The authority for the issue of any form of instrument under the Great Seal is ultimately that of a minister. (1) In certain cases the Chancellor issues the writ without any further authority, as in summoning members of the peerage to attend Parliament on succeeding to the peerage. (2) A warrant by the Speaker is authority for the issue by the Crown Office of writs for by-elections. (3) An Order in Council authorises the issue of proclamations, as for the summoning of a new Parliament, and an Order is also made directing the issue of the necessary writs. (4) Usually a warrant signed by the King (sign-manual warrant) is necessary as the preliminary to sealing; thus for instruments to treat and ratifications a warrant is signed by the King and countersigned by the Secretary of State for Foreign Affairs. In other cases another Secretary of State may sign, occasionally the Lord Chancellor. (5) In certain cases, such as the grant of a charter to a town and the creation of a colonial constitution, an Order in Council must precede the issue of the warrant. Elaborate as these precautions are, they are only a small remnant of the old procedure, under which the use of the Signet (abolished in 1851) and of the Privy Seal (abolished in 1884) were involved, as well as a warrant by the Attorney-General (abolished 1880).

The actual sealing is carried out in the office of the Clerk of the Crown in Chancery, whose signature authenticates the sealing; hence issue the writs for election of members of Parliament. But instruments to treat and ratifications are an exception.

Very many acts of State take the form of Orders in Council. These are attested by the signature of the Clerk and the Council seal. Orders may be embodied in proclamations, when they deal with matters of general public interest.

Sign-manual warrants are used also for substantive acts, such as the grant of pardon, or certain appointments such as that of Paymaster-General, when two Lords of the Treasury countersign, or stipendiary magistrate when the Home Secretary countersigns. A variant form of appointment is by commission, as in the case of the Governor-General and the Governors in India. A colonial Governor is appointed by commission under the sign-manual and the Signet,[1] the Colonial Secretary countersigning; an officer in the army is commissioned under the sign-manual and the second secretarial seal. A royal order under the sign-manual is used only for the authorisation of expenditure of money appropriated by Parliament, and is countersigned by two Lords of the Treasury.

In all cases, whether the Council or an individual minister is formally concerned, the responsibility rests with the minister who advises the action taken. Thus an Order in Council is enacted on the authority of the

---

[1] His instructions are signed by the King and sealed with the Signet, but not countersigned. Like letters patent, their issue is approved normally by Order in Council. For procedure in case of royal incapacity, as in 1928 during the King's illness when a commission was appointed to sign for him, see Anson, *The Crown* (ed. Keith), i. 70-72.

minister who sends the draft to the President of the Council with a request for its enactment.

Orders not involving royal action are made by ministers in various names, orders, rules, regulations, decisions, etc. In the Dominions and other oversea territories the more formal determinations of Governments are made by Orders in Council; in the Dominion of Canada the Governor-General, contrary to royal practice and general oversea usage, does not preside in Council but signs the orders at his office or elsewhere. Other instruments which require his signature are countersigned by a minister on the British analogy. The Union of South Africa, by the Royal Executive Functions and Seals Act, 1934, makes provision on the British analogy of special authority for affixing the Great Seal of the Union, and for determining what seals shall be used, both a Great Seal and a Signet being provided for. As in the United Kingdom, the use of a wafer seal in lieu of the Great Seal is permitted in definite classes of documents.

2. *The Privy Council and the Cabinet*

From the first the King was wont to act in conjunction with councillors of one sort or another, and from these diverse forms of council can be traced such institutions as the Judges, the House of Lords, Parliament itself, and the Privy Council, of which the Cabinet is an informal Committee, while in the Judicial Committee there lingers a relic of the once formidable jurisdiction of the King in Council, with its memories of the Star Chamber. The Privy Council now consists of all Cabinet ministers and ex-Cabinet ministers,

high Church dignitaries, the Lords of Appeal in Ordinary, certain other judges, various other politicians
and public servants, and a certain number of men of
eminence in one department or other of public life,
economics and finance, on whom membership has
been conferred as a mark of distinction. As an advisory or deliberative body it had ceased to function
by the time of Anne, though it revived for a moment
at her death, when Argyll and Somerset asserted
membership and it successfully secured the appointment of Shrewsbury as Lord High Treasurer, and then
took steps to secure the failure of any attempt to
defeat George I.'s accession. But it still exists to perform the executive act of the enactment of orders,
which are, however, laid before it on the authority of
ministers, and are not discussed by it. Four councillors
—three suffice—are normally summoned for such
meetings, and only for formal occasions, as on the
accession of a sovereign, are large numbers invited to
be present. It is usual to summon the minister concerned when any departmental matter of special
importance is dealt with.

The foundation of the Cabinet system was laid when
George I., who depended for his throne on the Whigs,
and whose linguistic defects prevented his deliberating
with ministers, gave up attending meetings of the
Council, thus leaving to ministers the initiation of
policy and rendering necessary the appointment of a
president, who ripened into a Prime Minister. The
doctrine of Cabinet unity and collective responsibility
was slow to develop; it was not clearly recognised as
late as 1801, when the idea of the Cabinet as necessarily confined to a group of ministers working in

T

harmony was asserted by Addington, who excluded Lord Loughborough from its membership on this score. In 1806 the Lord Chief Justice was included in the Cabinet, and it was argued that this appointment was unobjectionable as there was no collective responsibility. But in 1803 Pitt clearly saw that there must be "an avowed and real minister possessing the chief weight in the council, and the principal place in the confidence of the king". The power of the Prime Minister has grown with the transfer of power from the House of Commons to the electors in consequence of the Reform Acts; the election now of a new House of Commons is essentially coupled with the obligation, more or less avowedly, undertaken by candidates to support some great political leader's claims to the Premiership, and the man thus favoured is clearly in a position of dominant strength as regards the Cabinet.

The responsibility of the Cabinet being collective, its advice to the Crown must be unanimous; the Prime Minister [1] reports on its decisions to the King in more or less detail, and it rests with him to disclose or withhold any indication of divergent views. The Crown is entitled to demand the advice of the Cabinet, but George IV. was denied the right to learn individual opinions. It is, however, not rare to divulge to the Crown the existence of dissent. Secrecy as to Cabinet proceedings is theoretically inviolable unless permission is given by the Crown, through the Prime Minister preferably, for the divulgation of some particular facts, but the rule is more formal than real,

---

[1] To consult a colleague behind the back of the Prime Minister and to urge him to counteract his proposals is now unconstitutional, though Queen Victoria occasionally resorted to this form of tactics; cf. Fitzmaurice, *Life of Lord Granville*, i. 350, 459 (in 1859 and 1864).

though an effort to penalise revelations during the war was actually made. The keeping of formal records of Cabinet proceedings was begun only in the Coalition Ministry of Mr Lloyd George (1916–22), when a Cabinet Secretariat came into existence. At the same time the old rule, which rigidly excluded any save Privy Councillors from presence at Cabinet meetings, was relaxed and various outsiders, civil and military, were permitted to be present at what would normally have been deemed Cabinet discussions. The same emergency produced a temporary disappearance of the normal Cabinet, and the creation of a War Cabinet of five or six members, not holding portfolios, with the exception of Mr Bonar Law, to deal with the conduct of hostilities, leaving other matters to individual ministers; the necessity of consultation and unity of action led to the appearance of a quasi-counterpart of the War Cabinet, or Home Affairs Cabinet to deal with domestic issues; with the disappearance of war conditions the War Cabinet was dropped.

The unity of the Cabinet is bound up with the person of the Prime Minister, the keystone of the Cabinet arch, who attains that position by kissing the King's hands and accepting the commission to form a ministry. It rests with him to determine his colleagues,[1] though in practice his choice is definitely limited by the claims of his party followers, and the necessity of securing such colleagues as will command the attention of the House of Commons, whose power over finance necessarily gives it the right to determine the ministry. Even Gladstone had to admit the demands

---

[1] Queen Victoria exercised the right to veto appointments, *e.g.* that of H. Labouchere.

of Dilke and Chamberlain, but Sir H. Campbell-Bannerman resisted effectively the intrigue to transfer him to the House of Lords. The special position of the Commons renders it necessary that the Prime Minister shall either be a commoner, or if a peer shall possess a loyal colleague capable of leading the Commons and yet willing to work under another. The selection of Mr Baldwin in 1923, despite the strong claims of Lord Curzon, indicates that the emergence of the Labour Party as the official Opposition renders the presence of the Prime Minister in the Commons practically essential. The pressure of duties on Mr Lloyd George after the armistice induced him, even on the restoration of Cabinet rule, to leave to another the leadership of the Commons, but the result proves that detachment from the Commons inevitably undermines the position of a minister.[1] A further innovation by Mr Lloyd George lay in his exercising through a large secretariat a detailed supervision over the business of the departments, a revival of the policy of Peel, but with the fatal distinction that the supervision of the latter was, and could be, personal, while that of the former could not be made anything but sporadic and the work of subordinates. The advent of Mr Bonar Law to power, in October 1922, was followed by the decision to revert to more normal conditions.

The Prime Minister is the proper medium of communication between the Crown and the Cabinet, but each minister in charge of a department is entitled to direct access to the Crown on all departmental business. When matters of common concern, often involving

---

[1] Mr MacDonald's position in 1931–5 was weakened by reason of Mr Baldwin's closer contact with the Commons.

disputes between departments, are involved, committees of the Cabinet, to which non-members of that
body may be summoned freely, are deputed to secure
a common policy or to prepare the issues for decision
by the whole of the Cabinet. Decisions may be taken
by majority votes, but the Prime Minister can always
threaten resignation if his views are defeated, and the
threat is a more serious one than that of dissident
members, unless, as in Mr Gladstone's last Cabinet,
these are by far the most important members of the
body. The majority may, of course, be wrong, as when
Mr Bonar Law was overruled on the American debt
settlement; his failure then to resign was a regrettable
error, as his son has admitted. A member who will
not accept the decision must resign, or the Crown will
authorise his removal, and a member who, like Mr
Montagu in 1922, acts in a matter of high importance against the views of another minister without
consulting the Cabinet, may be summarily removed
from office. Ministers should not in public give vent
to contradictory views, but the degree of discipline
exacted varies from Premier to Premier. The effort,
however, in 1931–2 to combine free trade ministers
with advocates of protection in a National Government ended in the resignation of the former.

Prior to 1832, the Crown exercised no small influence on the Cabinet through its powers of control by
more or less corrupt means over the unreformed House
of Commons, whose constituencies had often fallen
into the hands of a few voters, who were under effective control by territorial magnates. From 1832 to
1885 the Commons became the dominating factor in
determining the Cabinet; the franchise secured the

political power to the middle classes, and the system of two-member constituencies, while party organisation was defective and went little beyond registration of voters, allowed considerable freedom of choice to the electors and independence to the candidate. The extension of the franchise and the redistribution of seats into one-member constituencies in 1885 have strengthened the electorate or the party organisations, and diminished the independence of the Commons; the increase of electioneering costs, with the extension of the franchise in 1918, and the payment of members, have conspired to render members extremely sensitive to the threat of a dissolution, and have compelled them in the main to follow loyally the leaders whose party aims they have bound themselves to support. The Commons thus has, on the one hand, become more sensitive to the control of the electors; on the other, it has ceased to control Cabinets, and it dare not reject or substantially amend governmental measures. The adoption of rules of procedure, which more and more abstract the rights of the private member to secure discussions or legislation, and the absorption of the time of the Commons by the Government have contributed to the subordination of the Commons to the Cabinet.

In addition to the committees which prepare business for the Cabinet, the Committee of Imperial Defence, which itself works largely through sub-committees, serves to collect and frame advice on all defence questions which transcend mere departmental interests. It is not technically a committee of the Cabinet and has no executive powers, but its composition, which includes the Prime Minister, the political and technical heads of the fighting services, and the Chancellor of the Exchequer, with the Secretaries of State for Dominion Affairs, the Colonies, India, and Foreign Affairs, as occasion may require—the Prime Minister being the only indispensable element— renders its position of great importance. Agreement reached in its deliberations can at once be carried out by the departments, and in case of a deadlock its dis- cussions can be laid before the Cabinet for disposal.

While the Cabinet is an informal committee of the Privy Council, with distinctive title and formerly summoned by the Prime Minister's secretary, and not by the Clerk of the Council,[1] there exist certain com- mittees of the Privy Council with advisory powers. One of these, on the affairs of the Channel Islands, is of ancient lineage, and is not regulated by statute; the Judicial Committee, a Court of Appeal from over- sea possessions, and the Committees for the Scottish Universities and the Universities of Oxford and Cam- bridge exist under statute. There is a Committee for the Baronetage, which controls the official list.

Privy Councillors are named by the King on the Prime Minister's advice; they take the oath of office and the oath of allegiance and kiss the King's hand at a council meeting; the King may remove a councillor by striking out the name in the council roll, or the name may be deleted by Order in Council as was that of Sir E. Speyer in 1918 on the ground of his attitude during the war. Since 1870, an alien, if naturalised, may be made a Privy Councillor, as decided in Sir E. Speyer's case.[2]

---

[1] Since 1923 the offices of Secretary to the Cabinet and Clerk of the Council have been combined.   [2] [1916] 2 K.B. 858.

3. *The Departments of State*

The exact composition of a Cabinet is a matter changing from time to time, and dependent on the will of the Prime Minister, and the pressure of his colleagues upon him to provide them with places in that body, but the exigencies of the public service demand that all the most important officers of State should be included in it. It was only in emergency in 1931 that a Cabinet of ten for the time sufficed; the normal number is twenty. Thus a Cabinet, in addition to the Prime Minister, who normally is First Lord of the Treasury, the holding of a departmental post like the Foreign Secretaryship being rarely combined,[1] would naturally include the Lord Chancellor, the Lord President, the Chancellor of the Exchequer, the Secretaries of State, the First Lord of the Admiralty, and probably the Ministers of Agriculture and Fisheries, Health, and Labour, and the Presidents of the Boards of Education and Trade. Ministers without portfolio have become rare since the war, while the Lord Privy Seal and Chancellor of the Duchy of Lancaster are offices which may at any time be of Cabinet rank. But the Postmaster-General, the First Commissioner of Works, and one or other of the Parliamentary Secretaries may conceivably attain this position.

The Lord High Chancellor is Speaker of the House of Lords, and presides over that body in its judicial capacity. He is responsible for the appointment of

---

[1] Mr MacDonald's combination of the two offices in 1924 was a patent failure.

judges,[1] justices of peace, and county court judges, and
for the exercise of the ecclesiastical patronage of the
Crown, as well as the custody and use of the Great
Seal through the Crown Office in Chancery. The
confusion of judicial and political functions is noteworthy, and it is very undesirable that he should
sit in cases where Cabinet policy is involved, but he
is not concerned with criminal jurisdiction, and the
practical objections to separating the two offices are
strong.

The Lord Privy Seal has now no functions to perform as such, but the office has not rarely been held by
a minister of distinction, or even by the Prime Minister,
in order to secure full time to devote to Cabinet work
proper. In 1935 Mr Eden held it to act for the Foreign
Office in League issues.

The Secretaries of State for Home and Foreign
Affairs received these distinctive functions in 1782;
from 1801–54, colonial and war matters occupied the
attention of a third Secretary, while in 1854 a separate
Secretaryship for War was created and given the
powers of the Board of Ordnance and a Secretary at
War who then existed. In 1858 the Secretary of State
for India came into being to replace the old Board of
Control, which under a President, the one real member,
supervised the government of India by the East India
Company. The war saw the creation of a Secretary
for Air in 1917; the office of Secretary of State for
the Colonies was divided in 1925, and the Secretary
for Scotland became a Secretary of State in 1926. He

---

[1] Lords of Appeal, Lords Justices, Master of the Rolls, Lord Chief
Justice, and President of the Probate, Divorce and Admiralty Division
are chosen by the Prime Minister.

has the custody of the Great Seal of Scotland and is in control of the Departments of Health, Agriculture, Education, etc. The other Secretaries are appointed by delivery of Seals, the Signet, the lesser Seal,[1] and the Cachet; the Signet is used in the full powers and instruments of ratification issued in the Foreign Office regarding treaties, and by the Colonial Office in commissions and instructions to Governors. Save where expressly otherwise provided, any Secretary of State can exercise the functions of another. The Chief Secretary to the Lord-Lieutenant, who was in effect Minister for Irish Affairs, disappeared with the revolutionary changes in Ireland in 1922, the Home Secretary becoming responsible for such fraction of his functions as remained.

The Treasury is a Commission appointed by letters patent for executing the duties of the Treasurer of the Exchequer of Great Britain and formerly of the Lord High Treasurer of Ireland. It consists of the First Lord, who has much patronage but no departmental duties, the Chancellor of the Exchequer, and a varying number of Junior Lords. The Chancellor's importance is modern; he has now the responsibility of supervising the estimates of revenue and expenditure, of securing that they shall be made to balance, of deciding as to loans and financial policy generally; he has also the duty of selecting sheriffs with the aid of the judges. The Junior Lords are at present five in number, two unpaid, and mainly act as assistants to the Chief Whip of the Government, who is Parliamentary Secretary

---

[1] Used in the Foreign, Home, War, Air, and Colonial Office for commissions. The Cachet is used only to seal envelopes of royal letters to foreign courts.

to the First Lord, while there is also a Financial Secretary who aids the Chancellor of the Exchequer and performs much of the detailed work of supervision of finance, holding necessarily an office of great moment. These two secretaries, however, hold office neither from or under the Crown, but are called into the Treasury Board. Effective Treasury control is possible only through the activity of the permanent staff of the Treasury under a permanent Secretary, who is the head of the Civil Service, while the control of the Treasury is supported by the action of the Comptroller and Auditor-General. Under the Treasury as collectors of revenue are the Commissioners of Crown Lands[1] (formerly Woods and Forests), and the Boards of Customs and Inland Revenue, without political chiefs, the department of the Paymaster-General, who has himself no functions and could always sit in Parliament without re-election, and the Post Office, whose chief, the Postmaster-General, aided by a Parliamentary Assistant, is a political officer, subject, formerly, to very close Treasury control in regard to the management of his monopoly of conveyance of letters, telegrams, radiograms, and telephone messages. By a recent arrangement much wider authority is enjoyed by the department, subject to an agreed payment to the Treasury. The office collects licence dues for the Customs and Excise Department and County Councils, pays widows', orphans', and old-age pensions, etc. Broadcasting is carried on under licence by a corporation, subject only to certain defined limits.

The Admiralty is a Board charged with performing

---

[1] The Minister of Agriculture and Fisheries is *ex officio* a Commissioner.

the duties of the Lord High Admiral; the essential head is the First Lord, despite the presence on the Board of four Sea Lords, the Deputy Chief of Naval Staff, a Civil Lord, and the existence of a Parliamentary Secretary, who is appointed by the Board, although in importance he ranks higher than any save the First Lord, and the First Sea Lord. The First Lord is responsible to the Crown and to Parliament for the business of the Admiralty, and his Sea Lords[1] are his subordinates, though their views, if they dissent, are presented to the Cabinet, and they are freely allowed to argue their case at meetings of the Committee of Imperial Defence; the Dardanelles Commission[2] asserted generally in regard to military and naval matters the right and duty of technical advisers at conferences with ministers to express their own views, when in disagreement with the responsible minister.

Other departments represent modern developments of the old system of entrusting matters to committees of the Privy Council. The most important is the Board of Trade, which is still technically such a committee, while the powers are exercised by the President alone; its sphere embraces statistics, patents, copyrights, companies, and all kinds of commercial interests, as regards which it is closely connected with the Foreign Office in relation to foreign trade. The Overseas Trade Department under a Secretary was set up to

---

[1] The First Sea Lord is also Chief of the Naval Staff and responsible for advice on all fundamental problems, so that the other Lords are much inferior to him in authority. The Second Lord is Chief of Naval Personnel, the Third is Controller, the Fourth is Chief of Supplies and Transport.

[2] Cf. *Parl. Pap.* Cd. 8490, 8502; Cmd. 371.

co-ordinate governmental activity as regards trade abroad; it supervises the consular service and the trade commissioners in British possessions, and is also in charge of emigration under the Empire Settlement Act, 1922. Transport in all its forms became, as the outcome of the war, a separate ministry, and it has continued in being owing to important developments of governmental control of traffic, passenger and goods. Merchant shipping has always been an essential part of the duties of the Board. The Board of Works, under a First Commissioner, has care of all public buildings at home and abroad and royal palaces; the importance of the office has increased largely owing to the enormous outlays on governmental buildings during the war. The Board of Education, under a President, has become one of the great spending departments of the State. The Ministry, formerly Board, of Agriculture and Fisheries has controlled these subjects since 1889 and 1903 respectively; it also assumed large powers in the war, only to lose them temporarily on the realisation, in 1921,[1] of the impossibility of proceeding with grandiose schemes of agricultural regeneration in view of financial stringency. In 1931–5 it assumed great activity in promoting agricultural protection, the limitation by quota or otherwise of foreign imports, especially wheat, and marketing schemes. The Ministry of Health, as a result of the war, replaced the Local Government Board, but its functions embrace those of the old Board together with the complex business of national health insurance in all its ramifications of a quasi-State medical service.[2] It has handed

---

[1] The Agriculture (Amendment) Act, 1921 (11 & 12 Geo. V. c. 17).

[2] The Ministry of Health Act, 1919 (9 & 10 Geo. V. c. 21).

over to the Home Office control of elections and registration. There are Ministers of Labour and Pensions.

In all legal matters the Government has the advice
of the Law Officers, the Attorney- and the Solicitor-
General, the former of whom is sometimes, but only
very rarely, a member of the Cabinet; both posts are
of high emolument and great importance. The actual
drafting of governmental measures is left to the Parliamentary Counsel, who are under Treasury control, and
who aid ministers in all matters of drafting amendments. While the Law Officers, though extremely important in many aspects, are not essential for membership of a Cabinet, the sinecure office of Chancellor of the
Duchy of Lancaster is often filled by a politician of
Cabinet importance. The Lord President of the Council
holds a place of high dignity, with a number of multifarious but no very onerous duties, and is usually a
minister of high importance, as was Mr (later Lord)
Balfour in the coalition ministry of Mr Lloyd George,
and Mr Baldwin in the National Government of 1931.

The necessity of a minister finding a seat in the
House of Commons, if not a peer, is now regarded as
extremely urgent, and even a brief period of exclusion
from the Commons normally results in resignation of
office.[1] There are, however, some offices where membership of the Commons is optional; the Scottish Law
Officers are the Lord Advocate and the Solicitor-
General, and it is not at all necessary for both to be in
Parliament. The holding of a peerage is not a bar to

---

[1] *E.g.* the Under-Secretary for Health, Scotland, the Minister of Agri-
culture, and other ministers had to resign in 1923 on this score. W. E.
Gladstone in 1845–6 as Colonial Secretary was without seat. But Sir W.
Jowitt in 1931, as Attorney-General, had to resign.

high office,[1] and a positive advantage in some cases such as the Foreign Office, but the presence of an excessive number of peers in Mr Bonar Law's administration of October 1922 was, somewhat hypercritically, made a ground of complaint. In such cases it is practically essential that an effective voice be given to the Commons by having an Under-Secretary or Parliamentary or Financial Secretary in the Commons, or entrusting representation of the department to the Junior Lords of the Treasury. These subordinate ministers are of much greater importance in cases where they have chiefs in the Lords. The representation of ministries in the Lords is a matter of less concern, and an important department may consider it more important to concentrate its Parliamentary strength in the Commons, and leave its business in the Lords to some minister without portfolio, or a holder of an office in the royal household, for certain of these offices (Treasurer, Comptroller of the Household and Vice-Chamberlain) also change with the ministry. Under-Secretaries formerly had the advantage that their offices were not regarded as held from the Crown, and, therefore, did not necessitate any re-election even before 1926.

4. *The Civil Service*

It is an essential feature of the constitution that for every exercise of the executive power of the Crown there must be responsibility to Parliament, and every public department, therefore, must have a political

[1] Only six Secretaries and Under-Secretaries of State can sit in the Commons: hence two must be peers even in a Labour régime: *e.g.* Lord Passfield and Lord Thomson. See 16 & 17 Geo. V. c. 18.

head or be subordinate to a department which has such a head. The actual business of each department must be performed by the permanent staff, whose importance in the business of government has grown enormously of recent years. The present system of the Civil Service is due to reforms suggested in 1849 but carried through only in 1870. The principles then applied involved (1) the abolition of patronage; (2) the admission of candidates at prescribed ages and by competitive examination; and (3) the drawing of distinction between intellectual and routine work. The undertaking by the State of social activities of every type has enormously increased the number of Government servants. In addition to huge staffs of industrial workers, manipulative workers, messengers, and so forth, there are the classes which make up the Civil Service in the narrower sense of that term. As at present organised there are the administrative class whose function it is to assist in the framing of policy, to supervise its execution, and to control the activities of the subordinate staff. Members of this class are recruited by competitive examinations held by the Civil Service Commission, first established in 1855. The standard of examination is that of Honours degrees at the Universities and the age limits are 22-24. The executive class is recruited by examination from young persons of a sound school education. Below them are the clerical class; the writing assistant class; the shorthand typist class, and the typist class. There are also professional, scientific, and technical officers who are recruited either by competitive examination or on the basis of their technical qualifications by competitive interviews. All Civil servants are subject normally to probation. They are appointed informally; after selection by the Civil Service Commission their appointments are notified by the office concerned. Promotion is not subject to the control of the Civil Service Commission, but on the whole is managed without undue political influence. Since the war of 1914–18 the Whitley Council system has been applied to the Civil Service. There is a National Council for the administrative and legal departments, with departmental councils in the respective departments. The National Council of fifty-four members is appointed, half by the Government and half to represent the staff. The Council may consider the principles of promotion and discipline, but may not deal with officers on scales of salaries rising to £700 a year. Since 1925 the industrial court deals with salaries, hours of work, and leave of classes of Civil servants up to £700 a year. It remains, however, with the Treasury to determine the effect to be given to recommendations of the Whitley Council or the Court, as Parliament must vote the additional amounts requisite and will do so only on the recommendation of the Chancellor of the Exchequer. It will be noted that the remuneration of Civil servants is largely decided by themselves; it has been greatly increased in late years without any obvious corresponding increase in efficiency or devotion to duty. Moreover the Service enjoys the advantage of a generous pension system; retirement is normally compulsory at age 65 and is frequent at age 60. Women are eligible for most Civil Service posts, excluding those in the Foreign Office and Diplomatic and Consular Services and the Colonial and Indian Service.

Civil servants hold office at the pleasure of the

Crown, unless expressly given a different tenure by statute, and in theory may be dismissed without assigning any ground.[1] But in practice they enjoy a security of tenure which is unparalleled in business life. This principle, invaluable within due limits, is unsatisfactory in the case of those departments which deal with matters of a business character.

Civil servants owe a duty of loyalty to any Government which may be in office, and on that ground they must not be political partisans; accordingly, resignation from the Service is required if a Civil servant announces himself as a Parliamentary candidate. Moreover, as the result of the General Strike of 1926, the Trade Disputes and Trade Unions Act of 1927 forbids a Civil servant to be a member of any organisation the primary object of which is to influence the remuneration and conditions of its members, unless the Association confines its membership to Crown employees, has no political objects, and is not associated with any political party.[2]

The permanent tenure of the Civil servant is an essential feature of the British political system. It lies at the basis of the possibility of the successful carrying-out of the complex business of modern government. Its merits have led it to be widely copied in the Dominions, and the satisfactory character of the Civil Services in Australia marks the completeness of the system as it is practised; Canada, which adopted it later, suffers in consequence from less efficient service.

[1] *Reilly* v. *R.*, [1934] A.C. 176. No action lies to recover pension: *Nixon* v. *Att.-Gen.*, [1931] A.C. 184; or salary: *Kynaston* v. *Att.-Gen.* (1933), 49 T.L.R. 300.

[2] The Police Act, 1919, forbade strikes by the police and precluded them joining trade unions, giving them an organisation of their own.

On the other hand bureaucracy has not gone without attack. It is asserted that it tends to arrogate to itself excessive power; by its knowledge and competence it dominates ministers and dictates policy. Again, departmentalism is a danger; departments strive with unwise insistence to secure the carrying-out of a particular point of view to the detriment of the interests of the State as a whole. Red tape and routine tend to flourish, and it is hard to break away from tradition, even when new needs demand fresh treatment. Some Civil servants, again, become high-handed; collectors of income tax forget that they are performing a delicate duty and seek excessive powers. There is some truth in these assertions, and the increased remuneration of Civil servants unquestionably helps the tendency to regard themselves as a distinctly superior class of society as compared with those whose work it is to amass wealth.

5. *The Functions of the Executive*

The Executive derives its powers from two sources: (1) the Royal Prerogative; (2) Statute. The powers which it exercises are far from being confined to the mere execution of laws. The Executive at the present day is charged with planning to secure the national safety against external enemies and internal disorder, involving the conduct of external relations and the maintenance of peace and security, which may be deemed the primary function of government. Further, as the business of the State is now held to include all matters involving the economic, social, and intellectual welfare of the people, the Executive is charged with the duty of securing the expansion and direction of commerce and industry, of extending the means of transport and communications, by sea, land, and air, of promoting public health and of furthering public enlightenment, by education and broadcasting. To accomplish its tasks the Executive must plan and procure as well as carry out the necessary legislation. Moreover it requires itself to enact measures of legislative character, and by comparatively recent innovation it has attained power, especially in connection with this delegated legislative power, to act as the interpreter of its own enactments; a combination of functions which has given rise to judicial criticism of the New Despotism.[1] Exaggerated as this criticism no doubt sometimes is, it calls attention to a fundamental fact. The Executive, through the Cabinet and Civil Service, has come largely to control the whole sovereign authority of the State. The Cabinet dictates legislation, whether spontaneously or, as often no doubt, on the prompting of the heads of the Civil Service, that legislation assigns to the Executive a power of subordinate law-making, and permits the Executive to interpret the law. There is unquestionably in this the potentiality of misuse of power by a ministry which is placed in office by the vote of the electorate under stress of some, perhaps temporary, feeling. Some anxiety was felt in 1931 when the Government used the emergency powers conceded to them to impose upon the judiciary reductions in salary. It is significant that Sir Stafford Cripps has proposed that a system of socialisation of industry should be brought into force in the United Kingdom

---

[1] Lord Hewart, *The New Despotism* (1929); C. K. Allen, *Bureaucracy Triumphant* (1931).

through the instrumentality of Orders in Council, Chapter I. issued under the authority of an Emergency Powers Act, such orders to be immune from judicial review.

The royal prerogative is the special pre-eminence which the King under the common law possesses in right of his royal dignity, or, in more modern terms, is the residue of discretionary authority which at any time is legally left in the hands of the Crown. The prerogative can be traced to three sources: (1) the system of tribal leadership, whence are derived the executive, legislative, and judicial powers of the Crown; (2) the feudal chieftaincy which is the source of the King's right to treasure trove and the custody of infants and idiots, and which is bound up historically with the doctrines of treason and allegiance; and (3) certain legal principles evolved by lawyers, *e.g.* "The King never dies" or "The King can do no wrong". The constitutional history of England is in large measure the record of the limitation of the prerogative;[1] the King's right of arbitrary imprisonment, arbitrary taxation, the issuing of commissions of martial law, the granting of monopolies, the suspension of and dispensing with Acts of Parliament, and the control of the judiciary, and the right of independent legislation, have all suffered vital limitation, but there remain large fields in which the prerogative has still a wide application. In the matter of foreign relations and of defence, legal restrictions of the prerogative have hardly been attempted. The King can declare war or neutrality, or make peace, without Parliamentary authority, and the practice of rendering important treaties subject to Parliamentary approval is of comparatively recent

[1] See Ridges, *Constitutional Law of England* (ed. Keith), pp. 184 ff.

date. The Labour Government in 1929 accepted the Optional Clause of the Statute of the Permanent Court of International Justice, which imposes an obligation of compulsory reference to arbitration of certain international disputes, on the authority of the House of Commons only in the face of the opposition of the great majority of the House of Lords. It is the practice of all ministries to conclude important international arrangements,[1] leaving it to the House of Commons to exercise merely the function of according formal approval, as was the case of the Locarno Pact in 1925 and the London Treaty on the Limitation of Naval Armaments in 1930. Similarly the Executive has almost unlimited authority in the sphere of Dominion relations and colonial government. The vital transformation of the Empire into a commonwealth of equal units was carried out by the Imperial Conference of 1926 on the authority of the British Government, which did not even submit its action for approval *ex post facto* to Parliament for approval, and consulted it only when the Statute of Westminster had to be enacted in 1931. Similarly the grant of responsible government in 1906–7 to the Transvaal and Orange River Colonies was carried out in the teeth of the bitter opposition of the House of Lords. The Executive also wields without control by Parliament the most important power of making appointments to the high offices of State which fall outside the field of action of the Civil Service Commission. It exercises the royal prerogative as to honours, can confer charters of incorporation, and exercises an important influence on

---

[1] Egypt in 1922 was given independence without preliminary approval by Parliament.

ecclesiastical affairs through the power of appointing bishops.

The legislative powers of the Executive are in the main derived from statutes; it is only in respect of conquered and ceded Colonies that a normal power of legislation still exists. The Crown may regulate by Order in Council the Civil Service, but its action is based on the Executive power, and it cannot impose any criminal sanction for its regulations. It can also regulate trade and commerce in war-time, but that takes the form of the waiving of the strict terms of the common law. The regulation by Order in Council of appeals to the King from oversea courts is now statutory under the Judicial Committee Act, 1844; formerly it was part of the judicial prerogative, and currency regulation is now statutory under the Coinage Acts, 1870 and 1920. The right to annex territory, as in the case of Kenya Colony in 1920 or Southern Rhodesia in 1923, is an exercise rather of executive prerogative. In the United Kingdom the King, by proclamation, can call attention to the provisions of existing legislation, and it appears that violation of such legislation may deserve more severe punishment, if despite the proclamation it is violated, but no fresh crime can be created by proclamation. The more usual use of proclamations is to call attention to such matters as the declaration of war or peace or new currency regulations.

From statute, however, the Crown derives very wide powers for the maintenance of public order in cases of emergency.[1] The King may issue a proclamation of

[1] Emergency Powers Act, 1920 (10 & 11 Geo. V. c. 55). It was widely used in 1926, and was based on the wide powers under the Defence of the Realm Act, 1914.

emergency, if satisfied that there is risk of action by any persons calculated to deprive the community of the essentials of life, by interfering with the supply of food, water, fuel, or light, or with the means of locomotion. When such a proclamation is made, Orders in Council may be issued, making regulations to secure the essentials of life to the community and to confer powers on any person for this purpose, but no form of compulsory military service or industrial conscription may be imposed, nor may the act of striking or peaceful persuasion to strike be made an offence. Full control is assured to Parliament, to which a proclamation must forthwith be communicated; the Parliament must be summoned to meet specially, if not in session, and regulations must be confirmed by both Houses. A proclamation has effect for one month only, but may be extended.

More normal in character is the power given to make regulations, rules, or orders under statute.[1] Such a delegation is, under modern conditions of legislation, absolutely indispensable. Parliament has not the time to enact in detail codes of regulations on technical matters, such as communications, public health, education, agricultural questions, etc.; it has not the technical knowledge requisite. Moreover, experimental regulations, for example as regards housing and town-planning, are often essential, which can be readily modified; unforeseen contingencies must be provided for, as when a new Trade Board has to be set up. The process has dangers. The powers given are often too vague, so that the Executive may invade unduly

---

[1] J. Willis, *Parliamentary Powers of English Government Departments* (1933).

private rights without the control of the courts being available to restrict their operation. Further, there is a tendency to grant authority, exclusive of the right of access to the law courts for protection. There are strong objections to the provision, which provides that orders are to have the same force as if enacted in the Act itself. But this famous clause has been reduced by judicial interpretation to permit only enactments within the purport of the Act.[1] It still remains to be seen what effect will be given by the courts to the power of a minister to confirm an order, for example, as to housing, such confirmation to be conclusive evidence [2] that the order has been duly made and is within the powers of the Act. Much more satisfactory is the type of delegation which restricts the power to enactment of subordinate details, the fixing of dates of commencement, or the determination of spheres of application; which gives no power to provide financial obligations; and which does not permit any alteration of the Act itself or other Acts. Certain safeguards have been provided by Parliament. In some cases regulations must be made in draft and may not operate until approved by resolutions of both Houses. In the case of resolutions affecting finance,

---

[1] *Minister of Health* v. *R.*; *Yaffé, Ex parte*, [1931] A.C. 494. The Housing Act, 1930, s. 11, permits application to the court within a limited time after a confirming order to test its conformity to the Act or to establish that the applicant's interests have been substantially prejudiced by noncompliance with the requirements of the Act. So also the Land Drainage Act, 1930; Public Works Facilities Act, 1930; Poor Law Act, 1930, s. 142. No other action by the court than quashing an order on such an application is allowed.

[2] *Ringer, Ex parte* (1909), 27 T.L.R. 718. Cf. the Agricultural Marketing Act, 1931, s. 1(8), but no scheme can take effect without approval by both Houses, and the registered dealers may reject a scheme by a poll.

for example, imposing duties under the Import Duties Act, 1932, the resolution is that of the Commons only. Much less effective is the provision for laying regulations with power to either House to disallow or modify, for the private member in the Commons has virtually no effective means of securing action. Some security, however, is provided by the rule of antecedent publication under the Rules Publication Act, 1893, which, however, is of limited operation. Of greater value is the customary practice by which rules are drafted by Government departments in consultation with representatives of interested parties, as in the case of merchant shipping, of public health, of agriculture, and other questions.

It has of late been suggested that it is necessary to secure further control over subordinate legislation, and that for this purpose there should be attached to each of the great departments a Parliamentary Committee to which should be submitted in draft all proposed regulations and which would be empowered to make suggestions to the department for the issue of regulations, and to study such regulations as were made in their operation. The objections which so far have prevented the adoption of any such scheme, rest on the dislike of ministers and of Civil servants alike of any interference with the plenitude of their authority. Alternatively, the excuse is made that any such Committe would tend to lessen the responsibility of the department, an excuse which assumes that the present system of nominal responsibility has much greater value than in all probability it has in point of fact.

The judicial powers of departments are essentially a development from their legislative functions. It would be absurd to expect the courts to deal with the vast mass of technical issues which arise under the legislation as to old age, invalid, and disability pensions, under the regulations as to education, or the complex issues affecting sanitation, public health, town planning, and construction of houses. No court could effectively decide whether a new school was necessary in any locality; the Board of Education can do so, after considering the views of the local authority, parents, and ratepayers; so it alone can decide questions of the dismissal of teachers, or the efficiency of non-provided schools. The Minister of Transport must determine issues regarding the grant of licences for transport; claims for unemployment allowances go through insurance officials, via courts of referees, to an umpire, whose decision is final. The Minister for Health has important decisions to take regarding orders made by local authorities requiring private persons to carry out sanitary matters. Often the decision is given to a body which is not strictly a court, but is in effect independent of the ministry, as indeed is the umpire under the insurance procedure. Such tribunals are the Traffic Commissioners under the Road Traffic Acts or the referees under the Widows', Orphans', and Old-Age Contributory Pensions Act, 1925.

The merits of such tribunals as these are undeniable.[1] They are more easy of access than the ordinary courts; their procedure is less technical, and much less expensive; they decide more rapidly; their members are possessed of specialised knowledge, and have not to rely on conflicting expert evidence adduced at great cost, the tribunal can secure uniformity more effectively

---

[1] See *Committee on Ministers' Powers Report*, 1932 (Cmd. 4060).

than any court, and can follow out a definite line of policy. It is pointed out that there is really in many cases no room for a strict judicial decision. That involves (1) statement of the case by each party; (2) the ascertainment of the facts if need be by argument; (3) the decision of any legal issue; and (4) a finding based on the facts and the application of law to the facts. Some issues dealt with by ministers, such as the determination of insurable employment, admit of legal decisions proper, but in many cases the final decision must depend on policy, and the discretion of the minister or the tribunal, for example, in regard to competitive claims for road licences by rival firms. Such issues can properly be left to ministers or preferably ministerial tribunals, provided that they are subject to the control of the courts to prevent them extending their jurisdiction outside the permitted sphere, that an appeal lies to the courts on any disputed issue of law, and provided that they observe the rules of natural justice. These demand that no person shall act as judge in his own case; thus it is undesirable that a minister himself or a tribunal under his direct control should decide issues where his policy comes into question. Further, any party must be allowed to present fully his case, and to know what case he has to meet; this does not, however, demand that he shall be entitled to an oral hearing nor that the judicial laws of evidence shall be applied. The decision when communicated should normally be accompanied by a statement of the grounds on which it rests. But the Committee of Ministers' Powers, which laid down these principles, declined to rule that reports by inspectors of Government departments on questions

referred to them should necessarily be made public.
After all, such reports form part only of the material
on which a decision is arrived at, and no finality could
be reached if every step of the process of reaching a
decision were subject to meticulous examination.

As against this extension of the functions of the
executive into the spheres of legislation and judicial
activity may be set the fact that in various ways
efforts have been made to vest executive powers in
the hands of bodies not subject to detailed control by
the executive. Instances of this may be seen in the
Electricity Commissioners, who are given very important functions in connection with the execution of
the great scheme for the supply in bulk throughout
the United Kingdom of cheap electric power. The
control of mining exploitation and the preparation
of amalgamation schemes have been entrusted to an
authority not immediately dependent on the ministry
responsible. Of great importance is the British Broadcasting Corporation, which operates since 1927 under
a royal charter and a licence from the Postmaster-
General. The control of the programmes of the Corporation is not undertaken by the Government, but it
reserves power to forbid the broadcasting of any
matter, and in emergency it could take full charge, and
broadcast nothing save what it thought fit. The importance of such a power in the case of a general
strike appeared clearly from the experience of the
general strike in 1926, when the newspapers were
prevented from publication by strike action. Mention
may also be made of the system of Marketing Boards
which deal with the disposal of agricultural produce,
including milk. These organisations are to a certain

extent democratically controlled, and only in certain respects are they subject to ministerial authority.

Wide as is the power of the Executive, there is one direction in which it is subject to an effective check. It cannot dispose of public moneys validly without eventual Parliamentary authority.[1] Any contract which it makes is subject to the implied condition that Parliament will provide the funds; if it will not do so the other party has no grievance and no remedy by petition of right or otherwise.[2] Similarly if money is paid away without proper authority, it can be recovered from the payee.[3] The same rule results in the principle that a pledge by an Attorney-General of a province of Canada that his province will pay the cost of troops requisitioned on the occasion of a riot cannot be enforced if the legislature does not vote the sum,[4] and in the Commonwealth of Australia the rule is interpreted very closely.[5] Nor may the Executive charge fees for its actions without legal authority.[6]

6. *The House of Commons*

The reform legislation of 1832 which gave an electorate of a million introduced a modified but real element of control by the people over the House of Commons which had almost disappeared under various forms of

---

[1] *Churchyard* v. *The Queen* (1865), L.R. 1 Q.B. 173; *Eastern Trust Co.* v. *Mackenzie, Mann & Co.*, [1915] A.C. at p. 759.

[2] *Commercial Cable Co.* v. *Newfoundland Govt.*, [1916] 2 A.C. 601.

[3] *Auckland Harbour Board* v. *R.*, [1924] A.C. 318.

[4] *Troops in Cape Breton Reference*, [1930] S.C.R. 554.

[5] *Commonwealth* v. *Colonial Ammunition Co.* (1923), 34 C.L.R. 198; for this principle in its application to the Anglo-Irish annuities dispute see Keith, *Letters on Imperial Relations, 1916–1935*, pp. 132, 133.

[6] *Att.-Gen.* v. *Wilts United Dairies, Ltd.* (1922), 91 L.J.K.B. 897.

governmental interference and corruption. But it was
not until 1867 that the middle class with an electorate
of 2,500,000 became fully masters of the composition
of the Commons, a position modified in 1884 by the
extension of the franchise on a generous scale to
5,000,000 so that the workers attained effective voting
power. The question of further extensions was inevitably raised, and became combined with the issue of
female suffrage, whose supporters before the war successfully blocked any reform which did not include
women. The opposition to enfranchisement, based as it
was on sound if not conclusive grounds, was largely
mitigated by the services rendered by women during
the war, illogically enough since it was precisely war
conditions which made it clear that the true burden of
maintaining the State fell on men, and the supporters
of the franchise for women made skilful use of the
power they had in the Commons to oppose any proposal
for allowing the registration of military and naval
voters, who by their absence on these services had lost
their votes under the existing legislation. As a result
the Representation of the People Act, 1918,[1] effected a
revolution in the size of the electorate by practically
trebling it, raising the electorate to 21,392,322, of
whom 8,479,156 were women over age thirty. In 1928
equal franchise was accorded to give 28,850,000 voters.
In 1931, 21,704,000 votes were recorded.

The franchise is, therefore, conceded to every person
over twenty-one years of age, in respect of three
months' residence in any constituency or in another
constituency in the same or a contiguous Parliamentary
borough or county. A vote is also given in respect of

[1] 8 Geo. V. c. 64.

occupation of business premises of £10 value. The wife or husband of a person who has a business premises qualification receives a vote on that score. Further, a vote in University constituencies is given to any men who are over twenty-one and have taken a degree, other than an Honorary degree, and to women over twenty-one who have taken a degree or passed the necessary examinations in cases where the University did not confer degrees on women. While a voter may be registered in several constituencies, if qualified in each, at a general election he or she can only vote twice, in respect of a residential qualification, and either of a business or University qualification. Special provision was in 1918 made for naval and military voters, but these were mainly of transitory character. Registration is effected in each Parliamentary borough by the Town Clerk, in each County by the Clerk. Provision is made for absent voters' lists, chiefly for defence service voters. Disqualifications are limited to infancy, lunacy, conviction for either treason or felony until the sentence is served or a pardon granted, peerage (save in the case of an Irish peer who is a member of the Commons), alienage, and employment for electoral purposes, though the returning officer has a casting vote, or conviction of corrupt electoral practices. The receipt of poor relief as a disqualification was abolished in 1918.

Disqualifications for membership are infancy, the rule being observed strictly since 1832; peerage, other than an Irish peerage; alienage; the status of a clergyman of the Church of England, minister of the Church of Scotland, or Roman Catholic priest; lunacy or idiocy; conviction of felony or treason or corrupt practices; interest in a Government contract; holding of a pension other than a Civil Service or diplomatic pension; and employment in a variety of offices of profit under the Crown. In some cases the disqualification is absolute, in some re-election after appointment was formerly necessary, and in others there is no disqualification at all.[1] A bankrupt is disqualified from election; if elected already he may not sit or vote, and his seat is vacated in six months after adjudication, unless the adjudication is meanwhile annulled or an honourable discharge granted.

Election is normally based on single-member constituencies, though twelve boroughs and the City of London have two members; the University constituencies of Oxford and Cambridge and the combined English Universities have two members apiece, the Scottish Universities three; in the University contests proportional representation with the single transferable vote prevails. Elsewhere its use has so far been negatived, though the existing system undoubtedly places undue power in the hands of the party organisations, preventing any individuality on the part of candidates, and where there are three parties or more resulting in the representation of the constituency often by a candidate who is merely a spokesman for a decided minority, having secured his seat by the splitting of the votes of electors, who are agreed in preferring either of the other two candidates to him.[2] In England there are 254 county (24 Wales) and 266 borough (11 Wales)

---

[1] Cf. the Re-election of Ministers Act, 1919 (9 Geo. V. c. 2.), which dispensed with re-election if the appointment to office was made within nine months after the summons of a new Parliament, and on appointment as Minister without Portfolio. In 1926 all requirement of re-election was dropped: 16 & 17 Geo. V. c. 19.

[2] The Government of 1922 was thus elected on a minority vote.

members; in Scotland thirty-eight and thirty-three; eight University members in England and Wales and three in Scotland. The exclusion of the Irish Free State from the House of Commons has reduced Irish representation to four borough, eight county, and one University member. Voting is by ballot, and each candidate must be nominated by two and supported by eight electors. Unjustifiable candidatures are limited by the rule that a candidate must deposit £150 which is returned if he receives one-eighth of the votes cast. Election expenses are limited by statute according to type of constituency and number of voters.

The chief officer of the House, who presides over its proceedings, save in Committee, when a Chairman of Committees takes his place, and who communicates its resolutions and carries out the duties of asserting its privileges, is the Speaker, elected, though not on a party vote, for each Parliament. The Clerk of the House and the Serjeant-at-Arms are his agencies, the one to record the proceedings of the House and advise as to precedents of procedure, the other to bring to the bar of the House persons directed to attend for examination, and to execute warrants for bringing recalcitrants to the bar, for detaining them, or committing them to such place of custody as the Commons may order.

The Commons claim the formal privileges of collective access to the person of the sovereign, and the most favourable construction of their proceedings; further, freedom from arrest, save for indictable offences and contempt of court, for the session and a period of forty days before and after; and freedom of speech. The latter privilege means freedom from external con-

trol and liability to legal proceedings at the instance
of third parties; the House itself by censure, suspension,
commitment, or expulsion vindicates such limits as it
thinks fit to impose on the licence of its members. By
statute of 1840,[1] passed as the outcome of a bitter
struggle arising from legal proceedings taken against
Hansard, the publisher of *Parliamentary Papers*, for an
alleged libel therein,[2] any papers published by order of
either house of Parliament are absolutely privileged,
and by judicial decision any fair report in the press of
Parliamentary proceedings is privileged, even if the
speeches reported are defamatory, but this has no
application to a reprint by a private member of a
defamatory speech. To protect members the Speaker or
Chairman may at any time order the withdrawal of
strangers, including the press, and any member may
take notice of the presence of strangers, whereupon an
immediate vote is taken. Secret sessions are, however,
practically unknown; the attempt during the war to
use them was not a marked success.

Privileges not formally claimed from the Crown, but
essential, are the right to regulate the filling of vacancies
by ordering the issue of warrants by the Speaker to the
Clerk of the Crown in Chancery for the issue of writs
whenever a seat is vacated; out of session this is done
under statute by the Speaker in case of vacation of
seats by death, peerage, bankruptcy, or acceptance
of office, other than the formal offices such as steward-
ship of the Chiltern Hundreds, which are bestowed
on members to meet the difficulty that no member
can resign his duties. Until 1868 the Commons further

---

[1] 3 & 4 Vict. c. 9.
[2] *Stockdale* v. *Hansard* (1839), 9 Ad. & E. 1.

exercised the right to decide all election petitions; in that year they gave the power to the courts, the tribunal being constituted of two judges, a singularly unfortunate decision when divergences of view arise between the judges, nor have all judges—who are often ex-members of political parties—shown in this matter full judicial qualities. The House also takes notice of any legal disqualification, such as conviction for felony, and it may expel any member for such reasons as it thinks fit, as in case of conviction for misdemeanour, thus vacating the seat, but not creating any incapacity for re-election.[1] Further, the House regulates its own affairs, exempt from judicial intervention save in the case of crime; in Mr Bradlaugh's case it refused to allow the taking of the oath and his seat by that member, and it was held that he had no legal redress.[2]

The House has also power to punish disrespect to its members or itself, interference with its procedure or its officers, or with witnesses who have given, or are to give, evidence before it. It can admonish, reprimand, or commit offenders to prison for the duration of the session, and may fine, though the power is disused. It is clear that it is for the House to decide what matters are breaches of its privileges, and that it is a sufficient return to a writ of habeas corpus that a person is imprisoned on the Speaker's warrant, though conceivably, if the ground of commitment were stated in the warrant not merely generally as for contempt, the courts might feel entitled to examine whether the act could in any way be regarded as a contempt.[3] The

---

[1] This was admitted finally in Wilkes's case, the House expunging its declarations of ineligibility.

[2] *Bradlaugh* v. *Gossett* (1884), 12 Q.B.D. 271.

[3] *Burdett* v. *Abbot* (1811–12), 14 East 1, 150.

House may commit persons for exercising legal rights,
but they cannot deprive them in any way of such
rights, and disputes of this sort are now obsolete.

7. *The House of Lords*

Menaced and condemned by general political
opinion as an effective second chamber, the House of
Lords has remained unchanged in composition through
the difficulty of any agreement on the alterations to
be effected. The root of the hereditary character of the
Lords is to be found in the rule of dubious date that,
when a summons to sit in Parliament had been addressed to any person individually by the Crown and
the summons had been obeyed, a right to be summoned was conferred upon his heirs.[1] In the case of
earls charters or letters patent were issued, and the
same practice was adopted when dukes, marquises,
and viscounts were created, the same rule ultimately
being applied also to barons. The patents normally
defined the descent, confining it to heirs male, in lieu
of heirs lineal, as in the case of baronies by summons,
but there was long doubt whether, if a barony by
summons had been created, it was not bound up with
the tenure of the estate of the first baron by summons,
so that the title passed with the estate, a doctrine
finally negatived in the Berkeley peerage case in 1861,
while in the Wensleydale peerage case in 1856 the very
questionable doctrine was asserted that the Crown
could not create a life peerage giving right to sit and
vote in the House of Lords. It has also been decided

[1] *Clifton Case* (1673), Collins' Baronies by Writ 271; *Freschville Case*
(1677), Lds. Rep. iii. 29.

that a peerage cannot be surrendered or extinguished by any voluntary action either of the holder or of the Crown.

The power of the Crown to create peerages is limited by statute in that a Scottish peerage cannot now be created, and an Irish peerage only subject to conditions as to number laid down in the Act of Union, viz. that one such peerage may be created for every three which become extinct, until the number falls to 100. The Crown, however, cannot issue writs of summons to peers who are aliens or bankrupt, and the House of Lords forbids infants or felons or persons expelled by its own sentence to sit.

The House of Lords consists of the peers[1] of the United Kingdom; sixteen Scottish peers elected for each Parliament by their fellows; twenty-eight Irish peers elected for life by their fellows, but there is now no machinery for their election; the Archbishops of Canterbury and York, the Bishops of London, Durham, and Winchester, and twenty-one other bishops by seniority; and seven Lords of Appeal appointed for life, whose chief function is to sit in the House of Lords as a judicial body.

The Lord Chancellor is Speaker of the House of Lords, but with very much less authority than the Speaker of the Commons. The Lords possess also, without formal claim, the privileges of freedom from

---

[1] That a peeress in her own right cannot sit in the Lords, despite the general removal of restrictions based on grounds of sex by the Sex Disqualification (Removal) Act, 1919, was determined by the Committee of Privileges in *Viscountess Rhondda's case*, [1922] 2 A.C. 337. The Lords now considerably outnumber the Commons; in 1935 there were 684 hereditary peers, 17 minors, and 68 representative peers, viz. 2 archbishops, 24 bishops, 16 Scottish and 18 Irish representatives, and 8 Law Lords.

arrest, freedom of speech, personal access to the Crown, of deciding the validity of new peerages, of insisting on the summoning of persons entitled to be summoned, of settling disputes regarding Irish peerages and claims to vote at elections of Scottish peers, and of committing to prison for contempt for any specified period and not merely until prorogation. They can deal with claims to old peerages only on the reference of the Crown. It is still open to any peer to record a protest from decisions of which he disapproves but not to vote by proxy.

As a judicial body, peers without legal qualifications by custom are excluded from taking part; the House acts as an appellate tribunal, as the court for trial of peers accused of treason or felony; as arbiter on peerage claims it acts by a Committee of Privileges, including lay members, and is not strictly bound by its own decisions as it is when hearing appeals, and it is theoretically the court in impeachments by the Commons.

8. *The Crown in Parliament*

Parliament is summoned by royal proclamation issued on the advice of the Privy Council under the Great Seal, which dissolves the existing Parliament and declares the royal pleasure to summon a new one, reciting an Order in Council requiring the Chancellor of Great Britain, and now also the Governor of Northern Ireland, to issue writs to the returning officers and others for calling a new Parliament. The writs are addressed to the temporal peers of the United Kingdom, to the spiritual peers, to the Irish representative peers, to returning officers for the return of members of the House of Commons, and in the shape of writs of attendance to the Judges, and the Attorney- and Solicitor-General, who may be called upon to advise, but are not members of Parliament. The Houses meet on the day fixed by proclamation, and the House of Commons selects its Speaker, who is confirmed by the Lord Chancellor in the name of the Crown, demands the privileges of the Commons, and receives assurances of their grant. The Speech from the Throne, and debates on it, usher in the regular work of the session.

Adjournments of Parliament are entirely within the power of the Houses, but the Crown has the right to compel meetings before the expiration of adjournments, when both Houses stand adjourned, by summoning them to meet not less than six days from the date of the proclamation. Prorogation, usually effected through Commissioners, which ends the session of both Houses simultaneously, and brings all business to an end, save in such cases as special agreement has been arrived at to carry over a Bill from one session to another, is entirely a matter of the prerogative, as normally is dissolution, which, however, might be effected automatically by expiry of the five years, which is the maximum duration of the House of Commons since 1911; under the Septennial Act, 1716, it was seven years. The demise of the Crown no longer affects the duration of Parliament.

The annual meeting of Parliament is secured, not by statute, but by the necessity of securing the appropriation of money for the most important needs of government, and the maintenance of a standing army and air force, which is legalised each year by the Army and Air Force (Annual) Act, and above all by the necessity that ministers have of satisfying the demands of the electorate for control through Parliament over administration, and legislative enactments to meet the constantly growing social needs of the people.

The prerogative of dissolution is now one to be exercised on ministerial advice only, and never at the royal discretion. The Cabinet, not the Prime Minister alone, has the right to advise. There are no binding rules as to ministerial advice; the passing of reform measures, however, as in 1832, 1867, 1884, and 1918, has been the cause of appeals to the new electorate. But a ministry may, if it deem it right, proceed with any programme it thinks fit, despite the fact that it has not received any mandate on the special Bills proposed from the electorate, unless, of course, like the Governments of 1905–10 or 1923, or 1924–9, it is precluded from dealing with some measure, such as Home Rule or Protection or Food Taxation, by a pledge to the electors before the elections took place; such a restriction, however, is merely binding in honour, not in law. On any issue of great importance which arises after an election, an appeal to the people is justifiable, and sometimes almost essential; thus the two elections of 1910 were both called for by the exceptional importance of the struggle between the Houses over the financial powers of the Lords and the taxation of land policy of the administration. The dissolution of 1918 was justified on the score not merely of the new electorate, but also of the necessity of the administration receiving a fresh mandate for making peace, and undertaking internal reconstruction, seeing that Parliament, which by efflux of time should have expired in January 1916, had been prolonged in existence as, owing to war conditions, an election during hostilities would have in effect disfranchised many hundreds of thousands of voters. That of 1922 was rendered inevitable by the decision of the Unionists to terminate the coalition and the resignation of the ministry; that of 1923 by the adoption of the policy of protection; that of 1924 by the defeat of a minority Government and the need of a decision as to future policy. In 1931 the National Ministry required a mandate for drastic economic reforms to meet the emergency which the Labour Government had failed to face. Even so, difficulties arose as to the interpretation of the mandate, and the Free Trade supporters in the Cabinet felt bound first to resign office, and later to go into definite opposition in view of the Ottawa agreements.

The sovereign is never present in Parliament save for the opening speech, and—very rarely—at a prorogation or dissolution, all of which acts can be, and often are, performed by Commission. By Commission also is the royal assent expressed to Bills passed by the two Houses, or over the head of the Lords under the Parliament Act, 1911. A public Act receives assent in the terms, *"Le roy le veult"*; a private Bill in the terms, *"soit fait comme il est désiré"*, and the appropriation Bill with *"Le roy remercie ses bons sujets, accepte leur bénévolence, et ainsi le veult"*, interesting relics of ancient relations between a subservient legislature and a powerful monarch. The words of the veto have never been used since, in 1707, Queen Anne responded to a Scottish Militia Bill with *"La reyne s'avisera"*. The Crown in fact has no discretion in

legislation and no power to stop any legislation desired by ministers, for it cannot constitutionally dismiss ministers—unless they are patently defying the
will of the people—or dissolve a House of Commons
save on ministerial advice. Nor would ministers ven-
ture to advise the Crown to refuse to accept a public
Bill passed by both Houses; if they desire to defeat
any measure it must be done in one House or other,
not by the prerogative.

The assent of the Crown is obtained in advance to
any Bill dealing with the position or property of the
Crown, or vitally affecting the royal prerogative (*e.g.*
of creation[1] of peers), as in 1934–35, and to all proposals to vote money or raise taxation the initiative of
the Crown is essential. Crown communications to the
Houses deal, apart from speeches at the opening or
close of the session, merely with such formal matters;
they may be under the sign-manual or reported
verbatim by a minister; mention of the private wishes
of the Crown in debate is forbidden save with the
express sanction of the Houses.

9. *The Functions and Procedure of Parliament*

From being a means by which the Crown obtained
legislation or taxation which it desired, Parliament,
especially the House of Commons, has developed into
the means by which the electorate secures the conduct
of the administration according to the will of the
majority, as well as the passing of such legislation as

---

[1] The process of procedure by Bill in the Lords by a private member
in such cases is open to much objection: Keith, *Letters on Imperial Relations, 1916–1935*, pp. 255-7.

appeals to that majority. The weapon of impeachment of ministers or others by the Commons before the Lords is indeed obsolete, and never was satisfactory, but ministers are now in such effective touch with the Commons that its disappearance is immaterial. The constant use of questions and supplementary questions, motions of all sorts, and proposed votes of censure or non-confidence are sufficient to secure that in administration due regard is had to the will of the majority in Parliament, and that little opportunity for complaint is given to the minority. A detailed management of affairs by the Commons is neither aimed at nor desirable, and ministries have never welcomed committees of enquiry into executive matters as opposed to general investigations such as, sufficiently prolonged, may serve to tide over a period of difficulty. Such committees have since 1871 full power to examine witnesses on oath, and the procedure of commitment may be used to enforce this power. The appointment of Parliamentary Committees, however, is often evaded by the appointment of Royal Commissions under the prerogative, as the Honours Commission of 1922, a procedure having the advantage of permitting the association of persons not members of Parliament with members. Power to compel evidence on oath may be given by statute. Or a Tribunal of Inquiry may be set up on resolutions by both Houses, with full powers to obtain evidence given by legislation of 1921, rendering unnecessary such special legislation as that of 1916 for the Dardanelles Commission.

It is seldom, indeed, that the passing of votes of want of confidence is necessary to terminate a minis-

try, though instances occurred in 1841, 1859, 1892,
and 1924. The legal value of such a vote is nil, but
no ministry could defy it without shortly finding
itself unable to carry on the administration by reason
of its discredit in the country and abroad. If it does
not accept the motion and resign, it must secure a dissolution as a last resort. This obviously would be a
wholly unjustifiable proceeding in a newly elected
Parliament; the King could not properly grant a dissolution; and hence it is the rule that a ministry
defeated at the polls resigns, in lieu of meeting Parliament and being formally defeated, provided that there
is available an alternative ministry. Thus in 1929
Mr Baldwin resigned on defeat, but in 1924 he held
office until formally defeated on the opening of Parliament. A mere defeat on some lesser issue in Parliament
involves resignation only when a ministry does not
desire to remain in office, as in 1895, when the reverse
suffered by the Liberal Government on a minor War
Office vote resulted in the disappearance of the Government, because its members were hopelessly at variance,[1]
and the Premier, Lord Rosebery, and the Leader of the
Commons, Sir W. Harcourt, were scarcely friends.
Normally the ministry will in one form or other secure
a vote of confidence after such a *contretemps*, or if
preferred merely ignore it,[2] accepting the vote as
decisive on the issue, as did the Government in 1922,
on several occasions of no real consequence. The posi-

[1] The Secretary for War, Sir H. Campbell-Bannerman, refused to
remain in office in any event.

[2] This is, however, probably an unwise course, due only to weakness
in the Cabinet, as in 1922. Mr Mackenzie King (Canadian House of
Commons, February 12, 1923) strongly opposed a motion deprecating
resignation save on a direct confidence issue.

tion, of course, is different where there is, as in 1924 and 1929–31, minority government; in these circumstances resignation is only necessary on a vital issue, and Mr R. MacDonald's action in 1924 was due in great measure to personal causes.

The resignation of a ministry with an adequate majority in the Commons, because it had no constructive legislative programme to propose, occurred in 1905, but the ministry had been weakened a couple of years earlier by the retirement of five important members, including Mr Chamberlain, on tariff disagreements.

The resignation of the ministry rests ultimately with the Prime Minister; as long as he remains, individual resignations are of minor consequence; with his resignation all ministers merely retain their offices as carrying on routine administration, pending the decision of the new Prime Minister as to filling them. If he is a member of the same party, then, of course, the ministers may be asked to retain, without reappointment, the offices which they hold.[1] In 1931 Mr MacDonald resigned and thus dissolved his Labour ministry; he was then asked to form a new Government, from which most of his former colleagues were omitted.

The power whence ministries derive their compact following and the possibility of their own existence is largely that of party organisations.

Party organisation can only be traced in a few instances prior to the increase of the electorate by the legislation of 1832. That measure rendered it necessary

---

[1] So in June 1935 on Mr MacDonald's resignation, and Mr Baldwin's reconstruction of the National Government.

to secure the registration of voters, and local societies sprung up which undertook this obligation, adding to it canvassing electors, distributing information as to candidates, and inducing electors to proceed to the polls. The necessity of such work was increased by the extension of the electorate in 1867, 1884, and especially in 1918 and 1928. Nomination of candidates only slowly developed, suggested chiefly by the experience at Birmingham of Mr Joseph Chamberlain, who borrowed the caucus idea from the United States. A central association bound together local ward parties, and by its guidance secured all three seats in 1868 for Liberalism. The Act of 1867 produced also the creation of the National Union of Conservatives and Constitutional (now Unionist) Societies, while the National Liberal Federation was brought into being in 1877. Both bodies have had vicissitudes; the Liberal Federation on the whole has always been more democratic in outlook, and, while the Conservative organisation has recognised that the framing of policy is for the leaders of the party, the Liberal Federation in 1891 drew up a Newcastle programme which deeply embarrassed by the richness of its contents the feeble Liberal Government of 1892–5. Recently the Federation has again claimed to prescribe policy, but the enfeebled condition of the party has deprived its claim of much value. Both bodies have, of course, opened their doors to the representation of women, and Scotland is treated as a distinct unit.

The Labour Party, of course, is of much more recent origin. In 1883 the Fabian Society, a bourgeois group, came into being with socialistic views, and the

Social Democratic Federation, founded in 1884, ran unsuccessful candidates for Parliament. In 1893 the Independent Labour Party was called into being by J. Keir Hardie, and sought to dissolve the existing alliance of trade unionism with the Liberal Party. In 1899 the Trade Union Congress was induced to summon a meeting of trade unions and socialistic societies to discuss the formation of a Labour Party, and a Labour Representation Committee came into being in 1900. But it was only after the success of Liberals and Labour at the election of 1906 that a Labour Party became definitely established, and in 1908 it adopted socialism as its creed. In view of the passing of the Representation of the People Act of 1918, the basis of the party was widened by the admission of members as individuals, and the insistence that workers included workers by brain as well as those by hand. The Labour Party thus consists of affiliated organisations, essentially trade unions and socialistic societies, with since 1927 co-operative societies, and individual members who are organised in local labour parties with the members of trade unions and socialist societies. These parties exist side by side with local trades councils, and both are entitled to send a delegate to the annual Labour Conference, at which trade unions and societies are represented according to their numerical strength. The Conference elects the National Executive, thirteen members representing the societies, five local labour parties, four women representatives, and the treasurer *ex officio*. The predominant position of the trade unions is maintained by the fact that they provide much of the organised voting strength and the funds necessary to win elections. The party has a definite creed, formally adopted as *Labour and the Nation* in 1928 by the Conference, The Executive is charged with seeing that each constituency has a party organisation, with which it lies to select a candidate, but he must be approved by the Executive, and he is bound to stand as a Labour candidate only, to stress in his election address the issues picked out by the Executive to be stressed, and to undertake, if elected, to be bound by the party constitution and standing orders. Refusal to accept this obligation has led to the disaffiliation of the Independent Labour Party.

The Labour Party's Central Office is virtually under the control of the National Executive. In the case of the Conservative Party the Central Office is subject directly to the Prime Minister, who appoints a politician of distinction to guide its activities. It has control of the funds contributed—often in return for titles or other material advantages—by leading supporters of the party, and it can withhold recognition of candidates chosen by local associations. To minimise this possibility, in 1935 the National Council of the Union secured the appointment of an Advisory Committee whose function it would be to keep local chairmen and the central authorities in touch, the Government having felt objections to the adoption of candidates opposed to the national policy on India. A joint propaganda was also arranged for the National Government which could be shared by Liberal and Labour supporters of that Government. In the case of the Liberal Party various vicissitudes have marked the head control, in part due to the desirability of securing aid from the campaign fund acquired person-

ally by Mr Lloyd George during the Coalition Government, but the scanty funds available to the party have
now fallen under the final authority of the Federation.

Through the party funds a close control is exercised
on members of the party who are aspirants for Parliamentary honours. An orthodox candidate expects to
have part at least of the cost of an election defrayed
thence, and his loyalty in Parliament is strengthened
by the fact that if he fails in this regard support will
be withheld at the general election. Moreover, this
consideration lends great force to a threat of dissolution as a means of bringing unruly members to
heel. Small as is the salary of the member—maximum
£400—it is to many useful, while Labour members
receive supplements from their trade unions or party
funds. Even if pecuniary considerations have no
weight on an independently minded member, he is
moved by his former pledges, by his desire to obtain
the aid of the Government in passing legislation, by
ambition for office or an honour; he must reckon with
the fact that, if he ceases to be orthodox, the whole
weight of the local organisation will be cast against
him, and often it is effectively prepared for canvassing
the electorate. Such is the general system of organisation both for Liberals and for Conservatives or Unionists. The Labour organisation is complicated by the fact
that the great trade unions supply the greater part of
the funds available for electioneering, and, accordingly,
local organisation is affected by this domination.

With the progress of time the private member's
initiative in legislation, once of first-rate importance,
has been largely diminished; it is the normal practice
of the Government to appropriate by far the largest

part of the time available, leaving him the odd chance of succeeding in the ballot for private members' Bills, and in having a Bill read a second time, with the possibility then that the Government may consent to take it up and find time for its subsequent stages. Further, the Government possesses large powers of defeating opposition to its measures by the use of the closure, it being possible since 1888 for any member to move that the question be now put, when a division takes place, unless the Chair holds that the rights of the minority will thus be infringed. Further, it is possible to move that a clause or part of a clause shall stand part of a Bill, and thus to exclude any amendments without consideration in detail. Since 1887 the "guillotine" closure has been available, under which a definite period is fixed for debate on a Bill. Or the House may fix a time-table by which sections of a Bill are to be finished at specified times, and this closure by compartment in use since 1893 may shut out masses of amendments. Or since 1911 authority to select amendments of a representative character may be given to the Chair, others thus automatically being shut out, the "Kangaroo" closure.

The procedure in public legislation is complex; notice of intention to introduce a Bill must first be given; then leave to introduce must be obtained, and this on controversial topics is sometimes debated; if leave is given, the Bill is presented, and the questions that it be read a first time and be printed are put without debate, and a date fixed for the second reading.[1] At that reading

[1] Minor Bills may be introduced by a minister or a private person in a speech of ten minutes' limit; one speech in reply only is allowed. The Speaker will decline to allow important Bills thus to be dealt with.

the Bill is discussed from the point of view of its general principles, and may be rejected or accepted, and in the latter event instructions may be given to the Committee to introduce ancillary and supplementary matter. The Bill then goes either to a Standing Committee,[1] or to a Select Committee, usually of fifteen members, if it is desired to take evidence on the Bill, or in the important cases to a Committee of the whole House, which is merely the House sitting under the Chairman of Committees. It is there amended if necessary in detail and reported to the House; a fresh discussion can then take place and new amendments be made, while the Bill may be recommitted for further examination, and again reported. When the report stage ends, the Bill goes for third reading, and if passed is sent to the Lords. If no amendments are made in Committee, there is no report stage, and the Bill goes at once for third reading.

A Bill from the Commons is at once read a first time in the Lords, and then, if sponsored by a member of that House, passes through a procedure analogous to that in the Commons. If no changes are made after third reading, concurrence is intimated to the Commons; if changes are made, the Bill goes back to the Commons, who may accept, or agree to reject, the amendments, which then become the subject of interchanges of messages, with reasons, between the Houses,

---

[1] The use of Standing Committees, begun in 1882 and extended in 1907, as the normal fate of Bills is a result of war pressure on Parliamentary time. In this way Scottish Bills are dealt with by a body in which Scottish members preponderate, 10 to 15 others being added, and in which the Government may, as in 1923, be in a minority. At present there are four Committees of 30 to 50 members, to which from 10 to 35 members may be added for any special Bill.

the procedure which has superseded formal or free conferences between the Houses. Bills other than money
Bills may originate in the Lords, when the procedure is
analogous to that followed in the more frequent case of
Bills going from the Commons to the Lords.

Disputes between the two Houses on general legislation are obviously inevitable, and in the nineteenth
century the convention gradually became established
that the Lords should reject or freely amend only such
Bills as excited no popular interest, while on matters
on which the electorate had clearly declared itself, they
must yield to the popular will. The Lords interpreted
this convention as implying that, if they doubted the
will of the people, they could force a dissolution on the
Government or compel the ministry to abandon the
Bill, as they did in 1894–5 when the Liberal Government did not even appeal to the people when the Bill
to confer Home Rule on Ireland was rejected. This
view was not shared by the Commons, and the struggle
came to a head over the resistance of the Lords, reinforced by creations from the ranks of commerce and
finance, lacking in political tact, to both the financial
and general legislation of the Liberal Government of
1905–10, that Government being determined to obtain
the power to overcome the resistance of the Lords to
any Home Rule scheme. Success was attained, as in
1832 over the Reform Bill, only by the promise of the
Crown in 1910 to create sufficient peers to compel the
passage of the Parliament Bill through the Upper
House. The measure provides that if any public Bill,
not being a money Bill or a Bill to extend the duration
of Parliament beyond five years, is passed by the
Commons in three successive sessions, whether in one

Parliament or not, and sent up to the Lords at least one month before the close of the session and is rejected by the Lords, then it shall, after the third rejection, be presented for the royal assent and become an Act, provided that two years elapse between the first second reading in the Commons and the final passage of the Bill there in the third session. A Bill is to be deemed rejected if not passed without amendment, or with agreed amendments only, and a Bill is to be deemed the same if it contains only amendments certified by the Speaker to be necessary through lapse of time or such as in the preceding session were accepted by the Lords, or were made by agreement at the third session. Under this legislation, which secured the enactment of the Welsh Church Act, 1914,[1] and, but for the war, would have been employed to bring the Government of Ireland Act, 1914, into operation despite the Lords, the Upper House has merely suspensory powers, though these are of considerable importance, and the reduction of the duration of Parliament to five years ensures that the electorate shall be masters of the legislature.

The paramount position of the Commons in finance was early asserted, and made perfectly definite in 1678, when it was claimed that aids and supplies were the sole gifts of the Commons, and should not be altered by the Lords. This left the right of rejection intact, but, in 1860, when the Lords rejected Gladstone's proposed repeal of the paper duties, the Commons asserted that it had the right so to frame tax or appropriation measures as to defeat the power of rejection, and in 1861 they exercised this power by including their pro-

---

[1] That the Act has been of great advantage to the Church is not denied.

posals in one Bill which the Lords could not reject. In
1894 they also carried their death duties against the
bitter opposition, largely on personal grounds, of the
Lords to that beneficent and wise measure. In 1909,
however, the Lords refused to yield and to accept the
Finance Bill, largely because it included proposals—
later found unworkable and repealed—for taxation of
land values. A dissolution followed, and the Government, not content with securing its Bills, proceeded
with the permanent deposition of the Lords from
financial power by the Parliament Bill. The passage of
this measure necessitated another appeal at the end of
1910 to the people, and victory then secured the Parliament Act,[1] which provides that, if a money Bill is sent
up to the Lords a month before the close of the session,
and is not passed by them as it stands within a month,
it shall be presented for the royal assent, unless the
House otherwise directs, and shall become an Act
without the concurrence of the Lords. A money Bill
means a Bill which is certified by the Speaker of the
Commons to deal only with the imposition, repeal,
remission, alteration, or regulation of taxation; the
imposition for the payment of debt or other financial
purposes of charges on the consolidated fund, or on
money provided by Parliament, or the variation or
repeal of any such charges; supply; the appropriation,
receipt, custody, issue, or audit of accounts of public
money; the raising or guarantee of any loan or repayment thereof; or subordinate matters incidental to
those subjects or any of them. Taxation and appropriation of local authorities are not covered by the Act. In
certifying that any Bill is a money Bill, the Speaker is

[1] 1 & 2 Geo. V. c. 13.

to consult, if practicable, two members appointed from the panel of Chairmen at the beginning of each session by the Committee of Selection, a body representing in due proportion the various sections of the House; but his certificate either as to a money Bill or the due observance of the rules regarding other Bills is not to be questioned in any court. On several occasions financial measures have not been certified. The exclusion of the Lords from financial control is thus complete; the composition of the House rendered it *ab initio* wholly indefensible.

To create any House whether wholly elected, *e.g.* by proportional representation by the electors or by the members of the Commons, or partly elected and partly nominated, or even in part hereditary, which would satisfy popular opinion generally and be an effective revising chamber, while not opposing the public will, is a problem of the utmost difficulty of solution.[1] The permanent maintenance of the hereditary principle seems utterly impossible of defence in face of the manifest failure of hereditary ability in the community at large, and not least in the peerage, and to defend it on the analogy of the Crown is to ignore the essential fact that the Crown has grown in popular affection precisely

[1] The plan of Lord Bryce's Committee (Cd. 9038) in 1918 was left practically dormant by the Governments of 1918–23, and the suggestions of Lords Birkenhead in 1925 and Cave in 1927 were not pressed. In 1934 Lord Salisbury proposed to reduce hereditary peers to 150 elected by the peerage, to add 150 otherwise selected, retaining the Law Lords and some spiritual lords, 330 in all. This house was to be empowered to delay until a general election a Commons Bill which it was desired to pass by the Parliament Act procedure. In 1935 Lord Rockley proposed to give the Crown power to create 5 life peers a year, and Lord Rankeillour wished to exclude from the Parliament Act Bills affecting the Civil List, the succession, the constitution of either House and their relations. The Government insisted that it had no policy to propose.

in proportion as it has ceased, since George III.'s lack of insight destroyed the first Empire, to seek to assert any hereditary capacity of claim to rule, and has accepted honestly and ably the rôle of acting in all official matters in accordance with the popular will. Far from strengthening, as Lord Birkenhead argued, the position of the monarch, the erratic tactics of the Lords on selfish grounds have rather weakened it than otherwise. The merits of the Lords are derived from the presence in it of many able and experienced politicians whose services would be secured in any satisfactory second chamber.

The Commons, as masters in finance, are careful to safeguard themselves against improvident expenditure; no grant will be voted save on the recommendation of the Crown, that is, of the ministry, though motions may be passed urging on the House expenditure of funds on some specified object, in the hope that thus ministers will be compelled to make definite proposals, and Bills come down from the Lords with italicised clauses as to expenditure, these being strictly merely waste paper. Similarly no taxation can be proposed by any private member. This is the crucial safeguard of Cabinet responsibility. Further, the House considers all matters of supply and ways and means in Committees of the whole House, whose resolutions are reported to, and approved by, the House from time to time. The Committee of Supply decides the amounts to be granted for each service; that of Ways and Means decides how to provide these funds, whether by charges on the consolidated fund created in 1787, into which the proceeds of taxation, much of which is provided for in permanent legislation, automatically go, or by fresh taxes or loans. Legal sanction is given to taxation by taxing Acts, and to appropriations by the Appropriation Act of the session, which is preceded by Ways and Means, or Consolidated Fund Bills, placing certain amounts at the disposal of the Government pending the final appropriation Act. That money is duly spent as voted is secured by the co-operation of the Treasury with the Comptroller and Auditor-General, who holds office independently of the executive, while the public accounts are reviewed *ex post facto* by a Committee of the Commons which animadverts on any errors committed, without producing much impression on the administration. The actual framing of estimates lies with the departments subject to Treasury control, but this has been relaxed of late years, and spasmodic attempts by Cabinet Committees, or by outside bodies appointed *ad hoc*, such as Sir Eric Geddes's Committee in 1921, to cut down the expenditure, have not been very successful. In 1931 drastic economies were effected in the crisis, but mainly by reducing salaries, which were soon restored, and real economy was hardly attempted. That any Parliamentary Committee should be given control over policy in framing estimates is repudiated by the administration, and a committee without any voice in policy seems to find it hard to secure any economies, since their suggestions can always be asserted to involve matters of policy. Moreover, lack of skilled advice hampers useful work, though an Estimates Committee is annually appointed. This is emphasised by the fact that the defence services are among the great sources of expenditure and any economy in them really depends on foreign policy and defence preparations.

Bills of a private character, dealing with naturalisation, divorce, or trust estates, and local Bills covering
an enormous variety of matters of local interest, are
subjected to a special procedure. In this matter the
work is divided between the two Houses in practice.
In both there are rigid standing orders[1] to ensure that
due notice is given to all interested for or against the
proposal; the second reading merely prevents the
further progress of some really objectionable feature,[2]
and the Committee stage is a judicial investigation
of the Bill by four specially selected members, arguments from promoters and opponents being carefully
weighed. Provisional Orders on questions of public
health, transportation, poor relief, finance, etc., and
local legislation for Scotland, under the Private Legislation Procedure (Scotland) Act, 1899 and 1933, are enacted normally on the faith of their being put forward
after full enquiry by a Government department without special scrutiny, but, if opposed, the normal procedure of private Bills is in effect applied, so careful is
Parliament not to ignore local and private interests.

10. *Parliamentary Reform and Governmental Reorganisation*

It is unquestionable that Parliament has ceased to
command the respect which was its share up to the
close of last century. There are many causes of this

---

[1] *House of Commons Standing Orders*, Part II. Cf. Bannington, *English Public Health Administration*, chaps. iii. and iv.

[2] Thus in March 1935 a Bill of the Municipality of Glasgow was rejected because it proposed to set up a municipal bank unnecessarily,
and in any case it was argued a matter of this kind should be dealt with
in a Public Act as a matter of general policy.

untoward feature. Experience shows that Parliament is unable to carry out necessary legislative activity, that many measures fail to be enacted for lack of time, that others are carried by the process of the closure inadequately discussed, and that private members have little chance of securing legislation unless it can be given an attractive character in the interests of some party. Drafting is often faulty; the Housing Acts present an impenetrable jungle. Control over finance is negligible; indeed the House of Commons is always prone to rash expenditure. It appears to better advantage in general control of administration, and in bringing home to the Government popular feeling, as in 1935 when it was the indignation felt without distinction of party in the Commons that secured the hasty cancellation of the scales of assistance laid down by the Unemployment Assistance Board. Again in 1935 its unanimity lent weight to the representations of the Foreign Secretary on his mission after the announcement of the German defiance of the Treaty of Versailles by rearmament, and the creation of an air force.

The decline in the reputation of Parliament is seen in the growing reluctance of men of wealth and position to become members, unless they can be assured at an early date of ministerial rank; the House appeals far less than formerly to the average member, who is not like Labour members a professional politician, interested in his remuneration as a member. In the country the decline in the prestige of Parliament has revealed itself in the efforts to overthrow its authority; in 1920 a Council of Action claimed the right, with the approval of men like Mr J. H. Thomas, to order the

Government to desist from its alleged intention of carrying on hostilities against the Soviet Government; in 1926, after many threats, a general strike was proclaimed by the trade unions with the assent of the Labour Party, though it was defeated by the active hostility of the middle classes and the indifference of the majority of the workers.

It is natural therefore that many projects to restore the prestige of Parliamentary government should have been mooted.

I. Devolution of authority to local units has often been recommended. As regards Scotland such action would be fairly easy, for that country has already its own courts, its own legal system, its own form of local government, and a national tradition. A scheme of a practical kind was adumbrated by a Conference under the Speaker in 1918, and it might have been adapted to Wales, in which education is administered already on specifically Welsh lines. But devolution would be of little advantage to Parliament unless it was extended to England, and it has been suggested to break up England into seven areas [1] (London, Mercia, Wessex, etc.) and to entrust to local authorities therein the charge of matters such as agriculture, education, local government, public health, order, and police. But apart from the difficulty of arranging finance, there is the grave objection that England is so essentially an economic unit that to break it up would be most difficult and probably disadvantageous, and the project has been rendered more difficult by the adoption of the new economic system, for that demands that all internal production, *e.g.* as regards agriculture, should

---

[1] R. Muir, *How Britain is Governed*, pp. 279-306.

be definitely related to control of imports whether by tariff or quota. Moreover, the lack of any real local demand for autonomy is probably an insuperable obstacle to any reform. It is possible that Scotland and Wales should be granted devolution of powers; the demand for some concession is growing in Scotland, where a Nationalist Party has emerged, some of whose members demand Dominion status, others a federal constitution, and others assimilation to Northern Ireland. The success of that experiment in devolution is clear, but it must be admitted that it has been due in part to the extreme generosity with which on political grounds that territory has been treated by the United Kingdom.

Functional devolution has also been advocated. The crudest form contemplates a system of guilds managing great branches of life, subject to the control of a political Parliament; S. and B. Webb have drafted a constitution for a Socialist Commonwealth, based on the functioning side by side of an industrial and a political Parliament, but the impracticability of their proposals is commonly admitted. There is possibly room for action on lines advocated by Mr W. Churchill,[1] the creation of a body which would discuss all governmental economic projects, and have the right to suggest measures to Parliament; but grave difficulties would arise in composing such a body as to represent fairly not merely capital and labour, but also the interests of technicians and consumers, and its proceedings might easily prove unfruitful, as the outcome of the complete divergence between the capitalistic and the socialistic outlook on life, or dangerous to consumers.

[1] *Parliamentary Government and the Economic Problem* (1930).

II. From another point of view proportional repre- sentation[1] is advocated as the necessary antidote to the weakness of Parliament against executive control. On this theory proportional representation would terminate the domination of the Cabinet by ending the régime of large shifting majorities. The two-party system would thus cease to be effective. It is unnatural, being based on the artificial assumption that one set of extreme views or another is held by the electorate, whereas middle courses appeal to many minds. The elections would return members in fair proportion to the views of the electors; Governments would probably have small majorities, or be able to carry on only by arrangements with one or other of the various groups. This would mean the adoption of new conventions; ministries would have to concentrate on measures of appeal beyond their own party group; they would have to accept defeat on minor issues as being without effect on their fate; they could no longer claim a dissolution at their discretion, but should resign so long as it was possible to find another grouping to afford support to another ministry. The opposition in its turn would have to cease merely to oppose, and instead regard its duty as one of co-operation for national ends.

It is clear that the present system tends to secure disproportionate majorities, which fluctuate without any relation to the votes cast, a slight change of view often producing a complete change of ministry. In 1900 the Conservatives obtained a majority of 154, while on the basis of votes it should not have exceeded 16; the Liberals in 1906 had a majority of 354 as against 95;

[1] Muir, *op. cit.* pp. 163-70, 179-96.

in 1918 the Government obtained 52 per cent of the votes, but 472 seats; in 1922 the Conservatives with 38 per cent of the votes secured 347 seats, in 1923 with practically the same votes 257 seats; in 1924 47 per cent of the votes gave 415 seats; in 1929 the Conservatives with 38 per cent of the votes had 253 seats, Labour with 36 per cent 288 seats, and the Liberals with 23 per cent 58 seats. In 1931 the Conservatives obtained 473 seats instead of 270, the Liberals 68 instead of 110, and National Labour 13 instead of 50, while Labour was completely under-represented. This is on the whole dangerous, now that the State is sharply divided between parties which differ essentially on the economic and social bases of the State; the divergencies of former times were consistent with a unity of outlook on the essential necessity of capitalism. Moreover, experience in the Irish Free State[1] proves that this form of proportional representation reduces the violence of party conflict, and secures the presence in the legislature of moderate elements. The complexity of counting votes is irrelevant, and the voter who cannot cast his vote correctly deserves disfranchisement. The objection that the power of the party organisation is increased may be disregarded, for the organisation is already predominant, and it is quite possible that in fact its influence might be lessened, and more place be left for moderate candidates. The difficulty that a candidate is divorced from his electorate as a result of its increased size is of minor weight in regard to urban areas, where a candidate would identify himself with a local division; in country areas—already often too large—there would be more difficulty and the system

[1] N. Mansergh, *The Irish Free State* (1934), pp. 59-73.

could be tried first in urban areas. By-elections offer difficulties, but that is a minor point. The real objection, which so far has prevented any success in the efforts made, as in 1918 and 1930–31, to secure legislation, is the feeling in the Conservative and Labour Parties that the two-party system tells to their advantage, and the reluctance to have weak ministries. But it is not clear that the progress of any country is necessarily best secured by the alternation in power of parties with strongly conflicting ideals, and the exclusion of moderate men from politics.

III. An alternative scheme [1] contemplates the association with the Government departments of advisory Committees made up of members of Parliament. These Committees would be small, not over thirty in number; they would specialise in the problems of the department to which they were attached, review all regulations which it drafted under its statutory powers, consider as part of the legislative process in Committee any Bills promoted on the subjects within their range, and study questions of the execution of the laws and regulations, and the desirability of new measures. On the same plan a Finance Committee would supersede the present procedure in Committee of Ways and Means and of Supply, and might exercise a far more effective control on the preparation of estimates with a view to effect economies within the limits of policy decided upon by the ministry. A drafting committee would deal with all legislation in order to remove needless defects such as are inevitable in the process of enactment; on it might sit experts from outside Parliament as well as members of Parliament. The project has to face the

---

[1] W. I. Jennings, *Parliamentary Reform* (1934), pp. 140-60.

strong hostility felt by ministers of all parties to the idea of being under any form of control in respect of their departmental work, and the objections of departments to the criticism of members of Parliament, especially if they are more or less expert on the matter in hand.

IV. Yet another suggestion involves the use of the referendum.[1] That was stressed in 1910–11 as a possible method of settling disputes between the two houses of Parliament, but was naturally objected to by the Liberal Party as imposing on it an unfair disability, which would not be shared by the Conservative Party through its effective control of the House of Lords. The referendum, however, has also been recommended on general grounds for the decision of great issues which transcend or should transcend party barriers, and the case has been strengthened by arguments of successful use in Switzerland and certain American States. But the project has never commanded much attention. It is clearly most difficult to segregate an issue so as to present the possibility of an intelligent answer at a referendum; a project of the nationalisation of industry could not intelligibly be presented save as a Bill which would be extremely hard to appreciate at its true value. The system also if operative would tend to lessen ministerial sense of responsibility; it would probably also be held to lower rather than rehabilitate the reputation of Parliament and confusion would probably result if a referendum and general election were held together. If the electors rejected referendum proposals of a ministry but returned it to power, it would

[1] For its use in the Dominions, see Keith, *Responsible Government* (2nd ed.), i. 305-7; ii. 690-701.

none the less lack prestige, and the same result would
be reached if it approved the referendum proposals,
but returned an opposition ministry, as happened in
Western Australia in 1934, when the electors voted for
secession from the Commonwealth but gave power to
a Labour Premier who was an avowed opponent of
secession.

V. Another view [1] insists that the reform required
is that of reducing the Cabinet in size, so that its members would be engaged in consideration of fundamental
problems, while execution of policy resolved on by the
Cabinet might be left with departmental ministers. A
suggestion along these lines was made by Lord Haldane,
who was chairman of a Committee charged with considering the possibility of governmental reorganisation
after the war. But the suggestion seems fatally open
to objection. To work out practically the relations of
the Cabinet and the non-Cabinet ministers would be
very hard; the confusion and chaos of the War Cabinet
system might be tolerated in a war, never in peace.
Moreover, the proposal rests on a fundamental lack of
appreciation of the character and capacity of political
leaders. There would be endless difficulty in deciding
who should form the Cabinet; the level of capacity produced by political warfare is not such as to bring into
being seven to ten men [2] markedly superior in general
thinking power to the rest of their colleagues. Moreover, even if the men were there, their colleagues would

[1] Cf. Muir, *op. cit.* pp. 108-15: Prime Minister; Treasury; Imperial
Relations; Defence; Justice and Police; Scottish Office; Industry and
Commerce; Agriculture, Fisheries, Forestry, Water Resources; Social
Services.

[2] The presence of a woman would be demanded, irrespective of real
capacity.

never be persuaded of the fact, and intrigue—bad enough under present conditions—would be intolerable. The patent fact is that with the general level of political capacity a large Cabinet is necessary so that the defects of individuals may become of less gravity to the interests of the State.

11. *Finance*

The revenues of the United Kingdom have been drawn during its history from many sources, and the emphasis has recently been altered by reason of the adoption of a system of protection for manufactures and agriculture alike. In the financial year ending March 31, 1936, it was estimated that from income tax would be received £232,500,000; from surtax levied on incomes over £2000, £51,500,000; from estates duty, £80,000,000, a figure attesting remarkably the love of accumulation of money for the sake of power and prestige; from stamps, levied on a wide variety of transactions, including stock exchange business, £25,000,000; from the old land tax, now largely commuted, £800,000; from excess profits duty and corporation profits tax —two remnants of war taxation—£1,700,000, large sums being hopelessly lost. From customs £188,570,000 was expected; from excise, £106,350,000; from Crown Lands, £1,330,000; from sundry loans, £3,900,000; from miscellaneous sources, £25,970,000; to which must be added the Exchequer share of the motor vehicle duties, £5,000,000, and the net receipt of the Post Office, £11,850,000. The total revenue estimated was £734,470,000.

The estimated expenditure was for interest and man-

agement of the national debt, £224,000,000; payments
to the Northern Ireland Exchequer, including net share
of reserved taxation, £6,750,000; miscellaneous consolidated fund services, £3,700,000; payments to the Post
Office Fund, £1,130,000—making a total of £235,580,000
for consolidated fund services. Defence, including pensions, took £124,250,000; civil votes, £352,979,000, with
£4,000,000 margin for supplementary estimates; tax
collection, £13,161,000, and £4,000,000 for the cost of
the restoration of cuts in pay. There remained over a
surplus of half a million estimated.

In the result of the working of the year ended March
31, 1935, £12,342,768 was saved on interest of debt,
and paid to reduce debt, while an accrued balance of
£7,561,879 was applied to the same purpose.

The revenue of the country is collected under the
control of the Treasury. The three great collecting departments are those of Customs and Excise; the Commissioners of Inland Revenue; and the Post Office. The
payments received by them are normally lodged day
to day with the Bank of England for the credit of the
consolidated fund, or in the case of Northern Ireland
with the Bank of Ireland. The Commissioners of Crown
Lands pay over only net receipts periodically. Other
departments may receive miscellaneous revenues,
which are paid to the cash account of the Paymaster-
General[1] as appropriations in aid.

---

[1] This officer's duties are carried out by the Assistant Paymaster-
General under power of attorney, or written delegation or tradition.
In its present form the office dates from 1848. It either pays or advances
to other officers for payment all moneys for the public service not pro-
vided in the Votes for the Revenue Departments or issued for the
National Debt. In Scotland payments are made by the King's and Lord
Treasurer's Remembrancer, reorganised in 1854.

Of the expenditure of the State part is authorised by permanent Acts, and is described as charged on the consolidated fund, that is, the fund to which all payments on account of the State are credited at the Bank. Such items include the interest, etc., on the public debt, certain payments to Northern Ireland, to the Road Fund and in relief of local taxation, the King's Civil List, the salaries of the Judges, of the Comptroller and Auditor-General, and of a number of less important officers, whose position is due to historical accident rather than principle. Other expenditure must be authorised each year by legislation, and these services are known as "supply services" as opposed to "consolidated fund services".

Payment of the sums authorised by permanent Act takes place under a procedure intended to secure a check on the spending authority. The Lords of the Treasury request the Comptroller and Auditor-General to give them a credit on the Exchequer account (*i.e.* the Consolidated Fund Account) at the Bank. The Comptroller must then satisfy himself that authority exists, and if so satisfied gives the credit. The Treasury then, and then only, can require the Bank to transfer the amount needed for the purpose in hand from the Exchequer account to that of a principal accountant, usually the Paymaster-General, but the Banks of England and Ireland pay direct interest on the public debt. The Bank sends to the Comptroller the authority for the transfer, so that he can record the issues. Ultimately he is furnished with a full account for examination, the Consolidated Fund Account.

In the case of supply services the estimates as mentioned above are prepared from October of the preceding year, and are adjusted with the Treasury by the department concerned, which is usually in close touch with that body. The essential principles of military, air, and naval expenditure, however, are decided by the Cabinet, which can use the Imperial Defence Committee; the Treasury as such is concerned only with details. In case of conflict with other departments the Cabinet again may have to decide; recent regulations have secured that the Cabinet shall not be allowed to commit itself to approve policies involving expenditure without the issue being first reported on by the Treasury. When the estimates are agreed upon they are submitted to the Commons in heads, styled votes, by the Treasury for the Civil and Revenue departments, by each defence department for itself, examined in Committee of Supply, and provided for in Committee of Ways and Means by resolutions reported to and approved by the House. When some votes [1] have been discussed, a Consolidated Fund Bill is presented and passed. It gives power to expend sums on a few large votes in the case of the defence services, and for each civil department or revenue department vote. The reason for the difference of treatment is that the defence departments are authorised to use sums on one vote to provide for others for the time being. Eventually an Appropriation Act is passed at the close of the session which sets out all the votes approved, appropriates them, and provides for their payment from the consolidated fund, authorising any necessary temporary borrowing.

The Appropriation Act, however, has other functions

---

[1] There are 15 for War, 15 for the Navy, 11 for Air, 127 for the Civil departments and the Revenue.

to perform. As it is passed about the end of July, it may well happen that it proves necessary to have supplementary expenditure provided for before the end of the financial year on March 31, and for that purpose a Consolidated Fund Act will be passed before the close of the year. The formal appropriation of the amounts so provided for will then be included in the Appropriation Act of the following year. Further, after the close of a year it may prove that excesses have been incurred on Civil department votes, and it is necessary that these excesses should be approved in the Appropriation Act. This is preceded by examination of the excesses by the Public Accounts Committee, which recommends that a vote be taken, and included in a Consolidated Fund Act. As the Committee deals with the accounts only about a year after the close of the year in which the excess was incurred, the Appropriation Act which approves them is the Act not of the following year but of the next year but one; thus the Act of 1934 approves excesses for the year 1932–3. In the case of defence votes the Act authorises the use of surpluses, arising on any vote through extra appropriations in aid or under-spending, with the sanction of the Treasury to meet deficiencies in appropriations in aid under another vote in the same department or to provide for some urgent new expenditure. But the action of the Treasury under this power must be submitted to Parliament with the appropriation accounts of the year in order that Parliamentary sanction may be accorded, and the Appropriation Act accords such approval for action taken in respect of the year preceding.

The Act also appropriates all sums which under the

Public Accounts and Charges Act, 1891, are paid to departments as appropriations in aid, thus securing due control over the disposal of these sums.

The mode of expenditure of the moneys provided by Parliament is elaborate. A royal order countersigned by two Lords of the Treasury recites the grant and requires the Treasury to authorise the Bank of England to make payments from time to time in accordance with the terms of the grant. The Treasury then obtains from the Comptroller and Auditor-General credit for the sums required upon the Exchequer account at the Bank of England. It then directs the Bank from time to time to transfer sums to the supply account[1] of the Paymaster-General—in the case of the Revenue departments to their accounts at the Bank of England—and to communicate the transfers to the Comptroller. The departments are notified by the Treasury of the sums placed at their disposal and they then dispose of them subject to the control of the Comptroller and Auditor-General.

The control of expenditure is carried out by the Comptroller and Auditor-General. He receives daily from the Banks accounts of receipts and issues of the consolidated fund, and reports from the Revenue departments of their payments. In the larger departments he has a local audit staff which audits concurrently expenditure, and in the lesser departments he has a periodic audit.

The Civil departments by November 30, and the defence departments by December 31, prepare appro-

---

[1] Also called Exchequer Credit Account; this with the cash account into which appropriations in aid are paid constitutes the Paymaster-General's accounts for supply of credit.

priation accounts showing their expenditure, and these the Comptroller and Auditor-General audits, to see if the sums paid out are properly classified under the appropriate heads; if they are duly vouched for by receipts; if they are duly authorised, and if any Acts of Parliament, Orders in Council, royal warrants or other regulations have been complied with or new appointments made or salaries altered without Treasury sanction. He calls attention in his report to any irregularity or expenditure not properly authorised. There is, of course, great difficulty in regard to cases where expenditure cannot be said to be illegal, but where extravagance seems possible. Observations on such topics and on trading accounts may be made by the Comptroller and Auditor-General, but it must be admitted that the national accounts are not so prepared as to allow of effective criticism based on accurate costing. Many suggestions for improving the mode of drawing up the accounts have been made, but with little result.

The accounts cannot be presented to Parliament until February in the year following, *e.g.* in February 1935 for the accounts of 1933–4. They are then examined by the Public Accounts Committee, which may be presided over by the Opposition member who has been Parliamentary Secretary to the Treasury. The Committee can question officers and enjoys the aid of the Comptroller and Auditor-General and the Treasury. Its reports are considered by the Treasury, which normally uses its advice to strengthen the system of control; where it differs, it explains its reasons and may induce the Committee next year to modify its views. Parliament itself treats the reports of the Committee with indifference, born of the reluctance of any member

of Parliament to economise. Efforts to insist on dis- Chapter
I.
cussions of the Committee's reports have failed to
achieve success.

The Comptroller and Auditor-General examines also
and reports on the consolidated fund accounts, and the
Treasury presents in June to Parliament finance accounts which show the receipts and issues for both
consolidated fund and supply services for the preceding
financial year.

In order to meet emergencies the Treasury has at its
disposal a Civil Contingencies Fund of defined amount
(£1,500,000), whence it can advance sums urgently required for unexpected services.[1] These sums must be
repaid in the following year by the departments which
have received advances, when provision has been made
by Parliament. The Treasury also has a Treasury Chest
Fund (£700,000–£1,000,000) available from which it
makes advances to sub-accountants of the defence and
Civil services overseas. These advances are reclaimed
from the departments according as money is voted by
Parliament, and the Treasury renders an account at
the close of the year to the Comptroller and Auditor-
General.

Collectors of revenue are authorised within certain
limits to make payment in their districts out of the
revenue received, either for departmental expenses or
for the service of other departments, in order to save
needless transit of funds. These advances are repaid
by the departments and credited to the consolidated
fund.

The national accounts are kept on a cash basis, so

---

[1] *E.g.* the purchase of the *Codex Sinaiticus*, in 1934; *H.C. Pap.*
No. 39 of 1935.

that receipts are credited to the year in which they were paid, though due in respect of an earlier period, and expenditure is charged against the revenue of the year of payment, regardless of the year in which it was incurred. Any surplus of revenue over expenditure—unless special provision is made—goes to pay off debt, and grants all lapse at the close of the year for which they are made. Special conditions, however, apply to certain funds. The Road Fund receives the proceeds of motor vehicle licences, less a contribution to the State, and borrowing has taken place on the security of its anticipated receipts, expenditure on roads—£26,500,000 in 1935-6—being defrayed from its resources. This permits of an ordered programme, but is open to criticism on the ground that expenditure should be varied according to national needs, and a source of income such as motor-vehicle duties should not be pledged mainly to meet the interests of road users.

Unemployment insurance is provided for by the creation of a fund contributed to by the State, the employer, and the employed. Under the Unemployment Act of 1934 it is controlled by a body known as the Unemployment Insurance Statutory Committee, subject to the Minister of Labour and Parliament. Its duty is so to adjust contributions as to maintain solvency and the gradual extinction of the debt which had been incurred by the fund during the period of reckless finance prior to 1931, when borrowing for the fund raised doubts of the ultimate solvency of the Exchequer. There is also an Unemployment Assistance Fund administered under the minister by an Unemployment Assistance Board; its initial proceedings raised strong Parliamentary protests and involved

legislation postponing the operation of new rates of
assistance, pending fresh examination of the issue.

Of abnormal character is the Exchange Equalisation
Fund created under the Finance Act, 1932, under which
the Treasury has unfettered disposal, unquestioned by
Parliament, of large sums, to use them to prevent
extreme variations of exchange.

The National Debt on an organised basis dates from
the establishment of the Bank of England in 1694,
when it lent £1,200,000 to the State at 8 per cent. It
was never repaid, and wars steadily increased its
amount until at the close of the Seven Years' War it
reached £146,000,000. The War of American Independence added £121,000,000; those of the French Revolution, during which British finance was conducted
with deplorable indifference to the public welfare and
enormous profits to the ruling classes, £601,000,000,
added to by the absurd sinking fund of £1,000,000
devised by the younger Pitt. Efforts from 1829 were
made to diminish the debt from surplus revenue, and
in 1875 Sir Stafford Northcote devised the new sinking
fund, consisting of the balance over of the annual
charge after providing for interest and cost of management; the sum thus provided has become of great importance of recent years through the prevalence of
unexpectedly low rates of interest. The old sinking
fund of 1829 is any balance on the year's accounts
which Parliament determines shall be devoted to paying off debt. The reduction of debt was arrested by
the Boer War, but by 1914 it was brought down to
£708,000,000, only to increase enormously owing to the
vast cost of the Great War, and to the large sums lent
to allied powers, the Dominions, etc. Calculation of

the exact amount is difficult, but the Treasury version gives the National Debt as £7,800,565,000 on March 31, 1935, a reduction since March 31, 1934, of £21,733,060. It is now classified as (1) permanent funded debt, the result of Goschen's conversion scheme, which created $2\frac{1}{2}$ per cent consols; (2) terminable annuities; and (3) short-term unfunded debt. In addition to the sinking funds already referred to, there are a number of specific sinking funds, but provision for these has not been regularly maintained of late years.[1] Moreover, payment for death duties may be made in securities under the War Loan Act, 1919. A National Debt Redemption Fund was created by a private donor of £500,000 in 1927 with a view to the accumulation of a sum to relieve posterity; it has received singularly little encouragement since. The management of the National Debt for the Government is undertaken by the National Debt Office,[2] which is under the control of Commissioners, high officers of State, including the Chancellor of the Exchequer, who virtually exercises control, and the Governor and Deputy-Governor of the Bank of England.

12. *Defence*

The question of defence is rendered supremely difficult for the United Kingdom because, while the Dominions are concerned only with their own defence, the British Government regards itself still as bound to make provision for the defence from foreign aggression of the whole of the Empire. Primarily reliance used

---

[1] Cf. Mr N. Chamberlain, House of Commons, April 15, 1935.

[2] Established under 26 Geo. III. c. 31. The Public Works Loan Board, created in 1817 to advance money to local authorities, is also independent of the Treasury, but acts under general rules laid down by it.

to be placed on the employment of the British navy, which in peace-time served also the valuable function of displaying the British flag abroad. Even now, despite the rise to importance of the air arm, the supremacy of the navy is not yet obsolete. The army is charged with the duties of providing and maintaining garrisons both in the United Kingdom and in the network of Imperial military stations, which, in conjunction with the fleet, provide for effective defence, and of which India makes by far the greatest numerical drain on British resources; at the same time it is required to provide a small, but mobile and highly qualified expeditionary force which can be sent abroad if hostilities break out, while it must be so organised as to allow of effective expansion with the least delay in the event of a great European conflagration. The Air Force is not merely essential for home defence and reprisals against attack by a hostile power, but it has proved possible in places such as Iraq, Somaliland, the Sudan, or the North-West Frontier of India, to maintain order at less cost in men and money than when infantry are employed. The problem of Imperial defence has been vitally affected by the restrictions placed on German armaments by the Treaty of Peace, now abrogated, and by the limitation of naval armaments in certain respects by the Treaties of Washington and of London, while the readiness of the Imperial Government to consider limitations of air forces by convention has been expressed.

The Bill of Rights expressly declares that the maintenance of a standing army in time of peace without the consent of Parliament is illegal; the old feudal and national forces have been obsolete since the Civil

War; moreover, the common law does not recognise any power to maintain discipline in an illegal force, and the Crown has no funds with which to pay an army. The maintenance of troops, therefore, involves annual application to Parliament for a code of rules, the Army and Air Force (Annual) Act, for authority to maintain a specific number of men, and for funds to pay them. The number specified cannot be exceeded, but the forces detached from the British army and serving in India are not included, and, though they could not be employed in the United Kingdom without statutory sanction, they can be used elsewhere.[1] But under Section 22 of the Government of India Act, the revenues of India could not be employed, save in urgent necessity, on military operations beyond the frontier save with the assent of Parliament, so that when such forces were used Parliament must find the money or authorise it being found by India, and under the new federal system the rule will apply. Save during the war of 1914–18 enlistment was, and is, voluntary; an officer holds during pleasure, but may not resign his commission without sanction;[2] a soldier enlists for a definite period, but may sooner be discharged by the Crown, or permitted to purchase his discharge. He serves for a time in the active army, then completes his service in the army reserve. In 1934 there were at home 110,089, in India 57,565, Bermuda and Jamaica 1070, Gibraltar 2608, Malta 3276, Egypt 10,001, Sudan 1686, Palestine 1967, Malaya 2322, China 7472, other stations 779. The reserve numbered 124,500,

---

[1] See below, Chap. XI. s. 15.

[2] *Cuming, Ex parte* (1887), 19 Q.B.D. 13 (naval officer); *Vertue* v. *Lord Clive* (1769), 4 Burr. 2472; *Hearson* v. *Churchill*, [1892] 2 Q.B. 144.

with a supplementary reserve of skilled workers, 17,500.
The Air Force, which was essentially as an independent
body a creation of the war, is subject under the Air
Force Act in essentials to the same position as the
military forces of the Crown. Units are maintained in
India, Iraq, Egypt, Palestine and Trans-Jordan, Aden,
and Singapore; part serves as the fleet air arm. Behind
the small regular army with its multifarious duties,
there is the Territorial Army, in 1934 136,000, also
voluntarily recruited, but unlike the pre-war militia or
volunteers, undertaking obligation for foreign service
in the event of war. Reserves provide for immediate
expansion of the army on the outbreak of war, but
only on a modest scale.

The naval forces have never been the object of
jealousy, and impressment of seafaring men under
common law was permitted and formerly practised.[1]
But for funds annual application is needed to Parliament, while discipline is provided for by Naval
Discipline Acts. There is a Home fleet and fleets in
the Mediterranean, China, America and West Indies,
East Indies, and Africa; reserves are supplied by the
Royal Naval Reserve and Volunteer Reserve. The
cost for 1935–6 is estimated at £62,915,380.

Both soldiers and sailors are subjected to a more
elaborate code of law than civilians; the criminal law
is applicable to them wherever they are serving, and
can be administered by courts-martial, though not so
as to oust the jurisdiction of the civil courts.[2] They

---

[1] *Broadfoot's Case* (1743), Foster, 154.

[2] The gravest crimes (treason, murder, manslaughter, rape) can in
the United Kingdom only be tried by a civil court; overseas they can
be tried on active service or if the nearest city for trial is over a hundred
miles away.

2 A

are subject also to pains and penalties peculiar to themselves, and administered by courts-martial. The civil courts, however, have power to control these courts if they attempt to deal with civilians, or if they deal with persons subject to military law, but exceed their jurisdiction, or fail to observe the due forms.[1] On the other hand, even if the courts, when they have jurisdiction, act on accusations made without reasonable ground or even maliciously, no redress against those responsible can be given by civil courts.[2] To prevent miscarriages of justice, military and air force judgments by courts-martial fall to be confirmed before execution and are scrutinised by the Judge-Advocate-General and his assistants on this score. In the case of the navy, the Lords of the Admiralty may disapprove acquittals[3] and mitigate punishments.

The control of the forces is ultimately vested in the Lords Commissioners of the Admiralty, the Army Council, and the Air Council, all bodies constructed on the basis of having at their heads a minister responsible finally to Parliament, and technical advisers, combative and civil, though the exact nature of the functions of these members and the personnel have been frequently varied of late. The Army

---

[1] Cf. *Heddon* v. *Evans* (1919), 35 T.L.R. 642; *Warden* v. *Bailey* (1811), 4 Taunt. 67. The court will not interfere because evidence is wrongly rejected or law misinterpreted: *R.* v. *Murphy*, [1921] 2 I.R. 190.

[2] See *Dawkins* v. *Lord Rokeby* (1875), L.R. 7 H.L. 744; *Fraser* v. *Hamilton* (1917), 33 T.L.R. 431; *Fraser* v. *Balfour* (1919), 34 T.L.R. (H.L.) 502; *Sutton* v. *Johnstone* (1786), 1 T.R. 541.

[3] As in the case of Rear-Admiral Bailey and Captain Tower, see House of Commons Debates, March 21, 1935. Precedents of 1862 and 1893 approved by Lord Palmerston and Mr Asquith were adduced by Sir B. Eyres-Monsell.

Council comprises the Secretary of State, the Parliamentary Under-Secretary, the Chief of the Imperial
General Staff, Adjutant-General, Quartermaster-
General, Master-General of the Ordnance, Financial
Secretary, and the Permanent Under-Secretary, who
is Secretary of the Council. The Air Council includes
the Secretary of State, the Under-Secretary, Chief
of the Air Staff, Air Member for Personnel, Air
Member for Supply and Research, and, since 1935,
Air Member for Organisation, and the Secretary of
the Council. The obvious advantages[1] of creating a
single ministry of defence, with subordinate ministers
for the three branches of the service, has been recognised, but the jealousies of the different arms renders
the task a very difficult one. Efforts to suppress the
individuality of the air service have been frustrated,
though, when either military or naval operations are
being undertaken, the air service is to act in subordination. In defence from aircraft it is to be the
primary arm and to be aided by the sister services, and
in attacks on enemy harbours or inland towns or in
commerce protection the arms are to co-operate. It is
in special the business of the Committee of Imperial
Defence and its sub-committees to endeavour to
secure that the funds of the country are not—as is
sometimes the case—needlessly expended in duplication of defence, and in competition among the services
for men and material.

The strength and expenditure on the army and naval
and air forces[2] are inevitably decided in the ultimate

---

[1] Cf. House of Lords Debates, May 15, 1935.

[2] In 1935 considerable increases in defence expenditure were announced as essential in order to induce respect in Europe for British
capacity to act as a factor in securing peace. See *Parl. Pap.* Cmd. 4827.

issue by the Cabinet, after they have given the fullest consideration to the views urged by the technical members of the boards in every case. These members are under no obligation to surrender their views to those of their Parliamentary chief, and when overruled they are entitled to remain in office and carry out the governmental programme without loss of honour, though, of course, they may feel it incumbent on them to resign if reductions of excessive amount are ordered, but this contretemps is extremely rare; an officer who feels dissatisfied can usually arrange to be allocated to some other work, relieving him of any responsibility for general preparations. Ever-increasing importance has been laid recently on the work of the War Staffs in each department in preparing schemes for effective offensive and defensive in war.

Since 1923 the rule has been laid down regarding the Imperial Defence Committee that, while the Committee continues to consist of the Prime Minister and such persons as he thinks fit to summon, membership should normally be enjoyed by the Secretaries of State for War, Air, Foreign Affairs, the Dominions, the Colonies, and India, the First Lord of the Admiralty, the Chancellor of the Exchequer or the Financial Secretary to the Treasury, the three Chiefs of Staff, and the Permanent Secretary to the Treasury, while other British or Dominion ministers or officials or experts might be summoned as the occasion demanded, and a Chairman might as deputy of the Prime Minister be

The total was: Army, £35,267,000; Navy, £50,542,000; Air Force, £20,245,000. On May 22 the Government intimated that in two years the air force would be increased from 1020 to 2000 machines (1500 for home defence), involving an addition of 22,500 men and much expenditure.

a permanent member.[1] The Prime Minister reports to the Cabinet the recommendations of the Committee, interprets to the departments the decisions of the Cabinet, and, aided by the Chiefs of Staff, keeps the defence situation as a whole constantly under review so as to ensure that defence preparations and plans and the expenditure thereupon are co-ordinated and framed to meet policy, that full information as to the changing naval, military, and air situation shall always be available to the Committee, and that resolutions for the requisite action thereupon may be submitted for its consideration. In addition to their functions as advisers to their own Boards or Council, the three Chiefs of Staff are made individually and collectively responsible for advising on defence policy as a whole, the three constituting, as it were, the super-chief of a War Staff in Commission, and meeting together to discuss questions which affect their joint responsibilities. Questions relating to the co-ordination of expenditure may be considered by the Committee on reference by the Cabinet, and the Committee will consider such questions in the light of the general defence policy of the Government, and the strategical plans drawn up to give effect to the policy in time of war.[2]

13. *The Judicature and the Laws*

Since 1881, under the Judicature Acts of 1873 and 1875, consolidated in 1925, the Supreme Court of Judicature has consisted of a High Court of Justice,

---

[1] This project was not adopted in 1923–35. It has been suggested as an alternative to a single Minister of Defence.

[2] See *Parl. Pap.* Cmd. 1938.

with original civil and criminal jurisdiction and appellate jurisdiction from inferior courts, and the Court of Appeal with appellate jurisdiction from the High Court, and in certain classes of cases from inferior courts, expecially the County Courts. The High Court is divided into three divisions, King's Bench, in which are merged the old Exchequer and Common Pleas, Chancery, and Probate, Divorce, and Admiralty, but law is no longer different according to the court in which it is administered; statutory provisions define which body of law is to prevail in certain cases, and generally equity supersedes common law in case of conflict. The Lord Chancellor presides in the Chancery division with six judges, the Lord Chief-Justice in the King's Bench with nineteen judges, and a President in the small division of Probate, Divorce, and Admiralty with two judges. The Court of Appeal consists of the Master of the Rolls and five Lords Justices. All puisne judges of the High Court are appointed on the Chancellor's recommendation by the Crown by letters patent, and hold office for life during good behaviour, subject to removal on addresses from both houses of Parliament to the Crown. Commissioners representing the High Court go on circuit for civil and criminal business.

Inferior civil jurisdiction, gradually extended of recent years, is exercised by County Court judges subject to appeal to the Court of Appeal. Inferior criminal jurisdiction is exercised in the counties by justices of the peace, at least two in number at petty sessions in minor cases, an appeal by way of re-hearing lying to the justices at Quarter-Sessions, or by a stated case to the High Court; in certain small offences one justice acts. More serious cases are dealt with by Quarter-Sessions,

where offences are tried with a jury on indictment,
subject to appeal by case stated to the High Court.
In boroughs of importance Quarter-Sessions are held
by a Recorder, a paid magistrate, while in London
stipendiary magistrates exercise a jurisdiction analogous to that of petty sessions, and so in less degree
elsewhere. These magistrates are appointed by and can
be removed by the Crown on the advice of the Home
Secretary, while justices of the peace are appointed and
removed on the advice of the Lord Chancellor, who
consults the Lords-Lieutenant of the counties, who in
turn consult advisory committees in order to secure a
fair distribution. But the more important criminal cases
must be tried before a Commissioner or a judge of the
High Court. Originally no appeal was allowed from
criminal cases decided by the verdict of a jury, but
appeal now lies to a Court of Criminal Appeal, both as
regards conviction and sentence, on certain conditions.

The courts of Northern Ireland, as regards superior
jurisdiction, resemble those of England. In Scotland
the supreme original and appellate civil jurisdiction
belongs to the Court of Session, whose Outer and Inner
Houses correspond roughly to the High Court and
Court of Appeal; criminal jurisdiction rests with the
High Court of Justiciary. Inferior criminal and civil
jurisdiction is exercised by the Sheriffs Principal and
Substitute, and there are minor courts of justices of the
peace. The judges are appointed by the Crown on the
recommendation of the Lord Advocate, and hold office
on the same tenure as in England; the position of the
Sheriffs is analogous, but the removal may be more
simply effected.

As a final Court of Appeal from the English Court of

Appeal and the Court of Session, and from the Irish
Court of Appeal for Northern Ireland, there is the
House of Lords, which, when sitting for judicial business, must contain at least three Lords of Appeal. This
definition covers the Lord Chancellor, the seven Lords
of Appeal in Ordinary, and any peer who has held high
judicial office, *i.e.* the Lord Chancellorship of Great
Britain or Ireland or a judgeship. The proceedings are
part of the ordinary business of the House; the decision
is based on a motion, and dissenting views are therefore expressed; it takes the form of an order, while the
Judicial Committee of the Privy Council must pro-
nounce a single opinion, which takes the form of advice
to the Crown, carried into effect by an Order in Council.
The House of Lords is bound by its own decisions,[1] and
these are binding on all lower courts, as are the judgments of the Court of Appeal. The House has normally
no appellate criminal jurisdiction, but an appeal lies
from the Court of Criminal Appeal on the granting of
permission by the Attorney-General only; such permission has only in 1919 and 1935 been accorded.[2] It
possesses, however, jurisdiction in all cases of treason
and felony over peers; in session it is presided over by
the Lord High Steward, appointed *pro hac vice* by the
Crown, and all the peers who attend are judges; out of

---

[1] *London Street Tramways Co.* v. *London County Council*, [1898] A.C.
375. Contrast for the Privy Council's right to review a decision, *Transferred Civil Servants (Ireland) Compensation, In re*, [1929] A.C. 242.

[2] Both cases of murder, the first involving the question of the effect
of intoxication on criminal intent, the second the onus of proof. The
Court of Appeal's views on criminal law do not bind the Court of Criminal
Appeal: see *R.* v. *Denyer*, [1926] 2 K.B. 258 (C.C.A.), and *Hardie and
Lane* v. *Chilton* (No. 2), [1928] 2 K.B. 306; Hewart, L.C.J. 20 Cr. App.
Rep. at pp. 185, 186. For divergence of view with the Privy Council see
Keith, *Journ. Comp. Leg.* xvi. 133, 134.

session he presides as judge, settles all points of law,
and the other peers act as jurors.

In certain classes of cases issues which are of a
technical character are disposed of by specialised
courts of law. Thus appeals against Inland Revenue
valuations are heard by referees appointed by the
Lord Chief Justice, the Master of the Rolls, and the
President of the Surveyors' Institution, and disputes
as to compensation for land compulsorily acquired by
a public authority are determined by an arbitrator
appointed by these authorities. Questions affecting
railways and canals were dealt with from 1854 to 1873
by the Court of Common Pleas, but it was found more
satisfactory to have a court with technical qualifications, and the present Railway and Canal Commission
is composed of a High Court judge and two experts
chosen by the Home Secretary; the court deals with
questions of facilities and through traffic, and more
recently with questions of working facilities in mines
and important questions affecting amalgamations.
Appeal lies from its decisions only on points of law to
the Court of Appeal. Questions of railway rates are
assigned to the Railway Rates Tribunal, consisting of
three experts, one appointed by the Lord Chancellor,
one by the Board of Trade, and one by the Ministry
of Transport. Appeal lies on points of law to the Court
of Appeal. Income-tax appeals are dealt with by the
Special Commissioners, appointed by the Treasury,
who are Government officials, but they can be required to state a point of law for the opinion of the
High Court, and stand in high repute for competence
and impartiality. The Treasury appoints also the
Board of Referees to whom certain income-tax points

go; they are professional and business men sitting under a King's Counsel. The Chief Registrar of Friendly Societies is given a considerable number of judicial functions and may order the dissolution of a society.

The law of England and Wales is the common law, *i.e.* the system evolved by the judges of the King's Courts from the conflict of local custom, as deeply and radically modified by statute, and regulations made under statute, and by judicial interpretation. Scotland stands in like case, but its common law differs greatly from that of England, being far more deeply affected by the civil law; there has been a substantial assimilation of the law of contract, of torts, and criminal law, while there are many differences as regards the law of real and personal property, testamentary law, intestate succession, and matrimonial relations, especially on the constitution of marriage and divorce. Northern Ireland has the English common law deeply modified by statute, but otherwise closely in accord with English law.

CHAPTER II

NORTHERN IRELAND, THE CHANNEL ISLANDS, AND
THE ISLE OF MAN

1. *Northern Ireland*

NORTHERN IRELAND, the Channel Islands, and the Chapter II.
Isle of Man, each with distinctive constitutional
features of its own, agree in being subject to the undisputed legislative supremacy of the Imperial Parliament within such limits as it chooses to impose on its
own activity in regard to them. Northern Ireland,
however, stands in a much more immediate relation
to that Parliament than the island territories, whose
insignificance in any material sense renders it a matter
of indifference that they should exercise a considerable
measure of independence.

Northern Ireland owes its existence to the Government of Ireland Act, 1920,[1] the effect of which, as
regards that territory, has been preserved intact
under the arrangements for the creation of the Irish
Free State, as a result of the decision of the Northern
Parliament to remain in close connection with the
Imperial Parliament in lieu of falling under the
supreme control of the Free State. The Parliament
of Northern Ireland is essentially a subordinate legis-

---

[1] See also the Irish Free State (Consequential Provisions) Act, 1922;
the Ireland (Confirmation of Agreement) Act, 1925; the Northern Ireland
(Miscellaneous Provisions) Acts, 1928 and 1932.

lature, and stands in no true federal relation to that of the United Kingdom, for the latter retains undiminished its authority over Northern Ireland, and in so far as it refrains from legislating on matters within the province of the local Parliament, it does so in virtue merely of a constitutional understanding that it is idle to create a legislature and then interfere with it. But the power to override is clear, and no Imperial Act can be questioned because it infringes directly or indirectly a topic dealt with by Irish legislation.

The power of legislation of the Northern Parliament is strictly limited both in area and subject matter. It can deal only with matters relating exclusively to the area allotted to it, the counties of Antrim, Armagh, Down, Fermanagh, Londonderry, and Tyrone, and the boroughs of Belfast and Londonderry, or some portion thereof. It may not legislate regarding (1) the Crown, the succession, the regency, Crown property, or the Governor, save as regards the exercise of his executive power in relation to Irish services; (2) peace or war or matters arising from a state of war, or the observance of neutrality; (3) naval, military, or air forces of any kind; (4) treaties, relations with foreign States or other parts of the King's dominions, extradition, and fugitive offenders rendition; (5) titles of honour; (6) treason, naturalisation, alienage, aliens as such, or domicile; (7) foreign trade, export bounties, navigation, and quarantine; (8) submarine cables; (9) wireless telegraphy; (10) aerial navigation; (11) lighthouses, buoys, or beacons; (12) coinage, negotiable instruments, legal tender, and weights and measures; (13) trade marks, designs, copyrights, or patents; and (14) temporarily certain reserved matters. The severity of these restrictions is a little modified by the rule that the Parliament may indirectly affect foreign trade by powers of taxation generally, or by measures to exclude contagious disease, or regulate harbours and inland waters; it may regulate booking of cinematograph films. The most drastic prohibition is imposed on any legislation endowing religion, hindering its free exercise, giving preference or imposing disabilities in regard of religious belief or status, affecting prejudicially the right of education without receiving religious instruction, interfering with religious property, or taking any property whatever without compensation. The Parliament may repeal Imperial Acts and regulations dealing with topics not excluded from its scope, if passed before it came into being, but not such enactments passed thereafter. The financial legislation of the Parliament is limited by the exclusion of customs duties, excise, profits tax, and save to a limited extent income tax, and elaborate arrangements were made for the determination by a Joint Exchequer Board of the Irish share of the revenues reserved and for the payment of a contribution to Imperial expenditure by Northern Ireland. In fact the Colwyn Committee advised the adoption of a principle which has relieved Northern Ireland from any substantial payment.[1] There are also excluded postal services, post office and trustee savings banks, designs of stamps, deed registration and public records, while to the Council of Ireland were reserved private Bill legislation for matters affecting both parts of Ireland, fisheries, contagious diseases of animals,

---

[1] Quekett, *Constitution of Northern Ireland*, i. 48-50; *Parl. Pap.* Cmd. 2389.

and railways common to both parts of the country. The Council, proposed as a means of furthering Irish unity, was to be composed of a President, nominated by the Lord-Lieutenant, and forty members, twenty for each part of Ireland, those from Northern Ireland being elected by the two houses of Parliament, to the number of seven and thirteen respectively. The Council, however, never became operative, and the powers mentioned passed in 1925 to Northern Ireland. Land purchase remained within Imperial control.

The executive powers of Northern Ireland are co-extensive with the legislative powers, and are vested in the King, who may delegate them to the Lord-Lieutenant, for whom, under the legislation of 1922, a Governor is substituted, or other officer. In the exercise of his powers the Governor acts on the advice of ministers, whether heads of departments or not, constituting an Executive Committee of the Privy Council for Northern Ireland. No minister can retain that position for more than six months unless he becomes a member of Parliament. The position of the Governor as regards the executive government is analogous to that of the Crown in the United Kingdom. He has a conditional delegation of the prerogative of mercy under Instructions, December 9, 1922.

In his capacity as part of the legislature the Governor summons, prorogues, and dissolves Parliament, subject to the rule of annual Parliaments, and a maximum duration of five years for the House of Commons. In regard to Bills he is under the obligation of giving or withholding assent according to his instructions from the Imperial Government,[1] and, if so

---

[1] Represented by the Secretary of State for Home Affairs.

instructed, he must reserve any Bill, which will then
lapse, unless assented to within a year. The control
over legislation thus given is analogous to that exercised in Canada by the Dominion over the provinces,
and is intended to be effectual. In other cases the Governor will clearly have no discretion save to assent.[1]

The Senate is composed of the Lord Mayor of Belfast,
and the Mayor of Londonderry *ex officio*, and twenty-
four Senators elected by the House of Commons, on
the principle of proportional representation with the
single transferable vote. Elected senators hold office
for eight years, one-half retiring every fourth year, and
casual vacancies are filled by election. The House of
Commons consists of fifty-two members, the franchise
being as in the United Kingdom, the elections until
1929 were by the system of proportional representation; now that applies only to the four members of the
University constituency; the other members are chosen
in single-member constituencies. Ministers may speak
in either House, but must vote only in the House of
which they are members, and provision is made to obviate the necessity of re-election on acceptance of office.
Peers are eligible for election to either House, and enjoy the franchise. A seven years' residential qualification
is now enacted. The privileges of members are as in the
United Kingdom House of Commons.

The relations of the two Houses require taxation and
revenue Bills, which must be recommended by the
Governor, to originate in the Lower House; the Upper
House may not amend such Bills or any Bill so as to
impose increased charges on the people, but any Bill

[1] His assent is written and kept with the Bill, not as in the Dominions
written on the Bill. It is notified by a minister to either House.

appropriating moneys for the ordinary annual services of the Government shall deal with that subject only, an attempt to avoid tacking. If the Lower House pass a Bill, and it is not accepted by the Senate, then on the Bill being passed in the subsequent session, a joint session may be held, at which the Bill may be passed by a majority of votes of the members present; in the case of a tax or appropriation Bill the sitting may be held during the same session. This procedure has not yet been employed.

The judicial arrangements include a Supreme Court of Judicature, consisting of the High Court and the Court of Appeal, to which a Court of Criminal Appeal was added by the Criminal Appeal (Northern Ireland) Act, 1930. The Act of 1920 provided an appeal to a High Court of Appeal for Ireland as a whole, whence appeals might be taken to the House of Lords, but this court has disappeared under the Act of 1922, and appeals go direct to the House of Lords. The constitutionality of any legislation might also be referred to the Judicial Committee of the Privy Council for a binding decision.

2. *The Channel Islands*

The Crown stands to the Channel Islands in a somewhat abnormal position, the result of the historical connection with the Crown as possessions of the Duke of Normandy, which remained loyal when Normandy itself passed away. The Crown is represented in the Governments of Jersey and Guernsey by Lieutenant-Governors, who are responsible to the War[1] and Home

---

[1] The Secretary of State for War submits the name to the King with Home Office concurrence; the Home Office later submits the warrant for

Offices in respect of their exercise of their executive functions, and who possess the right of assenting to or vetoing legislation. These officers control the executive, but the powers of the administration are limited by the existence of legislative and judicial institutions of equal age and imperfection.

No legislation, temporary or permanent, may be passed save by the Assembly of the States in Jersey. This body includes as Crown nominees the Lieutenant-Governor with power of veto, but no vote; the Bailiff, who presides, with a casting vote only; the Attorney- and Solicitor-General, who may speak but not vote; and the Visconte, who is in effect Sheriff and Coroner, and who may neither speak nor vote. There are also the members of the Royal Court, twelve jurats elected for life, natives of the island with property worth £720, and the States, namely twelve rectors holding their positions for life; twelve constables elected by the principal parishioners for three years; and fourteen members elected triennially, three for St. Helier, and one for each other parish, the franchise being extended to women. The powers of the legislature are limited; permanent legislation requires the assent of the Crown in Council, though provisional ordinances may be made for local or temporary purposes; these fall into abeyance unless renewed in three years. Either form of legislation is subject to the Lieutenant-Governor's veto if it may affect Crown interests or the royal prerogative, and in any case is subject to the Bailiff's dissent; in the latter case it cannot have effect unless approved by the King in Council. Taxation requires, save for

the civil appointment, and it is through it that the King exercises the prerogative of mercy, and makes ecclesiastical appointments.

2 B

urgent needs, the assent of the Crown in Council, while the hereditary revenues of the Crown are still under its control, and are used to defray expenses of the official Government. Duties on wines and spirits are provided for, the proceeds being allocated to local purposes.

The power of the Crown to legislate by Order in Council for the territory is disputed; it is claimed that no Order in Council is valid unless it is registered by the Royal Court, which may refuse registration if its terms infringe the ancient privileges of the islands, and that to legislate without the concurrence of the Straits is such an infringement.[1] The matter has been left undecided by the Privy Council; a similar claim as regards Parliament is ludicrous;[2] though it is the practice to send Acts applying to the islands to the court for registration, this affects in no wise their validity.

The judiciary consists of the Bailiff appointed by the Crown, a paid official and twelve unpaid jurats, who hold office for life, and need have no legal qualifications, though they have an equal voice in all decisions, the Bailiff in theory having none save when there is disagreement. He sits with two or three in first instance, with seven in appeals.

The constitution of Guernsey, which includes Herm and Jethou as integral parts, is still more complicated. The Royal Court, constituted as in Jersey, may enact Ordonnances, for the better enforcement of the existing law, and suggest legislation for the States. This body

---

[1] Cf. *Jersey States, Re* (1853), 9 Moo.P.C. 185; *Guernsey States Petition, Re* (1861), 14 Moo.P.C. 368.

[2] Keith, *Constitutional History of First British Empire*, pp. 382, 383. Legislation as to extradition, fugitive offenders, nationality, air navigation, merchant shipping, etc., is applied.

consists of the États d'Élection, comprising the Bailiff and jurats, the rectors of eight parishes, 180 parish councillors, elected by the ratepayers for life from ex-constables, and twenty constables elected for three years. These bodies, the councillors being represented by deputies, six for the town and nine for the country parishes, and eighteen directly elected members, make up the États de Délibération, which may accept or reject proposals of the Royal Court or Chefs Plaids and tax within limits; taxation above these limits and legislation need the assent of the Crown in Council. The Royal Court,[1] in addition to jurisdiction in Guernsey, acts as an appellate tribunal from the Royal Court of Alderney, which has also local States. But the States of Guernsey can legislate for Alderney, and for Sark, subject to royal allowance.

Sark is a feudal seignory;[2] its constitution provides for States constituted of holders by tenure and election; it has a court of limited jurisdiction; important matters fall to the Royal Court of Guernsey. From both Jersey and Guernsey appeal lies to the Crown in Council. The Courts and the States use old French in their proceedings, though English may be used in the States, and the law of the Channel Islands is so largely based on the old law of Normandy that lawyers study in the school of Caen.

Local militia, recruited as a rule voluntarily, are maintained at local expense, while the Imperial Government defrays the cost of the Imperial forces and

[1] In murder trials as many as eleven jurats may sit with the Bailiff, as in April 1935 (trial of Mrs de la Mare).

[2] The holder has a veto on legislation, but this may be overruled by the States of Guernsey.

the fortifications.[1] Ecclesiastically the islands fall within the diocese of Winchester and have been brought within the operation of legislation by the Church Assembly.[2] Tenacious of their local rights and traditions, the islanders are deeply attached to the British Crown, since under it they can retain the local privileges they value, while as parts of France these peculiarities would have been eradicated.

3. *The Isle of Man*

The Isle of Man from 1406 until 1765 was held of the Crown first by the House of Stanley, and then by the Dukes of Atholl; in that year the feudal rights of government were surrendered, and the Crown assumed direct control. In 1829 the outstanding manorial rights and ecclesiastical patronage were purchased by the Crown. The executive government is exercised by a Lieutenant-Governor, acting under the Home Office, who has control of the police and prison departments and of the local militia. The whole control of customs, legislative [3] and executive, rests with the Imperial Parliament and Government; the surplus revenue after meeting the expenses of government, and a contribution (£10,000) to the Imperial Exchequer, is at the

---

[1] In 1923 the islands were vainly invited to contribute small annual sums to the Imperial Exchequer, in view of the war debt. For the Isle of Man contribution see *Parl. Pap.* Cmd. 1331; in all £750,000 was paid by 1933–4 in final discharge.

[2] Church Measure 21 & 22 Geo. V. No. 4.

[3] Other legislation is rare, but may be passed in emergency, as was the Isle of Man (War Legislation) Act, 1914 (4 & 5 Geo. V. c. 62). The local legislature has a limited power of imposing customs, subject to confirmation by Parliament. Legislation is submitted through the Home Secretary for the approval of the King in Council; it is then promulgated on the Tynwald Hill in English and Manx.

disposal of the Court of Tynwald, which constitutes the legislature of the island. This body consists of two houses besides the Lieutenant-Governor; the Legislative Council, under a reform of 1919, is composed of the Bishop, the Attorney-General, the first and second Deemsters, four members elected by the House of Keys and two nominated by the Governor, the latter classes holding office for four years. Any person so elected or nominated must be at least twenty-one years of age, and resident in the island; a nominated member must not be in receipt of a salary from the Imperial or Insular Government. Any member of the Council, if authorised by the Governor, may appear before the House of Keys when a Government measure is to be discussed, in order to explain its terms. The Lower House consists of twenty-four members elected, sixteen for the six sheadings, five for Douglas, and one each for the other three towns, on adult franchise. Women are eligible as members or voters, and the normal duration of the House is five years, but it may be dissolved earlier by the Governor.

The island has its own peculiar laws.[1] Under legislation of 1921 the chief criminal courts are the Court of General Gaol Delivery and the Court of Criminal Appeal, consisting of one and three judges of the High Court of Justice respectively. The Deemsters hold weekly courts of criminal jurisdiction. Civil jurisdiction is exercised by the High Court with appeal to the Staff of Government. Appeal lies to the Crown in Council, and the writ of habeas corpus runs in the island.[2]

[1] Its land tenure is based on Norse custom; cf. Farrant, *Law Quarterly Review*, xxxv. 239 ff.

[2] The Home Secretary is responsible for the use of the prerogative and the appointment of the Judges and Attorney-General.

CHAPTER III

THE IRISH FREE STATE

THE aspirations of a majority of the Irish people for the severance of the relations with Great Britain established by the Act of Union seemed for a time to have received fruition in the Government of Ireland Act, 1914. But the outbreak of war, which prevented the application of that Act in any form, was followed by an intensification of separatist feeling, which, after a prolonged and embittered conflict and various efforts at settlement, resulted in the Treaty of December 6, 1921, the fundamental principle of which is the concession to Ireland of the same constitutional position in the Empire as Canada, the Commonwealth of Australia, New Zealand, and the Union of South Africa and the establishment of the rule that the relation of the Free State to the Imperial Parliament and Government shall, when not otherwise expressly provided, be that of the Dominion of Canada. The Free State, therefore, is essentially a Dominion in point of status, but the proximity of Ireland to Britain, taken in conjunction with the history of the relations of the countries, has resulted in the creation of a constitution of a special type and in some variation of the normal relations existing between a Dominion and Great Britain. Moreover, by the terms of the treaty, the northern portion of Ireland, as has been seen, exists as part of the United

Kingdom,[1] wholly detached from the control of the
Irish Free State.

The Free State constitution [2] was enacted subject to
one paramount principle,[3] that, so far as it or any law
passed under it was repugnant to the Treaty of 1921,
it should be void and inoperative, but this restriction
disappeared in 1933. The constitution is marked by
the effort to innovate, especially in the direction of
enunciating fundamental rights and of rendering responsible government statutory, so as to eliminate any
power of independent action by the representative of
the Crown. The rights asserted include the co-equal
membership of the State in the British Commonwealth
of Nations, and the derivation of all powers of government and authority from the people, to be exercised
in accordance with the organisation established by the
constitution. Political rights are given to Irish citizens
only, thus restricting their range. Irish is the national
language, but English has equal rights as an official
language.[4] It has been necessary by legislation to insist
on the use of Irish in education and in the law-courts,
and the moribund vernacular is being turned into a
language of law and literature, a process hampered by
its extremely deplorable spelling. No title of honour in
respect of services rendered in, or in relation to, the
State may be conferred on an Irish citizen save on the

---

[1] Provision is made in the Order in Council of March 27, 1923, and
amending orders issued under s. 6 of 13 Geo. V. c. 2 regarding the signification of the terms "United Kingdom" and "British Islands" in view of
the change in legal relationships.

[2] The Irish Free State Constitution Act, 1922 (Session 2). See also
the Irish Free State (Consequential Provisions) Act, 1922; Keith, *Journ.
Comp. Leg.* iv. 233 ff.; v. 120 ff.

[3] Repealed by the Constitution (Removal of Oath) Act, 1933.

[4] *O'Foghludha* v. *McClean*, [1934] I.R. 469.

advice or with the approval of the Executive Council. Freedom of the person is to be safeguarded by habeas corpus; there is an exception in the case of war or armed rebellion. The domicile is to be inviolable; freedom of conscience and religious equality are assured, much as in the case of Northern Ireland. Freedom of expression of opinion and of peaceful assembly without arms is guaranteed, as well as free elementary education, and the natural resources of the State may not be alienated outright.

Provision was made for a bicameral legislature, the Senate and Chamber of Deputies, Dail Eireann.[1] The composition of the Senate has varied; the first Senate of sixty members was nominated as to half by the President of the Council, and the others were elected by the Chamber, so that fifteen would retire every three years. The next appointments were made by the State as a single electorate, with most unsatisfactory results. In 1928 was adopted the plan of election by the two Chambers by proportional voting, senators to sit for nine years, a third retiring every three years. Its powers have also varied. In regard to money Bills it was given only the opportunity of suggesting amendments within twenty-one days, but the Dail was free to reject and pass the Bill unaltered. For other legislation its power of delay was extended to 270 days, and in certain circumstances a three-fifths majority could secure a referendum on a Bill. But in 1928 that right was swept away, and in return the Senate's power of delay was extended to some twenty months—less if a general election intervened. In 1934–5 the Dail

---

[1] The treaty provided for an oath of fidelity to the King, but this was abrogated in 1933 by Irish Act.

passed the Constitution Amendment (No. 24) Act to abolish the Senate outright. It had played a useful part in improving legislation, but it was unquestionably biased in favour of Mr Cosgrave's Government, under whose auspices most of its members had been elected.

The Chamber itself as first constituted was based on assigning one member to from 20,000 to 30,000 electors, the constituencies being arranged to allow of proportional representation with the single transferable vote. In lieu of 153 members the redistribution of seats in 1935 provides for 136, reducing the largest constituencies to five members only. The franchise is given to adults over twenty-one, subject to the usual disqualifications; the maximum duration of the Dail is five years. Prior to the election of the Chamber in 1923 under the constitution, the work of legislation rested with the Constituent Assembly, which enacted the constitution, and which was the House of Parliament elected under the terms of the Irish Free State (Agreement) Act, 1922, of the Imperial Parliament.

Parliament was given by the constitution various powers of which it has made so far no use. It may create subordinate legislatures with such powers as it thinks fit, so that if agreement were reached it could find a place for Northern Ireland. It may provide for the existence of functional or vocational councils and determine their rights and powers. It alone controls the armed forces of the State, which may not under the Treaty of 1921 exceed a figure bearing the same proportion to the Imperial establishment as the Irish population bears to the population of the United Kingdom. It is forbidden to make acts criminal which were not so at the time when they were committed.

The constitution made provision for the creation of a fund corresponding to the Consolidated Fund of the United Kingdom, and for the appropriation of moneys therefrom according to law; an elaborate system similar to the British has been built up to protect the public. The Dail appoints a Comptroller and Auditor-General to control all disbursements and to audit accounts of money administered by or under the authority of Parliament; he may only be removed from office for stated misbehaviour or incapacity on Parliamentary resolutions.

Save in the case of actual invasion, the State may not be committed to active participation in war without the assent of Parliament. This is in entire harmony with the Canadian doctrine as expressed by Mr Mackenzie King in the Canadian House of Commons of February 1, 1923, with general assent.

Power to amend the constitution was given in the constitution to the legislature to be exercised by simple Act for the first eight years; thereafter any amendment must be submitted to a referendum, and could only have effect if approved by a majority of the voters on the register, or by two-thirds of those voting, provided that a majority of voters recorded votes. In 1929 the time for amendment by simple Act was extended to eight years more. As noted above, amendment under the constitution was to be subject to the terms of the Treaty of 1921; that provision was deliberately removed—whether validly or not[1]—by the Constitution (Removal of Oath) Act, 1933.

The Governor-General, appointed by the King on

[1] Keith, *Letters on Imperial Relations, 1916–1935*, p. 157. Held valid in *Moore* v. *Att.-Gen.*, June 6, 1935; [1935] A.C. 484.

the advice of the Irish Government, was given by the constitution the right to reserve Bills, but only in accordance with Canadian constitutional usage, and this power was removed formally in 1933. The right of the Government to remove the Governor-General was asserted in 1932; the status of the present holder of the office has been reduced to minimal proportions; of the salary of £10,000 payable under the constitution £8000 is refunded, and the Seneschal, as he styles himself, takes no part in official functions. He summons and dissolves Parliament, but the Chamber itself fixes the day of meeting and the close of the session. He may dissolve the legislature only on the advice of the Executive Council, and the Council cannot advise a dissolution unless it still commands a majority in the Dail. A defeated Government is, therefore, deprived of one of the regular rights of Dominion or British Governments, to take the verdict of the electorate on its position; in 1927 grave difficulties arose on this point, and pressure had to be brought to bear on a deputy to refrain from casting, as he had promised, his vote against the Government. The Council is bound to resign when it ceases to command the confidence of the Dail; how this obligation could be enforced is uncertain, as the power to dismiss ministers does not appear to be granted to the Governor-General, and in any case as a servant of the Government he could hardly use it. The President of the Council, which is of not less than five nor more than twelve members, is elected by the Dail; he then selects his colleagues, who are submitted *en masse* to the approval of the Dail, to which they are collectively responsible in the usual way. It was contemplated in the constitution that the Council should not exceed seven in number, leaving room for the selection by the Chamber of other ministers who would hold office for the duration of Parliament and need not be members thereof. This project, intended to secure continuity in the administration of non-political departments such as Agriculture, Local Government, or Education, was badly conceived from the first. Finance is so essential in all Government business that the scheme would never have worked, if the extern ministers had not been treated as virtually part of the Executive Council, and it was a prudent step when the number of members of the Council was increased to twelve, leaving it open in future to make all ministers members of the Council, as is now done.

The judiciary has been extensively modified by legislation.[1] The High Court consists of six judges; it has a wide original civil jurisdiction in important causes, and its judges preside at the Central Criminal Court in Dublin, where the more serious crimes are dealt with. In constitutional questions it has exclusive original jurisdiction. Appeal lies from it to the Supreme Court of three judges—an increase to five is proposed and is desirable. The appeal can be regulated by law, but not so as to cut off appeal in constitutional issues. Circuit courts, ten in number, deal with most civil causes and criminal charges save murder, treason, and piracy. Minor civil causes and petty offences are disposed of by District courts. Grand juries are not used,[2] but special action has been necessary at times to safeguard jurors.

---

[1] Courts of Justice Acts, 1924, 1926, and 1928.

[2] In civil cases a majority vote of nine out of twelve suffices (Act of 1924, s. 95), and so in criminal cases under the Juries (Protection) Act, 1929, but the latter Act was temporary. Under the Juries Act, 1927, women serve on juries only if they so desire.

From the Supreme Court appeal lay by special leave of Chapter
the King in Council. It was bitterly resented in the III.
State and abolished in 1933.

The law of the Irish Free State is English law, which
was introduced piecemeal as conquest proceeded, and
was finally extended to the whole of Ireland by James I.[1]
It has, however, been extensively modified by legislation, though it remains essentially English in texture,
and Irish cases are often cited as of weight in the
English courts.

The higher judges, including District judges, hold
office during good behaviour, and may be removed only
for stated misbehaviour or known incapacity by resolution of Parliament. A retiring age is fixed at seventy-
two for High and Supreme Court judges, seventy for
Circuit judges and sixty-five for District judges. Judges
are subject only to the constitution and the law in
their conduct of their duties.

No one may be tried save in due course of law, and
under the constitution extraordinary courts may not
be established. But this rule has been nullified by
Constitution Amendment (No. 17) Act, 1931,[2] which
permitted the setting-up of courts composed of military
officers with powers to punish actions with penalties
more severe than provided in existing legislation. The
jurisdiction of courts-martial cannot extend to the civil
population save in time of war or armed rebellion and
for acts then committed, and is to be exercised under
regulations prescribed by law. Nor may such jurisdiction be exercised in any area where the civil courts

[1] See *Moore* v. *Att.-Gen.*, [1934] I.R. 44; Keith, *Journ. Comp. Leg.*
xvii. 121.

[2] *O'Duffy, In re*, [1934] I.R. 550; Keith, *Journ. Comp. Leg.* xvii.
119, 120.

are open or capable of being held, nor may any person be removed from such an area for trial elsewhere by court-martial. A member of the army, not on active service, may not be tried, save under special legal provision, by any but a civil court for any offence cognisable by such a court. Save for minor offences no person may be tried without a jury.

In distinction from the ordinary arrangements affecting the Dominions, Irish defence is regulated by the treaty, which, as mentioned above, specified the maximum number of Irish troops which may be maintained. Naval defence was reserved by the treaty for the British forces, but five years later it was to be open to the Free State to discuss the taking upon her shoulders of a share in the burden of her defence. Nothing so far has eventuated from this right. In peace certain harbour defence and aviation facilities are stipulated for, and British garrisons and ships make use of these facilities, the Irish Government treating them on the basis of a force in occupation by agreement. In time of war or of strained relations the British Government is entitled to such further harbour and other facilities as it may deem necessary. The existence of these obligations, as Mr de Valera has stressed, is inconsistent with the right of the State to expect any declaration of neutrality on her part to receive international recognition.

The State under the treaty was bound to assume a share of the British National Debt, but was entitled to have the boundary adjusted by a Commission. The Commission was duly appointed, after the British Government in 1924 took power to replace the Commissioner whom Northern Ireland refused to appoint, but when its result proved likely to lead to loss of territory to the Free State, her representative withdrew. By a singularly paradoxical if practical outcome, the State was allowed to retain its existing area, and was excused all payment in respect of debt, while Northern Ireland was rewarded for her acquiescence in the *status quo* as to territory by further pecuniary concessions at the expense of the long-suffering British taxpayer, to whom Ireland has proved a *damnosa hereditas*.[1]

[1] See Agreement of December 3, 1925, in 15 & 16 Geo. V. c. 77.

CHAPTER IV

THE DOMINIONS

1. *The Development of Responsible Government*

THE alarm caused by the disloyalty of the New
England Colonies resulted in the adoption in Canada
in 1774 by the Imperial Government of a policy intended to prevent rebellion by the complete control
of the administration on behalf of the Crown, and,
although representative legislatures were established
in Upper and Lower Canada by the Act of 1791, it
was with no intention of subjecting the executive to
effective control by the legislature. Similarly, when
the colonisation of Australia was begun in 1788, the
peculiar conditions in which it was effected rendered
it almost inevitable that the Imperial Government
should retain full control of both the executive and
the legislature. In Canada the inevitable friction
between the executive, supported by the Imperial
Government, and the legislature resulted, in 1837–8,
in abortive insurrections in both provinces, and the
suspension by Imperial Act of the constitution of
Lower Canada. Fortunately Lord Durham, who was
sent out as Governor-General and High Commissioner,
inspired by R. Baldwin, realised the essential impossibility of conducting the Government of a large
and intelligent community on the old system, and.

after the Act of 1840 [1] had been passed uniting the provinces, the new Governor-General was authorised by the Imperial Government to "call to his counsels and employ in the public service those persons who, by their position and character, have obtained the general esteem of the inhabitants of the province". This meant that the Governor should no longer act with an irresponsible council of officials, but with ministers, and, though Lord Metcalfe for a period (1843-5) sought to limit the extent of the change, and to save the Civil Service from political control, Lord Elgin, in 1847, assumed office with full authority to make the system effective, and by the following year the maritime provinces also had been accorded the new régime. In 1867 the important step was taken of the federal union of Nova Scotia and New Brunswick with Canada, which was redivided into Ontario and Quebec. The decision was largely motived by the deadlocks which showed the impossibility of working the Act of 1840 effectively in a single province of Canada, owing to the racial divisions of the people, and the refusal of the French element to be absorbed in the English, as had been hoped by Durham when he advocated the union. But considerations of the necessity of uniting in defence against the growing power of the United States and of abolishing tariff barriers in order to replace American reciprocity were also important. Provision was made in the Imperial Act of 1867, sanctioning the federation for the eventual admission of other provinces and territories, and, in 1871, British Columbia became a province with responsible government; Prince Edward Island

[1] 3 & 4 Vict. c. 35.

2 c

also entered the federation in 1873. Moreover, the Imperial Government in 1870 made over to Canada the enormous area under the Hudson Bay Company, from which the Dominion created in 1870 the province of Manitoba, and in 1905 those of Alberta and Saskatchewan, all with responsible government from their inception. In 1912 the Dominion legislature extended the provincial boundaries of Ontario, Manitoba, and Quebec to cover most of the area not yet under provincial authority, so that only the Yukon territory and some other areas, largely in the Arctic, are outside the sphere of responsible provincial government.

In 1832 Newfoundland was granted representative government, and in 1855 responsible government was introduced. From 1934 it was superseded temporarily.

In Australia, after autocratic rule, constitutional government was introduced in 1823 in New South Wales, and in 1842 representative government was established there; under the Act of 1850 of the Imperial Parliament, representative government was extended to Van Diemen's Land, renamed Tasmania in 1855, and to Victoria, which was severed from New South Wales in 1851; it was also conceded to South Australia, which was in 1836 erected into a distinct Colony under an imperial Act of 1834. In 1855 responsible government was conceded, coming into effective operation in the following year in all these Colonies. In 1859 Queensland was severed from New South Wales, and accorded responsible government from the outset. Western Australia, established in 1829, attained representative government in 1870, and responsible government in 1890. The six Colonies united under the Imperial Act of 1900, to form the Commonwealth of Australia, retaining separate existence as States.

New Zealand, created a distinct Colony in 1841, was granted representative government in 1852 by an Imperial Act, and in 1856 responsible government was fully established.

In South Africa the Cape of Good Hope, ceded in 1814, obtained a representative legislature in 1853, and responsible government in 1872; Natal, annexed in 1843 and made a separate Colony in 1845, received a measure of representative government in 1856, and responsible government in 1893; the Transvaal, after the conquest in 1902, was governed as a Crown Colony until given responsible government in 1906, and the Orange River Colony was similarly treated in 1907. By an Imperial Act of 1909 the four Colonies were merged in the Union, receiving a reduced provincial status.

In all these cases the essential feature of the introduction of responsible government was the instructions given by the Imperial Government to the Governor to conduct his administration on the advice of persons acceptable to Parliament, and hence it is that none of the constitutions provide in any effective manner for the maintenance of this form of government. The more recent constitutions, such as those of the Commonwealth and the Union, provide that ministers shall not remain in office longer than three months unless they become members of the legislature, but the essential rules of tenure of office by a Parliamentary majority, of action by the Governor on the advice of ministers, the solidarity of the

Cabinet, and so forth, are remarkable by their absence, nor is there any doubt that the conventions of the constitution are ill-suited for formal definition. Their enactment in the Irish Free State constitution has not had any clear advantage. That they shall be observed is sufficiently ensured by the fact that a ministry, which was not supported by the legislature, would find it practically impossible to carry on administration, for lack of funds and inability to obtain legislation, while a Governor who tried to act without ministers would be without any official help to perform his duties.

2. *The Governor-General*

In New Zealand and Newfoundland the King is represented by a single representative, styled Governor-General in the former, Governor in the latter Dominion. In Canada he is represented for the federation by a Governor-General, and for the provinces by Lieutenant-Governors; in the Commonwealth by a Governor-General and by Governors in the States; and in the Union of South Africa by a Governor-General, and in its provinces by Administrators. The Governors-General are appointed by the King on the advice of the Dominion Government, the Lieutenant-Governors and the Administrators by the Governors-General on the advice of their ministers; the State Governors by the King on the advice of the Imperial Government. All those appointed by the Crown hold office at pleasure, though a term of five or six years is normal; the others hold for five years subject to removal for cause assigned which must be communicated to either house of Parliament.

Powers exist for the appointment of deputies to exercise defined functions for their chiefs, and arrangements are made for the succession to the Government in case of the illness or incapacity, or death or absence of the holder of the office, the Chief Justice acting in default of any other appointment.

The Governor, or other chief executive officer, possesses all the authority inherent in the head of the executive government of the territory, whether it rests on prerogative or is inferred from statutes, and a grant to him of all necessary prerogative powers is assumed, including even powers generally held to be obsolete, such as the power to incorporate companies ascribed in 1916 to the Lieutenant-Governors in Canada by the Judicial Committee.[1] So these officers, without any express delegation of power, can exercise the prerogative of pardoning offences against provincial laws. There are, however, certain limitations to the powers conferred expressly or implicitly, corresponding with the fact that a Dominion is not an independent State; save on express authority from the King or under statute in the Union of South Africa, a Governor cannot declare war or make peace or conclude treaties; he cannot regulate coinage; nor can he confer any honorary distinction, or extend the boundaries of the Colony by annexing territory; Canadian annexations have been carried out under a general delegation of authority. Similarly during the war sovereign acts as regards neutral vessels required sanction by the Imperial Government.

The position of the Governor towards his ministers is closely analogous to that of the King towards the

[1] Keith, *Journ. Comp. Leg.* iv. 201 ff.

British Cabinet, on which it is based. This has been explicitly declared by the Imperial Conference of 1926. But the Governor suffers, as contrasted with the King, from the temporary character of his appointment, his selection by the Dominion Government, his lack of familiarity with local conditions, and the absence of that *éclat* which necessarily attends the person of a hereditary sovereign in a society rich with historical tradition. His ministers are often satisfied if his functions are reduced to those of a "rubber stamp", and his connection with the political side of Government becomes purely formal. The obligation to acquaint him with their decisions may exist in theory, as asserted by the Imperial Conference; in practice it is rarely observed, save when the Governor by personal character succeeds in winning the confidence of ministers, or a war induces an unusual degree of co-operation.

The Governor, however, had more power formerly than the King, if infinitely less opportunity of influence. The constitutional usage in the Dominions originally did not require that, as regards the demand for a dissolution, the Governor must act on ministerial advice; it expected him to refuse if he could find another ministry to carry on without a dissolution and so avoid the trouble of a general election. It was therefore notable in 1914 that Sir R. Munro-Ferguson (Viscount Novar) granted a double dissolution of the Commonwealth Parliament to a ministry with a bare majority in the Lower House, and scarcely any representation in the Upper. His predecessors in office had declined previous proposals for dissolution on the score that the possibilities of finding another ministry to carry on government, without troubling the electors, had not been exhausted, and, had he acted on the same principle, it might have been possible to avoid a dissolution, but he wisely conformed to the British precedents instead.

The development of Dominion practice on British lines was unexpectedly interrupted by an episode in 1926 in Canada. The Prime Minister applied for a dissolution, as his party was unable to carry on satisfactorily owing to the uncertain character of the Progressive Party's support of the ministry. The Governor-General objected to a dissolution in view of a pending vote of censure on the ministry on account of financial irregularities in the Customs department. The ministry resigned, and Mr Meighen, as leader of the Opposition, accepted office. But the one consideration which would have justified Lord Byng's action failed to be realised. Mr Meighen was unable to carry on without a dissolution, and was declared by the Commons not to have its confidence. He had, therefore, to secure a dissolution at which the constitutional propriety of the Governor-General's action was severely canvassed.[1] The election resulted in the decisive defeat of the new ministry, which had further been guilty of the impropriety of carrying on Government by means of acting ministers in order to avoid the necessity of its members seeking relection, and of spending large sums without Parliamentary sanction. The Imperial Conference of 1926 had this issue before it, and, by insisting that the position of the Governor-General must be regarded as similar to that of the King in regard to relation to his ministers, condemned Lord

[1] Keith, *Letters on Imperial Relations, 1916–1935*, pp. 56 ff., 67 ff.

Byng's action. The influence of this view was seen in 1931 when the Governor-General of the Commonwealth expressly relied on it to justify his grant of dissolution of Parliament to the Labour Prime Minister without seeking to find a ministry to carry on without the cost and trouble of a dissolution.

It may, therefore, safely be assumed that only in very remarkable circumstances would a dissolution be refused by a Governor-General; he could not, of course, accord one to a ministry which had failed by a recent dissolution to re-establish its command of the Lower House. Normally, however, to refuse the electorate the right of final decision involves a responsibility which no Governor-General could face. It must, however, be remembered that under the régime established by the Imperial Conference in 1930 the Governor-General is the nominee of the Government in office. There is thus possible the grave abuse of the power of a temporary majority. It might pass legislation to extend the life of Parliament and obtain the sanction of the Governor-General. That, however, does not apply to Canada or the Commonwealth, for in both the duration of Parliament is fixed by the constitution and cannot be altered by the will of Parliament alone. In New Zealand in 1934 the extension of the life of Parliament by the majority of the day was bitterly attacked by the Opposition, which quite fairly stressed the danger of such action.

The rule that the Governor is to be guided in his attitude towards ministers by the same principles as is the King is not applicable to the Governors of the States of Australia or the Lieutenant-Governors of the provinces of Canada. In point of fact there has long been a tendency to lessen the sphere of independent action in their cases also, but various considerations prevent full acceptance of the doctrine which has been adopted for the Dominions since 1926. It must be remembered that the grant of a dissolution involves in a State a serious waste of time and public money, seeing that the legislature has only a three years' term, except in South Australia, and popular opinion no doubt still expects the Governor not to dissolve unless he is satisfied that there is no means of carrying on the Government without a dissolution. Further, it must be remembered that in unicameral legislatures like that of Queensland and the provinces of Canada, there are risks in pressing too far the doctrine of automatic assent to ministerial proposals. A Governor could hardly assent to a Bill prolonging the life of a legislature which had ceased to express the views of the electors. Difficulties inviting action by the Governor have not been rare.[1] For example, Sir Dudley de Chair and Sir P. Game, as Governors of New South Wales, had both to resist efforts by Mr Lang to swamp the Legislative Council in order to secure its abolition; it was clearly unfair of the minister to ask for such action, especially as Sir D. de Chair actually conceded a large addition, with the unexpected result that the added members proved willing to vote for Labour measures, but not to end their own lives as legislators, though assured in any event of the privilege of free transport in the State. Though neither Governor would concede the minister's demands, both declined to dismiss the ministry, and the Secretary of State declined to interfere by altering

[1] Keith, *Letters on Imperial Relations, 1916–1935*, pp. 280-89.

the royal instructions which give the Governor the right of independent action. The value of that power was shortly afterwards seen when the State Government defied the Commonwealth legislation, compelling the State to provide funds to meet her obligations in respect of her debt; the Governor then dismissed the ministry for its refusal to obey the law of the Commonwealth. If the law violated had merely been State Law, the Governor might have relied on an Act of Indemnity to be secured by ministers, but there was no possibility of such action in that case. On the other hand, in 1924–5 occurred regrettable examples of disobedience by the Acting Governor and Governor of the constitutional law of Tasmania, for assent was accorded to two Bills, one for taxation, and one for appropriation, to which the Upper House had not accorded its assent. The episode is without parallel in Dominion history, and occurred under a Labour Government which hardly realised that it was striking a vital blow against the whole fabric of law and order.

Apart from their position as the constitutional representatives of the sovereign, the Governor-General in New Zealand and the Governors of the States and Newfoundland occupy the position of representatives of the Imperial Government, and the channel of communications between the central and oversea Governments, though, in the case of New Zealand and Newfoundland, Premiers can communicate on matters deemed by them of sufficient importance direct with the British Prime Minister, and there is a less fully authorised but not rare practice of dealing even with political matters through the High Commissioners or Agents-General in London. The

Governor must obey any directions from the Imperial Government, even if they conflict with ministerial advice, but in the field of executive action such conflicts are now almost unknown; the Governor has no means of making his will effective save perhaps as regards the grant of a pardon, without securing ministers willing to support him; this would rarely be possible and the intervention is incompatible with the status of the Dominions and the States. On the other hand, the Governor is bound by his instructions regarding the assent to, or reservation of, Bills, but friction on this account has largely been minimised by the restriction to the minimum of reservation, and by the willingness of ministers to recommend reservation in appropriate cases. The difficulty in question, whether the royal instructions render reservation necessary, is one on which the Governor is entitled to the legal advice of some law officer of his Government, based on legal considerations alone. He may also consult on this, and any other matter on which he feels doubt, the Dominions Secretary, a procedure which may obviate the need of reservation, or secure from his ministers the insertion of a suspending clause in the Bill. The gradual limitation of the sphere of Imperial intervention is illustrated by the abandonment of any attempt by that Government to prevent swamping of nominee Upper Houses, a process carried out in Queensland in 1920, and resulting in the following year in the inevitable passing of a Bill through both houses to abolish the Council. But there is no excuse for Mr Amery's action in refusing to disallow the Tasmanian Acts of 1924–5 to which, as mentioned, illegal assent had been given.

The reduction of the functions of the Governor to those of a constitutional monarch lessens the importance of appointing men of strong character and political or administrative experience, and strengthens the demand for local appointments. The position is still in a state of flux; no appointment has been made for many years without first ascertaining that the nominee of the Imperial Government will be welcomed locally, but the suggestion of several Australian State Governments for the appointment of local nominees, or the transfer of the functions to the Chief Justice, have not been accepted; a crisis in South Australia in 1922, owing to the resignation of the Governor on the score of inadequate emoluments, was met by the selection of an Australian officer of high distinction and popularity, for whom the legislature consented to increase the pay of the post; again ultimately success was achieved as regards a similar deadlock in Tasmania. On the other hand, it is now possible to appoint royal princes, such as the Duke of Connaught to Canada, and Prince Arthur of Connaught to the Union, the latter appointment a striking proof of the desire to keep the post free from any suspicion of intervention in the troubled waters of South African politics.[1] Similarly, it is, of course, most desirable to secure the impartiality of the officer appointed to succeed to the administration of the Government on the incapacity or absence of the Governor; thus the swamping of the Queensland Council in 1920 was rendered easy by the appointment as Lieutenant-Governor of an ex-Labour minister.[2]

[1] On the other hand, the last two appointments to Canada have been outspokenly democratic, one a financier, and one a novelist.

[2] The illegal assent to a Tasmanian Bill in 1924 was given by a Chief Justice who had been a Labour supporter.

3. *The Cabinet and the Public Departments*

The distinction between the Privy Council and the Cabinet, which is familiar in the United Kingdom, has no real parallel in the Dominions. It is true that in some cases, as in the federal executives of Canada, the Commonwealth, and the Union, and in Victoria and Tasmania, the Executive Council contains all persons who have ever been admitted to it as members, but only those who are actually in the Cabinet are summoned to its meetings. Ministers who are outside the Cabinet and Executive Council are a comparatively modern innovation in the Dominions, but ministers without portfolio were common when, before the war, they were comparatively unknown in the United Kingdom. The number of ministers, members of the Council, is sometimes legally restricted, as in Australia to nine, where, however, honorary ministers can also be appointed, in the Union to eleven, and in the Union they have the right to speak in either house of Parliament. At Cabinet meetings the Governor never presides, but, save in Canada, he is usually present at meetings of the Executive Council, at which formal business is transacted as in the Privy Council in the United Kingdom. But it is essential that he should sanction all proceedings of the Executive Council intended to have legal effect as Orders in Council; the Privy Council has emphatically asserted in the case of a Canadian province that no Cabinet consent can take the place of an order of the Lieutenant-Governor in Council.[1]

The cohesion of a Cabinet depends as in Great Britain

---

[1] Keith, *Journ. Comp. Leg.* iv. 240.

on the person of the Prime Minister, who is commissioned by the Governor, and who selects his own colleagues, save in the case of Labour Governments in Australia, where the Labour caucus selects the members, and virtually can force their own nominee on the Governor. The resignation of the Premier places all the ministries at the disposal of his successor, or of himself if recommissioned, to form a Government, points illustrated very clearly by the history of Mr Hughes's successive ministries in Australia from 1915 to 1922. So in 1928 General Hertzog by this procedure got rid of Mr Madeley. The ascendancy which a strong and able Premier may possess is illustrated by the cases of Sir John Macdonald, Sir Wilfrid Laurier, Mr Mackenzie King, and Mr Bennett in Canada, Mr Seddon in New Zealand, General Botha in the Union, and Mr Hughes in Australia. Party organisation is perhaps less effective in the Dominions than in Great Britain, and funds are far less freely available, except in Canada, but there is an exception in the case of the Labour Party, which in Australia is admirably organised both for State and federal purposes. The members work effectively in Parliament, determining by majority votes their policy in detail, while they are bound by the policy adopted by conferences of the labour organisation in the State or Commonwealth, subscription to which is an essential condition of nomination for election, and which is enforced by requiring in some cases the provision of resignations in blank. This cohesion and unity render a Labour Party a very formidable rival to parties which are distracted by individual jealousies, but it naturally exercises an unfavourable influence on the freedom of opinion and action of the members of the party. In

South Africa until 1933 racial divisions dominated party affiliation; but there is now a United South African Nationalist Party uniting moderate British and Dutch.

The Civil Service in the Dominions differs in certain respects from that of Great Britain. Ministers perform much more detailed work in their departments, and considerations of democracy and economy have operated to establish the principle that, apart from technical appointments, the Civil servant should be recruited by a comparatively low educational test, and then advanced by promotion, disregarding the British distinction of different educational tests according to the nature of intelligence required for the work to be accomplished. But there are signs of a change in this regard in the Dominions, though the rule of low salaries, until altered, will always depress the attainments of the service. In Australia the dread of political influence in the Civil Service has led to efforts to remove the service in large measure from ministerial control by conferring ample powers on Civil or Public Service Commissions both as regards appointment, promotion, and discipline, and the same attempt is made in the Union of South Africa,[1] but by no means in any case with complete success, various devices for introducing ministerial intervention being possible. In the Union since 1926 racialism has been marked in governmental appointments. In Canada it was only in 1918 that fairly effective means were taken to bring the outside services, as well as those at Ottawa, under the Civil Service Commission, and thus to destroy the grave abuse of

[1] See Act No. 27 of 1923. There is also a Public Service Advisory Council.

political patronage,[1] which caused numerous changes of incumbents of office on every change in the Government and destroyed the possibility of efficiency. The Canadian legislation, of course, presents many faults, but it has encouraged the provinces also to set their houses in order in this regard. Here also, however, the superior openings in private life retard the attainment of a really efficient service.

4. *The Lower Houses of Parliament*

The Parliaments of the Dominions and States are normally bicameral; there is an exception in the case of Queensland, where the Legislative Council was abolished as useless in 1922; the legislatures of the Canadian provinces, save Quebec, have either never been bicameral or have reduced themselves to a single chamber, and the provincial councils of South Africa are also unicameral.

In Canada the franchise, Dominion and provincial alike, is in the main adult suffrage; thus the Dominion Act of 1920 awards the franchise to every male and female British subject, aged twenty-one, resident in Canada for a year, and in the constituency for two months; persons personally naturalised in Canada are also eligible, but there are certain limitations as to wives and children of such persons, and alien women married to British subjects, and as to persons who are specially disqualified in any province, as are North American Indians in some provinces, Chinese in Saskatchewan, and British Indians, Japanese and Chinese naturalised subjects in British Columbia. For

---

[1] See Dawson, *The Civil Service of Canada* and *Constitutional Issues in Canada*, pp. 287-319.

provincial purposes Nova Scotia and Prince Edward Island, as regards half the Assembly in which the Council is merged, maintain a small property qualification, as in Quebec, which alone has not yet conceded the vote to women. Proportional representation was by an Act of 1920 introduced in Manitoba for the constituency of Winnipeg, which was given ten members for the purpose.[1] The average duration of Parliament falls little short of the normal five years' duration allowed to the Lower Houses.

Redistribution in the Dominion is required after each decennial census; it is based on the maintenance of the number of members for Quebec at sixty-five, and each province being allotted a proportionate number, provided that no province has fewer members than senators; under this arrangement Ontario has eighty-two members, Nova Scotia twelve, New Brunswick ten, Prince Edward Island four, Manitoba seventeen, Saskatchewan twenty-one, Alberta seventeen, British Columbia sixteen, and the Yukon one. The numbers of provincial members range downwards from ninety in Ontario;[2] in Prince Edward Island the Assembly repre-

[1] On February 19, 1923, the Canadian House of Commons passed a resolution in favour of the alternative vote, but rejected proportional representation by 90 to 72, against Mr Mackenzie King's advice. On February 23 the Union House of Assembly negatived it by 65 to 20, despite General Smuts's support.

[2] Quebec, 90; Nova Scotia, 30; New Brunswick, 48; Prince Edward Island, 30; Manitoba, 55; Saskatchewan, 63; Alberta, 63; British Columbia, 48. The Yukon, which is without provincial status, and is governed by a Comptroller, has a Council of 3 members elected for three years with limited powers. The North-West Territories include the rest of Canada outside the provinces; they are governed from Ottawa by a Commissioner, a Deputy, and five Councillors appointed by the Governor-General in Council, who may legislate on a variety of topics analogous to those of the provinces and differing only slightly from the powers of the Yukon.

2 D

sents a merger of the old Council and Assembly, and
there are two groups of members, the first elected on a
higher franchise.

Newfoundland under the suspended constitution
enjoys manhood suffrage with votes for women over
twenty-five years of age, subject to two years' residence; it has thirty-six members of Assembly, and its
duration is four years.

In the Commonwealth of Australia and the States
the franchise is possessed by adults, male and female,
but in Queensland and Western Australia and in federal
elections in these States, aboriginal natives of Africa,
Asia,[1] Australia, and the islands of the Pacific (save in
the case of federal elections, New Zealand) are excluded
from the vote. Preferential voting exists in the Commonwealth, Victoria, and New South Wales, where proportional representation failed after trial; it survives
in Tasmania; an elector may if he pleases give a contingent vote in Queensland and Western Australia, and
ordinary voting prevails in South Australia. The duration of the Lower Houses is uniformly three years,
save in South Australia, where in 1934 five years was
adopted.

New Zealand gives adult suffrage, with quadrennial
Parliaments, but provides for the Maoris by allocating
four seats to them exclusively.

The number of members of the Commonwealth
House of Representatives is seventy-five,[2] and under
the system of redistribution according to population,

---

[1] The Commonwealth and Queensland have given British Indians
the vote. Voting is now compulsory in the Commonwealth and the
States.

[2] A member without the right to vote sits for the Northern Territory
under an Act of 1922.

New South Wales has twenty-eight members, Victoria
twenty, Queensland ten, South Australia six, Western
Australia and Tasmania five each. In the States, New
South Wales has ninety members, Victoria sixty-five,
Queensland sixty-two, South Australia forty-six (eight
constituencies with three members, and eleven with
two), Western Australia fifty, and Tasmania thirty. In
New Zealand there are eighty members, four being
Maori representatives, with distribution between the
north and south islands by population.

Since 1931 in the Union of South Africa adult male
and female [1] suffrage for white persons exists in the
Cape, Natal, Transvaal, and Orange Free State provinces for both Union and provincial elections; for non-
Europeans in the Cape there are educational and property qualifications exacted, but no colour bar; in
Natal, besides property qualifications, there are effective exclusions of both African natives and British
Indians. In the Transvaal and Orange Free State non-
Europeans have no vote. The duration of Parliament is
five years, of the provincial councils three, and the
latter are not subject to dissolution save by efflux of
time. Under the redistribution scheme based on the
census returns the number of members of the Assembly
rose in 1934 to a hundred and fifty, the Cape having
sixty-one, Natal sixteen, the Transvaal fifty-seven, and
the Orange Free State sixteen. The provincial councils
have the same number, save the Orange Free State and
Natal, which have twenty-five as a minimum.

In all cases annual sessions of Parliament are required, and payment of members has been extended in

---

[1] The grant of female suffrage was largely dictated by the desire to
minimise the value of the native vote.

amount, until the Commonwealth grants £825 (in 1935) annually, this being the maximum amount. The legislatures are summoned, prorogued, and dissolved by the representative of the Crown, and their members enjoy privileges which are now generally assimilated to those of the House of Commons of the United Kingdom.[1] This is naturally not the case with the South African provincial councils, but the members are assured freedom of speech in council.

The adoption of time limits for speeches in the Dominions has been increasingly general of late years, where this form of abbreviation of debate is preferred to closure by compartment. Thus in the Union in 1922 a system was adopted which provides for a single general debate on the budget, five full days being allotted to it in addition to the time taken by the minister; in Committee of Supply members can as a rule speak only for ten minutes, but the number of times they can speak is not limited; in Committee of Ways and Means the allowance is two speeches, not exceeding fifteen minutes, on each vote put from the Chair; in general business there is a limit of forty minutes, when the Speaker is in the Chair, ten minutes in Committee, with no limit for the mover of a motion. Even these not drastic restrictions were only carried on a party vote, after protests by the Labour leader that the Prime Minister treated Parliament as "a sort of national excrescence or constitutional encumbrance".

Electors are normally qualified for membership; the disqualifications vary considerably in detail, but are generally similar to those in force in the United King-

---

[1] The Quebec legislature in 1922 enacted an Act for the imprisonment of a person charged with calumny of the Assembly.

dom, both as regards the right to vote and the right to be elected.

5. *The Upper Houses*

The Senate of Canada consists of ninety-six members nominated for life by the Crown on the advice of the Dominion Government, the members being not less than thirty years of age, and possessed of freehold property in land worth at least 4000 dollars. As reconstructed in 1915 Ontario and Quebec have each twenty-four members, Nova Scotia ten, New Brunswick ten, Prince Edward Island four, and the western provinces, Manitoba, British Columbia, Saskatchewan, and Alberta, six each; in case of deadlock the Crown may add four or eight members, one or two for each of the four groups returning twenty-four members apiece, but the power has never been exercised. The Legislative Council of Quebec consists of twenty-four members qualified as in the Dominion, nominated by the Lieutenant-Governor. In neither case can members be added. In Newfoundland, under the constitution now in abeyance, the number of members who may be nominated is unlimited; but the Governor can only make provisional appointments up to fifteen in all, and, therefore, any further additions must be made by the Crown, which in this matter acts on the advice of the Imperial Government, and, therefore, is in a position to maintain the independence within limits of the Council.

In the Commonwealth the franchise for the Senate is the same as in the House of Representatives, and any elector may be chosen. Each State has six members, who hold office for six years, three retiring every three years in rotation; each State is a single electorate for voting purposes, and preferential voting [1] exists. In New South Wales the Council was nominated, but is since 1932 elected [2] to the number of sixty, fifteen retiring each four years. In Victoria the Council consists of thirty-four members elected for seventeen constituencies, holding office for six years, half retiring every third year. A councillor must be a male, at least thirty, and own freehold of the clear annual value of £50; the electorate is composed of persons with a small property qualification, or of educational attainments, or of professional employment. In South Australia a member must be thirty years of age; the number is twenty, elected four each for five constituencies, for six years; there is a property qualification for electors with educational qualifications also. In Western Australia also a member must be thirty; the number is thirty, elected for ten districts, holding office for six years, one in each district retiring every two years; a property qualification is required from the electors. In Tasmania there is the same age qualification; the number is eighteen, elected for fifteen districts, for six years; there is a property or educational qualification for voters, and as in Victoria and Western Australia there is preferential voting for the Council. There is retirement by rotation, as also in South Australia.

The New Zealand Council was originally nominee for life, then in 1891 the term of new councillors was reduced to seven years. By an act of 1914, the opera-

---

[1] The names of candidates may be grouped according to their political predilection under an Act of 1922, but the elector's freedom of choice is not restricted in any way.

[2] The electorate is composed of the two Houses.

tion of which has been from time to time suspended, provision is made for election of forty councillors in four districts on the system of proportional representation, and the nomination of three male Maoris by the Governor. No property qualification is required either of electors or members.

In the Union a senator must be aged thirty at least, be registered as an elector, have resided for five years within the Union, be a Union national of European descent, and, if an elected senator, own real property worth £500 clear. The Senate is now composed of forty members, eight nominated by the Governor-General, half on account of their acquaintance with the needs of the natives, and eight elected by proportional representation for each province by the members of the Council and the provincial representatives in the Assembly sitting together; other proposals [1] for reconstituting the Senate have not attained success. Senators hold office for ten years, but the Senate may be dissolved within 120 days of the Assembly, and nominated senators vacate office on a change of Prime Minister, under provisions enacted in 1926.

Members of the Councils are normally paid, but in New South Wales and Victoria this is not the case. The privileges of the Councils are based on those of the British House of Commons, which they may not exceed.

---

[1] Mainly in the line of reducing nominees to four, and substituting direct election for the choice of eight representatives each of the provinces; a small number additional, to bring the Senate up to a third of the Lower House, might then be elected by that House. The matter was considered by a Select Committee of the Senate in 1918, and a Speaker's Conference (suggested by Lord Bryce's conference) in 1920. But General Smuts's Government contemplated no change, and it seems clear that no increase of authority is desired.

6. *The Functions and Procedure of the Parliaments*

The powers of the legislatures are, subject to limitations already examined, similar to those of the Imperial Parliament. The legislatures exist largely to control administration as well as to legislate, and their financial control occupies much of their time; in the Dominions, as opposed to the States and provinces, tariff-making imposes a serious burden on members. The general forms of procedure are essentially similar to those in the United Kingdom, and control of finance is secured to the Government by the limitation that no money votes can proceed save on the sanction of the Government. The predominance over the administration of the Lower House is secured by its sole initiative in matters of finance. But the existence of elective Upper Houses complicates relations between the Houses, and, when nominee Houses cannot be swamped, they have obviously a different and more independent position than the House of Lords, or the nominee Houses with unlimited numbers.

The nominee Houses are, however, all comparatively weak. That of New South Wales avoided swamping and threats of abolition by the Labour Party, by readiness to yield when the Lower House had a substantial majority and agreed with the people, and, despite occasional additions of members to secure the passing of disputed measures, lost its utility or power only in 1930–32, when it was reconstituted. The Queensland Council was swamped by the Lieutenant-Governor in 1920 in order to carry controversial and confiscatory land and tramway legislation; it never recovered from this treatment and was abolished in 1922.[1] In Newfoundland the Upper House has never seriously disputed the views of the popular chamber. In Canada, both federation and province, the Upper Houses are more independent because their numbers are limited and so they cannot be swamped; the Liberal Senate of 1912–13 defeated the Conservative Government's effort to contribute thirty-five million dollars to the Imperial navy, and proposals to abolish it as it stands, in view of its partisan character, have been repeatedly discussed without revealing any real agreement on a new course of action.[2] In New Zealand the nominee Council has shown a moderate amount of independence, but the principle that it should not indefinitely or provocatively oppose the popular will was asserted in 1892, when the Governor was over-ruled by the Colonial Secretary on demurring to make an increase in the number of the Council to secure adequate strength for the newly triumphant Liberal administration. In all these cases the Lower House denies the right of the Upper House to amend money Bills, and in Newfoundland the position of the Upper House was assimilated by an Act of 1917 to that of the House of Lords by the adoption of legislation on the basis of the Parliament Act, 1911. In Canada, how-ever, in 1922–30 the Senate, while a Conservative majority remained, asserted the right to amend or reject.

[1] Keith, *Journ. Comp. Leg.* iv. 235 ff. It was provided in 1934 that a Council could not be reconstituted without a referendum. This was sug-gested by the precedent of New South Wales, under whose legislation any change of the Council requires a referendum: Constitution (Legis-lative Council) Amendment Act, 1929.

[2] R. A. Mackay, *The Unreformed Senate of Canada* (1926).

Under the Commonwealth constitution proposed laws, appropriating revenue or money, or imposing taxation, may not originate in the Senate, nor may it amend Bills imposing taxation or appropriating revenue for the ordinary annual services of the Government, nor may it amend any law so as to increase the burden imposed on the people. But it may suggest, and persist in suggesting, amendments in such Bills, which the House of Representatives may accept. Otherwise the Senate has equal powers with the Lower House, and it is provided, in order to prevent tacking, that taxation measures must deal with one subject only, and the Bill appropriating revenue for the ordinary annual services must include nothing else. To meet deadlocks in other matters it is provided that, if the Lower House twice passes a Bill, an interval of three months intervening, and it is rejected by the Senate, the Governor-General may dissolve both Houses; if the Lower House then again passes the Bill, and the Senate rejects it, a joint sitting may be held, and if the Bill is approved by an absolute majority of members of the two Houses it may become law. If, however, the issue is a constitutional change, and either House twice passes a Bill by an absolute majority, and it is rejected by the other House, the Governor-General may refer the issue to a popular referendum forthwith; in practice, of course, he would only act as ministers advised. The deadlock provision for ordinary legislation was put into effect in 1914, with wholly disastrous results for the Government, on whose advice it was granted. In general the Senate has shown much strength, while the mode of its election has hitherto operated to give one party or the other a very large majority in its ranks. But it has developed very little State feeling, and like the Canadian Senate is divided on federal political party lines and does not act, as may the United States Senate, as a States House.

In Victoria the Council has, like the Senate, no financial initiative, but in both cases it is expressly provided that the imposition or appropriation of fines or penalties, or of fees for services or licences, is not to be taken as financial legislation so as to prevent the Council initiating such proposals. Further, the Council may not amend financial legislation, though it can reject it, but it may suggest amendments to the Assembly, provided that these do not increase the burden on the public, and in practice the power of suggestion is practically as useful as that of amendment, since it can be enforced by the right to reject. In case of deadlock provision is made that the Governor may dissolve the Assembly when a Bill has been rejected by the Council, not less than six months before the date of its dissolution by efflux of time; if after the election the Bill is again passed and again rejected, he may, not less than nine or more than twelve months after the dissolution, dissolve both Houses simultaneously. The procedure is clumsy and ineffective, but the Upper House, though strongly entrenched, is prepared to accept the popular will when it is clearly expressed.

In South Australia friction between the Houses has been often severe, since, unlike Victoria, South Australia is a State where Labour is often powerful in the Lower House; in 1911 an appeal was made by the Labour Government of the day to secure Imperial intervention to coerce the Upper House, but the idea was rejected by that Government on the ground that such action could only be taken if all other constitutional remedies had been exhausted; if it were desired by a large majority; and if it were necessary to enable the work of the State to be carried on. The powers of the Council are very substantial; an Act of 1913 provides that a money Bill or money clause in a Bill shall originate only in the House of Assembly, and the Legislative Council may not amend any money clause, but may return any Bill containing a money clause with a suggestion to omit or amend such clause, or to insert additional money clauses, or may send to the Assembly a Bill containing suggested money clauses, but only as requests. The power of the Council applies to the money clauses in an appropriation Bill only when such clauses contain some provision appropriating revenue for some new purpose, or dealing with some matter other than the appropriation of revenue. For general deadlocks there exists only the inadequate provision that, when a Bill has been passed by the Assembly, and fails to pass the Council, and is passed again by the Assembly after a general election, the second and third readings being passed by an absolute majority, and is again rejected by the Council, the Governor may within six months either dissolve both Houses or issue writs for the addition of nine members to the Council. This is clearly a cumbrous and ineffective proceeding.

In Western Australia, while the Council has no financial initiative, it may like the Senate suggest amendments, the principles of the Commonwealth constitution having been adopted in 1921. It is, in point of fact, a powerful body exercising a very considerable amount of control when Labour Governments are anxious to carry out socialistic undertakings at the public expense, though it is inevitable that no Upper House can really effectively deal with matters of this kind if the Lower House represents a strong popular feeling. No dead-lock provisions exist, and the same condition applies to Tasmania, where the Upper House is in a specially strong position, seeing that the use of proportional representation in the Lower results in the Government of the day having a microscopic majority, and, there-fore, practically no moral strength in conflicts with the Upper House. Proposals to abolish the Upper House or reduce its powers naturally had no success, until in 1924–5 Bills not accepted by the Council were illegally assented to. The result was an Act of 1926 declaring void clauses in appropriation Bills not confined to the ordinary annual supply and income-tax and land-tax rating Acts containing other provisions. Bills of these kinds the Council cannot amend nor can it amend any measure so as to increase or impose any burden on the people or appropriate revenue. But it can suggest amendments where it cannot amend. The Act is prob-ably without legal effect, but enunciates a constitu-tional principle.

Under the elective constitution contemplated for New Zealand by the Act of 1914, the Lower House may carry any money Bill, defined as in the Parliament Act, 1911, over the head of the Council. The Council, how-ever, while it may not initiate a money Bill (other than a Bill imposing or appropriating fines, penalties, or fees) may amend any money Bill, other than a taxation Bill, or one for the ordinary annual appropriation, pro-vided that it may not increase the burden on the people, and it may suggest amendments to any Bill it cannot amend. For deadlocks on general legislation it is provided that, if a Bill is passed in two successive sessions by the Lower House and rejected by the Council, the Governor may convene a joint sitting, when the Bill may be passed by an absolute majority of the members of both Houses, and if not, both Houses may be dissolved simultaneously, but not later than six months before the dissolution of the Lower House by efflux of time.

In the Union the Senate has no financial initiative, save as regards the imposition or appropriation of fines or penalties. It may not amend any Bill so as to increase any proposed charges or burden on the people, nor any Bill so far as it imposes taxation, or appropriates revenue or moneys for the service of the Government, but any Bill which appropriates revenue or moneys for the ordinary annual services of the Government shall deal only with such appropriation. It may, however, reject measures which it cannot amend. For deadlocks it is provided that, if a Bill is passed by the Assembly in two successive sessions and is rejected by the Senate, the Governor-General may convene a joint sitting, when the Bill may be passed if approved by a majority of the total number of members of both Houses;[1] if the Bill deals with the appropriation of revenue or moneys for the public service, the joint sitting may be held in the same session as the rejection. The Senate in point of fact has proved a comparatively weak and not very satisfactory body, but no suggestion to increase its powers would be acceptable.

An effort has been made, notably in the Commonwealth and in New South Wales, to meet the danger of

---

[1] As the Senate has only 40 members to 150 of the Lower House, its inferiority in power is clear.

the hasty undertaking of public works by the Government. Thus in New South Wales no such work, which
is likely to cost over £20,000, may be approved until
it has been referred on the motion of a minister to a
Committee consisting of three members of the Council
and four of the Assembly; on the report of this body
the decision of the Assembly is taken as to proceeding
with the work or not, and, if it resolves to do so, a
statutory obligation is cast upon the minister to introduce a separate Bill for this purpose, which can, of
course, be rejected by the Upper House [1] without the
complications resulting from the inclusion of the proposal in a general appropriation Bill. In the Commonwealth the limit is £25,000, and the procedure analogous.

English is normally the official language of the Dominion Parliaments and courts, but French has equal
rights in the Dominion of Canada and Quebec, and
English and Dutch, including under Act No. 8 of 1925,
Afrikaans, are equal official languages in the Union of
South Africa. In 1926 of those over age seven nearly
60 per cent were bilingual.

7. *The Federations and the Union*

In the case of New Zealand, where provincial government disappeared in 1876, and of Newfoundland,
there is but one legislature which may at pleasure
delegate powers of making by-laws to municipalities
and other local government bodies. In Canada, the
Commonwealth, and the Union, on the other hand,

---

[1] The practice as to the number of ministers in the Upper House
varies greatly. The Canadian Government of 1921 laid down the principle that as a rule only ministers without portfolio should sit in the
Senate. But that has not been rigidly followed.

there is a complex system in which legislative power is in some degree divided, and with it also executive authority. There is, however, a fundamental distinction between the cases of the federations and the Union. The Union Parliament has plenary powers to legislate on any topic, and to confer on its officials executive functions in this regard, so that the provincial councils are without any exclusive powers. Nevertheless they were under the South Africa Act, 1909, not liable to be abolished, nor might their powers be diminished, save by Bill reserved for the consideration of the Imperial Government,[1] and, as they represent the four Colonies which amalgamated in the Union, they possess a vitality of their own which renders the formal disabilities under which they suffer of less consequence than might have been expected, and which may secure their survival though reservation was abolished in 1934.

(a) The Dominion of Canada

In Canada federation was effected by men who, like Sir John Macdonald, would have willingly seen a much greater measure of unity brought about, but who recognised the strength of local feeling as forbidding this, and, therefore, compromised on the issue. All direct relations of the Imperial Government and the provinces were cut off, and a representation from a province reaches that Government only in so far as it pleases the Canadian Government to send it on. The Lieutenant-Governors are appointed by the Governor-General, paid by the Dominion, and may be removed from office at the discretion of the Dominion Govern-

---

[1] Thus Act No. 5 of 1921, depriving the Provincial Council of the Transvaal of the power to tax the profits of the gold-mines, was reserved.

ment. This fact does not give the Dominion Govern- ment as originally planned any direct hold over the provinces, but it does assure them the means of keeping in touch with provincial governments. But the Dominion has also the power of requiring the Lieutenant-Governors to reserve provincial Bills, though this is practically never done, and the originally much more important power of disallowing provincial Acts within a year after receipt by the Governor-General. The use of this power is mainly confined to Acts which infringe the principles of the distribution of legislative power in Canada, or contravene Imperial interests applicable to Canada, as, for example, British Columbian legislation directed against Japanese immigration or employment, and, more rarely, cases of Acts confiscating property without compensation on an adequate basis. The power is one to be discreetly exercised,[1] it has been used very rarely since 1896; in 1918 a British Columbia Act was disallowed as it interfered with an arrangement to which the federation was a party, and in 1923 a Nova Scotia Act as it interfered unfairly with property rights; but the local governments acquiesced.

The division of legislative and executive authority is based on the principle that the residuary authority lies with the Dominion, a deliberate deviation from the United States model, which in other regards greatly influenced the form of the Constitution; the revelation of the weakness of the central Government by the events leading up to the Civil War of 1861-5 had greatly impressed the creators of federation with the

---

[1] In April 1935 both in England and in Canada appeals were made for its use against Ontario legislation cancelling contracts for hydro-electric power. Cf. Dawson, *Constitutional Issues in Canada*, pp. 446-59.

2 E

necessity of a strong central power. The Dominion, therefore, has exclusive powers in all matters not expressly assigned to the provinces, and, without prejudice to this plenitude of authority, it has the sole right to legislate regarding military and naval defence; the postal service; the census and statistics; navigation and shipping, beacons, buoys, and lighthouses, quarantine, and the establishment of marine hospitals; sea-coast and inland fisheries; interprovincial and international ferries; currency, banking, bills of exchange, interest, legal tender, and weights and measures; patents, copyright, bankruptcy; marriage and divorce; criminal law, including procedure, but excluding the constitution of courts; naturalisation and alienage; and Indians and the lands reserved for them. Moreover, it has an absolutely unlimited right of taxation and of raising loans and of managing its property; it has also a general power to regulate trade and commerce, but this authority, which was intended to have wider scope, has been restricted by judicial interpretation to cover only regulations for political purposes, such as the imposition of restrictions on trade in arms, or in liquor or some similar end.[1] While the provinces have powers of regulation of immigration and agriculture, the Dominion has paramount legislative authority on both these topics. Finally, the Dominion possesses full legislative authority to carry out any obligations imposed by treaty on Canada, including, it appears, the right for this purpose to invade the sphere of authority of the provinces, though it is usual and obviously constitutional to obtain the concurrence of the provinces

---

[1] It has been held that federal regulation of prices is, in peace, incompetent; see Keith, *Journ. Comp. Leg.* iv. 238.

in the course proposed,[1] and for the necessary legislation to be passed by the provinces, as was proposed
in the case of labour conventions accepted by Canada.

It must, however, be noted that in 1935 the Conservative Government announced its adoption of a
policy of social legislation intended to confer on the
workers in the Dominion many advantages of the
type popular in Australia. The motive power for this
movement was largely supplied by the pressure of
economic difficulties, and the encouragement accorded
by the spectacle of the "New Deal" in the United
States, which has always exerted a profound influence
on Canada. It was announced that it was proposed to
use the power of ratifying arrangements as to social
legislation arrived at under the procedure of the
Labour organisation of the League of Nations so as to
confer legislative power overriding provincial law on
such issues as the eight-hours day. Reliance was also
placed on the decision of the Privy Council in the case
of radio control in Canada,[2] when it held that, though
the agreement respecting radio communication was
not an Empire treaty in the sense of Section 132 of the
British North America Act, it was sufficient basis for
the use of the general and residuary power of the
Dominion. How far this plan can succeed remains to be
seen. It can hardly be denied that it is unconstitutional

[1] Neither the Dominion nor the provinces can alone deal effectively
with liquor legislation, and a most complex system of concurrent legislation was found necessary, but unsatisfactory, to effect prohibition in
Ontario and other provinces. Since 1919 this system has been repealed
in favour of State control; the referendum has been freely used in this
connection.

[2] *Radio Communication in Canada, In re,* [1932] A.C. 304; cf. *Regulation and Control of Aeronautics in Canada, In re,* [1932] A.C. 54; Keith,
The Constitutional Law of the British Dominions, pp. 300 f.

in the sense that it gives a very changed force to the constitution, whose provisions were intended to cover only such cases as air navigation which was regulated by a convention made in the name of the Empire.

Resort to this device[1] is in part explained by the fact that it has proved impossible to secure any agreement on the method of altering the constitution and the extent of such alteration. It may be hoped that ultimately some accord may be reached on this account rather than the progress of necessary legislation remain subject to the complex difficulties of legal interpretation.

The provinces have exclusive powers of legislation on the whole topic of property and civil rights; the solemnisation of marriage; the incorporation of companies with provincial objects, *i.e.* whose sphere of action is primarily confined to the province; municipal institutions; the control of public lands belonging to the province; the establishment and maintenance of prisons, hospitals, asylums, and other charities; and local works and undertakings, excluding, however, railways or other works extending beyond provincial limits, steamship lines connecting the province with any other place, and such local works as the Parliament of Canada may declare to be for the general advantage of Canada or of two or more provinces. All matters of a merely local or private nature are also entrusted to the provinces, together with the ad-

---

[1] Another mode of federal intrusion into the provincial sphere has been by grants for local matters conditional on federal control, *e.g.* agricultural instruction (1913), technical education (1919), highways (1919), old-age pensions (1927), unemployment relief (1930–35), vocational education (1931). Cf. Dawson, *Constitutional Issues in Canada*, pp. 459-71.

ministration of justice, including the constitution and
maintenance of courts, both of civil and criminal jurisdiction, and civil procedure. Their powers of taxation
are limited to direct taxation and the imposing of shop,
saloon, tavern, auctioneer, or other licences, with a
view to raising revenue for provincial, local, or municipal purposes; they can also borrow money on the
sole credit of the province. Punishment by fine,
penalty (including confiscation), or imprisonment may
be imposed for breach of any enactment of the legislature within the ambit of its power. As regards immigration and agriculture, the provinces have powers subordinate to those of the Dominion. The provinces have
in general sole control of education, but no Act may
prejudicially affect any right or privilege with respect
to denominational schools enjoyed by any class of
persons at the date of union; moreover, when any
system of separate schools existed at the union as in
Ontario and Quebec, or has since been created, as in
Manitoba, Saskatchewan, and Alberta, an appeal lies
to the Dominion Government from any Act or decision
of a provincial authority, affecting any right or privilege of a Protestant or Roman Catholic minority; if
the award then made by the Dominion Government is
not carried out, the Dominion Parliament may pass
remedial legislation for the province. The privileges
referred to are essentially denominational, not of
language,[1] and the power of the Parliament to give
redress is extremely difficult of application, efforts to
do so in regard to Manitoba being one of the causes
leading to the Conservative *débâcle* in 1896.

[1] Decided by the Privy Council in 1917–20 in the case of the schools
of Ontario: *Ottawa Roman Catholic Separate Schools Trustees* v. *Royal
Bank,* [1920] A.C. 230.

Chapter
IV.
___

As the resources of the provinces are inadequate to maintain them in view of their limited powers of taxation,[1] subsidies are granted by the Dominion, growing with increase of population, the amounts being revised in 1907 generally. Special allowances are made also to Manitoba in view of the extension of her boundaries in 1912, and to Prince Edward Island as the least prosperous of the provinces, while the Maritime provinces have been promised special aid. As the main grants are contained in Imperial Acts, the Dominion cannot control in this way the actions of the provinces. The provinces also can amend freely their constitutions save as regards the office of Lieutenant-Governor; the Dominion has extremely limited powers of fundamental change, a fact due to the recognition of the British North America Act, 1867, as a legislative affirmation of a compact between the provinces, which ought only to be altered with practically unanimous provincial assent. Under their wide power the western provinces have experimented with limited schemes[2] of initiative and referendum, of which that in Manitoba,[3] however, has been pronounced invalid, since it deprived the Lieutenant-Governor of his

[1] Manitoba, Saskatchewan, and Alberta had the disadvantage of not owning the public domain, which was administered by the Dominion, until in 1930 its surrender was agreed upon and new subsidies arranged: British North America Act, 1930; Manitoba agreement, ss. 20, 21; Saskatchewan, ss. 21-4; Alberta, ss. 20-22.

[2] A useful variant is the power given by an Act (c. 35) of 1921 in Alberta to the Lieutenant-Governor in Council to take at pleasure a plebiscite, on the desirability of new legislation, or the amendment of the law.

[3] *Initiative and Referendum Act, In re*, [1919] A.C. 935. Yet the Alberta Liquor Act enacted as the result of a popular vote under the Direct Legislation Act, 4 Geo. V. c. 3, was held valid in *R.* v. *Nat Bell Liquors, Ltd.*, [1922] 2 A.C. 128.

power to assent or refuse to assent to provincial Bills. That officer, though a nominee of the Dominion Government, is a representative of the Crown in all matters of provincial concern, and possesses by implication a devolution of the royal prerogative so far as is necessary for the administration of the province.

(b) The Commonwealth of Australia

The federation of the Commonwealth was undertaken rather in recognition of the advantages of common action in external matters as against foreign interests in the Pacific and the influx of criminals, and in such questions as the tariff and communications, than for any pressing need of unity, and hence it is based on the principle of creating a new entity, which should leave to the Colonies, which became States, as much power as possible. The connection between the Imperial Crown and the States thus remains unbroken; the Governors are appointed by the Imperial Government, and they are in no sense subordinates of the Governor-General; they do not correspond with the Imperial Government through him, though normally they keep him supplied with copies of their despatches. The legislation of the States cannot be disallowed by the Commonwealth, and the powers of the States in all matters remain unaltered as before federation, save in so far as the constitution of 1900 grants exclusive powers to the Commonwealth. The Commonwealth, however, is also granted concurrent powers on a considerable range of topics, and when these powers are exercised they supersede State powers. The Governor-General and the Governors share the prerogative according to the same distinction; constitutionally, for instance, the Governor-General may pardon offences against Commonwealth laws, the Governors those against State laws, and the former only can exercise war prerogatives.

The Commonwealth has power over the postal service; the census and statistics; lighthouses, light-ships, beacons and buoys, quarantine; fisheries in Australian waters beyond territorial limits; astronomi-cal and meteorological observations; currency, legal tender, banking (other than State banking not extend-ing beyond the limits of the State), bills of exchange; weights and measures; patents, copyright, trade-marks, bankruptcy, insurance (other than State insurance con-fined to State limits); foreign corporations and trading or financial corporations formed within the limits of the Commonwealth; marriage and divorce; invalid and old-age pensions; naturalisation and aliens; immigra-tion and emigration; the influx of criminals; the control of railways with respect to military and naval trans-port; the acquisition on just terms of property from any State; and, subject to the consent of the State concerned, the acquisition or construction of railways in a State. It may also legislate for the people of any race (other than the aboriginal inhabitants of any State), for whom special legislation is deemed neces-sary, for the relations of the Commonwealth with the islands of the Pacific, and for external affairs, but it seems dubious if this power is sufficient to enable the Commonwealth to invade the spheres of the States even in order to carry out treaty obligations. A remedy for this lack of authority is, however, present in the power of the States to confer authority on the Commonwealth for any purpose, as was done by several States in regard to aerial navigation The Commonwealth powers as to trade and commerce are confined to the regulation of foreign and inter-State trade and navigation, excluding, therefore, the control of industry and shipping within a State, and to conciliation and arbitration for the settlement of industrial disputes extending beyond the limits of any one State. Indirectly, however, the Commonwealth can greatly influence trade by its exclusive power of imposing customs and excise duties, and of granting bounties, though the States are permitted to grant bounties on metals, and, with the consent of the Commonwealth, on other products also. The Commonwealth has a general power of taxation, but must not discriminate between States or parts of States, and it controls the naval and military forces which no State may maintain save with its consent. The grant of preferential treatment to any State by any law regarding revenue, trade, or commerce, is prohibited, nor may the Commonwealth deprive any State of the reasonable use of its waters for conservation or navigation, nor may it legislate as to religion. On the other hand no State may coin money, or make anything save gold or silver legal tender, nor may it discriminate between its own citizens and those of other States. The Commonwealth Parliament may forbid State authorities giving preferential treatment on State railways, if such treatment is held by the inter-State Commission, provided for in the constitution, to be undue and unreasonable, or unjust to any State; but the Commission has been allowed to lapse at present. Commonwealth property is exempt from State taxation, and *vice versa*, but State imports are subject to customs duties. The States may not impede freedom of intercourse and trade within the Commonwealth.

The interpretation of the constitution has remained in the hands of the High Court, which has refused save in one case to certify as fit for decision by the Privy Council any case involving the question of the rights *inter se* of the Commonwealth and a State, or of two or more States. In the early years of its existence it adopted from the American constitution, which greatly impressed the fathers of federation, the doctrines of immunity of instrumentalities and reserved powers. Thus it held that the federation could not by indirect means interfere with the authority over internal trade and production reserved to the States, and that the States could not tax Commonwealth instrumentalities, even to the extent of imposing the obligation to stamp a receipt for a federal salary or income tax on federal salaries. Similarly, it forbade the Commonwealth Court of Conciliation and Arbitration to deal with the terms of employment of State railway servants, and it ruled that the awards of the court could not override positive State law. In 1920, however, this interpretation was laid aside, and the court resorted to the principles of interpretation of statutes adopted in English courts and declared applicable by the Privy Council to the Australian constitution. This change of view has greatly weakened the position of the States. Their servants on the State railways and other undertakings are subject to determinations of wages by the courts, their loans are subject to Commonwealth taxation if the Commonwealth thinks fit, suits in tort can be brought against them without their consent. Moreover the exigencies of the war led to the wholesale invasion by the Commonwealth of the sphere of taxation which had originally in practice been left to the States. Use was made of the difficulties into which the States were thus reduced to secure their assent to a Financial Agreement, which was duly approved by legislation by all the States and the Commonwealth, and became part of the constitution by a constitutional amendment in 1929.

The agreement proved in 1932 of the utmost importance to the Commonwealth. Under it the Commonwealth undertook, in lieu of other subsidies, to pay a very large proportion of the interest on the States debts, the obligation of which it took over, and to contribute generously towards sinking funds for the extinction of existing and future debts. New South Wales under a Labour régime defaulted in its obligation to pay part of the interest, and refused to obey the decision of the High Court[1] that it must pay. Legislation was then passed under the constitutional amendment (s. 105 A.) authorising legislation to enforce the agreement, sequestering State revenues, and, when the State Premier endeavoured to frustrate the efforts to collect these revenues, he was dismissed for disobedience to law by the Governor. The ensuing general election approved his action, and the State resumed obedience to its obligations. It is, however, clear that the amendment has deeply interfered with State autonomy, by overriding the law that no appropriation of revenue or taxation can be imposed save by the State Parliament for State purposes.[2]

By the provision of equal representation in the

---

[1] Keith, *Journ. Comp. Leg.* xv. 118-20.

[2] See above, Chap. I. s. 5.

Senate for each State, regardless of size, there is a more formal recognition of State equality than in Canada, where the minor provinces are accorded much smaller representation than Ontario and Quebec, but the Senate has not proved in any sense a champion of State rights any more than has the Canadian Senate. The States retain power of constitutional alteration but their position is much less secure than that of the provinces, for the Commonwealth constitution itself may be altered, and the position of the States vitally affected, by laws passed by the Commonwealth Parliament by absolute majorities and approved at a referendum by a majority of voters and a majority of States. The States, however, are protected by the rule that no alteration diminishing the proportionate representation of any State in either house of Parliament, or the minimum number of representatives of a State in the House of Representatives, or increasing, diminishing, or otherwise altering the limits of the State, or in any manner affecting the provisions of the constitution in relation thereto, may become law unless the majority of the electors voting in the State approve the proposed law.

The restrictions on the activities of the Commonwealth under the constitution have proved considerable, and repeated efforts have been made to secure for the Commonwealth power to deal with all forms of trade and commerce, including intra-State trade; industrial matters generally, including the wages and conditions of labour; the control of corporations generally; and the power to regulate monopolies, and in suitable circumstances to operate the monopoly for the good of the Commonwealth. But proposals slightly varied in each case failed at referenda of 1911, 1913, 1919, and 1926, showing that the people are not prepared for the complete submergence of State autonomy, and a Royal Commission which considered the constitution did not recommend any vital changes. A demand for secession by Western Australia authorised by a referendum was vainly presented to the Imperial Parliament in 1935.

Territories of the Commonwealth and New Zealand

The Commonwealth controls certain territories, which in part are included in its area, in part are separate from it.

(1) The Northern Territory, with an area of 523,620 square miles and a European population little over 4000 in number, was transferred on January 1, 1911, from South Australia, which had held it since 1863. In 1926 it was subdivided into two parts, Central and North Australia, each administered by a Government Resident with an Advisory Council, and a Development Commission was instituted. In 1931 the project was abandoned, the Councils and Commission disappeared, and administration was restored to the hands of an Administrator. Legislation is effected by the Governor-General in Council.

(2) The Federal Capital Territory has attained especial importance since Parliament House was opened there in 1927, thus superseding the practice under which Parliament had sat at Melbourne. Under legislation of 1930 and action by ordinance taken thereunder the administration of the territory is vested in the Minister of the Interior, who has an Advisory Council of the Director-General of Health and three

officers of the Department of the Interior, together with three residents elected for two years by adult suffrage.

(3) Norfolk Island has an interesting history. Colonised in 1788, it was used as a penal settlement until 1813, and then again from 1826 to 1855, being formally annexed in 1844 to Tasmania. In 1856 it was transferred to the status of a separate settlement under New South Wales, and the descendants of the mutineers of the *Bounty* were removed thither from Pitcairn Island, now too small for their maintenance. In 1896 the island was placed under the control of the Governor of New South Wales, but in 1913 the Commonwealth Parliament passed the Norfolk Island Act to provide for the control of the island on its transfer by the Crown to the Commonwealth. From January 1, 1929, the island has been under the control of the Prime Minister's department. Acts of the Commonwealth Parliament do not, unless expressly so provided, apply to the island, and legislation is by ordinance of the Governor-General in Council. The laws of the island remain in force except as varied, and there is an Advisory Council to advise the Administrator and Chief Magistrate. The Magistrate's Court has jurisdiction in all criminal causes, not capital, and in all civil causes, with appeal to the High Court of the Commonwealth. The power of pardon is granted to the Governor-General.

(4) Like Norfolk Island, Papua—formerly British New Guinea—is not part of the Commonwealth but is controlled by it under the power given by Section 122 of the constitution to govern territories handed over by the Crown. Originally a Crown Colony, created in

1888, it was transferred to the Commonwealth under
the authority of letters patent of 1902 and the Papua
Act, 1905, with effect from September 1, 1906. The
Government retains the usual Crown Colony form.
The Lieutenant-Governor is aided by an Executive
Council of seven officials, and legislates with the aid
of a Legislative Council, which includes the members
of the Executive Council and five unofficial members
nominated by the Governor-General. The territory is
only in part under effective administration. There is
little organised native society, so that rule through
chiefs is impossible, and the most useful agency has
proved to be native police. The Lieutenant-Governor
is judge of the Central Court, which with the powers
of a Supreme Court sits where required for serious
offences and civil business. There are eight magisterial
divisions in which Resident Magistrates exercise both
executive and judicial powers, and there are for petty
matters Native Magistrates' courts. The island, however, does not enjoy, as does Norfolk Island, free
entry for its produce into the Commonwealth.

(5) Since 1933 the Commonwealth has been responsible under an Order in Council of February 7,
1933, for the government of the Australian Antarctic
Territory, being that territory south of the 60th
degree of south latitude which lies between the
160th degree of east longitude and the 45th degree of
east longitude, excluding Adelie Land. The Governor-
General may legislate by ordinance.[1] In the same year
provision was made for the acceptance of control over
the Ashmore and Cartier Islands in the Indian Ocean
off the north-west coast of Australia, under an Order

---

[1] Act No. 8 of 1933.

in Council of July 23, 1931. The Governor in Council of Western Australia legislates.[1]

New Zealand had earlier acquired under Imperial Order in Council of July 30, 1923, control over the Antarctic region south of the 60th degree of south latitude, and lying between the 160th degree of east longitude and the 150th degree of west longitude. The power to govern this area purports to be given under the British Settlements Act, 1887, and some doubt may exist as to the legitimacy of the delegation of legislative authority to a single officer in the area. Since February 11, 1926, under Imperial Orders in Council of November 4, 1925, New Zealand has administered from Apia, Western Samoa, the Union group of islands. The Cook Islands, whose administration has been dealt with above, are an integral part of New Zealand, to which they were annexed on June 11, 1901, having been under a British Protectorate since 1888.

Note will be taken below of the mandated territories of Australia and New Zealand, as well as that of the Union of South Africa.

(c) The Union of South Africa

The Union constitution provides for the appointment by the Governor-General in Council of an Administrator who is the head of the provincial executive, but must act with a committee of four persons appointed by proportional representation whether councillors or not; the Administrator has a casting vote in the discussions in case of equality but cannot act against the advice of the Committee. Nor has he any

---

[1] Act No. 60 of 1933.

power to dissolve the Council before the end of its three years' term. The Executive Committee has full executive authority in all matters within the sphere of the provincial council's authority to legislate. The Union Government may also impose other duties on the Administrator, but these he performs on his own authority, without consulting the Committee unless he desires. The Administrator is also given a definite control over provincial finance, for no appropriation, whether of moneys raised by provincial taxation or of Union grants, can be made save on his recommendation to the Council, and all moneys must be issued under warrant from him.

The legislative powers of the provincial councils extend to the borrowing of money on the sole credit of the province, with the consent of the Union Government and in accordance with regulations framed by Parliament; education, other than higher education; agriculture to the extent defined by Parliament; control of hospitals and charitable institutions; municipal and other local institutions; local works and undertakings, other than railways and harbours, and works extending beyond the provincial borders, and subject to the power of Parliament to declare any work a national work, and to provide for its construction by arrangement with the Council or otherwise; roads, outspans, ponts and bridges other than inter-provincial bridges; markets and pounds; fish and game preservation; the imposition of punishment by fine, penalty, or imprisonment for enforcing any law or any ordinance of the province made in relation to its subjects of control; and generally all matters which, in the opinion of the Union Government, are of merely local or private

2 F

nature in the province, or in respect of which Parliament may delegate the power of legislation. By legislation of 1913–25 the powers of the councils have been extended to include the destruction of noxious weeds and vermin, and the control of dogs; the experimental cultivation of sugar, tea, and vines; grants to agricultural and kindred societies; library, museum, and art gallery administration, with certain exceptions; the administration of cemetery and casualty wards; poor relief; the regulation of shop hours; the establishment and administration of townships. In 1925 town planning was authorised. It may also deal with the licensing and control of vehicles, horse-racing and betting, and of places of amusement. The provinces have also been given as sources of revenue the right to levy hospital and education fees, and licence fees for dog, sporting, motor, flower-picking, and game licences. They may raise auction dues, tax vehicles, amusements, betting, personal incomes and company receipts on defined conditions, the ownership of immovable property, and impose licence duties on the right to import non-Union goods for sale. The general power of direct taxation conceded in 1909 has disappeared; the Labour administration of the Transvaal had used it to tax mining profits, and its right to do so was upheld by the courts, which led to its annulment in 1921, and in 1922 direct taxation of natives was forbidden.

The provincial ordinances must be assented to by the Governor-General in Council; they may be reserved by him for consideration, but fall to the ground if not assented to within a year. The assent is not by any means a formality, and is of special importance, as it can be, and has been, used to secure the observance of the rule that the control and administration of native affairs and of matters specially or differently affecting Asiatics throughout the Union is vested in the Governor-General in Council. Any ordinance is valid only in so far as it does not disagree with an Act of Parliament, and may at any time be superseded by such an Act. A council may recommend to Parliament legislation which it cannot enact, and may take evidence in matters which have to be dealt with by private Bills, which will obviate the necessity of further investigation by Parliament.

In addition to revenues raised by themselves the provinces receive subsidies from Union funds, fixed in 1913 at a half the ordinary annual expenditure, since 1931 at £16 17s. 6d. per head for the first 30,000 pupils and £14 per head for the excess number in each province; the licence fees fixed since 1925 by the Union in respect of trades, professions, and occupations; and the proceeds of transfer duties, liquor licences, and, in Transvaal labour districts, native pass fees. In addition Natal and the Orange Free State are allocated £75,000 annually as extra allowances. The whole issue is under reconsideration.

Up to 1930 through the Governor-General the Union enjoyed contact with the native territories, which he administered as High Commissioner of the Imperial Government, Basutoland, which is a Colony, and the Protectorates of Swaziland and Bechuanaland.[1] Ad-

---

[1] The territories are now under the control of the High Commissioner for Basutoland, the Bechuanaland Protectorate, and Swaziland, who serves also as High Commissioner for the United Kingdom in the Union. The Union has pressed for the transfer of the territories but objections have been expressed by the natives: Keith, *Letters on Imperial Relations, 1916–1935*, pp. 161, 163, 169, 170.

mission to Southern Rhodesia with provincial status was offered in 1922, but rejected by a popular referendum; provision exists in the Union constitution for the admission of other territories on agreed terms.

8. *Defence*

(1) *Canadian* defence is based on the assumption that war with the United States can be ruled out of account and that Canada would not be requested by the Council of the League of Nations to send forces to Europe to enforce sanctions against a State which breaks the League Covenant.[1]

The National Defence Act, 1922, transferred to a Department of National Defence control of the militia, navy, and civil and military aeronautics. The department is controlled by a Minister and Deputy-Minister. By Order in Council in 1923 there was constituted the Defence Council to advise the Minister, of which the Deputy-Minister, the Chiefs of the General and Naval Staffs, are members and the Adjutant-General, Quarter-master-General, and the Director of the Royal Canadian Air Force are associate members.

Canadian policy renders a standing army unnecessary and renders it possible to rely on the non-permanent, active militia, supplemented to a certain extent from the small permanent force. The active militia, in 1934, had an establishment of 9029 officers and 125,722 other ranks; the active strength was over 51,000, but only 36,000 received training of twelve days. The forces are as far as possible organised and trained on British

[1] Palmer, *Consultation and Co-operation in the British Commonwealth*, pp. 84 ff.

lines, for which purpose the Government encourages interchange of officers, the attendance of officers at courses of instruction in England, and exchange visits between staff officers.

The air force of Canada in summer is almost entirely devoted to civil operations. Aeroplane photography in connection with the preparation of maps, fishery protection, a study of the spread of pine blister, wheat rust, etc. Military training is carried out in winter; the force in 1933 numbered 103 officers and 591 airmen.

The sea forces of Canada are intended to protect the focal points in Canadian waters at which Canadian shipping becomes congested. It is not proposed to contribute to general Imperial defence or to co-operate in the protection of Australia and New Zealand, despite the arguments in favour of this course urged from time to time by Australian ministers. The naval forces of the Dominion, therefore, in 1934, were reduced to four destroyers and three minesweepers. In 1934 the permanent force numbered 104 officers and 792 men; there was a naval reserve of 500 of all ranks and a volunteer reserve of 1000. The total cost for 1933–4 was 13,600,000 dollars.

In view of the constitutional advance of the Dominions, it is proposed that in any future war Canadian personnel will be reserved for Canadian units; the Canadian forces will be administratively self-controlled, with direct responsibility to the Canadian Government; and that, tactically, the Canadian commander will probably be under the orders of the Commander-in-Chief, but will not be free from responsibility to the Canadian Government for the safety of his command. These principles are, of course, an application of the system adopted in the last year of the Great War.

Compulsory service was enacted, but only for the latter part of the Great War, and, though in theory all able-bodied citizens between the ages of 18 and 60 are liable for service in case of war, no use has ever been made of this provision. Moreover, it is clear that the despatch of forces from Canada could only take place on the express authority of Parliament, and perhaps, as contended by Mr Meighen, on the authority of a general election, or even a referendum.

(2) *Australian* defence policy accepts primary responsibility of each Dominion to provide for local defence. It accepts the necessity of maintaining equality of the British Empire with any naval power and the provision of naval bases; recognises the vital necessity of preserving the Suez–Red Sea communication, and agrees that the preservation of Empire trade routes is a matter of common concern, and that equality of status carries some responsibility to share the common burden of defence. It therefore aims at securing uniformity of organisation and of training of its forces with those of the United Kingdom at Home and in India.

The services are administered by the Department of Defence, under a Minister and Secretary. There is a Council of Defence under the presidency of the Prime Minister, on which the three services are represented and which deals with policy co-ordinating the requirements of sea, air, and land. There is also a Defence Committee, whose Chairman is Chief of General Staff and the other members of which are the Chiefs of the Naval and Air Staff, the Finance Secretary of the Department of

Defence, and the Secretary. Each service has its own Board under the presidency of the Minister for Defence, and is responsible for the control and administration of the forces.

The principle of universal compulsory training of a citizen army adopted on the advice of Lord Kitchener from 1911 to 1929 has been abandoned and the forces constituted on a voluntary basis. Under this system men from 18 to 40 years of age are enlisted for three years, with possible re-engagement up to age 48. The normal period of training is sixteen days a year, including eight days' continuous camp training. The divisional organisation created in 1921 is retained, but the peace nucleus of the militia forces is reduced to 30,000 and in addition senior cadets up to 7000 may be enrolled from age 14 to 17. The permanent staff is merely sufficient for the administration and instruction of the military forces.

The Royal Australian Air Force maintains a flying training school, an aircraft depot, two service land-plane squadrons, and one service amphibian flight. The establishment of the permanent force is 102 officers; of the citizen force, 49 officers, and 261 airmen.

Naval defence since 1913 has been based on the supply and maintainance of a navy which remains under Commonwealth control in peace and in war unless it is placed under the British Admiralty. The Washington Conference of 1921 resulted in the reduction of the fleet and the sinking of the battle-cruiser *Australia*. Since 1925, however, steps have been taken to strengthen the navy and to exchange a cruiser periodically, so that Australian sailors who now make up the personnel of the sea-going forces may gain experience in fleet exercises on a large scale. The fleet now consists of two cruisers, *Australia* and *Canberra*, and some minor vessels. The total strength of the sea-going forces in 1934 was 334 officers and 2879 men. There are also a fleet reserve, a naval reserve, and a naval volunteer reserve. Training is given to midshipmen at the Naval College, which since 1930 is situated at the Flinders Naval Depot, Victoria. It performs for the navy similar services to those rendered by the Royal Military College, transferred in 1931 to Victoria Barracks, Sydney, from Duntroon.

A war railway council consisting of military and railway officers was instituted in 1911 to furnish advice regarding railway transport for military purposes, and to secure co-operation between the Defence and the Railway departments in regard to concentration and mobilisation of troops.

The total expenditure has risen considerably of recent years, and in 1933–4 was over £5,116,000.

(3) *New Zealand* defence stresses the importance of the protection of sea-borne trade and deprecates any excessive reduction of naval armaments. It aims at the greatest measure of similarity of organisation and material, and since 1933 a policy of strengthening the Dominion forces has been emphasised.

The three services are administered by the Minister of Defence through the Naval Board, constituted in 1921, and the General Headquarters New Zealand Military Forces. The Naval Board is composed of the Minister of Defence, the Commodore commanding the New Zealand station, and a Captain R.N. The military forces are commanded by a general officer responsible to the Minister of Defence, assisted by branches of

General Headquarters, which are the counterpart in New Zealand of the War Office.

The military forces of New Zealand are divided into the permanent forces, which provide commanders and staffs, instructional staff, and nucleus garrison. They are liable for service in New Zealand or overseas. The Territorial Force, which was recruited by compulsion from 1909 to 1930, is now recruited voluntarily for service within the Dominion. The New Zealand Air Force is maintained as an integral part of the military force. The Territorial Force in 1934 numbered 635 officers and 8634 other ranks.

The New Zealand division of the Royal Navy is at the disposal of the United Kingdom in time of war and its officers are derived from the Royal Navy. Financial resources compel the reduction of expenditure as far as practicable, but the Dominion endeavours to maintain two cruisers lent by the Admiralty in an efficient state, and to provide base and repair facilities at Auckland and facilities for training recruits. In 1933–4 naval defence cost £527,998. Two sloops are maintained by the British Government for duties in the South Pacific within the limits of the New Zealand stations.

(4) The defence of *South Africa* is organised on the basis of the defence of the Union in any part of South Africa, whether within or without the Union.[1] Since 1921 the Union has undertaken entire responsibility for its defence and maintains at Table Bay and at the naval base at Simon's Bay approved coastal defences,

---

[1] Act No. 13 of 1912; No. 22 of 1922. The code of military law now depends on the Defence Act (Amendment) and Dominion Forces Act, No. 32 of 1932: Keith, *Journ. Comp. Leg.* xv. 255, 256.

while at Durban a graving dock is provided, capable of taking anything except the largest type of battle-cruiser; but the British Government still maintains and staffs, under the Commander-in-Chief, the naval base at Simonstown. Military policy aims at maintaining a quickly mobilisable citizen army, capable of dealing with any internal war emergencies or danger on the land frontier, of discharging the responsibilities of the Union for coastal defence and that of the naval base, and affording military training to as many young citizens as Union finances permit. The Union Government is specially concerned to be able to control without delay any native unrest, whether in the Union in South-West Africa, or the adjacent territories, Basutoland, Swaziland, and the Bechuanaland Protectorate. Its view towards Imperial defence is to maintain military organisation in harmony with that of Great Britain and to discuss organisation with the War Office and Air Ministry, but without prejudice to the absolute freedom of the Union's decision, whether to participate in any particular eventuality. The ideal of undertaking a share in naval defence proper as a concomitant of Dominion status has been dropped and no naval forces proper are now maintained by the Union.

Responsibility for the Union's forces rests with the Department for Union Defence, presided over by a Minister. He is advised by a Council of Defence of four members. The Secretary for Defence is also the officer commanding the Union defence forces. The other principal officers are the Chief of the General Staff, Director of Air Services, Quartermaster-General, Adjutant-General, and Director of Military Services.

The defence system is based on liability of citizens

of European descent in war, if between age 17 and
60, to render personal service within or without the
Dominion. The citizens between 17 and 25 are liable
to undergo peace training for a period of four years;
but only some 50 per cent of those liable are required
to serve, others being required in their twenty-first
year to enrol as members of rifle associations. As an
alternative, citizens may enrol in the South African
Division R.N.V.R., which is administered under the
orders of the Commander-in-Chief Africa Station.
There is a small permanent force for which training
is given in the South African Military College, and a
Coast Garrison force. The citizen force is divided into
the active citizen force, the citizen force reserve, and
the national reserve, which may be called out in three
classes, according to age, after the whole of the active
citizen force and the citizen force reserve have been
mobilised in time of war.

The air force has recently been strongly developed
with a view to providing mobile forces to be used in the
case of unrest in any part of the Union or adjacent
territories. Recently the force has adopted aeroplanes
of other than British make.

(5) The *Irish Free State* Department of Defence
owes its origin to the revolutionary Ministry of Defence
organised in 1919 to combat British rule. After the
Treaty of 1921 the Provisional Government organised
the Republican forces and formed from them the regular army which took over charge of the areas evacuated
by the British forces in 1922 and overcame the resistance of Mr de Valera's following. The purpose of the
forces now maintained is internal defence, against local
disorder or attack; it is essentially a home defence force

which could not be used outside the State without express Parliamentary authority. The Free State has made no suggestion of desire to share in Imperial defence, and it has so far not availed itself of the right which it has enjoyed since 1926 of suggesting that it should assume a share in the burden of coastal defence. As has already been noted, the Free State is bound by treaty to permit British occupation of Berehaven, Queenstown, and Lough Swilly, where British warships are regularly stationed, and in time of war must afford such other facilities as may be claimed, a fact which involves the Free State in imminent risk of the refusal of any foreign State to allow of the validity of any claim she might assert to maintain neutrality in a British war.

The autonomy of the Free State is marked in the fact that the control of the forces is not associated with the name of the King, and the military oath ignores the Crown. The command-in-chief is vested in the Executive Council, which exercises it through the Minister of Defence, who is styled Commander-in-Chief, but may not assign to himself executive command, and who may not be an officer on full pay.

The Minister presides over the Council of Defence, which contains a civil member, who is Parliamentary Secretary, and three military members, whose tenure of office may not exceed three years. The army is organised on the basis of a professional force, with a strength in 1935 of 583 officers and 5300 other ranks. the cost being £980,500. The reserve force numbered some 6000 of all ranks. The Military College is staffed by officers trained in the United States Army Staff College; the head of the School of Music is a former officer of the Prussian Guards who has rendered great services to Irish military music. A recent development is that of a Volunteer force, apparently as a counter-blast to the Irish Republican Army, 22,000 in number.

(6) Newfoundland had a branch of the Royal Naval Volunteer Reserve, the revival of which is desirable, but through financial stress has not continued the beginnings of a military organisation undertaken during the war.

Very important gifts of war material have since the close of the war been made to the Dominions, both in ships, including submarines, and aeroplanes, the total value reaching many millions, while the naval and military property handed over in the Cape is of very considerable value. The gifts of material have been unconditional, and Canada has not thought it necessary to maintain in commission any of the flotilla presented to her. Similarly in the Commonwealth the naval reductions have included the transfer to British control of the submarines, and have evoked protests to the effect that the naval force has been diminished in a dangerous degree. It is clear that, as compared with the British forces, Dominion naval preparations are yet only in an embryo condition. Thus in 1930–31 British expenditure was 22s. 7d. per head of population, Canadian 36 cents, Australian 5s. 6d., New Zealand 9s. 1d., Union of South Africa 10¾d. (white population).

9. *The Judicature and the Laws*

In Canada the appointment of the judges of all superior, district, and county courts rests with the Governor-General; these posts are not within the control of the provincial legislatures, which, however, are responsible for the organisation of provincial courts, and have established Supreme Courts, usually with appellate divisions. The Dominion has also established a Supreme Court which is a general court of Canadian appeal, and an Exchequer Court,[1] while it has conferred on several Boards quasi-judicial functions. Appeals, however, lie direct to the Judicial Committee of the Privy Council from the provincial courts, either by special leave or as of right, on conditions as to the nature or value of the cause stated in Orders of the King in Council or local legislation in Ontario and Quebec, and it is in the option of the litigant to choose the tribunal he prefers. By special leave appeals lie from the Supreme Court of Canada, but a suitor who has preferred to go there from a provincial court is not normally, unless the cause involves principles of special importance, allowed to appeal from that court.[2] All the judges of superior courts hold office during good behaviour, but may be removed by the Governor-General on addresses from both houses of Parliament.

In Newfoundland judges also hold office during good behaviour, but subject to removal by the Crown on addresses from the legislature.

In the Australian Commonwealth the judges of the High Court and other federal courts are appointed by the Governor-General in Council, hold office during good behaviour, and may be removed only on addresses from the houses of Parliament, on the ground of proved misbehaviour or incapacity, but the Houses must

---

[1] It is a Court of Admiralty, with local judges in the provinces. From Colonial Courts of Admiralty appeal lies to the Privy Council as of right, and that is preserved in the Canadian Admiralty Court legislation of 1934.

[2] *Clergue* v. *Murray*, [1903] A.C. 521.

clearly be judges of what is proof. The judges in the States hold on a similar tenure, but removal is ascribed to the Crown in New South Wales, Queensland, South Australia, and Western Australia, and to the Governor, or Governor in Council, in Victoria and Tasmania, on simple addresses from both Houses; in the former case an obligation is thrown on the Imperial Government to advise the Crown and, therefore, to accept responsibility for the propriety of the proceedings. Appeals lie as in Canada, first from the State Supreme Courts either to the Commonwealth High Court, or to the Judicial Committee, but not in cases regarding the limits *inter se* of the constitutional powers of the Commonwealth and those of any State or States, or as to the limits *inter se* of the constitutional powers of any two or more States. Such cases under legislation in the Commonwealth in 1907 may not be decided by State Supreme Courts, but must be dealt with by the High Court. As no appeal lies from the decision of the High Court on these issues to the Privy Council, unless the High Court certifies that the case should be determined by the King in Council, and the High Court on principle refuses such certificates,[1] the determination of the interpretation of the constitution has rested with the High Court, which has largely followed the precedent of the United States, and not the principles of interpretation laid down in the case of Canada by the Judicial Committee.

In New Zealand judges hold office during good behaviour, but may be removed by the Governor on addresses from both Houses. Appeals to the Judicial Committee lie normally from the Court of Appeal, exceptionally from the Supreme Court.

[1] Keith, *Journ. Comp. Leg.* iv. 107 f.

In the Union the old colonial courts are merged in a Supreme Court with an appellate division and four provincial divisions, and a number of local divisions, all being superior courts whose judges are appointed by the Governor-General in Council, and may be removed only on addresses from both Houses on the ground of misbehaviour or incapacity. Appeals lie to the appellate division in every case in which they would before Union have lain to the King in Council, but the decisions of the appellate division are final save in so far as an appeal may be permitted by special leave to the King in Council, so that in the Union appeals come from one court only, and such appeals are not encouraged by the Judicial Committee.[1]

In addition to the jurisdiction which Dominion courts possess under local statutes, they can act as Colonial Courts of Admiralty under the Colonial Courts[2] of Admiralty Act, 1890, and have further a wide range of authority to deal with matters occurring outside the Dominions under various Imperial Acts, such as the Merchant Shipping Act, Foreign Enlistment Act, etc. Jurisdiction in prize was specially conferred on them during the late war. Admiralty jurisdiction in criminal matters they exercise under the Admiralty Offences (Colonial) Act, 1849.

The laws of the Dominions in the main rest upon English law, including the doctrines of equity and statutes of general application up to the date either of the introduction of English law on the creation of

[1] *Whittaker* v. *Durban Corpn.* (1920), 90 L.J.P.C. 119.

[2] This Act can be amended by those Dominions which adopt the Statute of Westminster, 1931, and they can regulate prize law. Canada has modernised her Admiralty law, preserving the appeal to the Privy Council as of right. It is not applicable to the Free State.

the Colony, or to some other date fixed by local legislation. But in Quebec the common law is the old French
law existing on the capitulation which was preserved
by agreement, while the criminal law was assimilated
to English law; naturally the law of Quebec has been
influenced greatly by the French Code, with which the
Civil Code of Quebec in large measure agrees. In South
Africa, Roman Dutch law is the common law of the
whole of the Union, and has been introduced into
Southern Rhodesia and South-West Africa, and for
Europeans the Bechuanaland Protectorate, Swaziland,
and Basutoland. But in all cases the common law has
been deeply affected by local legislation, and by regulations made under the force of such legislation, and to
a very minor degree by Imperial legislation and regulations under such legislation applying to the Dominions,
though it is to Imperial legislation that the greater part
of the Dominion constitutions is due. Indeed, the constitution [1] of Newfoundland alone can be said to rest
on the prerogative and local legislation, for in all other
cases the constitutions either rest entirely or in the
main on Imperial legislation, even where such legislation is now embodied in local Acts.

[1] At present in abeyance.

CHAPTER V

COLONIES POSSESSING RESPONSIBLE GOVERNMENT

1. *Malta*

Chapter V.

THE constitution of Malta, as granted in 1921, is complex in its attempt to reconcile the grant to Malta of responsible government in all internal affairs, while preserving effective and direct Imperial management of questions of Imperial concern. The Governor, accordingly, is assigned two quite different capacities, one as the constitutional head of the Maltese administration acting on ministerial advice, one as Imperial officer managing those affairs reserved to the Imperial Crown. The distinction is a vague one, and, as expressed in the constitution, presents difficulties of solution of the most formidable kind. The Maltese legislature may not legislate as to matters touching the public safety and defence of the Empire, and the general interests of British subjects not resident in Malta, and specifically it may not deal with the control of naval, military, or air forces; defence including land acquisition on compensation; aerial navigation; defence surveys; submarine cables, wireless telegraphy and telephony; Imperial property for defence purposes and civil property required for Imperial purposes; trade out of the islands; importation of goods for the Imperial forces; currency and coinage; immigration; naturalisation and aliens; postal and telegraphic censorship; issue and visa of

passports; appropriation of revenues accruing in respect of any reserved matter; and treaties or any relations with foreign States, save in so far as local legislation may be necessary to give effect to treaty obligations
affecting the island. In 1932 control of the police force
was made a subject which could be treated as Imperial.
Legislation on local government matters, roads and
harbours, shipping and quarantine may be passed, but
must be reserved. Religious toleration is laid down as a
fundamental principle, and a superior position as an
official language is assured to English, save in the law
courts, while in the original constitution Italian was
recognised in official use in the law courts and in education, and in a minor degree Maltese also. In 1932 fresh
provision was made to secure the position of the English and Maltese languages, but in 1934 it became
necessary to make Maltese the official language of the
courts, and in 1935 the use of Maltese in education was
extended. The legislature is given constituent powers,
but may not alter the division of subjects as reserved
and non-reserved, or the provisions as to religion or
language, or the Civil Lists reserved to the control of
the Crown. Any legislation contravening the limits set
is invalid, in so far as the contravention exists.

The executive control of matters not reserved rests
with the Governor in Executive Council, consisting of
not more than seven ministers, who must be members
of the legislature, re-election on acceptance of office
being dispensed with, while all other matters fall within
the power of the Governor. He may legislate, and is
aided in administration by a nominated council of five,
the Lieutenant-Governor, the Legal Adviser, military,
naval, and air officers; in matters of administration not

exclusively pertaining to the Executive Council he may convene joint meetings of both bodies as his Privy Council, and a committee of that body consisting of three ministers and three members of the nominated council is created to consider questions of legislation or executive action proposed which may affect reserved subjects. Since 1932 control of judicial appointments has rested with the Governor.

The legislature consists of a Senate of seventeen members, chosen to secure representation of the clergy, nobility, learned classes, merchants, and trade unions, by a limited electorate, and an Assembly of thirty-two members elected on a very low franchise, confined to men. The Senate may suggest amendments in money Bills, but must accept or reject simply the Bill, as returned from the Assembly after consideration of the suggestions. In case of the rejection in a subsequent session of a measure rejected in a previous session, a joint session may be held in which the Bill may be passed by a majority of the votes of the total members of both Houses, or the Governor may dissolve the Assembly, or both Senate and Assembly, and convene a joint session. The rules clearly give wide power to the Senate to force its will on the Assembly. The Senate lasts for six, the Assembly for three years, unless sooner dissolved.

The Crown retains the right to legislate on any reserved subject by Order in Council, and also to alter the provisions of the constitution regarding the division of subjects, religion, language, and the Civil List which provides for the salary of the Governor, Lieutenant-Governor, Legal Adviser, and the Judges, and secures to the Governor the power to have appropriated such sums as may be necessary for reserved heads, this being the only contribution of Malta to Imperial expenditure, whence, of course, the islands derive great advantages through the expenditure there of money by the naval and military forces. In 1930, owing to serious unrest over the election, the constitution was suspended by Order in Council, June 26, and when restored in 1932 it was subject to certain changes validated by the Malta Constitution Act, 1932. The elections of 1932 were conducted under ecclesiastical pressure, and the new Government endeavoured to defy the constitutional restrictions on the use of Italian in primary education; in November 1933 it was dismissed and all power vested in the Governor.[1]

As Malta was the seat of an ancient civilisation before its acquisition by the British Crown, naturally enough no attempt was made to introduce English law as the common law of the island, which thus has a legal system based in part on ancient custom, in part on Roman law as developed by Italian jurisprudence, the culture of the islands having been essentially Italian. A relic of the ancient constitution is seen in the existence of a local nobility, whose titles have received recognition from the British Crown, though they give no claim to precedence of any kind outside the islands themselves. The local militia serves to supplement the Imperial forces, and is paid from Imperial funds.

2. *Southern Rhodesia*

The history of Rhodesia gives it a peculiar position in the Empire; it was acquired by the British South

[1] See Keith, *Journ. Comp. Leg.* xiv. 276; xvi. 131, 132, 294.

Africa Company under the authority of a charter of October 29, 1889,[1] which gave wide administrative powers; the influx of population, following on the successful termination of the Matabeleland wars, necessitated the grant of a revised form of administration, which was conceded by the Southern Rhodesia Order in Council of 1898 and amending orders. Under these the executive government was vested in an Administrator, with an executive council of three members appointed by the Company, with the approval of the Secretary of State for the Colonies, while legislation was entrusted to a legislature of six nominees of the Company, and thirteen elective members, the interests of the Company being secured by provisions which prevented their proprietary rights being affected by legislation without their approval. The administration was supervised for the Imperial Government by a Resident Commissioner, under the direction of the High Commissioner for South Africa, more especially in regard to native policy, and the control of police and armed forces was placed in the hands of an Imperial Commandant-General.

In 1915 the powers of the Company, granted in the first instance for twenty-five years by the Crown, were continued by a supplemental charter in accordance with the wish of the people, but only on condition that the Crown might, if it desired, establish responsible government before the end of the ten years, for which the extension of Company government would normally run. In 1920, however, the legislature showed a clear demand for the change of government, and ultimately

[1] Amended by Orders in Council, May 9, July 30, 1891; July 18, 1894.

the Secretary of State pledged himself to concede it, if the demand were persisted in in face of the difficulties which had arisen regarding the local finances. In 1914 the long-discussed questions of the rights of the Company in unalienated lands and minerals were referred to the Judicial Committee, which in 1918 [1] reported that the lands were the property of the Crown, but that, if the Company ceased to be entrusted with the administration, it was entitled to ask the Crown to reimburse it either from land sales or, if the lands were given away, from public funds for the balance of its advances for the necessary and proper administration of the country, a surprising judgment, which proved, after investigation by a Commission, to involve a liability for £4,400,000, less certain unascertained amounts, but plus the value of such public works as the new administration might take over. In view of the desire of the legislature to proceed with responsible government, a draft constitution was prepared based on the recommendations of a Committee under Lord Buxton, and submitted to the electorate, while overtures were made by the Union Government for the entry of Rhodesia into the Union. The issue was decided by a referendum on October 27, 1922, by 8744 to 5989 votes in favour of the alternative of responsible government, which was conceded by letters patent, September 1, 1923, and became operative on October 1, 1923.

There remained the serious difficulty of providing for the repayment to the Company of the sums held due under the Privy Council judgment, in respect of past administrative deficits.[2] In July 1923, however, the matter was disposed of by the decision of the

---

[1] [1919] A.C. 211.   [2] *Parl. Pap.* Cmd. 1914, 1984.

Imperial Government to compromise the Company's claims for a payment of £3,750,000 and recognition of its mineral rights throughout the territory, while the Company in return transferred all buildings used for administrative purposes and administrative funds, and received a waiver of the Imperial Government's claim for the refund of advances made in respect of war expenditure by the Company. At the same time it was agreed that the Company should transfer to the Crown its claim to lands in Northern Rhodesia, retaining the mineral rights and being assured against unfair competition in respect of the railway system, the Imperial Government undertaking that no new railway would be constructed which would unduly affect the railways in Southern and Northern Rhodesia.[1]

As in the case of Southern Rhodesia the creation of responsible government would normally have left to the legislature unfettered discretion as to the mode in which mineral rights and railway construction should be controlled, even to the extent of expropriation at an arbitrarily fixed rate, express provision was made in the Southern Rhodesian constitution, requiring the reservation by the Governor of any Bill altering or amending the law as to the collection or allocation of mining revenues in force in the Colony on the coming into operation of responsible government, or imposing any special tax on minerals. In the case of railways any Bill must similarly be reserved, until there had been enacted by the legislature a measure adopting the provisions of the law in force in the United Kingdom relating to the Railway and Canal Commissioners,

Parl. Pap. Cmd. 1914.

and to the Rates Tribunal, provided by the Railways Act, 1921.[1] The sale of mineral rights by the Company to the Government in 1933 and the enactment of the requisite railway legislation have rendered obsolete these restrictions, and the latter was abrogated by letters patent, May 28, 1927. The Imperial Government undertook to provide similar restrictions in any constitution of Northern Rhodesia.

The constitution necessarily differs from that usual under responsible government by one important reservation. The enormous native population requires special protection, such as was given under the Company's régime, and, accordingly, this arrangement is continued. The approval of the High Commissioner is required for all appointments in the Native Department, and the salaries, functions, and removal of such officers are subject to his concurrence. The native reserves set out in the Imperial Order in Council of 1920 shall remain inalienable save for the purposes laid down in that order, and only then in exchange for other lands.[2] A native may acquire, encumber, and dispose of land like a non-native with safeguards that he receives due consideration for sale or encumbrance. But this rule is varied by letters patent of 1930 permitting the setting aside of areas for European and native occupation respectively, and lands have been allocated accordingly. Fines on chiefs or tribes require the assent of the High Commissioner. No conditions, restrictions, or disabilities may be imposed on natives to which Europeans are not also subjected, without the previous assent of the High Commissioner, by any proclamation or other instru-

[1] 11 & 12 Geo. V. c. 55.   [2] Compare *Parl. Pap.* Cmd. 547.

ment under a law, unless the law expressly provides for such regulations, and any such law must be reserved by the Governor, but these rules do not apply to restrictions as regards arms, ammunition, and liquor. The summoning of native councils and the giving to them of powers of passing regulations is also contemplated.

The constitution is otherwise of the normal type, contemplating Legislative Council and Assembly,[1] the former having no financial initiative, and merely the right to suggest amendments in appropriation and taxation Bills which it must either accept or reject after the suggested amendments have been considered. But the Council is at present in abeyance, and its creation is hardly likely. The legislature has large constituent powers, but alterations in the constitution must be passed by two-thirds majorities in both Houses, and the legislature may not repeal the provisions regarding natives, lands, the reservation of Bills, or the salary of the Governor, and the Crown reserves to itself the power of revoking these sections or altering them. Ministers may not hold office for more than four months if they have not seats in the legislature; they may speak in either House, and do not vacate office on selection. Judges are appointed by the Governor in Council, and may be removed only on addresses from both Houses on the ground of proved misbehaviour or incapacity. Appeal lies to the Appellate Division of the Supreme Court of the Union of South Africa. Defence is provided for on the basis

[1] The franchise since 1928 is based on occupancy qualifications, ownership of mining locations, or income of £100, thus in practice excluding most natives. There are 30 seats (4 two-member). Its duration is five years.

of compulsory training between ages 19 and 23 and Chapter
compulsory service in war from age 18 to 60.[1]

The position in Northern Rhodesia differs vitally
from that of Southern Rhodesia, for in the 287,950
square miles of territory there are only 13,000 Europeans
settled along the railway line connecting Bulawayo
and Cape Town with the Belgian Congo, while the
natives number about 1,331,000. The territory was
formerly controlled, subject to the legislative authority
of the High Commissioner, by an administrator of the
British South Africa Company, with the aid of an
advisory council of five Europeans elected by the
white community, which, however, had no legal control of legislation or administration. A decision as to
its future was long delayed by the dubiety of the
rights of the Company as regards minerals and land
in the absence of any conquest, and the validity of
their claim to be reimbursed the amount of administrative deficiencies. In July 1923 it was arranged by the
Crown to take over the administration from the Company with effect from April 1, 1924, equitable conditions having been arranged regarding the Company's property rights. The constitution now includes
a Governor, an Executive Council of five members,
and a Legislative Council, composed of the Executive Councillors, four nominated officials, and seven
elected members. The territory has no real unity;
the west, Barotseland, must, it is clear, in effect remain a native reserve, somewhat on the lines of
Basutoland, certain powers being exercised by the
Paramount Chief aided by a Khotla, or Native

_____

[1] Act No. 23 of 1926. A contribution in cash to the Imperial navy is
contemplated.

Council; the east might be united with Nyasaland, and the railway strip with Southern Rhodesia.

Roman Dutch law is in force in Southern Rhodesia, the laws of the Cape having been introduced by proclamation of June 10, 1891. In Northern Rhodesia the law of England, including the statutes up to August 17, 1911, is in force, and appeal lies direct to the Privy Council.

3. *Ceylon*

The constitution of Ceylon represents a unique experiment. Originally governed under the regular Crown Colony system, the island felt the impulse to constitutional reform which was born in India during the war of 1914–18, and the representations of the Ceylon National Congress and other bodies eventuated in 1923 in the grant of a constitution in which there was a large majority of elective members in the legislature, though paramount power of legislation and executive authority remained vested in the Governor. In practice, however, executive control passed largely into the hands of committees of the legislature. Enquiry by a Commission under Lord Donoughmore resulted in 1931 in the concession of a new constitution based on a very wide extension of the franchise to men and women alike. By election as regards fifty seats, and nomination as regards eight, is constituted a Council of State in which sit also three Officers of State, Chief, Legal, and Financial Secretaries, but without vote. The Council elects seven Committees, charged each with a branch of functions of the State, while the Officers of State control the remaining activities of government, such as defence, external relations, public order, legal proceedings, elections and law-drafting, and finance and audit. The Committees elect chairmen who together with the Officers of State constitute a Board which is collectively responsible for the estimates, original and supplementary, and the allocation of time in legislative proceedings. The Committees deal with all important executive issues, reporting on the graver issues to the whole Council, and then to the Governor, who has a final voice in all matters. The Board of Ministers falls to be removed by the Governor if it cannot carry its estimates, if the Council passes a motion of non-confidence, or if on other grounds he is satisfied that it no longer possesses the confidence of the Council; in that event a dissolution follows. The Governor has a paramount power of legislation and of taking full executive control of any department; he can not only refuse assent to legislation, but reserve it or require that it shall be passed by a two-thirds majority before presentation for assent. With the aid of a Public Services Commission he controls the Civil Service. The Crown reserves full power to alter the constitution by Order in Council or to legislate, and in 1934 this power was unexpectedly used to impose quota restrictions on Japanese imports in order to assist British exports. The system has evoked protests from the Council, which demands the elimination of the Officers of State, the placing of full financial power in the hands of the Council, and the abolition of the special legislative powers of the Governor. But there is much less unanimity in criticism of the Committee system of executive control, which is still preferred by many to normal responsible government, for which, in the absence of political parties, the island seems hardly to be ripe.

Ceylon enjoys Roman Dutch law, much modified by legislation and judicial interpretation, but regard is had to Sinhalese law, to the law of the Kandy Sinhalese, and to that of the Indian Tamils.

The Maldive Archipelago, south-west of Ceylon, is tributary to that government, but is not affected by the new constitution.

The Council of State may alter the constitution by reserved Bills.

CHAPTER VI

THE CROWN COLONIES

1. *Colony and Protectorate*

IT is impossible to draw any clear logical distinction
between a Colony[1] and a Protectorate in the British
Empire system, for the status of the different parts of
the Empire has been largely determined by historical
accident, and not regulated by any definite legal theory.
A Colony doubtless suggests British settlement overseas; but Gibraltar, whose importance is military, and
which is entirely removed from British settlement, is a
Colony, as are Basutoland, which is almost closed to
Europeans, and the Gilbert and Ellice Islands, where
British settlers are few and far between. On the other
hand Southern Rhodesia, with its active and loyal
British people, was left a Protectorate so long as it was
under the control of the British South Africa Company. Or again, the term Colony suggests organised
administration, and Protectorate a mere control of a
native administration, but even this distinction is inadequate. Southern Rhodesia before annexation was
excellently administered by European officials, while
the Colony of Papua remained largely unexplored and
inhabited by tribes which had only the faintest idea

---

[1] Crown Colonies is used in the convenient sense covering all Colonies
whose administration is subject to the control of the Crown as represented by the Secretary of State for the Colonies.

that they were natural-born subjects of the Crown. In Gambia, by an ordinance of 1902, much of the colonial area was appointed to be administered as Protectorate.

There is, however, one clear distinction in law between a Colony and a Protectorate. The former is part of the possessions [1] of the Crown; all persons born therein are British subjects; and all British legislation for British possessions extends to it, while in the case of Protectorates legislation by the Imperial Parliament is only applicable when it is clearly apparent from the Act in question that it was intended to apply to Protectorates. The Slavery Abolition Act, 1833, and the Slave Trade Acts, 1824 and 1843, for instance, apply to any British Colony, and one motive for delaying the transition from Colony to Protectorate has doubtless been the doubt whether domestic slavery, which has on occasion lingered on in Protectorates, would not become a grave crime by the establishment of a Colony. In 1927 it was found necessary to extinguish the system by legislation in Sierra Leone Protectorate. Historically the creation of Protectorates is best exemplified by the case of Africa. When after 1880 the competition of European powers for territory there became acute, there was every temptation to adopt the loose form of connection with the Crown, suggested by the term Protectorate. The native chief, ignorant as he was, was much more likely to sign an agreement promising him protection than to agree to an annexation out and out, and, when foreign claims came into competition, it was infinitely easier to abandon a mere obligation or right

---

[1] The Crown determines boundaries in the letters patent constituting Governments; changes can be effected under the Colonial Boundaries Act, 1895, as when in 1904 Sombrero was attached to the Virgin Islands.

of protection of a chief than to abandon territory which
had been made part of the Empire, and which perhaps
should not be surrendered without the assent of Parliament. Historically these considerations explain the
existence of the Protectorates of the Gambia, the Gold
Coast, Sierra Leone, and Nigeria, of Uganda, Nyasaland, and Somaliland, and of the Bechuanaland Protectorate, while Swaziland, which was a Protectorate
of the Transvaal, fell to the British Crown with the
conquest of that territory.[1] In the Western Pacific the
Solomon Islands owe their position as a Protectorate
mainly to the imperfect efforts yet made to reduce the
people to civilisation; the Gilbert and Ellice Islands
have already emerged into the distinction of a Colony.
On the other hand, there were excellent reasons of
an international character for making Papua, on its
annexation in 1887, a British Colony, and not relying
on the form of a Protectorate, which would else have
better accorded with the barbarism of the people.

In accordance with its historical origin a Protectorate is normally administered on different lines from a
Colony; the distinction is seen at its best in the case
of Nigeria, where the Colony represents in effect the
territory of Lagos, with its semi-Europeanised population, and the Protectorate covers the vast areas of the
Fula States; the Colony with the Southern Provinces
has a Legislative Council with native members; for the
Northern Provinces the Governor alone legislates, a
distinction justified on the score that it would be unjust
to deprive the natives of the coast of influence on

[1] The East Africa Protectorate was of the same type; by Order in
Council of June 11, 1920, it became the Kenya Colony, save as regards
the mainland dominions of the Sultan of Zanzibar, which form the
Kenya Protectorate.

2 H

legislation affecting themselves, and equally unjust to give them a voice in determining legislation for the people of the Fula States, who have little in common with them. Similarly, in the case of the Northern Territories of the Gold Coast, though the Executive Council acts for the Territories, the Governor alone legislates, and not the Legislative Council of the Colony, but the evanescence of the distinction of Colony and Protectorate is shown by the fact that Ashanti, which is similarly legislated for by the Governor, is a Colony, having been annexed on its reduction in 1901. When it is possible to establish a Legislative Council in which expression can be given to the needs of the population, the time for annexation is normally present, as in the case of the creation of the Kenya Colony from the East Africa Protectorate. But the colonial status is also compatible with Protectorate modes of government, as in Basutoland, and the Gilbert and Ellice Islands, where British rule is essentially a supervision and regulation of native institutions.

2. *The Sources of Colonial Constitutions*

The sources of colonial constitutions are curiously varied as a consequence of the complex history of the Empire.

(1) Early colonial law was dominated by the conception that Englishmen carried with them the law of England, and that, if they settled anywhere, the only constitution which the Crown had the right to grant was one based on the English model of a representative legislature.[1] Hence the bicameral legislatures with

---

[1] Keith, *Constitutional History of the First British Empire*, pp. 9-17.

nominee Upper Houses of the New England States, and the introduction of similar institutions into the other American and West Indian territories. In the case of a conquered or ceded Colony the Crown could bestow such constitution as it deemed fit, but it was not unusual to grant even such a Colony the normal form of constitution; thus, though Jamaica was taken by force of arms and eventually formally ceded to the Crown, it was given in 1662 a representative constitution. Such constitutions could not be changed by the Crown, unless it expressly reserved power to do so, as is now the rule; it stood towards them in no higher position than it did to the constitution of the United Kingdom.[1] But circumstances of varied kinds, the abolition of slavery and economic troubles, accompanied in Jamaica by a native rising, repressed with needless cruelty by the Governor, combined to force many of the colonies to resign their independence, especially as the Imperial Government adopted the perfectly natural attitude that no pecuniary aid could be advanced to colonies in which the executive government was at the mercy of the legislature for effecting necessary reforms of any kind. Jamaica after the rebellion surrendered her legislature in 1866, when an Imperial Act (29 & 30 Vict. c. 12) gave full constitutional authority to create any form of government to the Crown. Ten years later Grenada and St. Vincent followed suit, and another Imperial Act (39 & 40 Vict. c. 47) gave full power to the Crown to erect new governments. After valiant efforts to stand out, one by one, British Honduras, the Leeward Islands, Antigua, Dominica, St. Kitts, Nevis, Montserrat, and the Virgin Islands surrendered their

[1] *Campbell* v. *Hall* (1774), 1 Cowp. 204.

representative legislatures, themselves remodelling them so as to leave a decisive authority in the hands of the Crown.

(2) In other cases the power to create constitutions rests simply on the prerogative to assign the form of government of a conquered or ceded Colony, as in the cases of Ceylon,[1] Kenya, Mauritius, Seychelles, Hongkong, Fiji, Gibraltar, Malta, Ashanti, Basutoland, St. Lucia, Trinidad, and formerly British Guiana.

(3) In other cases it rests on express statutory authority,[2] as in the case of the Straits Settlements when they were transferred from the care of India to the Colonial Office in 1867, and in that of the Falkland Islands. These islands were, it is true, settled territories, but the manifest absurdity of creating a representative legislature for a tiny population presented itself, and a similar question arose regarding the control of British settlers in West Africa; the existing legislation is represented by the British Settlements Act, 1887, which gives power to the Crown to legislate by Order in Council for any British settlement, not under an established Government, and to establish in it a legislature of not less than three persons. It is by virtue of this legislation, if not the prerogative in respect of conquest or cession, that legislatures were set up in the Gambia, Gold Coast, and Sierra Leone. Full power over St. Helena was given to the Crown in 1833 by Act of Parliament, when control was taken over from the East India Company, and an Act of 1928 gave authority to remodel the constitution of British Guiana. Tobago, formerly an independent Colony, was under Im-

---

[1] *Abeyesekera* v. *Jayatilake,* [1932] A.C. 260.
[2] 29 & 30 Vict. c. 115.

perial legislation[1] in 1899 made an integral part of Trinidad.

Chapter VI.

The wide power of the Crown to create constitutions has resulted in the existence for the vast majority of existing Colonies of a double power. The constitution recognises the necessity of, and provides, a local legislature, but at the same time the right of the Crown to legislate by Order in Council is asserted. Such legislation may be used to enact some measure which it would be difficult to press through the local legislature without raising undue resentment, or merely for some ground of convenience. The power is possessed by the Crown in regard to all the Crown Colonies save Barbados, Bahamas, Bermuda, the Leeward Islands, and British Honduras.

Imperial constitutional legislation for these Colonies, other than in general terms conferring authority on the Crown, is rare; the most important exception is the Act of 1871, conferring a constitution on the Leeward Islands, Imperial legislation being necessary to create a federal body, and the Act of 1919 providing for a West Indian Court of Appeal.

General Imperial legislation for these territories is rare, but on subjects of general concern, such as shipping, whaling, copyright, and aerial navigation, power is normally taken to adapt the enactments to the Colonies by Order in Council. It is, however, characteristic of the unwillingness of Parliament to legislate vaguely that the measures of compulsory service enforced in the Colonies during the war were passed by the local legislatures, not by the Imperial Parliament.

[1] 50 & 51 Vict. c. 44; Order in Council, October 20, 1898.

3. *The Different Classes of Governments*

The fundamental similarity which justified the classification together of these Colonies is the existence in each of an executive government, which is subordinate to the Crown, and is effectively under the control of the Secretary of State for the Colonies. The executive, of course, must act within the limits of the law, though it must be noted that it possesses a considerable measure of power to mitigate the application of the law by the refusal of the law officer to prosecute, and the power of the Governor to pardon, an offender. But the executive can effectively prevent the enactment of any law, and in the vast majority of cases it can control the legislature; even where this is not possible, the power of legislating by Order in Council can be employed to provide the executive with any necessary powers. This authority was freely invoked in the disputes in Malta which unluckily were inevitable, until the decision to grant Malta a considerable measure of responsible government in domestic issues.

I. In the case of the Bahamas, Barbados, and Bermuda alone is the true type of representative government to be found, in which the legislature cannot be controlled in a positive direction by the executive, these territories having managed to preserve their independence during varied vicissitudes. In each, therefore, there is a constitution, consisting of the Governor, a nominee Legislative Council, and a House of Assembly, elected, in Barbados annually, in Bermuda quinquennially, in Bahamas septennially, on the basis of a male franchise, which in Bahamas is very low, but more substantial in the other two Colonies, Bermuda demanding a £60 freehold; the Councils number nine members, the Houses twenty-nine in Bahamas, twenty-four in Barbados, and thirty-six in Bermuda. The Governors have the aid of Executive Councils, and to these, with a view to establishing some harmony between the executive and the legislatures, and to facilitate the passing of governmental measures, some members of the legislature are when possible added. As a remnant of early privileges, the members of the Lower Houses are not bound by the rule of the Imperial Parliament that the assent of the Crown is necessary for proposing money votes, and to remedy the possibility of confusion in the finances thus involved the experiment was made, first in Barbados, of creating an Executive Committee, composed of the members of the Executive Council, one member of the Legislative Council, and four of the Assembly, selected by the Government, which prepares the estimates, introduces all money votes, and initiates all governmental measures, a suggestion also mooted in Bermuda. The possibilities of friction in this form of government are by no means negligible, especially when the legislatures are anxious to incur expenditures beyond their means to support, but in the main the existence of these anomalous Governments is open to no exception; the loyalty of the Barbadians is proverbial. Bermuda as a naval station is governed by a military Governor, but as regards the civil administration he is entirely under the control of the Colonial Office.

II. Until 1928 British Guiana enjoyed a complicated constitution, based on the Dutch régime, though by an ordinance of 1891 it was much simplified and modernised. The executive authority was vested in the Governor and an Executive Council, and legislative authority generally in a Court of Policy, consisting of the Governor, seven nominated and eight elected members, chosen on a moderate franchise; but the annual tax ordinance was passed by that body aided by six financial representatives, who formed the combined court. That body had also the right of discussing freely all the items in the annual estimates prepared by the Governor in Executive Council, a privilege, however, which was only conferred periodically for a fixed time by Order in Council in return for a Civil List. A real measure of control over finance was thus possessed by the legislature, but the Crown had power to legislate by Order in Council, and thus deadlocks were impossible. The Court of Policy had a maximum duration of five years. In 1928, in order to give the Government the power to control finance in order to raise a loan for development purposes, power was taken by Imperial Act to remodel the constitution by Order in Council. It now consists of a Governor, an Executive Council in which sit three elected members of the Legislative Council, and a Legislative Council of ten official members, fourteen elected on a moderate franchise and five nominated members. The Governor in Executive Council, with the Colonial Secretary's approval, may decide against the refusal of the Council to vote any enactment.

In Cyprus the legislature contained a majority of elected members, fifteen to six, with the High Commissioner, now Governor, being three elected by Muhammadan electors and the rest by Christian electors, but the Crown had the necessary power to legislate by Order in Council in the improbable event of an effective combination against the administration.

Such a power was also essential in view of the racial issue and the desire of the Greek inhabitants for union with Greece, which was indeed at one time offered by the Imperial Government as an inducement to Greece to enter the war on the allied side. In 1931 the occurrence of rioting resulted in the transfer of all legislative power to the Governor.

III. In general, however, the executive government can effectively enough, without recourse to the use of Orders in Council, secure any desired legislation through the influence it possesses with the legislature. Even when a part of the legislature is elective, it is insufficient in strength to defeat the deliberate will of the administration: such are the constitutions, though varying in detail, of Jamaica,[1] Leeward Islands, Dominica, Trinidad, Grenada, St. Lucia, St. Vincent, Mauritius,[2] Straits Settlements,[3] Nigeria, Gold Coast, Sierra Leone, Fiji,[4] and Kenya.[5]

IV. In other cases the Council is nominated, and therefore still less likely to disagree with the administration, as in British Honduras, Gambia, the Falkland Islands, Hongkong, and Seychelles.[6]

V. In yet other cases there is no Legislative Council, the Governor being granted sole legislative authority, as in Gibraltar, St. Helena, Ashanti, Basutoland, the

---

[1] See below, s. 5.

[2] 8 officials, 9 nominated, 10 elected.

[3] 13 officials, 13 non-officials, 2 selected by the Chambers of Commerce.

[4] 13 nominated officials, 3 nominated Fijians, 6 elected Europeans, 3 elected Indians.

[5] 11 *ex officio*, 9 nominated officials, 11 elected Europeans, 5 elected Indians, 1 Arab elected, and 2 nominated representatives of the natives.

[6] Of the Leeward Islands Presidencies, Antigua, St. Christopher (St. Kitts)-Nevis, and Montserrat have nominee councils; for the Virgin Islands the Governor legislates.

Gilbert and Ellice Islands in the Western Pacific High Commission; Aden is in like case, but may be given a nominated Legislative Council.[1]

The legislative activities of all these territories are necessarily subjected to close scrutiny by the Colonial Office, which is responsible for the administration of the Colonies to Parliament. In addition to the effective powers of control over the legislature, care is taken to secure that the executive government shall not err in its management of the legislature. Apart from the principle that legislation of any important character or novel nature should not be undertaken without the approval of the Secretary of State, it is expressly provided in all recent constitutions that the Governor shall not assent, without previous instructions, to numerous classes of Bills, including as a rule Bills for divorce, the grant of any land or money to himself, currency, differential duties, imposing obligations contrary to treaty, interfering with the discipline of military, air, or naval forces, or imposing restrictions on non-Europeans to which persons of European birth or descent are not subjected, and any Bill of an extraordinary nature whereby the prerogative, or the rights of British subjects not resident in the territory, or the trade and shipping of the Empire, may be prejudiced. Such Bills must be reserved if assent is not withheld or postponed for instructions, unless they contain a suspending clause providing that they shall not come into operation without special approval. In cases of emergency a Governor may assent even to such a Bill if not contrary to treaty, but he must report at once his reasons for acting, and any Act or ordinance may be disallowed by the Crown.

[1] See below, s. 8.

The control over the legislatures is exercised, it will Chapter
VI. be seen, not by restricting the scope of their authority[1] to legislate, but by securing that the powers enjoyed shall be exercised as desired by the executive in any vital matter. The legal limitations on the powers of colonial and protectorate legislatures, as contrasted with Dominion Parliaments, to which the Statute of Westminster is applied, are (1) subjection to the Colonial Laws Validity Act, 1865; (2) territorial limitation; and (3) the restriction of their constituent powers. This last restriction is not applicable to Colonies with representative legislatures, such as Bahamas, Barbados, and Bermuda, and the power of constitutional change seems clearly to appertain to those legislatures whose present non-representative condition is due to the legislation passed by the legislatures at times when they were representative, such as the island legislatures in the Leeward Islands, St. Vincent, Grenada, and British Honduras. The Leeward Islands federation has by statute wide constituent powers. But it is the normal condition of all legislatures created under the British Settlements Acts, 1887, to lack constituent power.[2]

4. The Leeward Islands Federation and West Indian Constitutional Reform

Despite the many efforts which have been made to devise federal schemes for the British possessions in the

---

[1] Thus it was held by the Privy Council that the legislature of Gibraltar had power to provide for the internment there of the Egyptian patriot Zaghlul Pasha, despite the fact that he had committed no crime against the local law: *Zaghlul Pasha, Re* (1923), 67 Sol. Jo. 382.

[2] Protectorate legislatures created under the Foreign Jurisdiction Act, 1890, are in like condition.

West Indies, which would give these Colonies a higher status and a more effective voice in Imperial affairs, the Leeward Islands federation remains the only result of these aspirations. The connection of the islands is old, for they were all, save Dominica, colonised from St. Kitts, and, from the time of William and Mary, possessed a common legislature as well as local legislatures; this body expired in 1798, and was only revived by an Imperial Act of 1871,[1] which created a federal Colony of Antigua, Dominica, St. Kitts and Nevis (united into one Government in 1882), Montserrat, and the Virgin Islands. The legislature thus created, as since remodelled, includes ten official members and ten unofficial members, elected by the unofficial members of the island legislatures of Antigua, Dominica, St. Kitts-Nevis, and Montserrat, from among their own numbers, and one selected for the Virgin Islands by the Governor. The federal legislature is given concurrent but paramount powers with the island legislatures on such topics as justice, property, commercial and criminal law, quarantine, status, the maintenance of a general police force, and a common convict establishment, posts and telegraphs, currency, weights and measures, audit, education, care of lunatics, copyright, patents, immigration, and its own constitution and procedure. The federal expenses, defrayed from island contributions, are regulated by the legislature, and any island legislature may confer upon it power to legislate on any topic not included in the list of matters assigned to the federation. The island legislatures retain their powers, but any Act repugnant to an enactment of the federal legislature is void, and a

[1] 34 & 35 Vict. c. 107.

federal Act may repeal or amend a local Act. The Council may not last more than three years; a weekly session is usual in each year.

The legislature may alter its constitution by an ordinary Act to be reserved for the royal approval, and, on addresses from the legislature of any West Indian island, the Crown may, with the concurrence of the Council, include that territory in the federation on such terms as may be agreed upon, and set out in the Order of Council providing for admission. But this power has not been used, and a federal scheme for the West Indies would have to be brought into existence by fresh legislation. The federation does not effect any close union of the islands generally, but it provides for federal departments for some important matters, audit, police, agriculture, though the objection has been made that greater prosperity could be attained by leaving the island greater autonomy. Efforts to form a union of the Windward Islands have failed, though the three Colonies, St. Vincent, St. Lucia, and Grenada, are placed under one Governor with local Administrators, as in the Leeward Islands, but without any federal link, even in the shape of a general legislature.

The whole question of West Indian federation and constitutional reform was examined by Mr E. F. L. Wood (Lord Halifax) in the report on his journey in December 1921 to February 1922, on a visit to the West Indian Colonies, the first formally undertaken by a Parliamentary Under-Secretary of State.[1] The conclusion achieved on the issue of federation was that

---

[1] *Parl. Pap.* Cmd. 1679. A later but quite inconclusive investigation by a Commission in 1933 is recorded in Cmd. 4383; Keith, *Journ. Comp. Leg.* xvi. 132, 133.

which must be accepted by any impartial judgment. The advantages of federation are completely outweighed by the difficulties presented by the lack of adequate communications, and the absence of economic possibilities of improving these communications in view of the inevitable tendency of trade, and by the political repugnance to federation felt in the several territories as the outcome of different historical traditions among other factors. He was only able to record a certain amount of willingness in the Colonies of the Windwards group to consider federation in some form with Trinidad, and this mainly due, it would appear, to the jealousy felt by St. Vincent and St. Lucia of the position of Grenada as the seat of the Governor.

The West Indies, Mr Wood found, evinced no real demand for responsible government, for which the communities are unsuited, both by reason of the mingling of races, religion, and colour, especially marked in Trinidad but not absent anywhere, and by considerations of an administrative character. The population is too small, and the leisured class too infinitesimal, to permit of effective government without an impartial official class, under the control of the Crown through the Secretary of State, which can secure equal justice for all interests. Moreover, the franchise even in Jamaica is exercised by a remarkably low proportion of the registered voters. Hence it was only possible to recommend the use of election for a minority of nominee members on the Councils. This was done and to associate the position of the nominated and elective members with responsibility, the Governors were informed that, save in the case of extreme urgency, no measure should be carried against the unanimous opposition of all the unofficial members. Mr Wood did not suggest that any rule should be laid down as regards placing elective members on the Executive Councils; the plan might be adopted where convenient, the question being always of the balance between inconvenience of introducing elective members to an executive body, and the advantages of securing their participation in business and facilitating relations between the Government and the electorate. Dyarchy on the Indian model was rejected on the score that the administrations are on too small a scale to allow scope for it; a more serious objection would appear to be the fact that it has any validity which it possesses only as a stepping-stone to responsible government, which is not contemplated for the West Indies.

More interesting is the position of Jamaica,[1] where in 1919 female suffrage was conceded, and the body of the electorate is large, the franchise resting in the main on the payment of not less than 10s. taxes in respect of occupation of a dwelling-house. Under the constitution as amended by Order of Council of 1895 the Council consists of the Governor with five officials *ex officio*, not over ten nominated officials and non-officials, who are usually bound to vote for the Government when desired, and fourteen elected members, any nine of whom can block any new appropriation or proposed tax, while, if the whole elected members are opposed

---

[1] Under 26 & 27 Vict. c. 31 Jamaica controls the Cayman Islands, which have a local legislature, the justices of the peace and elected vestrymen, the Governor's assent being requisite to legislation. Under 36 & 37 Vict. c. 6 it controls the Turks and Caicos Islands, which under Jamaica Law No. 6 of 1926 have a local legislature of the Commissioner, 3 officials and 4 nominated non-officials. Jamaica laws can apply to all these islands.

to any measure, it can be carried by the Governor by the other votes only by the device of declaring it to be of paramount importance, a right also available against the veto of the members on financial issues. This power, though dormant, undoubtedly has served on occasion to obviate the occurrence of a deadlock. The disadvantages of the position are obvious, since the elective members can obstruct without in any way having the power effectively to aid the Government in constructive ways, but a new scheme devised by the Under-Secretary was rejected by the legislature.

5. *The Governor and the Executive*

The powers of the Governor are various; he is granted by letters patent constituting his office the executive authority of the Crown so far as necessary for the government of the territory, to be exercised according to the laws in force[1] and to the instructions of the Crown, which normally are given in two forms, one in a formal instrument of Instructions, and the other directions contained in despatches and telegrams. The Instructions are given in the King's name, but directions are issued under the general authority of the Secretary of State, as charged with His Majesty's commands in colonial affairs. In the performance of his duties the Governor has the aid of an Executive Council, which normally consists of the chief executive officers with, in some cases, especially where the legislature contains elected members, representatives of the non-official community. All hold office at the pleasure of the Crown

---

[1] When the Governor acts within his powers, no court can review his discretion: *De Verteuil* v. *Knaggs*, [1918] A.C. 557.

and may be suspended from the Council by the Governor, whose action must be confirmed by the Crown. Appointments of members who do not hold seats *ex officio* may be made provisionally by the Governor subject to confirmation, and it is usually possible for him to summon for a special purpose an extraordinary member.

The Governor is required to consult the Council save on unimportant or urgent matters, or where consultation would cause material prejudice to the public interest; he alone may submit questions, subject to the right of any member to have entered in the minutes any question he desired to submit with the Governor's reply to his request; he may disregard the advice of the majority, but must report his reasons for doing so to the Secretary of State, and any member may enter in the minutes the grounds of his advice on the issue.

In addition to his voice in legislative matters the Governor is normally empowered to make grants of land [1] in accordance with any law or instructions; to appoint, suspend, remove, or interdict officers; and to exercise the prerogative of pardon. In these matters he is, of course, subject to control in varying degrees; as regards pardon in all capital cases he is required to consult his Council, but to take the burden of decision on himself; on this subject Imperial intervention is practically, for sound reasons, unknown. Appointments and dismissals, however, are carefully supervised; full authority exists as a rule only as regards appointments not exceeding £200 a year in value; in

---

[1] The King by prerogative is ultimate owner of all colonial land, and absolute owner of ungranted land. Cf. *R.* v. *Clarke* (1851), 7 Moo.P.C. 79. By legislation he may have similar rights in a Protectorate: *Southern Rhodesia, In re*, [1919] A.C. 211.

2 I

other cases the power of appointment is provisional, and important offices are filled at the direction of the Secretary of State. A Governor may interdict an officer, when he deems it necessary, from carrying on his duties, but normally in the case of officers whose pensionable emoluments exceed £200 a year, procedure is by suspension, with a full investigation by an Executive Council Committee, a review by the Council, and finally a decision by the Secretary of State. Greater discretion naturally is conceded in such cases as that of Ceylon, but on the whole very ample safeguards against injustice exist, and as in the Imperial Civil Service it is difficult to dispense with the services of an officer whose only fault is incompetence.

Elaborate provisions exist to secure that, in the event of the death or incapacity of the Governor, there may be an officer—sometimes styled Lieutenant-Governor—legally entitled to act in that capacity, and the power is given to the Governor to appoint a Deputy with specific powers during his pleasure in case of the Governor's temporary absence from the seat of government or on a visit to adjacent territories.

The Governor, even if a military officer, has, of course, no direct authority over the Imperial military forces, if any, stationed in the territory, though, as the King's representative, he gives the "word" in all places, and is entitled to receive information as to the strength and condition of the troops and the military defences. When a military command includes several Colonies, the officer in supreme command may transfer troops from one Colony to another on the application of the Governor, but he should normally

obtain the assent of the Governor of the Colony in
which troops are stationed. The Governor has similarly no right to give orders to His Majesty's naval
forces or require their presence. But these considerations are subject to the mutual obligation of the
services of the Crown to render aid to one another, and,
accordingly, both naval and military officers, in cases
of emergency, may be asked to assist in meeting local
disorders which the forces of the Colony cannot repress.
The introduction of telegraphic communication by
cable and wireless has rendered it easy to secure the
assent of the War Office or Admiralty for movements
of troops or ships and operations, but the occurrence
of an emergency may render action necessary without
such authority.

It is the duty of the Governor to secure by his
personal attention to all matters of importance the
effective working of the several departments of the
Colony, and he is specially enjoined to promote religion and education among any natives of the territory, to protect them in their persons and the free enjoyment of their possessions, and to repress by every
lawful means violence and injustice against them. In
recent years especial importance has come to be
attached to the development of colonial areas, and it
has become an anxious part of a Governor's duty to
consider the complex issues presented by applications
for concessions, and by schemes of railways, roads, and
harbour construction, involving large financial outlays, and therefore necessitating careful calculations of
ways and means. Moreover there is always the risk of
overtaxing the native labour supplies. He has the aid
of efficient heads of departments, the advice of experts

in the United Kingdom, and general guidance from the Secretary of State. The business transactions outside the territory are in the main conducted through the Crown Agents for the Colonies in London under the general supervision of the Secretary of State.

6. *Defence*

As in the case of the Dominions and India, the responsibility for the defence of the Crown Colonies and adjacent Protectorates from foreign aggression rests with the Imperial Government, but order locally is preserved as a rule by military or police forces raised in each territory, and controlled by its Government,[1] under final supervision by the Colonial Office. Guidance as to the organisation of these forces, inspectors-general, staff officers, and officers and non-commissioned officers to serve in them, are obtained from the Imperial Government, but the local forces do not normally form part of the Imperial army, nor are they under the control of the War Office.[2] The character and nature of the forces differs considerably according to the circumstances of the territories, and in certain cases Imperial garrisons are maintained which, though intended primarily to serve general Imperial

---

[1] The Bahamas, and Basutoland, have police forces which can be used for military service; Cyprus and Seychelles have only police forces, not liable to military service.

[2] Where there are Imperial garrisons, the control of the local forces may be delegated to the O.C. troops, as in Malta, where the units are part of the British forces, and Malaya. The O.C. Jamaica is Inspector-General of the West Indian local forces, save in Bermuda and Falkland Islands.

The forces in the Colonies are made in certain conditions subject to the Army or Air Force Act, especially when on active service.

purposes, are none the less available in time of emergency for local purposes. In the case of West Africa there exists a native force of very considerable value, the Royal West African Frontier Force, units of which are kept in all the territories. It is administered through the Inspector-General at the Colonial Office, but in each area it is under the Governor's control. A similar service is performed under an Inspector-General for the East African territories by the King's African Rifles and the Somaliland Camel Corps, whose task has been rendered easier by the suppression, through the use of the air force in 1920, of the long-drawn-out revolt in Somaliland. Imperial garrisons secure the position of Gibraltar, Malta, Cyprus, Ceylon, Mauritius, the Straits Settlements, Hongkong, Bermuda, and Jamaica. The war gave an impetus to defence organisation, and as in India to the imposition of compulsory training or liability for defence in the Eastern, West Indian, and Pacific Colonies as regards the European population. Since 1928 a defence force is raised under compulsion in Kenya.

Naval bases exist at Gibraltar, Malta, Bermuda, Hongkong, and Singapore. Recognition of the services rendered by the Imperial navy was shown before the war by the action of the Malay States in presenting H.M.S. *Malaya* to the Crown, and during the war by the numerous grants in kind and money, made or undertaken as contributions to the cost of the war. Similar large contributions have been made by Hongkong and Malaya to the Singapore base. The use of colonial naval forces in conjunction with the Royal Navy is provided for by the Colonial Naval Defence Act, 1931.

7. *The Judicature and the Laws*

In accordance with the individuality of the Colonies is the rule that each has normally a Supreme Court, which as a full court serves as a Court of Appeal[1] and review in the case of inferior jurisdictions, and also has original jurisdiction in important civil and criminal cases, with power to issue the prerogative writs of habeas corpus, mandamus, etc.

Appeals lie from these courts normally direct to the Judicial Committee of the Privy Council, but an effort to reduce such appeals and to create some measure of co-operation in judicial matters is provided by the West Indian Courts of Appeal Act, 1919, which, enlarging an earlier scheme of 1889 applicable to the Windwards, creates a Court of Appeal for the Leewards, the Windwards, Trinidad, and Tobago, Barbados, and British Guiana, consisting of the Chief Justices of these territories, and provides for the application of the scheme to other Colonies, if legislation is passed to that effect by their legislatures. The Colonies may require that any appeals shall first go to the Court of Appeal, but, subject to that right, an aggrieved litigant retains the power of carrying his case direct to the Judicial Committee. The Court of Appeal, however, should be able to develop a jurisprudence of its own, and avoid needless diversity in the interpretation of Acts. In the case of the British territories in East Africa a similar service of unification

---

[1] In the Straits Settlements a special Court of Criminal Appeal was created in 1931; the judges of the Straits and the Federated Malay States sit together for purposes of appeals. In Hongkong the Consular judge at Shanghai is added to the Supreme Court for appeals.

is rendered by His Majesty's Court of Appeal for Eastern Africa, from which an appeal lies to the Judicial Committee. Similarly,[1] from the West African territories appeal lies to the West African Court of Appeal. This system was applied from 1934–5 to Nigeria.

Each Colony has, as a rule, as the basis of its law the English common law, the doctrines of equity, and the older statutory law,[2] and in statutory law in recent years a certain assimilation has been brought about by the practice of the preparation of model enactments by the Colonial Office, which the colonial legislatures are invited to follow in drawing up fresh legislation, and by the slow realisation of the advantages of uniformity in such matters as commercial law, bills of exchange, sale of goods, and so on. In the case of the Presidencies of the Leeward Islands, each has its separate system of laws, but the federal legislature enacts on certain matters laws for the whole of the Colony. In some cases of Colonies which had a settled system of laws when they came into the possession of the British Crown, the base of the law is some other system than English; thus in Ceylon the Roman Dutch law prevails, and formerly this was the case in British Guiana, but save as regards land rights from January 1, 1917, the English law has there been substituted for Roman Dutch law by express enactment. In St. Lucia the Coutume de Paris formed the basis of the civil law until, in 1879, a code based on it was introduced. In the case of Mauritius and its

---

[1] Orders in Council, November 1, 1928; January 20, 1930.

[2] The law up to a certain date is often specifically declared applicable; *e.g.* in Nigeria, January 1, 1900, is the date.

former dependency, Seychelles, the French civil code is the basis of the civil law. In Trinidad the laws of Spain, as they existed in 1797, when the island became British, prevail so far as not superseded by legislation, as has, however, been almost, if not entirely, the case. Cyprus has the Turkish law of 1878 as basis. In Gibraltar English law, as it stood on December 31, 1883, was introduced by an Order in Council of February 2, 1884. It is in the sphere of civil law that, as a rule, the old law has been allowed to remain in operation; criminal law is more intimately connected with the changed conditions induced by an alteration in sovereignty.[1] The Indian penal, and criminal, and civil procedure codes have exercised a considerable influence in bringing about codification of criminal law in East Africa, and in the Eastern Colonies, and have thus modified ordinary English law.

In all those cases in which there is a considerable native population with laws and customs of its own full consideration is given in the courts to such institutions; thus in a Colony such as Fiji the courts have to take into consideration the native laws and customs of the Fijians, the usages of the Indian immigrants, and the English law of the European settlers. In Ceylon there are four systems applicable to the native population, and in the Straits Settlements and Hongkong regard has to be had to Chinese law.

8. *Miscellaneous Territories*

Reference has been made above to Aden, which it has been finally decided to separate from India. Ac-

---

[1] Ceylon, Mauritius, Seychelles, and St. Lucia retain foreign law.

quired by occupation and purchase between 1839 and 1888, the settlement is only 75 square miles in extent, but to the north and north-east a Protectorate is exercised over 9000 square miles. The settlement, originally treated as part of Bombay, was placed under the Government of India in 1932 as a Chief Commissionership, while in 1927 the military affairs of Aden and the business of the Protectorate were handed over to the Colonial Office. The decision to terminate connection with the Indian Empire under the Government of India Act, 1935, was not unnatural. The constitution contemplated to be given by Order in Council is of the usual colonial type under the British Settlements Act, 1887, but appeal from Aden is to lie to an Indian court, and thence to the Privy Council. Perim, occupied in 1857, is part of the settlement.

Tristan da Cunha was occupied in 1816 in connection with Napoleon's residence at St. Helena; on the withdrawal in 1817 of the garrison, Corporal Glass with his family remained behind, and a small community grew up through the arrival of coloured persons from St. Helena and the Cape. Until his death in 1853, Glass governed the community; thereafter until 1933 the oldest inhabitant took charge; the rule is now that there is a council of four, the chairman acting as spokesman of the islanders—some 160 in number—and conducting marriages in the absence of a chaplain. There is also a women's council for the affairs of women and children. Offers of removal to the Cape have been rejected and British solicitude keeps the islanders fairly well off.

Ascension, formerly controlled by the Admiralty, is now a dependency of St. Helena.[1] Other islands like the

[1] Letters patent, September 12, 1922.

Ashmore and Cartier group have been placed under the control of the Commonwealth of Australia. At the Great and Little Basses and Minicoy in the Indian Ocean the Board of Trade maintains lighthouses, the cost being met in part by dues levied on passing vessels and collected at Ceylon, Mauritius, Straits, and Indian ports. Amboyna Cay and Sprattley Island, sandbanks in the China Sea, are leased for guano collection, having been annexed in 1877. Other islands—some leased by the Treasury—are Bird and Cato Islands in the Norfolk group, Raine Island, Bell Cay and Bramble Cay, near British New Guinea, Caroline Island, Flint Island, Vostock Island, Malden Island, Starbuck Island; and in the South Atlantic, Gough, Nightingale, and Inaccessible Islands.

Ocean, Fanning, Washington and Christmas Islands are now included in the Gilbert and Ellice Islands; Pitcairn and the Phoenix group fall directly under the High Commissioner for the Western Pacific.

CHAPTER VII

FOREIGN JURISDICTION

THE powers of extra-territorial jurisdiction exercised by the Crown at the present day are historically closely connected with the privileges first granted in 1583 by the Sultan of Turkey to the British Levant Company, under which that body was permitted a measure of self-government, and the right of exercising jurisdiction over British subjects sojourning in the Ottoman Dominions. These concessions, which were analogous to those acquired earlier by the French, were consolidated and extended in course of time, until before the war the system of capitulations—a term originally denoting no more than heads of agreements—secured large and comprehensive privileges to the Crown in all the Turkish territories. The powers of jurisdiction, exercised by Consuls appointed by the Levant Company, were in 1825 transferred by an Imperial Act to the Crown on the dissolution of the Levant Company, and in 1843 the opening of treaty ports in China was the cause of the passing of an Act in general terms for the exercise of British jurisdiction in any foreign countries in which "by treaty, capitulation, grant, usage, sufferance, and other lawful means" the Crown had power and jurisdiction. This measure was succeeded in 1890 by a still more comprehensive enactment,[1] which ap-

---

[1] The Foreign Jurisdiction Act, 1890 (53 & 54 Vict. c. 37), amended by 3 & 4 Geo. V. c. 16.

plies also to the case in which there exists in any country no Government from which a grant of jurisdiction can be obtained.

The exercise of such jurisdiction,[1] of course, is compatible only with cases of semi-barbarous countries, or countries under conditions of civilisation so disparate from British conditions as to render it unjust and unfair to subject British subjects to the control of their courts. Accordingly the progress of civilisation in Japan was followed by the Treaty of 1894, which provided for the extinction, in 1900, of all British extra-territorial jurisdiction there, and assurances[2] have been given to China that the British Government is prepared to abandon jurisdiction if and when China establishes suitable conditions ensuring fair trial of Europeans. In the case of Turkey extra-territorial jurisdiction was surrendered by the Treaty of Lausanne of 1923; a special régime reserving issues of status to British courts outside Turkey was terminated in 1930.[3] In the case of former Turkish territory now under mandate to the United Kingdom or foreign powers and of Iraq arrangements have been made for effective jurisdiction, which renders consular jurisdiction obsolete. Albania secured its termination in 1926. In Persia, now Iran, the system ended by unilateral denunciation in 1928, when the United Kingdom also conceded full fiscal autonomy to the State. In Siam in 1909 treaty pro-

[1] Jurisdiction necessarily includes the right to legislate and the Act of 1890 includes a list of Acts which can be applied as well as the general power to legislate. See, *e.g.*, the Foreign Jurisdiction (Neutrality) Order in Council, October 24, 1904, or the Foreign Jurisdiction (Military Forces) Order in Council, 1927, restricting the power of the courts as regards troops on active service.

[2] *Parl. Pap.* Cmd. 2774, 2797, 3480.

[3] Dicey and Keith, *Conflict of Laws* (5th ed.), pp. 392, 904.

visions arranged for its gradual complete extinction, codes based on European law taking the place of native law.

Where it still remains, jurisdiction depends on express treaty and usage. In China all questions of property and personal rights of British subjects *inter se* and crimes committed by British subjects shall be dealt with by consular courts. Chinese subjects who commit crimes against British subjects fall to be punished by Chinese courts; in disputes between Chinese and British of a civil character the Consuls are enjoined to seek to procure pacific settlements with the aid of the Chinese authorities. Thus under the Order in Council of 1925 governing jurisdiction in China, the courts are given authority over all British subjects, including natives of British Protectorates and of the Indian States; over the personal and proprietary rights of such subjects wherever resident; over foreigners in whose case jurisdiction is conceded by their sovereign; and over British ships and persons and property connected with them. Provincial courts are held by the Consuls; there is a Supreme Court at Shanghai to which appeal lies, and from which, as in every case of this jurisdiction, appeal can be brought to the King in Council. From the operation of the China Order in Council Kashgar is excluded; a Consul-General stationed there is paid by India and exercises jurisdiction under the Kashgar Order in Council, 1920, under which powers are conferred on the High Court of the Punjab to hear appeals, whence further appeal may be brought to the King in Council.

India is also interested in Maskat, Bahrein, and Kuwait, all States in the Persian Gulf under treaty relations with India. In them consular jurisdiction is exercised under Orders in Council.[1] The Political Resident in the Persian Gulf is in control of political relations and from his court appeal lies to the King in Council. He is also charged with relations with the "trucial" chiefs on the Pirate Coast who since 1893 are under treaty not to enter into relations with or cede land to any foreign State, and the Kuria Muria Islands, annexed in 1854, are under his charge. Since the termination of the arrangement with Persia for the use of the Persian coast for air services, British relations with the Arab coast have been rendered more intimate, and the British Government has repelled the claims of Persia to sovereignty over Bahrein.

Consular jurisdiction is still exercised in Egypt through consular courts and a Supreme Court, sitting at Cairo, Alexandria, and Port Said, which hears appeals and from which appeal lies to the King in Council.[2] These courts alone deal with questions of personal status and crimes proper committed by British subjects and protected persons. But jurisdiction in matters between British subjects and foreigners are the business of the mixed courts, which exercise a very wide jurisdiction, though efforts have been made by Egypt to have the capitulations abandoned outright and control over the mixed courts given to Egypt.

Consular jurisdiction is also exercised in Ethiopia (Abyssinia)[3] and in the case of Morocco,[4] outside the

---

[1] February 3, 1915 (Maskat); August 12, 1913 (Bahrein); March 17, 1925 (Kuwait). Indian as well as English law is applied to persons subject to jurisdiction.

[2] Order in Council, July 28, 1930. As in all cases power to legislate, subject to the control of the Secretary of State, is delegated.

[3] Order in Council, December 19, 1913.

[4] Order in Council, March 21, 1929, consolidating older legislation.

Tangier zone. That zone has a special judicial system of international character under a convention of December 18, 1923, as modified by a protocol of July 25, 1928, under which Italy shares with the United Kingdom, France, and Spain control of the Tangier régime.

Foreign jurisdiction in China was formerly closely connected with the existence of spheres of influence, as was shown in 1898 when as a counter-weight to the Russian acquisition of Port Arthur the United Kingdom obtained a lease of Wei-hai-wei. In 1922, however, the treaties reached at Washington substituted for this doctrine that of equality of opportunity and the open door for all trade, and led to the Japanese evacuation of Shantung, and the British rendition of Wei-hai-wei. The issue, however, has been revived by the creation under Japanese influence of Manchukuo and the enunciation of the doctrine of the special interests of Japan in China. Russia in like manner has interests in Mongolia. Siam since 1904 has been recognised as falling in part within the British, in part within the French sphere of influence, but the State seems destined to preserve its independence. The declaration of zones of interest in Persia by the agreement of 1907 between the United Kingdom and Russia was followed by the diminution of Russian authority and by a Treaty of 1919 which if ratified would have placed Persia definitely under British influence. But it was not accepted by the Persian legislature, and the usurpation of power by Reza Khan Pahlavi in 1925 has established Iran as an independent State. The United Kingdom, however, as already noted, has interests in the Persian Gulf which it will not surrender. Moreover, through the Chief Commissioner and Resident at Aden, it is in close relations with the Arab tribes; he controls Sokotra, a Protectorate since 1886, and Perim, annexed in 1857. Britain also is interested in the Kingdom[1] of the Hedjaz and of Nejd, and in the ruler of Yemen,[2] tendering good offices in their recent warfare with a view to accelerating the conclusion of peace.

In Africa spheres of influence have ceased to be of consequence, since the United Kingdom in 1904 agreed to recognise the rights of France in Morocco; similarly she has conceded Spanish rights in her share of that area. On the other hand, Egypt is definitely in the British sphere of influence, as is Iraq, and though in India since 1919 the British Government claims no rights over Afghanistan, and Nepal has been recognised by Treaty of 1923 as absolutely sovereign, Britain remains definitely concerned with the foreign relations of Bhutan, and is not prepared to see Tibet fall into the power of China to such an extent as to render possible any danger to India.[3]

[1] See Treaty of May 20, 1927, recognising Ibn Saud.

[2] See Treaty of February 11, 1934.

[3] Relations between Tibet and China remain indeterminate, but the British view in 1912 against Chinese control of internal affairs remains unaltered.

CHAPTER VIII

PROTECTORATES OF COLONIAL CHARACTER

The doctrine of foreign jurisdiction explained in the preceding chapter has been employed to justify the control exercised over a large number of territories which are under the protection of the British Crown, but which are not reckoned as British territories.[1] These areas may conveniently be called colonial Protectorates, though the phrase has no official sanction.

The essential feature of these Protectorates, which, together with Protected States dealt with in the following chapter, are regularly referred to officially as territories under His Majesty's protection, is that these areas do not form an integral portion of the territory of the protecting State. Protectorates of both classes have certain characteristics in common: (1) Internationally, protection precludes the acquisition by any foreign State of the protected territory. (2) The protecting State assumes full external sovereignty over the protected State and no foreign State can enter into diplomatic or political relations with the protected State, save through the protecting State. (3) In consequence, the protecting State is bound to secure such an organisation of government in its Protectorate as will secure due regard to the rights of subjects of the foreign States. (4) Protectorates are often a prelimin-

[1] See above, Chap. VI. s. 1.

2 K

ary to annexation of the territories concerned by the protecting State. The plan of asserting Protectorates instead of formal annexation became regular on the part of European powers in the period after 1880, and the Berlin Conference of 1884–5 lent it authority by requiring powers signatory to the treaty to notify to the other powers their declaration of any fresh Protectorate within the area dealt with by the treaty. Other European powers in this period adopted the doctrine that the declaration of Protectorate rendered proper the assumption of full jurisdiction, civil and criminal, over both protected subjects and foreigners in the protected area. But the British Government at first took a much more limited view. It was held that, while jurisdiction could be exercised over British subjects and subjects of the Protectorates, in the case of foreigners jurisdiction should be dependent on their consent and on that of their Government.[1] But this doctrine, though it might be applied to the case of States with a fairly well organised system of government, as in the Zanzibar and Brunei Orders in Council 1884 and 1890, became hard to operate in the case of territories occupied by tribes without an effective central Government. The necessity of maintaining effective order in such territories to comply with the terms of the Treaty of Berlin, and the more exacting requirements of the Brussels Conference Treaty of 1890, compelled the British Government to adopt a wider point of view, which was shown in the terms of the Order in Council of 1891, passed to provide for the control of the territories in Bechuanaland and the areas in

[1] Africa Order in Council, October 15, 1889. It was extended to foreigners by Order in Council, June 28, 1892.

respect of which the British South Africa Company, established by royal charter in 1889, had obtained, or proposed to obtain, the power to exercise jurisdiction and political control. That order is definitely based on the view that, subject to the respect which must be shown to any Agreements with native rulers, the Crown may, by its authority, impose legislation upon, or establish its jurisdiction over, protected territories.

The basis of this right may be regarded as an exercise of prerogative founded in the case of British subjects on the doctrine of allegiance, which gives the Crown power to govern those whom it protects, and as regards other persons on the power to accept cession of jurisdiction, to acquire it by force of arms, or to exercise it where it is not challenged. Apart, however, from the prerogative, the authority of the Crown is rendered effective by the Foreign Jurisdiction Act, 1890, which consolidates earlier Acts. The Act (s. 1) authorises the Crown to exercise any jurisdiction which it possesses within a foreign country in as ample a manner as if the jurisdiction had been acquired by the cession or conquest of territory. Every act done in pursuance of any jurisdiction in a foreign country shall have the validity of acts done according to the local law. Where a foreign country is not subject to any Government from which the Crown might obtain jurisdiction by any lawful means, the Crown may exercise jurisdiction over British subjects in that country, and such jurisdiction is reckoned as foreign jurisdiction (s. 2). Power is given to assign to any court in a British possession, or held under the authority of the Crown, any jurisdiction which could lawfully be conferred on a British court in a foreign country. Validity is given to authorise the deportation of persons by order of British courts in foreign countries, and Orders in Council made under the Act are given full validity save in so far as they may be repugnant to Acts of Parliament or orders or regulations made thereunder extending to the subjects of the Crown (s. 12). The Crown therefore has, in respect of its jurisdiction, authority almost unfettered.

The modes in which jurisdiction can be acquired are specified in the preamble as treaty, capitulation, grant, usage, sufferance, and other lawful means, and the wideness of this enumeration serves to render it possible to ignore the suggestion in Section 2, that in some cases jurisdiction may apply to British subjects only. At any rate, since 1891, it has been the regular practice in issuing Orders in Council to ignore earlier limitations, and in the Protectorates of colonial type the exercise of sovereignty is absolute, subject always to the invariable practice of the observance of such treaty rights as may be conferred on local rulers by express agreement. It must, however, be noted that these agreements are not regarded as treaties of international law, and that, should the British Crown determine to override them, it could do so without incurring international liability, nor would there lie against the Crown any form of procedure under the constitutional law of the Empire.

It would appear that the chiefs in the African Protectorates are not regarded by the British Government as being in the possession of such a degree of sovereignty as would exempt them from the jurisdiction of British courts.[1] The result is a clear contrast between

---

[1] *Tshekedi Khama* v. *Ratshosa*, [1931] A.C. 784.

them and the princes of the Indian States, or of the Malay States,[1] who are not held to be subject to municipal jurisdiction; even in British India jurisdiction over Indian princes is exercised only in respect of their land holdings.

As the territory of Protectorates is not British territory, its inhabitants are not British subjects by birth thereon. They are reckoned as British protected persons and are entitled to British diplomatic protection when in foreign countries, and in foreign countries with independent Governments in which the Crown exercises extra-territorial jurisdiction they are treated as entitled to the same exemption from local law as are British subjects; in this respect they are treated in the same manner as the subjects of the Indian States, who, by statute, are reckoned as British protected persons.

It is not customary for British legislation to deal directly with the Protectorates, the more normal procedure being to authorise the Crown by Order in Council to apply to the Protectorate new legislation of general character, such as is applied to the Colonies. Large numbers of such statutes have been made applicable to the Protectorates, and by the Orders in Council which provide generally for their government the system of English common law, or of the Indian Codes, has from time to time been introduced for application generally, except in those cases affecting natives which are normally left to the operation of native law and custom. The form of government which is provided is based on the colonial system to which it has been progressively assimilated, the terms Governor and

[1] *Duff Development Co.* v. *Kelantan Government*, [1924] A.C. 797.

Government being usually substituted in recent constitution for the older High Commissioner and Administration.

The intimacy between Protectorates and colonial Government is shown by the fact that control may be exercised by the Governor of an adjacent Colony.[1] The judicial system is regulated by Order in Council or local ordinance on the colonial model. Appeal lies in some cases to the Supreme Court of an adjacent Colony or Protectorate and thence to His Majesty in Council, or in some cases direct to His Majesty in Council. In the West African territories there is a West African Court of Appeal and as regards East Africa an Eastern African Court of Appeal, but Somaliland has direct access to the Privy Council.[1] The Eastern African Court of Appeal acts also for the mandated territory of Tanganyika and the protected State of Zanzibar.

As noted above, as much use as possible is made of the principle of indirect rule of the native population by the instrumentality of local chiefs to whom is assigned authority of administration, of the raising of taxation and the exercise of criminal and civil justice, subject to the supervision of European officers. Power to make local regulations is also conceded to the chiefs with their councils, or in places where no chiefs exist, as in Southern Nigeria, to district councils. The widest authority is that accorded to the Kabaka of Buganda in Uganda and the Emirs of Northern Nigeria and to certain chiefs of Lagos, such as the rulers of Abeokuta and Ibadan.

The degree of development of the colonial Protector-

---

[1] Territorial areas are defined by Orders in Council from time to time.

ates and the character of their population determine the extent to which the use of executive and legislative councils is provided for. Nigeria, as now constituted, consists of the merger into one administration of the Colony of Lagos, ceded by the local ruler in 1861 and created a Colony in 1862; the Protectorate of Southern Nigeria, which was an extension of the Oil Rivers Protectorate of 1885; and the Protectorate of Northern Nigeria, representing the territories acquired by the Niger Company. In 1906 Lagos and Southern Nigeria were merged as the Colony and Protectorate of Southern Nigeria, and in 1914 they were merged with Northern Nigeria into the Colony and Protectorate of Nigeria. The present constitution, which rests on Orders in Council of 1922 and 1928, and letters patent and royal instructions, as regards the Colony, provides for an executive council and for a legislative council, for the Colony and the southern provinces of the Protectorate, which is also given control over Protectorate Government expenditure in the northern provinces, though for these provinces the Governor alone legislates. The Council is presided over by the Governor and consists of official members, including the members of the executive council, the senior Residents, five other officials and three nominated officials; three members elected by persons resident within the municipal area of Lagos, and one member elected by residents within the area of Calabar; and not more than fifteen nominated unofficial members. The nominations are made to secure representation of the four Chambers of Commerce, the local Chamber of Mines, banking interests, shipping interests, and the rest to represent African interests. The franchise is confined to male

British subjects with not less than £100 per annum gross income.

Northern Rhodesia,[1] established as a distinct Protectorate in 1924, has executive and legislative councils, with an elective minority on the latter, seven out of sixteen members.

In the case of Sierra Leone, a single legislative council acts for the Colony and the Protectorate. As reconstituted in 1924, the legislative council consists of the Governor as president, eleven official members, and ten unofficial members, of whom two are elected as urban members, while the others include three paramount chiefs, securing direct representation of Protectorate interests.

In the Nyasaland Protectorate, proclaimed in 1891, the Order in Council of 1907 established an executive council and a legislative council. The latter consists of the Governor, *ex officio* members, and four unofficial members nominated by the Governor.

In Uganda, declared a Protectorate in 1894, the present constitution under an Order in Council of 1920 includes an executive council of officials and a legislative council, consisting of the Governor, six official members, and three nominated members.

The remaining Protectorates have no legislative councils of their own. The Kenya Protectorate is now constituted of the mainland dominions of the Sultan of Zanzibar, over which a Protectorate was proclaimed in 1890. The legislative council of Kenya legislates for the Protectorate.[2]

Somaliland, a Protectorate since 1884, administered

---

[1] See above, Chap. V. s. 2.
[2] Order in Council, August 13, 1920.

by the Resident at Aden till 1898, was not brought under effective control until 1920–22, when air power was first successfully employed to meet dervish attacks. It is administered and legislated for by a Governor.[1] The Northern Territories of the Gold Coast are administered by a Chief Commissioner under the control of the Governor of the Gold Coast, who has legislative authority.[2] The laws of the Gold Coast were applied to the territories by Order in Council of 1901. The Gambia Protectorate is legislated for by the legislative council of the Gambia Colony.

The British Solomon Islands Protectorate is administered by a Resident Commissioner, who has the assistance of an advisory council inaugurated in 1921, composed of three official members and four nominated members, including the Bishop of Melanesia. Legislation is passed by the High Commissioner for the Western Pacific.

There are also two Protectorates in South Africa which are still under the control of the British Government, the Bechuanaland Protectorate and Swaziland. Both, together with the Colony of Basutoland, are controlled by a High Commissioner, formerly styled High Commissioner for South Africa, but now High Commissioner for Basutoland, the Bechuanaland Protectorate, and Swaziland.[3]

The Bechuanaland Protectorate was proclaimed in

---

[1] Orders in Council, December 17, 1929; April 23, 1932. The title Governor was restored in 1935.

[2] Order in Council, November 9, 1934. The executive council of the Colony now acts also for the Northern Territories.

[3] Order in Council, December 20, 1934. He is succeeded in absence by the Naval Commander-in-Chief, but his duties as High Commissioner for the United Kingdom are undertaken by one of his subordinates.

1885 and its area defined in 1891. It was administered for certain purposes as if part of the Bechuanaland Colony until the latter was annexed to the Cape in 1895. Since then the territory has been administered by a Resident Commissioner on lines similar to those of Basutoland. A number of important chiefs are recognised and permitted to exercise, within defined limits, powers of administration, legislation, taxation, and jurisdiction, acting with their councils in accordance with native law; but native courts are forbidden to authorise destruction of property, and jurisdiction over Europeans[1] is excluded. There is an elaborate judicial system, but the jurisdiction of an assistant resident magistrate does not extend to cases affecting natives of the same tribe, except when necessary to prevent acts of violence. More important civil and criminal cases, especially those affecting Europeans, are dealt with since 1912 by the special court of the Bechuanaland Protectorate, which is presided over by a judge or advocate of the Supreme Court of South Africa.

Swaziland was a Protectorate of the South African Republic, and on conquest the Protectorate became vested in the British Crown.[2] The administration is vested in a Resident Commissioner, who is advised in purely European matters by an elected advisory council of nine members. Legislation for Swaziland, as

---

[1] Disregard of this rule in 1933 led to the suspension of Tshekedi Khama by the Acting High Commissioner. He was, however, reinstated, and in 1934 two proclamations were drawn up dealing with the powers of chiefs and their jurisdiction. On the economic difficulties of the area see *Parl. Pap.* Cmd. 4368.

[2] Orders in Council, June 25, 1903; December 1, 1906; October 18, 1909; December 20, 1934.

for Bechuanaland, is passed by the High Commissioner only. Since 1912 civil and criminal jurisdiction in more important cases is exercised by a special court, presided over by a trained lawyer. In native disputes of a civil character, the chiefs continue to exercise jurisdiction, subject to appeal to the Resident Commissioner.

CHAPTER IX

THE PROTECTED STATES AND EGYPT

1. *The Protected States*

ESSENTIALLY distinct from Protectorates of the colonial type are a number of protected States, chiefly in Borneo and the Malay Peninsula. The essential characteristic of the Protectorate is that the Crown assumes and exercises full sovereign authority, though without annexing the territory. In the case of the protected States the sovereign authority belongs to the sovereign of the State, and not in any sense to the British Crown, and the rôle of the latter is derived from treaty arrangements with the States which do not confer any sovereignty over them, but give powers and duties in respect either of both internal and external affairs, or the latter almost exclusively. Historical accident largely explains the distinction between the two cases; in these Eastern territories there was a longer tradition of governmental forms which presented the possibility of preserving the existing State form, while the British Government was most anxious not to extend its responsibilities. In Africa, where such a policy would have been willingly followed, it proved impracticable of maintenance in the long run owing to the inferiority of political organisation and capacity of those concerned.

By far the most important group of protected States

is that in the Malay Peninsula, composed of the Federated Malay States and the States outside the federation, all of which are under the sphere of action of the
High Commissioner for the States, whose office is combined with that of Governor of the Straits Settlements.
In 1874 the first effective steps to bring these States
under British protection were taken, when Residents
to advise respecting collection of revenue and general
administration were appointed to Perak, Selangor, and
Sungei Ujong; in 1887 the external affairs of Pahang
were entrusted to British control, and next year fuller
protection and a British Resident were accepted. In
1895 the federal State of Negri Sembilan came into
being, including Sungei Ujong and other States which
had received British protection in 1883–9. The administration in each State is carried on by the State Council
presided over by the Sultan, assisted by the Resident,
and also, in Perak and Selangor, the Secretary to the
Resident. The council includes members of the royal
family, high chiefs, and, in the three older States,
Chinese representatives, and it has legislative power
for the State. The Residents are appointed by the
Secretary of State and are controlled by the High
Commissioner through the Chief Secretary, and through
their influence the administration is largely conducted
on Crown Colony lines, there being a large European
staff. The Chief Secretary's functions as a controller
of the Residents in the interests of unity of policy were
provided for in a Treaty of 1895, by which a federation
was created, each State agreeing to a system of mutual
aid in men and money, and the provision of an Indian
force for general service in the States and for the
defence of the Straits Settlements in the event of war.

Arrangements were then made for periodic meetings of the rulers for consultation, and in 1909 this ripened into the creation of a Federal Council, consisting of the High Commissioner, the heads of the four States, and others. In 1927 it was, by agreement, reconstructed. The High Commissioner is president, and there are twelve official and eleven unofficial members nominated by him with the King's approval. The council meets thrice a year to consider legislation which is to apply to more than one State, and the estimates of all the four States. There is a federal judiciary.

The other Malay States include Johore,[1] with which a Treaty of December 11, 1885, was concluded, placing its foreign affairs in British hands and providing for the appointment of a British Agent, not, however, actually carried out until 1910; in 1914 a General Adviser with enlarged powers was appointed. Further, there are the States of Kedah, Perlis, Kelantan,[2] and Trengganu, over which Siam claimed a measure of suzerainty, which was surrendered by the Treaty of March 10, 1909. Since 1902 Kelantan had been under the obligation to act on the advice of a British officer in the Siamese service, and his powers are now exercised by a British adviser. The position of Kedah is similar. The relation of Trengganu to Siam, on the other hand, was nominal and a Treaty of April 22, 1910, regulates the Sultan's relations with the British

[1] There is a constitution of 1895, with a Council of Ministers, composed of Malay officers of State, an Executive Council of British and Malay officers, a Council of State to which European and Asiatic official and unofficial members are appointed, and a judicial system analogous to that of the Federated Malay States.

[2] The legal position of Kelantan and of the other States is fully set out in the case *Duff Development Co.* v. *Government of Kelantan*, [1923] 1 Ch. 385; [1924] A.C. 797.

Crown. All political relations with foreign powers are handed over to British hands, and in 1919 the State accepted an adviser, whose advice on administration and finance must be adopted. In 1930 Perlis adopted a similar arrangement. Under the advice of the British advisers the States have largely prospered since detachment from Siam. Each ruler has a State Council for advice and legislation.

Brunei, once a powerful State, now diminished to a mere fraction of itself by cessions to Sarawak and North Borneo, surrendered in 1888 control of its foreign relations, and in 1905 accepted guidance in internal affairs to be given by a Resident under the directions of the High Commissioner.

As contrasted with these territories, Sarawak occupies a position of self-determination. Its history is curious, for when Sir James Brooke acquired in 1842 a large cession of territory from the Sultan of Brunei, the question arose whether any British recognition could be extended to him, seeing that any territory acquired by a British subject must be acquired, on the strict legal theory, for the Crown. The knot, which legal ability failed to untie, was finally cut; protection was refused, but recognition as an independent sovereign was granted in 1863. Later, an agreement of June 14, 1888, placed Sarawak under British protection. The Crown undertakes not to interfere in internal affairs, but is to determine any question arising as to the succession, to control the foreign relations of the State, and to have the right to appoint consular officers. British subjects are assured most-favoured-nation treatment, and no part of the State may be alienated without the consent of the Crown. The administration is conducted in the usual manner of the Malay States by the ruler with a supreme council of nine members (four European and five Malay magistrates) and a general council of fifty (European and Malay officers and native chiefs) meeting triennially, and the history of its development by successive acquisitions to an area of 40,000 square miles, under the rule of the Brookes, is a picturesque interlude.

Much more prosaic is the record of British North Borneo, which had its origin in cessions made by the Sultan of Brunei and Sulu to Baron Overbeck and Sir A. Dent in 1877–8; these in 1882 came into the hands of the British North Borneo Company, which was established by a charter from the Crown of November 1, 1881. By an agreement of May 12, 1888, a formal protection was afforded to the Company, the Crown undertaking control of all foreign relations and obtaining the right to appoint consular officers, but refraining from intervention in internal affairs.[1] The charter gave legislative authority to the Company, which is exercised by the Governor with the consent of the board of directors in London; the Governor is aided by a legislative council of eight official and five unofficial members; representing the trading communities, European and Asiatic, but their function is advisory. English law was introduced under the charter but subject to due regard for native law, especially in matters of property, succession, and status, and the Indian codes have been largely adapted for use. Allegations of unsatisfactory treatment of the natives were recently disproved on investigation for

---

[1] Appeal lies from the High Court to the Privy Council: Order in Council, November 28, 1914.

the Secretary of State for the Colonies. There exists an Imam's Court for the administration of Muhammadan law, and native courts to settle cases by native custom. The selection of the Governor is subject to the approval of the Crown.

In the Western Pacific the little State of Tonga under a queen has been protected since 1900. It has a constitution with Privy Council and Parliament. The British Government exercises a certain control through an agent and consul, who is subject to the High Commissioner for the Western Pacific.

In these protected States it is not the practice normally to secure formal rights of jurisdiction over British subjects, the influence of the Crown on the administration being sufficient to secure due execution of justice, though there is manifestly nothing in the status of a protected State to render such exercise of jurisdiction improper if it were found necessary; and it is exercised in Tonga. There the Tonga courts punish offences against the Tongan law, not punishable with death or imprisonment over two years.[1] In other cases non-Tongans are subject to the High Commissioner's Court. In Brunei, a local law[2] confers on the Resident's Court full jurisdiction. From the courts of the Federated Malay States and Johore appeal lies to the Privy Council. From Tonga appeal lies through Fiji to the Council.

In the New Hebrides a most complex condominium

---

[1] *Parl. Pap.* C. 6594.

[2] The Courts Enactment Act, 1908, provides for the jurisdiction of the Resident's Court, the application of laws of the Straits Settlements and the Federated Malay States, and allows appeal to the Supreme Court of the Straits Settlements, and thence to the Privy Council; Order in Council, September 26, 1908.

or joint Protectorate is shared with France under Conventions of October 20, 1906, and August 6, 1914, jurisdiction being exercised in certain matters by a special international tribunal, in others by consular courts, but the system is wholly unsatisfactory.

2. *Egypt and the Sudan*

The anomalous and complex position occupied by Egypt towards the British Crown was, to a certain extent, more effectively defined in 1914 when the connection, shadowy but real, between Egypt and Turkey was severed and a British Protectorate was established over the country. The grave difficulties of effective control over the European residents in view of existing treaty rights, were solved by the plan of declaring martial law, under which the necessary measures for effective control could be taken. The termination of hostilities raised inevitably the issue of the future of Egypt, having regard to the principle of self-determination enunciated by the allies; and the inability of the British Government, on the plea of the pressure of the peace settlement, to come to any arrangement with the Egyptian ministry in 1919 heralded a period of great strain in Anglo-Egyptian relations. A deadlock was imminent, in view of the difficulty of forming any Egyptian ministry to carry on the government unless independence was conceded, and the practical impossibility of managing affairs merely through the relatively small number of British officials, nearly all employed solely in advisory capacities and dependent on the Egyptian services for the carrying out of the actual administration. Finally, through a visit of the High Commissioner to England in February 1922, it was found possible to arrange a settlement as between the views of the British administrators on the spot and the Imperial Government. As no Egyptian ministry would accept responsibility for negotiating a treaty to acknowledge Egyptian independence, the procedure was adopted of a unilateral declaration of the termination of the British Protectorate and the establishment of Egyptian independence. An undertaking was given to withdraw absolutely martial law as proclaimed on November 2, 1914, on the passing of a General Act of Indemnity. At the same time the British Government reserved the questions of the security of the communications of the British Empire in Egypt; the defence of Egypt against all foreign aggression and interference, direct and indirect; the protection of foreign interests in Egypt, and of minorities; and the Sudan. On March 15, 1922, notification of Egyptian independence was made to foreign States by the British Government, and it was stated that Egypt could now establish a Ministry of Foreign Affairs and prepare the way for diplomatic and consular representation abroad. It was, however, pointed out that the welfare and integrity of Egypt were necessary to the peace and safety of the British Empire, which would, therefore, always retain as an essential British interest the special relations between itself and Egypt, long recognised by other governments. In pursuance of this principle they would regard as an unfriendly act any attempt at interference in the affairs of Egypt by another power, and would consider any aggression against the territory of Egypt as an act to be repelled with all the means at their command. On April 19, 1923, a new constitution for Egypt as an independent State was signed by the sovereign, establishing a constitutional monarchy with a bicameral legislature and a responsible ministry.

The ministry of Zaghlul Pasha established as the result of the elections in 1924, was followed by negotiations to secure for Egypt complete independence and the realisation of the national aspirations for Egypt and the Sudan. But the insistence of the British Government on maintaining its views both as to Egypt and the Sudan was followed on November 19 by the assassination of Sir L. Lee Stack, Sirdar of the Egyptian army and Governor-General of the Sudan. The British Government insisted on payment of an indemnity of £500,000, the withdrawal from the Sudan of Egyptian officers and units, and the revision of conditions affecting the status of officers in the Civil Service of Egypt, including the maintenance of the posts of financial and judicial advisers, together with the increase of the area of irrigation in the Sudan. The British terms were, in substance, carried out, but the appointment of the Sirdar to the Egyptian army was dropped, it being held sufficient to maintain an Inspector-General of the Egyptian Army. A very large number of British officials took the opportunity to retire.[1]

Internal difficulties, due to the King's desire for autocracy, led to the suspension of constitutional government until 1926, when Zaghlul Pasha resumed power. In 1927 it was necessary to make it clear that the *status quo* regarding the Egyptian army must be

[1] See Lord Lloyd, *Egypt since Cromer*, vol. ii. chap. vi.

maintained, but this was followed by proposals for a definite treaty, which were accepted by Sarwat Pasha, but proved unacceptable to the Egyptian Government as a whole. In 1929, however, the question of control of the waters of the Nile was at last adjusted,[1] and in 1930 a fresh attempt at treaty settlement was made, which contemplated the removal of British troops[2] from Cairo and Alexandria to the deserts, east of longitude 32°, the withdrawal of British officers from the Egyptian army, and the suppression of the European Department in the Ministry of the Interior, involving the destruction of the power of the United Kingdom to protect foreign residents. It was further promised that the British Government would use its authority to secure the abolition of the capitulations. On the other hand, the King undertook to afford effective protection to the lives and property of foreigners in Egypt. The treaty, however, proved unacceptable and negotiations remained incomplete. The King's renewed efforts to establish autocracy led in 1930 to the promulgation of a new constitution. The British Government refused to interfere with his action, as a matter of domestic interest, but in 1934 the King cancelled, on the advice of his new ministry, the constitution of 1930, with a view to the introduction of a more constitutional régime.

The Sudan, whose future is regarded as affecting vitally British interests, is under a condominium of Great Britain and Egypt created by Agreement of January 19, 1899, which negatives any claim of Turkey to suzerainty, and rests the British right on

---

[1] *Parl. Pap.* Cmd. 3348.

[2] A force of about 11,420 is maintained. See *Parl. Pap.* Cmd. 3575.

conquest; this system was extended by Agreement of July 10, 1899, to Suakin.[1] The supreme military and civil authority is vested in a Governor-General, appointed by Egyptian decree with the consent of the British Government, and removable only in the same manner; he appoints the Provincial Governors and Inspectors, who, with the chief members of the civil staff, are British, and he legislates by proclamation. In the exercise of his executive powers, other than in military matters and as regards appointments, and in legislation he is aided since 1910 by a Council of four officials and five other nominees, but he has the final decision in all matters. Defence is entrusted to the native Sudan defence force and a small British force. The system of government employs direct rule through local chiefs. The Government of Egypt has no legislative or other control, beyond the fact that the budget is submitted to it for approval and audit, and that irrigation forms the subject of joint agreement between the two Governments. Civil and criminal law and procedure have been codified and, while the higher judges and magistrates are British, Muhammadan law is administered to Muhammadans in special courts, appeal, provincial, and district, by Kadis, and native sheikhs and chiefs administer customary law in their districts, subject to appeal to a British officer, and to the limitation that no death sentence may be pronounced. The more important criminal cases are tried by Governors of provinces and District Commissioners or Mamours of provinces and districts.

---

[1] The condominium has been allowed to stand despite the removal of Egyptian forces: Lloyd, *Egypt since Cromer*, ii. 136 ff. Egypt in 1923 agreed to pay £750,000 contribution to the cost of administration.

3. *Zanzibar*

Zanzibar, separated in 1861 from Maskat, preserves some of the appearance of a protected State with a very complete transfer of power into British control. A formal Protectorate was announced in 1890 and recognised by France and Germany. More detailed control of the administration was only assumed in 1906, while in 1913 the Foreign Office gave over control to the Colonial Office, and under an Order in Council of January 21, 1914, the administration was organised. As modified by Orders in Council, 1924 and 1925, Government is in effect carried on in the name of the Sultan by a British Resident, Legislation is enacted in the form of the Sultan's decrees, which are binding on all persons, when countersigned by the Resident; if he annuls his countersignature on the direction of the Colonial Office, the decree ceases to be valid. Under the Sultan's Decree of 1926 there is an executive council with the Sultan as president, the Resident as vice-president, and three official members. The legislative council is presided over by the Resident; there are three *ex officio*, five nominated official members, and six unofficial members representing their communities. The central administration is in the hands of British officers, but there are Arab Governors in the towns, and village headmen. The Indian Penal and Civil and Criminal Procedure Codes are in force, but the basis of civil law is Muhammadan law, and native law is recognised, if not unjust or immoral.

Over all cases in which a British subject or person

enjoying British protection or a foreigner is concerned, jurisdiction is exercised by His Majesty's High Court, subject to appeal to His Majesty's Court of Appeal for Eastern Africa; in cases affecting only subjects of the Sultan, the Sultan's courts have jurisdiction, subject to appeal to the British judge, sitting as the Sultan's Court for Zanzibar, from which appeal lies to the Court of Appeal for Eastern Africa. From it lies appeal to the Privy Council.

The subordinate courts are held by resident magistrates, administrative officers, and Arab Kathis. In addition district courts, composed of benches of local headmen, exercise a limited criminal jurisdiction.

CHAPTER X

1. *The Pacific and African Mandates*

IT would have been the wish of the Dominions that the territories conquered from Germany in the Pacific and Africa should have followed the usual fate of war, and been annexed on the defeat of Germany to the victors; but this policy was defeated by President Wilson's insistence on the system of mandate. The Imperial Government was prepared to accept that system in Central Africa, but desired annexation in the case of South-West Africa and the Pacific territories, but insistence on this proved impossible. The essential aims of the Dominions were, however, secured by the formulation of a "C" class of mandates applicable to territories which, "owing to the sparseness of their population, or their small size, or their remoteness from centres of civilisation, or their geographical contiguity to the territory of the mandatory and other circumstances, can be best administered under the laws of the mandatory as integral portions of its territory, subject to safeguards in the interests of the indigenous population". The safeguards referred to are set out in an earlier portion of Clause XXII. of the Covenant of the League of Nations, as "freedom of conscience and religion, subject only to the maintenance of public order and morals, the prohibition of abuses, such as

521

the slave trade, the arms traffic, and the liquor traffic, and the prevention of the establishment of fortifications, or military and naval bases, and the military training of the natives for other than police purposes, and the defence of territory". These are the conditions applicable to mandates of "B" type ruled to be applicable to the peoples of Central Africa, but in their case there is added the obligation to secure equal opportunities for the trade and commerce of other members of the League. This obligation [1] might be deemed to be applicable as a means of safeguarding the natives from commercial exploitation in the interests of nationals of the mandatory state, but this interpretation has not so far been admitted by the Imperial or Dominion Governments, and it is certain that it was never contemplated to apply this rule to these cases, which comprise the Australian mandate for New Guinea, the New Zealand mandate for Samoa, the mandate for Nauru to the Crown, and that for South-West Africa to the Union, all approved formally by the League of Nations in December 1920. The mandates, though approved by the League, were allocated by the principal allied and associated powers in virtue of the cession to them unconditionally of the territories in question by Germany. [2]

The terms of these mandates are essentially reproductions of the stipulations of the League Covenant. Full power of administration and legislation, as an integral part of the territory of the mandatory, is conceded, and the right to apply the laws of the mandatory to the territory. The mandatory must

---

[1] Cf. Keith, *Letters on Imperial Relations, 1916–1935*, pp. 312, 313.

[2] See Keith, *Journ. Comp. Leg.* iv. 71 ff.

promote to the utmost the material and moral well-
being and the social progress of the inhabitants. The
slave trade must be prohibited, and forced labour,
unless for essential public works and services, and then
only for adequate remuneration. The traffic in arms
and ammunition must be regulated by the principles
of the international convention of September 10, 1919,
and the supply of intoxicating spirits and beverages
to the natives must be prohibited. The natives may
not be trained in arms save for local police and internal
defence; no naval or military base, or fortification is
permitted. Freedom of worship and the free entry of
missionaries are imperative. An annual report must
be made to the Council of the League, whose consent is
necessary for any change in the terms of the mandate
and any dispute regarding the interpretation or application of the terms must be referred to the Permanent Court of International Justice under the
League Covenant. The annual report is a matter of
importance; it is examined by the Mandates Commission of the League, an impartial body on which a
majority of members are not nationals of mandatory
States, which obtains explanations from a responsible
officer of the mandatory, and the report of the Commission with any observations of that officer is submitted to the League. The Assembly meeting of 1922
was marked by the firm explanation by the representative of New Zealand that the Dominion was in
no way subject to the orders of the Commission or of
the League, and in 1926 the Dominions protested
against a proposed questionnaire. The position is, indeed, perfectly clear; the Commission or the League
have no power over the mandatory other than the

general rights in respect of international matters conferred in the Covenant generally. It is noteworthy that Japan has been ready to hold her mandated territory under the League despite her secession in March 1935. On the other hand, it is clearly the duty of each mandatory to make the conception of a mandate effective by frank discussion and consideration of all suggestions emanating from the Mandates Commission, a body of impartial critics. On these matters, of course, as on other League questions, direct communications proceed between the League and the Dominions.

(1) *New Guinea* is governed by the Commonwealth under the New Guinea Act, 1920, which creates New Guinea a territory of the Commonwealth, entrusts the administration to an Administrator, and, as amended in 1932, creates an Executive Council and a Legislative Council of eight official and seven unofficial nominated members. Legislation can be disallowed by the Governor-General. The Act also provides for the observance of the fundamental principles set out in the mandate, but goes further in absolutely forbidding compulsory labour under any conditions. Under the Act military administration ceased on May 9, 1921, when there came into operation ordinances substituting English law for German, applying various Commonwealth and Queensland Acts, and preserving the natives their land rights and their customs as regards cultivation, barter, hunting, and fishing. Tribal institutions, customs, and usages have also been preserved save where they conflict with the general principles of humanity. The supply of firearms, ammunition, liquor, and opium to natives is absolutely forbidden, and a system of law

courts has been created. One effect of the change of régime is important; the German Government made no objection to the entry of Japanese and other Asiatics, and accorded Japanese a privileged position almost equal to that of Europeans; Japan has, therefore, not unnaturally represented that the application of the immigration régime of the Commonwealth renders the position of her nationals inferior to what it was under the German régime.

(2) In the case of *New Zealand* the power to legislate for *Samoa* is derived, not as in the case of the Commonwealth[1] from the constitution, which provides for legislation for territories placed under the authority of the Commonwealth, but from an Imperial Order in Council of 1920,[2] under the Foreign Jurisdiction Act, 1890. Originally the constitution was embodied in an Order in Council of the New Zealand Government, but this was replaced by the Samoa Act, 1921. The executive government is vested in an administrator acting under the Minister of External Affairs of the Dominion. Legislative power belongs without restriction to the Governor-General in Council, while a Legislative Council of from four to six officials, and two elected Europeans and two nominated Samoans, is established. The powers of the Administrator in Legislative Council are limited; no ordinance may affect the royal prerogative or title to land; impose customs, or export duties; establish any body corporate; create any local authority

---

[1] There is some doubt as to the source of power. Cf. *Jolly* v. *Mainka* (1933), 49 C.L.R. 242, 274 ff.

[2] Probably this was unnecessary: the mandate would have sufficed to give legislative authority. Cf. *Tagaloa* v. *Inspector of Police*, [1927]; N.Z.L.R. 883; *Tamasese, In re*, [1929] N.Z.L.R. 209; *Nelson* v. *Braisby* (No. 2), [1934] N.Z.L.R. 559.

with rating or legislative authority; establish paper currency; or impose penalties over one year's imprisonment or £100 fine. English law is made applicable, subject, however, to the retention of Samoan land and succession laws, and the giving of discretion as to the enforcement of contracts to which natives are parties. Land is classified as Crown, European, and native, the latter being vested in the Crown, but merely as trustee for the beneficial title owners under the native title, and subject to the customs and usages of the native race. Restrictions are placed on the alienation of native land. Full provision is made for civil and criminal jurisdiction by a High Court with an appeal to the Supreme Court of New Zealand. All property rights of the German Government are vested in the King. Careful as the legislation is, there has been much feeling in the island, and a petition was presented to the King in 1921 asking, in effect, that the Imperial Government should assume direct administrative control, a request which was necessarily refused. There has been much unrest, due in part to agitation among half-castes, rendering drastic legislation and deportation thereunder of offenders necessary. But the Mandates Commission has not disapproved. A serious difficulty arises from the necessity of employing indentured Chinese labour to maintain cultivation of the estates, established under the German Government. Umbrage at this action has been taken in labour circles in New Zealand, and the policy is not popular even with the Government, which has adopted it merely *faute de mieux*. The moral difficulties involved are reflected in the inclusion, through the insistence of the Legislative Council, in the Samoa Act, 1921, of a section forbidding marriages between

Samoans and Chinese. The position of the Chinaman is not enviable, since he is forbidden to settle, and his employment accordingly presents in a minor degree the objections which led to the termination of Chinese labour in the South African mines. The Faipule, leading chiefs, representing every district, appointed by the Administrator, meet twice annually, and draft native orders for submission to the Government.

(3) In the Union legislation for *South-West Africa* has been passed, not as in the Commonwealth under the constitution power to deal with territories, nor under Imperial authority, as in New Zealand, but under the general power to legislate for the peace, order, and good government of the Union given in the South Africa Act, 1909. The validity of the exercise of this power might, before the Statute of Westminister, 1931, perhaps have been questioned on the score that it is extra-territorial legislation, but it may be defended on the ground that the mandate by inference confers the power to legislate. The government of the territory was rendered more than usually difficult through the existence of a large German population, beside the much reduced native races. It was possible under the Treaty of Peace to deport them, but it was preferred to encourage them to accept Union rule. Civil administration was introduced on December 31, 1920, in lieu of military law. By a proclamation of 1919, Roman Dutch law, civil and criminal, as existing in the Union in the Cape Province on January 1, 1920, was introduced into the territory, and an elaborate judicial system established; the magistrates in the districts act also as administrative officers in charge of native affairs. Land set aside for reserves for natives may not be

alienated from them, save with the assent of the Union Parliament. A number of reserves have been marked out, in which the tribal chief, or an elected or appointed headman, is responsible to the magistrate for law and order, and receives a small salary; these reserves are to serve as the means of securing a contented and settled population and a recruiting-ground for labour. The labour laws are decidedly drastic; in areas open to European settlement every native, not infirm or aged, must be in employment unless he has visible means of support, and a rigid pass law is enforced. Methods of enforcing obedience by use of air power evoked complaints at the League Assembly in 1922 and the enquiry then made elicited proof of grave errors of administration. There is also the fundamental difficulty that the Union makes the welfare of Europeans paramount to the sacred trust of civilising the natives under mandate.

The political development of the territory is of interest. In the early days of its government power was vested by statute in the Governor-General, who by proclamation No. 1 of 1921 delegated authority to the Administrator. By Act No. 42 of 1925[1] a generous measure of authority was given to the local government. Administration is on the model of the provincial system entrusted to the Executive Committee, consisting of the Administrator, and four members elected by proportional representation by the Legislative Assembly. This body carries on the administration of all matters within the legislative power of the Assembly. In dealing with other matters not within its sphere, and in regard to the exercise of his assent to or reservation of Bills, the Administrator is aided by an Advisory Committee

---

[1] Amended by No. 38 of 1931.

composed of the Executive Committee and three nominated members. The Assembly is composed of four nominated members and twelve elected by adult male European suffrage, and its normal tenure is five years. Its powers are restricted in certain matters in order to secure due regard to the terms of the mandate. The prior consent of the Governor-General is requisite for any legislation on native affairs, mines, railways, and harbours, the public service, courts of justice, posts, telegraphs and telephones, military organisation, defence force movements, immigration, customs and excise, currency and banking. Control of police, education, civil aviation, land or agricultural banks and lands, is subject to special authorisation by the Governor-General. Any ordinance may be referred back, or reserved by the Administrator, and even if assented to may be disallowed by the Governor-General.

There is a Territory Revenue Fund which can be appropriated only by ordinance, and expended under warrant of the Administrator. But the latter has defined powers of acting pending appropriation, and the Governor-General has authority to approve expenditure which the Assembly declines to authorise, and to enact taxation which the Assembly rejects. Moreover, the Governor-General retains the full powers of exercising or delegating administrative and legislative authority, and proclamations by him are superior in authority to any proclamation by the Administrator under delegated power or ordinance of the legislature. The Governor-General alone can remit death sentences.

This constitution followed on the assent obtained by General Smuts from the German Government for the naturalisation *en bloc* of all Germans who did not specifically reject such naturalisation.[1] As a result, the German population has exercised considerable authority, and lately has endeavoured to secure the placing of German on a footing of absolute equality with English and Dutch, including Afrikaans, as an official language. In 1934–5, however, this movement suffered a set-back, the Nazi organisation being dissolved by the Government on the ground that its aims were incompatible with the established status of the territory, and the general election returned a majority which applied for inclusion in the Union as a fifth province. Difficulties have, however, arisen regarding the suggestion, based on the fact that the financial position of the area is embarrassed and acceptance as a fifth province may raise a question with the League of Nations. At the instance of the Mandates Commission the issue of sovereignty over the territory has been discussed on several occasions between the Union Government and the Commission. The Union Supreme Court has held that the position of the Union in the territory is such that a native by resisting its authority may be guilty of treason,[2] and the Union in one or two official documents used the term sovereignty as describing its position in regard to the territory. It is clear that no great matter of substance was involved, and the Union gracefully conceded the point of form by an amendment of its railway legislation to negative an apparent claim of full dominion over the area. It is clear that, if there were to be any idea of returning the territory in whole or part to Germany, incorporation as a province would be undesirable, but it may be doubted if the official

---

[1] Act No. 30 of 1924; 3261 out of 3489 accepted naturalisation.
[2] *R.* v. *Christian*, [1924] S. Afr. A.D. 101.

sympathy with the restoration of German territory Chapter X.
expressed in 1935 by Mr Pirow refers to South-West
Africa or is not rather an expression of the willingness
of the Union to see the British Government surrender
Tanganyika.[1] Yet it must be remembered that it was
the use made of that area as a means of training
African troops for war that rendered General Smuts
determined in 1919 to see carried out the expulsion of
Germany from African territories.

Legally the incorporation of the Union as a fifth
province of the area appears consistent with the mandate, which permits administration as an integral part
of Union territory; but that view might not com-
mend itself to the League of Nations, especially so
long as Germany was a member of the League. Much,
however, depends on the strength of the demand of
Germany, raised again officially in March 1935, for the
restoration of some at least of her oversea territories,
which are desired, according to Dr Schacht, as sources
of raw material, without which Germany cannot long
hope to be able to maintain payments to her creditors,
public and private, and by Herr Hitler as a condition
of return of Germany to co-operation with the League.

(4) Nauru, an island $8\frac{1}{2}$ square miles in area, rich in
phosphate, presents peculiar features. Under agreement between His Majesty's Government in London,
and the Governments of the Commonwealth and
New Zealand, administrative, legislative, and judicial
authority are vested in an Administrator; the first

---

[1] Keith, *Letters on Imperial Relations, 1916–1935*, pp. 76, 331, 346.
On April 9 it was announced that the British Government would not
surrender any mandate ; on June 13 at Geneva the Union Government
pledged itself not to incorporate the territory without consultation with
the League.

holder of the office was appointed for five years by the Commonwealth Government, and the present Administrator is an officer of the Australian navy. The Administrator may establish ordinances for peace, order, and good government, subject to disallowance by the appointing Government, set up courts and magistrates, and maintain a police force. The native population is about 1500 in number, while 165 Europeans with 1000 Chinese are engaged in Government work and the extraction of phosphate. The legal basis of the arrangement is the Nauru Island Agreement Act, 1920, of the Imperial Parliament, and legislation to the same effect by the Commonwealth and New Zealand, which remove any possible doubt as to the powers of the Administrator. At the same time the three Governments purchased the rights, derived from a German company, of the Pacific Phosphate Company in the guano deposits, and their exploitation is conducted on their behalf by a Board of three Commissioners, whose duty is to dispose of the product for agricultural purposes in the three countries, in the proportions of 42 per cent for the United Kingdom and Australia, and 16 per cent for New Zealand, this representing the proportions in which the £3,500,000 purchase money was paid. The arrangement has been the source of misunderstanding in the League Mandates Commission and elsewhere, on the score that a monopoly was thus being created against the spirit of the League Covenant; but it is clear that the commercial side of the matter is purely one of the acquisition by the Governments of an existing valid monopoly, though it remains dubious whether the Governments should have deliberately placed themselves in a position in which their commercial interests may run counter to the effective care of the natives which is imposed on them by the mandate. The Administrator, however, is solely responsible for the moral and general welfare, labour conditions, and health of the inhabitants. The Governments are under an obligation in no wise to interfere in the activities of the Commissioners, an arrangement which may be productive of difficulty, if these operations ever come to run clearly counter to native needs.

(5) In Central Africa portions of the German territories of the Kamerun (Cameroons) and Togoland have been acquired under mandate by the United Kingdom, and arrangements have been made for their administration in connection with the adjacent territories in the Gold Coast and Nigeria, while the much more important acquisition of German East Africa, less portions handed over to Belgium under mandate, has been erected into the Tanganyika Territory, provision for whose administration is made by Order in Council of July 22, 1920, under the Foreign Jurisdiction Act, 1890, or the prerogative. The administration is entrusted to a Governor, with an Executive Council of the usual colonial type; legislative power by Order in Council of March 19, 1926, is vested in the Governor and a Legislative Council of thirteen officials and not more than ten nominated unofficial members; in legislating, it is required to respect native laws and customs, save where opposed to justice or morality, and may not alter any Order in Council without previous approval. A High Court with full jurisdiction is established in both civil and criminal matter, and the Indian Civil Procedure, Criminal Procedure, and

Penal Codes are introduced, together with the English common law, doctrines of equity, and statutes of general application so far as the circumstances of the territory permit. In all cases to which natives are parties the court is to be guided by native law so far as it is applicable, and is not repugnant to law and justice or any enactment, and to decide according to substantial justice without undue regard to technicalities or delay. Appeal lies to the Court of Appeal for Eastern Africa.

2. *The Mandates for Palestine, Trans-Jordan, and formerly for Iraq*

The mandates for Palestine, Trans-Jordan, and Iraq fall under the provisions of Clause XXII. of the League of Nations Covenant, which contemplates, in the case of mandates for portions of the Turkish Empire, the rendering of administrative advice and assistance to peoples not yet able to stand by themselves. The cases, however, have been treated very differently, for the British Government had pledged itself in 1917 to the establishment of a national home for the Jewish people, and this pledge was homologated by the other allied powers, and, therefore, has attained recognition in the mandate [1] for Palestine finally settled in 1922 by the approval of the League of Nations, after due arrangements had been made with the United States to secure the interests of American citizens, despite the failure of the United States to join the League. In the case of Iraq, on the other hand, the Imperial Government,

---

[1] *Parl. Pap.* Cmd. 1785. For Arab objections see Cmd. 1700, and for Church questions, Cmd. 1708.

after an apparent inclination to treat the territory as a colonial mandate, definitely abandoned the conception and adopted the scheme of an alliance, as a step towards independence.

(a) Palestine

The Palestine mandate of July 24, 1922, imposes the duties of securing such political administrative and economic conditions as will assure the establishment of a Jewish national home, the development of self-governing institutions, including self-government for localities, and the safeguarding of the civil and religious rights of all inhabitants of the territory. The Zionist organisation is recognised as an agency to co-operate with the administration in securing Jewish interests, and a policy of immigration of Jews is enjoined, but so as not to prejudice the rights and position of other sections of the population. A nationality law to favour Jews who immigrate becoming citizens has been passed. All privileges of foreigners, including rights of jurisdiction under the capitulations, are abrogated, the mandatory being required to secure the establishment of a judicial system which will safeguard the rights of foreigners and rights of religious denominations, especially as regards trust administration. The mandatory is required to secure the preservation of existing rights regarding the holy places of Palestine, to secure through a Commission appointed by the League Council the handing over of holy places to the permanent care of suitable custodians, and to provide freedom of conscience and the exercise of religion; no person may be penalised because of race, language, or religion, or forbidden to enter on religious grounds.

Missionary enterprise is only to be subject to considerations of public order and good government. Military forces can only be organised on a voluntary basis for the preservation of peace and defence. No discrimination between nationals of the League States is permissible in any matter of commerce, taxation, navigation, or exercise of professions, or the export or import of goods, but special customs arrangements may be made with any State formerly part of Asiatic Turkey or Arabia. The mandatory is bound to inaugurate a land system to promote closer settlement and intensive cultivation. All foreign relations are in the hands of the mandatory whose extradition treaties are to apply. English, Hebrew, and Arabic are official languages. An annual report to the League is required; any dispute must be submitted for arbitration to the Court of International Justice, and the mandate may not be altered without the assent of the Council of the League, which, even on a proposal by the mandatory, may not, it seems, act by a majority.

The constitution of 1922, provided by Order in Council of August 10, 1922, establishes the control of the administration in a High Commissioner, aided by an Executive Council, who is given full powers over the public lands and over mines, subject to valid concessions. For legislation a Council was provided consisting of ten official and twelve unofficial members, in addition to the High Commissioner, with a duration of three years.[1] The elected members were to be selected by an electorate, consisting of all male Palestinian

[1] The first elections were rendered invalid by the abstention of the Arab voters, as a protest against the denial of self-determination, and accordingly, in June 1923, they were cancelled, and a nominee advisory Council appointed *ad interim* pending effective elections, but the Muham-

citizens over twenty-five years of age, through a system of primary elections, by which in suitable voting districts secondary electors at the rate of one for 200 electors were to be selected. The electors were to be divided into twelve colleges, each religious denomination being assigned a number of these in proportion to its number of secondary electors, and these colleges were to elect the members. No ordinance might vary the terms of the mandate or restrict complete freedom of religion, or discriminate on grounds of religion, race, or language, and ordinances might be refused assent by the High Commissioner, or reserved, and, even if assented to, might be disallowed by the Crown; any ordinance affecting any matter dealt with in the mandate must be reserved. In addition to an elaborate series of civil [1] and criminal courts, there are established Moslem, Jewish, and Christian (Latin and Orthodox) religious courts, which deal with matters of status of Moslems, Jews, and Christians, and with religious endowments. On immigration questions the High Com-

---

madan and Christian members declined to act if their action was to be regarded as homologating the constitution. Viscount Grey (House of Lords, June 27, 1923) suggested a modification of the policy of the Government in favour of respecting the civil rights of the Arabs, while affording facilities for the establishment of a Jewish University and of a home of Jewish culture. In October 1923, an offer was made to the Arabs to create an Arab Agency with functions parallel to the Jewish Agency under the mandate, but this proposal was rejected by the Arabs. The territory is thus reduced to Crown Colony government, which cannot be permanent, but up to 1935 no change has been possible. The High Commissioner alone legislates with an advisory Council of Officials.

[1] The civil law is the Ottoman law in force on November 1, 1914, subsequent statutory law, and English law, so far as applicable. Special provisions secure foreigners, except in petty offences, the right of trial by a British magistrate or a court containing a majority of British judges; in the Court of Appeal he can claim such a majority and in matters of personal status that the question be heard by the British President.

missioner was to consult with a committee containing not less than half the unofficial members of the legislature, and, in the event of disagreement, a report must be made to the Secretary of State, whose views would be final.

The influx of large numbers of Jews was bound to have a serious effect on the economic conditions of the Arabs, and resulted in grave rioting, which elicited from the British Government the appointment of a strong British police force and enquiries into the possibility of so controlling immigration as to allow of the preservation of Arab land interests.[1] As the result of these enquiries, efforts were made to safeguard the Arabs from being reduced to the position of landless labourers, but the anti-Semitic campaign in Germany rendered it desirable to relax restrictions, and certain elements both in Palestine and outside have put forward the claim for Jewish domination in Palestine, even at the cost of expelling the Arabs. The British Government, however, has repeatedly asserted that it intends to honour its obligations to the Arabs, though it has failed to convince the latter of its sincerity. Since 1927 the Jews have been recognised as a community, religious, cultural, and communal, with power to levy rates on its members and to manage its internal affairs through a Chief Rabbinate, an Elected Assembly, and a General Council elected by the Assembly, which represents the community in its dealings with the Government. A number of Jews, however, have exercised the option to remain out of the community. The Moslems have no corresponding body of equal importance. The Supreme

---

[1] *Parl. Pap.* Cmd. 3560; Sir John Hope Simpson's report, Cmd. 3686, 3687.

Moslem Council, composed of a President and four members elected by secondary electors, is concerned with the management of charitable endowments, controls officers connected therewith, nominates the officers of the religious courts, maintains an orphanage, and undertakes tree-planting and repair of sacred edifices.

Certain legal issues of importance have been decided by the Privy Council. It has declared the validity of the Order in Council providing for appeals from the Supreme Court, and it had laid down the principle that it lies primarily with the executive government to determine what actions are within the terms of the mandate, and that it is not normally possible for a court to control that discretion.[1] An international issue of importance has also arisen out of the Mavromattis claim against the Palestine Government, for the Permanent Court of International Justice has naturally ruled that the Greek Government is entitled to take up a complaint of a national that the administration had deprived him of the benefit of a contract binding on the Turkish administration.

(b) Trans-Jordan

In the area of Palestine over the Jordan the British Government felt free from the obligations undertaken regarding a home for the Jewish people, and in September 1922 this fact was duly notified to the League of Nations, while assurances were given that the other terms of the mandate for Palestine would be given effect to in the territory. The present position is regu-

---

[1] *Jerusalem and Jaffa District Governor* v. *Suleiman Murra*, [1926] A.C. 321.

lated by agreement of February 20, 1928, with the Emir, under which the British Government is given assurances of the due execution of its mandatory liabilities. The agreement was duly accepted by the Legislative Council of six official and sixteen elected members created by the Emir Abdullah ibn Hussain, brother of King Faisal, and the Crown is represented in the territory by a British Resident with a small British staff, including financial and judicial advisers. For maintaining order since 1926 there has been created a Trans-Jordan Frontier Force, which acts for Palestine and Trans-Jordan, while civil police work in the latter is entrusted to the Arab Legion under British commanders. Supervision over the British Resident rests with the High Commissioner for Trans-Jordan, who is the High Commissioner for Palestine.

The legal system is based on the Ottoman Code, and the official language is Arabic.

(c) Iraq

The Mesopotamian mandate was originally presented to the League in a form implying the duty of the mandatory to prepare a constitution for the territory, and included much the same general provisions as in the case of Palestine but without the complications involved in the idea of a Jewish national home, and the issue of the holy places, with which the mandatory was to have no concern. But this proved to ignore the strength of local feeling, and the unwillingness of the British taxpayer to continue incurring the heavy expense which proved necessary in order to keep the people of Iraq under control, although free use of aeroplanes in lieu of troops reduced the cost considerably. An alliance,[1] therefore, was decided on and signed on October 10, 1922, while contemporaneously an assurance was given to the King that every effort would be made to determine the boundaries of the country in order that successful application might be made to the League of Nations for the admission of Iraq to membership, and the mandate thus brought to a close. Under the alliance, advice and assistance were to be afforded to the King, without impairing national sovereignty. A constitution was to be provided by the King and the Constituent Assembly, which must secure freedom of conscience and worship, forbid discrimination on the score of race, religion, or language, and secure to each community the right of educating its members in their own speech. The King must accept the advice of the High Commissioner for the duration of the treaty on all important matters affecting the international and financial obligations and interests of the British Crown, and must ensure the stability and good organisation of the finances of the Iraq Government, so long as that Government was under financial obligations to the British Government. Military aid to the Iraq Government was provided for by a separate agreement. The King might be represented diplomatically at London and elsewhere by agreement; in other places the British Government looked after Iraq interests. Foreign powers represented in Iraq under *exequaturs* from the King, but after agreement to their appointment by the British Government. No territory might be ceded or leased to any foreign power. The judicial system must respect the interests

[1] *Parl. Pap.* Cmd. 1757.

of foreigners, and be communicated to the Council of the League. But by a subsequent arrangement the effect of the treaty was limited to a maximum of four years, after the ratification of peace with Turkey, the intention being that it should terminate earlier on the admission of Iraq to the League, provision being made simultaneously for new treaty relations.

The Treaty of 1922 as modified in 1923 was accepted by the Constituent Assembly convened by King Faisal, but the situation was altered by the question of Mosul, for the League Council, in awarding the disputed area to Iraq, stipulated for the extension of the British mandate.[1] A new Treaty of January 13, 1926, accordingly provided for such extension, and the boundary was fixed with Turkish agreement in June. A further Treaty of 1927[2] was unacceptable to Iraq, and in 1929 it was allowed to lapse, and a promise given to support an application by Iraq for membership of the League in 1932. In 1930 a treaty was arranged to come into force when Iraq was admitted to the League, and to regulate for twenty-five years on a footing of equal alliance the relations between the two countries.[3] This arrangement took effect when Iraq was admitted to the League in 1932. Under it Iraq is bound to consult with the British Government on issues of foreign policy, and to afford facilities for the maintenance of British air bases in her territory; moreover, in accordance with the British declaration in 1928 in respect of the Paris Treaty for the Renunciation of War, the defence of

---

[1] *Parl. Pap.* Cmd. 2562, 2563, 2624.
[2] *Ibid.* Cmd. 2998, 3440.
[3] *Ibid.* Cmd. 3627, 3675, 3797, 3933.

Iraq is deemed by the British Government a part of defence of British interests of a vital kind, as in the case of Egypt. Iraq is also bound to maintain such a judicial system as shall secure equal justice to all foreigners. She is under pledge to the League to afford security for minorities, but this pledge was signally violated by massacres of Assyrians in 1933, and projects for saving this unfortunate minority, which unluckily rendered services to the British Government in the war on the strength of assurances of protection, failed in 1934–5 to reach any useful result.

CHAPTER XI

BRITISH INDIA, THE INDIAN STATES, AND BURMA

1. *The Origin of the Constitution of* 1919

THE acquisition of dominion over vast areas of India by the East India Company was effected under the authority of, and on behalf of, the British Crown, and Parliament, by a long series of Acts, from 1773 onwards, regulated the administration of the Government, and eventually reduced the company to a mere governmental agency, defended by Macaulay in 1833, when the renewal of the charter was under discussion, on the score that it was more convenient and effective than direct rule with the embarrassing patronage which it would throw into the hands of the Government. The Sepoy rebellion in 1857–8 deprived the maintenance of the form of Company administration of all validity; the Emperor accused of complicity in the revolt was deposed, his nominal authority passing to the Crown; and the Crown assumed full control under the Act of 1858, adopting the style of Empress of India under an Act of 1876. The control which the Company acquired over India was based in part on mere conquest, but in large measure under treaty and grants from the nominal Emperor at Delhi, and naturally enough the power which it acquired it exercised with Parliamentary sanction in the despotic fashion of the sovereigns whom it succeeded or represented. Centralisation of authority was also aimed at; in 1833 the sole legislative power in India was vested in the Governor-General's Council to the supersession of the power formerly exercised in Bombay and Madras.[1] In 1853 the Council was extended for legislative purposes[2] to the number of twelve, but it made the fatal error, in governmental eyes, of treating itself like a Parliament, and criticising the sacred mysteries of executive power, and in 1861 it was severely reduced to purely legislative functions, while similar restricted authority was restored to Madras and Bombay, but under strict control by the central Government.[3] Bengal was also given a Legislative Council distinct from that of the Governor-General in 1862, the North-Western Provinces and Oudh (now United Provinces of Agra and Oudh) in 1886, and in 1892 a real step in advance was taken by increasing the size of the legislatures and introducing indirectly the principle of election for some members of these bodies. Moreover, the power to ask questions and discuss but not vote on the budget was granted, and resolutions might be moved.[4] The Punjab obtained a Council in 1897, and in 1905 Bengal was partitioned into the Lieutenant-Governorships of Bengal, and Eastern Bengal and Assam. In 1909 Lord Morley's reform schemes largely increased the size of the legislatures, introduced openly election by selected bodies such as Chambers of Commerce, gave non-official majorities on the provincial councils, and even an elective majority in Bengal, and extended very considerably the deliberative and financial authority of

[1] 3 & 4 Will. IV. c. 85. [2] 16 & 17 Vict. c. 95.
[3] 24 & 25 Vict. c. 67. [4] 55 & 56 Vict. c. 14.

2 N

the Councils.[1] The reforms of 1911 made Delhi again the capital of India, reconstituted Bengal as a single area of Bengali speech, created the new province of Bihar, Chota Nagpur, and Orissa, and made Assam a Chief Commissionership. Bengal was further given the status of a Presidency under a Governor like Bombay and Madras, and in 1912 Assam, and in 1913 the Central Provinces, received Councils. Burma politically isolated, had already received a Council in 1897.

The apparatus of Councils, however, was not intended to do more than aid the executive in suitable legislation; the power of the executive, even in the provinces where the legislatures had non-official majorities, could always in the long run be made effective by the paramount authority of the central Government, the legislature of which contained an official majority even under Lord Morley's reforms, and Lord Morley deprecated any interpretation of his reforms as introducing Parliamentary institutions into India. The events of the war served to make public opinion in Britain realise how narrow was a conception that India could develop on any lines save those of responsible government. The Home Rule League was formally established in Madras in September 1916; a month later nineteen members of the Indian Legislative Council adumbrated reforms, while in December the Indian National Congress, and the Muslim League, in meetings at Lucknow, came to a momentous decision to ignore the bitterness of centuries of strife, and to co-operate for self-government. On August 20, 1917, recognition of India's services,

[1] 9 Edw. VII. c. 4.

which had already been signalised by her representation at the Imperial War Conference and Cabinet, was formally accorded by Mr Montagu's statement that the policy of His Majesty's Government was that of "the increasing association of Indians in every branch of the administration and the gradual development of self-governing institutions, with a view to the progressive realisation of responsible government in India as an integral part of the British Empire". Mr Montagu visited India in the autumn, and reported[1] with Lord Chelmsford, the Viceroy, on April 22, 1918, and at the close of 1919, after most elaborate examination by Committees and Parliament, the Act reforming the constitution of India became law. It was essentially a transition measure, meant to pave the way to the full responsible government which alone Indian opinion can be expected to accept. Its numerous defects from any logical point of view are explained by this fact, and need not be emphasised. It was in large measure a rigid constitution, because, as asserted in the preamble, Parliament was determined to keep the question of the rate of constitutional advance in its own hands.

2. *The Montagu-Chelmsford Reforms*

The essence of the system of Indian government[2] before the reforms was the complete authority of the central Government in executive and legislative matters as a necessary complement to its responsibility to the Secretary of State. The new system aimed at the gradual introduction of responsibility to the

---

[1] *Parl. Pap.* Cd. 9109.   [2] Government of India Act, 1919.

people, and for that reason it was necessary to provide a sphere of action in which the central Government would not normally interfere. It was therefore decided to draw a distinction between central and provincial subjects, and to endeavour in the sphere of the latter to introduce a measure of responsible government. Provincial subjects, therefore, were classified as transferred, and reserved, and in the former category were placed those topics of special social and economic importance, while in the latter were ranked those matters essentially connected with the maintenance of law and order and the preservation of financial stability. Thus local government, education, sanitation, public health, hospitals, asylums, public works, development of industries, agriculture, veterinary questions, and co-operative societies were transferred matters, while reserved topics included land, irrigation, famine relief, administration of justice, police, prisons, factory inspection, and labour matters in general.

In finance also a distinction was drawn; the centre received income tax, railway receipts, posts and telegraphs, customs, salt tax, and the tax on export of opium, while the provinces had excise, land revenue, irrigation and forests, and stamp duties and registration fees. They were assured of a share of increases in income tax, but were bound to pay contributions to the centre, until relieved of these by growth of central receipts.

In transferred matters the Governor acted with the advice of ministers responsible to the legislature, of which they must be, or become, members within six months. He could, however, disregard their advice if he considered that it unfairly affected the interests of race, religion, education, social conditions, wealth, or other circumstances, and, if he could not find ministers to accept his ruling, he could assume charge of the subject. Moreover, he could sanction any expenditure necessary for any department or for the peace and tranquility of the province, but he could not legislate on a transferred subject over the head of the legislature. Such legislation, however, could be passed by the Governor-General or the central legislature in case of need. In reserved matters he acted with his Executive Council usually equally composed of British and Indian members, and had full power to pass legislation and appropriate funds even over the head of the legislature. He decided the proportion of funds to be allocated as between transferred and reserved subjects, and financial correctness was ensured by the control in each province by an Executive Councillor of the Finance Department which scrutinised all proposals of ministers for expenditure, taxation and borrowing. A further control was exercised by the rule that alterations in conditions affecting officers appointed by the Secretary of State required his approval, and the Governor was responsible for securing due regard to the rights of such officers.

The legislatures were largely increased in number, and the franchise was widened. Bengal was given 139 members, and Assam, the smallest legislature, had 53; not more than 20 per cent could be nominated, and at least 70 per cent must be elected. Nomination was used to provide a considerable official bloc, and to secure spokesmen of the depressed classes, Anglo-Indians, and Indian Christians. It was necessary to provide constituencies separately for Hindus, Muhammadans, Sikhs, Europeans, Anglo-Indians, landholders, industrial interests, and Universities. It was laid down that taxation could be raised only by Act, and that rates of land revenue would be treated in future as subject to enactment. Appropriations were to be made in the form of votes granted by the legislature, but there were excepted ecclesiastical, political, and defence expenditure, interest on loans, salaries and pensions of officers appointed by the Secretary of State, and provincial contributions. A Public Accounts Committee was allowed to review the expenditure and report to the legislature.

Control over the provincial government in transferred matters was reserved to the central Government mainly for the purpose of safeguarding central subjects, while the Secretary of State had wider powers, including the right to intervene in regard to matters affecting the relations of India and other parts of the Empire or foreign countries.

In practice the system worked imperfectly.[1] The basis of effective responsible government is financial responsibility and reliance for support by ministers on effective party organisations. In India, responsibility of any kind was blurred by the duplication of governmental authority; it was impossible—and some Governors did not even try—to separate the aspects of Government and to make ministers definitely responsible in their spheres. Finance was difficult, and ministers could not perform nation-building without imposing unpopular taxation, for much of the revenue had to go in supporting law or order and in meeting

[1] Report of the Statutory Commission under Sir J. Simon (Cmd. 3568, 3569).

the costs of the central Government in respect of defence. The official bloc of experienced officers had so much weight in the legislature that ministers tended to secure its support by adopting lines of policy satisfactory to the Executive Council. In a few cases, at times, as in Bengal and the Central Provinces, where the policy of the Indian National Congress to refuse co-operation was adopted, ministers could not be appointed, and the administration had to be assumed by the Governor.

In the central Government responsibility was left entirely with the Governor-General in Council, which by custom has six members, three Indian. But the legislature was made bicameral and enlarged. Of the 60 members of the Council of State with a duration of five years, 34 were made elective; of the 145 of the Assembly with a duration of three years, 102. The powers of the legislature were assigned equally between the Houses, except that financial initiative was left to the Assembly, but the Council early claimed the right to discuss the budget and amend the Finance Bill; differences of this sort could be dealt with in joint session convened after six months. Previous sanction by the Governor-General was rendered requisite for any measure affecting revenue or expenditure, religion, military, naval, or air forces, external relations, provincial subjects, or any Act or ordinance passed by the Governor-General. His power to legislate was given in two forms; if any Act which he deems necessary is not passed, he can certify and send down a draft which is deemed law if accepted by either House or even if rejected by both. He can legislate by ordinance, with effect for six months, but with the right of renewal.

Such ordinances have been freely used to combat re-volutionary propaganda, and their justification is shown by the fact that later they have been embodied in Acts passed both by the central legislature and by certain provinces. He can also restore any financial grants which the legislature refuses to vote or reduces. These exceptional powers have been sparingly used; thus in 1922 it was necessary to legislate to protect Indian States from press attacks, and in 1935 the Governor-General had to certify the Finance Bill, as the Assembly had reduced the appropriations by £3,750,000.

A most important concession was made in permitting the legislature when in accord with the Government of India to determine fiscal policy.[1] The result of that fiscal convention was to permit the introduction and rapid development of a system of protection for Indian industry, involving great losses to Manchester exporters. It is probable also that the interests of Indian consumers have been overlooked, for the legislature represents necessarily a mere fraction of the people and the great mass of the workers, agricultural and industrial, are wholly unrepresented therein. In other matters also governmental co-operation has been marked, especially as regards the position of Indians overseas, where the Government has stressed without cessation Indian claims as against the British Government and the Dominions alike.

Inevitably the franchise for the central legislature has been high and the constituencies communal, as in the provinces. As in their case it has been utterly impossible to develop any close contact between members

[1] Cf. Joint Committee on India Constitutional Reform Report, i. 204.

and constituents. The aim of the authors of the reforms to stir India into political life has been signally falsified by the progress of events, politics remaining the preserve of a small intelligentsia.

3. *The Indian Federation*

The progress of events in India under the Act of 1919 was marked by incessant efforts on the part of Indian politicians to attain further concessions. The National Congress in 1927 developed a demand for independence, and an All Parties Congress approved the drafting of a constitution based on complete autonomy though not necessarily without the Empire. The British Government in its turn accelerated the despatch to India of the Statutory Committee envisaged in the Act of 1919, and Sir J. Simon acted as Chairman. Its report, issued in 1930, contemplated vital changes, involving complete responsible government in the provinces, the control of justice and police—popularly styled law and order—being transferred to ministers. At the same time the legislatures were to be based on a wider franchise and the official bloc was to disappear. At the centre, on the other hand, it was deemed essential to preserve full British control. It was, however, noted that any scheme of Indian government must be imperfect unless the question of an ultimate federation to include the Indian States were envisaged, and it was recommended that this topic should be further explored. The result was the summoning by the British Government to London of a Round Table Conference, the Indian rulers having intimated that they were prepared to envisage federation. The Conference held three sessions in 1930–32; the British Government presented in 1933 to Parliament its proposals, and they were examined fully by a Select Joint Committee of the two houses of Parliament, who were aided by assessors from India. Their report, confirming in most regards the governmental proposals of 1933, was issued in 1934, and on it was based the Government of India Act, 1935.

The motives which induced federation were complex. The princes [1] were actuated by the desire to secure a voice in such issues as defence and customs policy; under the existing régime in these matters they had no say, and the introduction of high protection had begun seriously to affect State interests. At the same time they were anxious to secure their rights against the process of authoritative interpretation by the Crown, as evidenced by the ruling of Lord Reading in 1926 that the Nizam of Hyderabad must accept without argument the decision of the British Government to refuse to hand back to him control of Berar. The opportunity of obtaining a definition and reduction of the powers of paramountcy seemed to be presented by the anxiety of the British Government to inaugurate a measure of responsibility in the central Government, for to make the experiment safe it was desirable to create a Conservative central legislature, and this could be best accomplished by granting more than numerically proportionate representation to the States. It was assumed that their representatives in the legislature would solidly support the wishes of the Crown. In return the princes felt that they might justly expect the Crown to consent to leave unused, save in case of grave misrule, its paramount authority. This co-operation of

[1] See below, s. 14.

motives was at first regarded without serious dissatisfaction in British India, where it was believed that the
princes would in practice unite with their fellow-
countrymen to oppose British interests if deemed inimical to Indian welfare; later, suspicions were aroused
that the result might be the creation of a federal body
essentially undemocratic in spirit, for the princes made
no secret of their determination not to accept democracy as an ideal. Hence in 1935 the newly elected
central Legislative Assembly condemned by a large
majority of the independent elected members the
federal part of the scheme.

4. *The Federal Government*

The scheme of the Act as regards federation contemplates its becoming operative [1] only after States
representing at least 52 of the 104 seats allocated
to the States in the Council of State, and having half
the population of the States, have declared their desire to accede. Accession is in every case dependent on
a free determination by the ruler being of age and not
under incapacity; the terms of accession may vary in
each case, but it is essential that a State should accept
the fundamental principles of the federation; latitude
lies chiefly in the power to accept or reject certain subjects, and to require that the duty of carrying out
federal obligations shall be left with the State, and not
placed in the hands of federal officers. The acceptance
of any accession rests with the Crown, but federation

[1] In 1935 it was not expected that the federation could become effective in less than two or three years. Pending it, the central legislature
will operate as in s. 2, but with powers as in s. 8.

can be proclaimed only on addresses from both houses of Parliament before which the instruments of accession must be laid. Subsequent accessions may be accepted by the Crown, but after twenty years from federation only if both Houses of the Indian legislature so desire.

The federal executive power extends to all matters on which the federation has legislative power, to the control of military, air, and naval forces, and the exercise of the powers of the Crown over the tribal areas on the frontier. Normally in his functions the Governor-General [1] will act on the advice of his Council of Ministers, not exceeding ten, whom he appoints to hold office at pleasure. But in matters of defence, of ecclesiastical affairs—ministration to the British forces and civil officers—and of external relations, other than relations with other parts of the King's dominions, and in respect of the tribal areas the Governor-General is to act at his discretion, having the power to appoint counsellors to aid him; he also may appoint a financial adviser whose function will be to advise him in the discharge of his special responsibility for safeguarding the financial stability and credit of the federal Government, and an advocate-general to advise the federal Government in legal matters. In the conduct of Government apart from his own sphere, the Governor-General is required to exercise his individual judgment regarding the action to be taken in any matter which involves his special responsibilities. These include (*a*) the prevention of any grave menace to the peace and tranquillity of India or any part thereof; (*b*) the safe-

---

[1] The style Viceroy is to remain ceremonial and not to be given any specific sense.

guarding of the financial stability and credit of the federal Government; (c) the safeguarding of the legitimate interests of minorities; (d) the securing to members of the public services of any rights provided for them by or under the Act; (e) the prevention of executive discrimination and (f) of action which would subject United Kingdom or Burmese goods imported into India to discriminatory or penal treatment; (g) the protection of the rights of any Indian State; and (h) the securing that the due discharge of his functions with respect to matters in which he is required to act at his discretion or exercise individual judgment is not prejudiced or impeded by any course of action taken in respect of any other matter. To secure that he may be fully informed, the Governor-General may make rules of business requiring not only ministers but secretaries to bring to his notice any questions affecting his special responsibilities. Whenever he acts in his discretion or individual judgment, he is, of course, subject to the control of the Secretary of State.

5. *The Federal Legislature*

The legislature consists of two Houses; the Council of State and the House of Assembly. The former has 156 representatives of British India, and up to 104 representatives of the States; the latter 250 representatives of British India and 125 members for the States, which thus are considerably over-represented in comparison with numbers. The British India members of the Upper House are elected with the exception of six chosen at the Governor-General's discretion; the Muhammadans have 49 seats, Sikhs, 4, women 6, and the scheduled castes 6; there are 75 general seats; one Anglo-Indian, 7 European, and 2 Indian Christian representatives are chosen by members of each type in the Councils or Assemblies of the provinces. An electorate of 100,000 is contemplated.

For the Assembly there are in each province general constituencies with seats specially reserved for the depressed classes; for these seats a preliminary vote by members of these classes selects four times the number of candidates as of seats; the final choice then lies with the whole general constituency, a device accepted by M. Gandhi as preventing the disruption of the Hindu community, into which his campaign of social reform is intended to bring the Untouchables. There are also constituencies for Muhammadans in every province, and where numbers justify, constituencies for the Sikhs, Anglo-Indians, Europeans, Indian Christians, commerce and industry, landholders, labour, and special arrangements are made for women. There are 105 general seats, 19 for the depressed classes; 6 Sikh seats; 82 Muhammadan; 4 Anglo-Indian; 8 European; 8 Indian Christian; 11 commerce; 10 labour; 7 landholders, and 9 women. In both Houses the States are free to arrange representation as they please; definite figures being ascribed to the great States or groups of lesser States; in the Council no State has more than 5; in the Assembly Hyderabad has 16, Mysore 7, Travancore 5, and Kashmir and Gwalior 4 each. For both Houses members must be British subjects or rulers or subjects of an Indian State; age 25 is requisite for the Assembly, age 30 for the Council of State. There are the usual disqualifications: holding of a non-ministerial office of profit under the Crown in India; unsoundness of mind; insolvency; conviction of certain electoral offences or of crime. Seats may be resigned and are vacated on occurrence of any disqualification, and on absence for sixty days may be declared vacant by either House.

The Council is a permanent body, it being arranged that members shall sit for nine years, with periodic retirements at each three years, while the maximum duration of the Assembly is five years. The privileges to be enjoyed by the Houses include freedom of speech and publication of papers by order of either House, but it is forbidden to confer judicial powers on any House or Committee; witnesses may be compelled to attend, but punitive power is restricted to the removal or exclusion of persons infringing the rules or otherwise behaving in a disorderly manner. This restriction is clearly carried too far. Each House appoints its own President or Speaker and his deputy; they and members are salaried. Ministers and counsellors may speak but not vote in either chamber. The President or Speaker has only a casting vote. English is the official language of the legislatures and of the Federal and High Courts, but in the former members may be permitted to use other languages.

The Governor-General may summon, prorogue, or dissolve at his discretion the Assembly, but annual sessions are required; he may require the attendance of members in order to address them or send messages.

In general the two Chambers have equal legislative rights. But, if they disagree, or six months passes without acceptance of the measure by the House to which it has come, the Governor-General may on notification convene in the next session, not earlier than six months

after his notification, a joint session, at which the Bill
may be passed by a majority of the members voting.
If the Bill affects finance or any matter which concerns
the discharge of functions in his discretion or subject
to his individual judgment, the Governor-General may
hold the joint session forthwith. On a Bill being passed,
he may assent, withhold assent or reserve; twelve
months are allowed for assent to a reserved Bill to be
notified, or for disallowance of an Act; but the Governor-General may request reconsideration of a Bill
and of amendments.

Financial arrangements are complex. The Governor-
General must lay before the Chambers an annual
financial statement showing the sums to be expended
which are charged on the federal revenues, and those
which it is proposed to expend from these revenues,
distinguishing expenditure on revenue account from
other expenditure. The former class includes: (*a*) the
salary and allowances of the Governor-General; (*b*) debt
charges of all kinds; (*c*) salaries and allowances of
ministers, counsellors, and certain other officers; (*d*)
salaries and pensions of judges of the Federal Court and
any High Court; (*e*) expenditure on defence, ecclesiastical affairs, and external relations and tribal areas;
(*f*) the cost of the performance of the duties of the
Crown in respect of the States; (*g*) grants for the
administration of excluded areas in provinces; (*h*) sums
requisite to meet awards of any court; and (*i*) any other
sums charged by federal Act. The legislature will not
vote these items, but may discuss all save those in (*a*)
and (*f*). Demands for grants shall first be laid before the
Assembly, which may assent, reduce, or refuse assent;
in the last event, the grant shall be submitted to the

Council only if the Governor-General so directs; if the grant is reduced, only the reduced amount shall be submitted unless the Governor-General directs otherwise. The Council has the same rights as the Assembly to assent, reject, or reduce; in case of disagreement, a joint session held thereafter decides. In all cases no demand for a grant can be made save on the recommendation of the Governor-General, and he can restore any grant refused or reduced by the legislature. Similarly no Bill to impose a tax, authorise borrowing or a guarantee, or impose a charge on federal revenue may be introduced without his assent, and no such Bill may originate in the Council.

The Governor-General is further empowered to make rules for the procedure of the Chambers in respect of matters in which he is required to act at his discretion or on his individual judgment; to secure the timely completion of financial business; the prohibition of questions on or discussion of matters affecting the States, outside the federal sphere, unless he holds that the matter affects federal interests or a British subject and consents to action; and the prohibition of questions on or discussion of matters affecting relations between the Crown or the Governor-General and foreign States, or the administration of excluded areas or his action at his discretion in relation to provincial issues. He may also forbid, in the exercise of his special responsibility for the tranquillity of India, the discussion of any Bill or amendment, and the legislature may not discuss the judicial action of any Federal or High Court judge. But the validity of any action taken by it may not be questioned in court on the score of irregularity of procedure.

2 o

Special legislative powers are given to the Governor-General. In case of emergency, at his discretion when the legislature is not sitting he may issue ordinances, which must be presented to the legislature when it reassembles, and which fall unless confirmed within six weeks or earlier disapproved by both Chambers. He may also, where matters within his personal discretion or individual judgment are concerned, promulgate ordinances which have effect for six months with possibility of renewal for six months, but in that case they must be laid before Parliament. He may even at his discretion, forthwith or after a month's notice and the consideration of any address presented to him, enact Acts with permanent effect; these also must be laid before Parliament. Further, in case of the failure of the constitutional machinery he may assume to himself, to be exercised at his discretion, any federal power save that of the Federal Court, but any proclamation under this power must be laid before Parliament and shall cease after six months unless approved by resolutions of both Houses from time to time. The suspension, however, of the constitution may not exceed three years; thereafter new provision must be made by Parliament, but no right of secession is accorded.

6. *The Governors' Provinces*

Additions bring the number of provinces[1] up to eleven; Madras, Bombay, Bengal, the United Provinces, the Punjab, Bihar, the Central Provinces and Berar—which remains under the nominal sovereignty of the Nizam, Assam, the North-West Frontier Pro-

---

[1] Provincial autonomy will begin even before federation.

vince, Orissa, and Sind. Burma ceases to be part of India.

The administration of the provinces is based on the principle of responsible government; the Governor selects ministers, but, as in the federation, a minister must be or become within six months a member of the legislature, the suggestion that non-Parliamentary ministers might be appointed having been negatived. The Governor has special responsibilities in which he must act at his discretion subject to the control of the Governor-General. These include the safeguarding of tranquillity, of the legitimate rights of minorities and of the public services, the securing in the sphere of executive action prevention against discrimination against British subjects domiciled in the United Kingdom, the securing the peace and good government of partially excluded areas, the protection of the rights of Indian States, and the execution of orders of the Governor-General under his authority in regard to the administrative relations between the federation and the provinces. The Governor of the Central Provinces is also bound to secure a fair share of revenue to be spent on Berar; the Governors of Bengal and Assam have a responsibility for the excluded areas in these provinces, the Governor of Sind for the Lloyd Barrage Scheme, and the Governor of the North-West Frontier Province for the unimpeded performance of his duties as agent of the Governor-General in respect of the tribal areas. All the Governors are bound to use individual judgment in respect of any changes of rules affecting the organisation or discipline of police forces. This is a provision intended to meet the fears necessarily felt regarding the effective administration of police under ministerial control in view of the strength of communal feeling. Moreover, the Governor may at his discretion take into his control matters necessary to combat crimes of violence intended to overthrow the Government, and may forbid the disclosure by any police officer of sources of information regarding such crimes to any other police officer save under the instruction of the Inspector-General, or to any other person save by the Governor's direction. Apart from these special powers, the Governor may make rules requiring ministers and secretaries to bring to his notice any matter which may affect his special responsibilities.

7. *The Provincial Legislatures*

In Madras, Bombay, Bengal, the United Provinces, Bihar and Assam two Chambers exist, in the other provinces one. The Upper Chambers have a perpetual existence, members holding for nine years with periodic triennial retirement, the Assemblies lasting five years as a maximum. The size of the Councils varies from 65 maximum in Bengal to 21 minimum in Assam; selection is in part by nomination by the Governor to a maximum of 8 in Bengal or 4 in Bihar; in part by election by general Muhammadan and European constituencies, and in Bengal and Bihar 27 and 12 members respectively are chosen by the Assemblies. The size of the Assemblies varies from 250 for Bengal, 228 United Provinces, 215 Madras, 175 Bombay and Punjab, to 50 for the North-West Frontier Province. The electorates according to need are general, with reservation for depressed classes; Muhammadan; Sikh; Anglo-Indian; European; Indian Christian; commerce, industry, mining, and planting; landholders; Universities; labour; women; and representatives of backward areas and tribes. The franchise, which is dealt with in the Act, extends very widely the vote as compared with the state of affairs under the Montagu-Chelmsford scheme, the aim being to give the vote to 14 per cent of the population (29,000,000 males, 6,000,000 females) as against 3 per cent under the existing franchise.

The provisions applicable to the federal legislature are, with the necessary changes, applied to those of the provinces. The relations of the Houses as to general legislation are similar to those in the federation, but the period which justifies a special session is fixed at twelve in lieu of six months. The Governor may assent, refuse assent, or reserve for the consideration of the Governor-General, who has like power with reference to the Crown; an Act assented to by either may be disallowed by the Crown. Either may refer back a Bill for consideration.

In financial matters the federal model is not wholly followed. The Legislative Councils have no voice in the matter of grants; but otherwise there is the same presentation of the annual financial statement, the distinction of sums charged on the revenues—on the same lines as in the federation—and those to be charged. The Governor, like the Governor-General, can restore items not accepted by the Assembly if his special responsibilities are affected. Moreover, he has like powers of making regulations to govern procedure in the legislature, to prevent discussion of Bills or amendments, and judicial officials are similarly protected from criticism in the legislature. There is, further, protection for maintenance of grants for Anglo-Indian and European education; these can be varied only by a three-fourths majority of the Assembly. The Governor has also power, when the legislature is not in session, to issue ordinances subject to submission to the legislature, and with the authority of the Governor-General he may issue ordinances or pass Acts in matters involving the exercise of his discretion or individual judgment.

Special provision is made in respect of areas declared to be excluded or partially excluded areas within any province. No federal or provincial Act applies to such areas except when so declared with or without modification by the Governor, who may, with the assent of the Governor-General, subject to disallowance by the Crown, make regulations for them which may override any federal or provincial Act. In his executive authority in regard to excluded areas he has to exercise his discretion.

The Governor has, with the approval of the Governor-General, the power to assume such functions as he thinks fit in the case of a break-down of the constitutional machinery.

There are also Chief Commissioners' Provinces: British Baluchistan, Delhi, Ajmer-Merwara, Coorg, the Andaman and Nicobar Islands, and Panth Piploda. The Governor-General controls at his discretion the administration, and may make regulations for British Baluchistan and the Andaman and Nicobar Islands, while Coorg retains its legislature.

8. *The Distribution of Legislative Powers*

The federal legislature has power to legislate for the whole or any part of British India or for any Federated

State, and the provincial legislatures may legislate for the provinces or any part thereof. In addition, the federal legislation may apply to any British subject or servant of the Crown in any part of India; to any Indian subject wherever he may be—a remarkable provision; in the case of a law dealing with a topic accepted by any State to subjects thereof anywhere; and in the case of a law on military, air, or naval forces raised in British India, to all members thereof and followers wherever they may be; and to ships or aircraft registered in British India or any Federated State.

There is drawn a distinction of legislative power according to subjects, there being (1) a list of subjects exclusively federal, (2) a list of provincial subjects, and (3) a list of concurrent powers. The federal list includes: armed forces; naval, military, and air force works; external affairs, including the implementing of treaties and extradition; ecclesiastical affairs; currency, coinage, and legal tender; public debt; posts and telegraphs; public services; pensions; federal property; certain museums and research institutions and surveys; the census; admission to and movements in India; quarantine; import and export; railways; control of vessels; maritime shipping and navigation, Admiralty jurisdiction; major ports; fishing and fisheries beyond territorial waters; aircraft and air navigation; lighthouses; carriage of passengers and goods by sea or by air; copyrights, inventions, designs, merchandise marks and trade-marks; cheques, bills of exchange, promissory notes; arms, firearms, ammunition; explosives; opium; petroleum; trading corporations; development of industry when declared federal by

Act; insurance; banking; elections; statistics; offences against laws under powers given in the list; and duties of customs, including export duties; excise duties except on alcohol, narcotic and non-narcotic drugs, and preparations containing these substances; corporation tax; and salt. These forty-seven subjects are those which the States are expected as a rule to accept as applicable to themselves if they desire to accede to the federation. Other subjects which may be accepted by the States are taxation on income other than income from agricultural land; taxation on the capital—other than agricultural land—of individuals or companies; duties in respect of succession to property other than agricultural land; rates of stamp duties in respect of bills of exchange and other similar instruments; terminal duties on goods or passengers carried by railways, or by air; taxes on railway rates and freights; State lotteries; naturalisation; migration within India; establishment of weight standards; jurisdiction of courts in respect of any federal powers; and fees, other than court fees.

The provinces for their part control public order and justice; the jurisdiction and powers of courts; prisons; reformatories; their public debt and services; public works; libraries; elections; local government; public health and sanitation; pilgrimages within India; burials; education; communications subject to the federal powers; water and water rights; agriculture; land; forests; mines; fisheries; protection of wild birds and animals; gas and gasworks; trade and commerce within the province, including money-lending; inns and innkeepers; production, supply, and distribution of commodities, and development of industries; adulteration of foodstuffs; intoxicating liquors; unemployment and poor relief; incorporation of companies not under federal power; theatres; betting and gambling; charities and charitable institutions; offences against laws dealing with any of these matters, and statistics in relation thereto. They deal also with land revenue; excise duties excluded from the federal list; taxes on income from agricultural land, on lands and buildings, hearths and windows; duties in respect of succession to agricultural land; taxes on mineral rights; capitation taxes; taxes on professions, trades, callings; on animals and boats; on the sale of commodities, on turnover, and on advertisements; cesses on the entry of goods into a local area; taxes on luxuries, including entertainments, betting, and gambling; and stamp duties outside the federal sphere.

The concurrent list includes criminal law and procedure; civil procedure, evidence, and oaths; marriage and divorce; infants and minors, adoption; wills, intestacy, and succession, save as regards agricultural land; transfer of property other than such land; registration of deeds; trusts; contracts; arbitration; bankruptcy; actionable wrongs; professions; newspapers and printing; lunacy and mental deficiency; poisons and dangerous drugs; mechanically propelled vehicles and boilers; prevention of cruelty to animals; European vagrancy and criminal tribes; and jurisdiction of courts in respect of matters in the list. A further group of subjects includes: factories; welfare of labour; health insurance and invalidity and old age pensions; trade unions; industrial and labour disputes; prevention of the extension into units of infectious or contagious diseases of men, plants, or animals;

electricity; the sanctioning of exhibition of cinematograph films, etc.

Normally the federation may not invade the provincial sphere, but if the Governor-General proclaims
an emergency in which the security of India is threat-
ened, whether by war or internal disturbance, the
federal legislature with his assent, at his discretion,
may legislate on any provincial subject with overriding effect. But a proclamation must be laid before
Parliament and falls unless confirmed within six
months by resolutions of both Houses, and any Act
expires six months after the lapsing of the proclamation. The federation may also legislate by consent for
two or more provinces, but any province may repeal or
vary such legislation. Any subject not included in the
list or topic of taxation may, at his discretion, be assigned by the Governor-General to either the federation or the provinces. The power of the federation to
implement treaties permits legislation only with the
prior assent of the ruler or Governor of a federated
unit; this is a dangerous limitation which may affect
most inconveniently Indian action. Federal Acts
within their sphere override provincial Acts, but a
provincial Act on a concurrent subject, if reserved
and duly assented to, overrides a federal Act thereon,
and no further federal Bill to alter such an Act may be
introduced save with the prior assent, at his discretion,
of the Governor-General. Federal Acts override State
legislation on the subjects accepted by the State as
federal.

As a precaution against hasty legislation [1] it is pro-

---

[1] Taxation of non-residents differentially is also subjected to the
requirement of prior sanction.

vided that the prior sanction, at his discretion, of the
Governor-General is necessary for the introduction
of any Bill repugnant to provisions of an Act of
Parliament, or Governor-General's or Governor's Act
or ordinance, or affecting matters reserved to the
Governor-General, or any Act relating to the police
force, or the criminal procedure affecting European
British subjects. Similarly the prior sanction of the
Governor-General, or, as regards his Acts or ordinances
or the police, of the Governor, is requisite in respect of
provincial legislation. But these provisions are matters
of procedure and their neglect does not invalidate
Acts duly assented to. No legislature may make any
law affecting the sovereign or the succession, or the
sovereignty, dominion, or suzerainty of the Crown in
any part of India, or the law of British nationality,
or the Army Act, the Air Force Act, or the Naval
Discipline Act, or the law of prize or prize courts; nor
may it amend, save as expressly provided in the
Government of India Act, the Act or any Order in
Council made thereunder, or rules made by the
Secretary of State or by the Governor-General or
a Governor in his discretion or the exercise of his
individual judgment, or the prerogative appeal.

The danger of legislative discrimination against
British subjects domiciled in the United Kingdom is
recognised, and the plan adopted is to exempt such
subjects from the operation of any federal or provincial Act which restricts entry into India, or imposes, by reference to place of birth, race, descent,
language, religion, domicile, residence or duration of
residence, any disability, restriction, or condition in
respect of travel, residence, the holding of property or

public office, or the carrying on of any occupation, trade, business, or profession. But this exemption does not apply in so far as Indian subjects are subject to restrictions in the United Kingdom, nor is it illegal to apply quarantine regulations or to exclude or deport undesirables. Moreover, in case of grave menace to tranquillity or to combat crimes of violence the Governor-General may suspend temporarily the security afforded. Taxation may not differentiate against British subjects or companies domiciled in the United Kingdom or Burman subjects or companies domiciled in Burma. British companies are afforded protection on the same basis of reciprocity, and the right of medical practitioners in British India and in the United Kingdom to practise in either country is placed on the same footing, because in either case practitioners refused the right may obtain a ruling by the Privy Council as to the propriety of their exclusion. Permission is given to Indian legislatures to confine subsidies for the encouragement of trade and industry, in the case of companies not engaged in such branches at the time of the legislation, to such bodies as are incorporated under the law of British India, offer facilities for training Indians, and have up to a half of their directors Indians. It is, however, recognised that these restrictions are unsatisfactory and that the real solution must lie in a convention based on reciprocity;[1] if such a convention is made, the provisions of the Act may be waived for its direction by Order in Council.

[1] See a draft in Keith, *Letters on Imperial Relations, 1916–1935*, pp. 232-44.

9. *Administrative Relations between the Federation and the Units*

The executive authority of each unit must be so exercised as to secure respect for federal laws. Federal Acts may impose duties on a province or State, subject to payment of cost of additional staff, to be decided by arbitration if necessary, and the Governor-General may agree to entrust executive federal functions to a State or province. Rulers may stipulate for the administration of federal laws, but the Governor-General must be able to satisfy himself as to the due execution of the law. The Governor-General has also power to give directions to rulers if they act so as to prejudice the exercise of the executive authority of the federation or fail to carry out obligations as to administering federal laws. Wider powers exist as regards the provinces, whose Governors may be instructed to use their executive power in any way necessary to prevent menace to the peace or tranquillity of India. The Governor-General is given special powers in respect of questions of broadcasting, the provinces and States being entitled to reasonable facilities of transmission, and issues affecting water rights, to the exclusion of judicial intervention. Moreover, on addresses from the provinces an Inter-Provincial Council may be established to deal with inter-provincial disputes, and discuss matters of common interest.

10. *The Finance of the Federation*

Though legislative power as to taxation is distributed as described above, the federation is not entitled to treat as its own its receipts as a whole. The produce of succession duties, stamp duties, terminal, etc., taxes must be handed over to the provinces and any States which accept these items as federal; but the federation may impose and retain the proceeds of a surtax on any of these items. The arrangements regarding income tax provide for the retention by the federation of the tax on federal incomes and that raised in Chief Commissioners' provinces, but the payment to the provinces of a certain portion of the tax, subject however to the retention therefrom for a prescribed period of a certain amount, which will in a second prescribed period be diminished to nil. The federation may also impose a surcharge, in which case it must require from each federated State which does not accept income tax as federal a sum equivalent to the probable yield of such a surcharge. Salt duties, excise duties, and export duties fall to the federation, subject to the power by Act to assign part to the provinces; half, however, of any export duty on jute falls to the province, a concession to the needs of Bengal. The federation also may grant aid to provinces in need of assistance, and provinces may make grants for federal objects and *vice versa*.

The federation must provide the Crown with sums necessary in respect of the conduct of its relations to the States, and sums receivable from the States may be paid to the federation. But in order to secure accessions to federation it is provided that the Crown may remit over a period, normally of twenty years, contributions due from any State, whether in acknowledgment of suzerainty, or in commutation of an obligation to afford military assistance, or in respect of the maintenance of forces by the Crown, or in respect of the creation of, or grant of territory to, a State, or due to the Crown as representing some other State formerly entitled. But no remission shall be granted save in so far as the contribution payable exceeds the value of State privileges, including the right to levy sea customs or duties on salt, or sums in commutation thereof, the privilege of free entry of goods, etc. It seems that ultimately, if federation becomes complete, the sum remitted will be some £750,000 at least.[1]

No burden may be placed on federal or provincial finance save for Indian purposes; hence it follows that if Indian forces are used outside India, a matter in the discretion of the Governor-General, the United Kingdom must pay.[2]

Financial stability is specially within the duty of the Governor-General, aided by his financial adviser. He is aided by the fact that a Reserve Bank[3] has been created to control exchange; he has discretionary authority in appointing the Governor and his deputy, the supersession of the Central Board, and the liquidation if necessary of the Bank. His previous sanction is necessary for the introduction of any Bill affecting currency or the Bank.

The federation may borrow on the credit of Indian revenues, a province on that of provincial revenues, but it requires the consent of the federation for borrowing outside India. The federation may lend to a province, and so long as any part of the loan is out-

---

[1] *Indian States Enquiry Committee (Financial) Report*, 1932 (Cmd. 4103).   [2] See below, s. 15.

[3] Reserve Bank of India Act, 1934.

standing, it may refuse permission to a province to borrow; but it must act reasonably, the Governor-General being the final arbiter. The federation may lend money to the States, and its sterling loans are eligible for ranking as trustee stocks in the United Kingdom.

Audit control is provided for by the appointment on judicial tenure of an Auditor-General who will act for the federation and the provinces, unless and until Provincial Auditors on like tenure are established. There is a special Auditor of Home Accounts.

Provision is made for the vesting in His Majesty for the purpose of the federation or province as the case may be of lands and buildings, for the acquisition of further property, the making of contracts, etc., and for direct suit against the federation or province on the same basis as under the existing law against the Secretary of State in Council.[1] Full provision is made as to liability already existing on the Secretary of State in Council.

The importance of railways is evidenced by the creation of a special Railway Authority, not less than three-sevenths of whose members and the President are appointed at his discretion by the Governor-General. Instructions can be given on policy by the federal Government, but the intention is that the railways shall be run on business principles with due regard to the interests of agriculture, commerce, industry and the general public. The Governor-General has power to give instructions to the authority in any matter affecting his special responsibilities. Issues be-

---

[1] For this cf. Eggar, *Government of India*, pp. 59-70. For political actions there is no liability.

tween the authority and owners of State railways are
to be decided by a special tribunal, subject to appeal
on a point of law only to the Federal Court, whose
decision is final.

11. *The Judicature*

Provision is made for the establishment of a Federal
Court under a Chief Justice and six puisne judges, to
hold office until age sixty-five, subject to removal by
the King by sign-manual warrant in case of infirmity
or misbehaviour if the Judicial Committee so recommends. The court has original jurisdiction exclusive of
any other court in any question between the federation
and a unit, or two or more units, if the issue is legal,
and in the case of a State if it concerns the interpretation of the Act or Order in Council or some matter
of federal power or an agreement. It can only in such
cases give a declaratory judgment. It can hear on
appeal, on certificate by any High Court that any
matter involving the interpretation of the Act or an
Order in Council under it is involved, causes from
such courts; no direct appeal then lies to the Judicial
Committee. From the High Court of a federated State
appeal lies if it is alleged that a question of law regarding the interpretation of the Act or an Order in Council
under it has been wrongly decided; the procedure is by
way of case stated either on the initiative of the High
Court or of the Federal Court. Provision may also be
made by federal Act to extend the appellate jurisdiction in civil cases from provincial High Courts; in such
cases the appeal to the Judicial Committee may be
abolished. From any decision of the Federal Court

2 P

appeal to the Judicial Committee may be brought by the leave of that body or of the court itself. The decisions of the court or the Privy Council shall bind all courts in India, and be given effect.

The Act similarly provides for the tenure of office of judges of the High Courts of the provinces, whose retiring age is fixed at sixty. The powers of the courts are continued, and full power of administrative superintendence over all courts subject to its appellate jurisdiction is given to each High Court. Power is given to constitute or reconstitute courts, and the expenses of courts are charged on provincial revenues, and controlled by the Governor in his individual judgment.

12. *The Services of the Crown*

The fullest control over conditions of service in the defence forces is reserved to His Majesty and the Secretary of State, and the expenses of the departments are charged on the federal revenues.

The Civil Services are accorded full protection. Office is held at pleasure, but no person can be removed by any authority subordinate to that which appointed him, and before dismissal or reduction in rank he must be given an opportunity to defend himself. In future, appointments will normally be made for federal services by the Governor-General, for provincial services by the Governor, and they will make regulations for their services. The Secretary of State will continue to recruit for the Indian Civil Service, the Indian Medical Service (Civil) and the Indian Police. He may determine what posts are to be filled by persons appointed by himself, and selection for these posts falls to be made by the Governor-General or Governor in the exercise of his individual judgment. The most complete security as to tenure, pay, pension,[1] etc., is accorded to such officers. The Governor is given the decision as to the appointment of district judges, and he makes rules regarding qualification for the subordinate civil judicial service whose promotion, transfer, and leave are controlled by the High Court. The political service remains under the full control of the Secretary of State.

Provision is made for the establishment of a Public Service Commission for the federation and similar Commissions for the provinces, though they may use the federal Commission or agree to establish one body for two or more provinces. Their duties include holding examinations for entrance to the services, and they are normally to be consulted on methods of recruitment, the principles of making appointments and promotions, and the suitability of candidates, disciplinary matters, and claims for payment of expenses incurred by officers in defending legal proceedings or pensions for injury. Their functions may be extended by Acts passed with previous sanction; their expenses are charged on the federal or provincial funds, and their personnel controlled by the Governor-General and the Governors.

The Secretary of State ceases to be advised by a Council, but has from three to six advisers, half qualified by ten years' service in India, who have not retired more than two years before appointment. He need not ask their advice save in matters affecting

---

[1] A British guarantee of pensions has been refused, but the obligation of the Secretary of State to secure payment is absolute.

service conditions specially provided for in the Act. Due provision is made for the charging to British funds of the cost of the Secretary of State's establishment.

The office of High Commissioner for India in the United Kingdom is continued, the extent of his activities to be decided by the Governor-General. He may also act for Burma.

13. *The Amendment of the Constitution*

Amendment of the constitution is in the main forbidden, but it is contemplated that change may be made by Order in Council with the assent of the British Parliament in certain matters on requests by the federal or provincial legislature, not earlier than ten years as a rule from the establishment of the federation or of the new provincial system. The matters concerned are: (1) The size and composition of the Chambers of the federation and the choice or qualification of members, but not so as to vary the relative proportions between the Council and Assembly or between the British Indian and State seats; (2) the number of Chambers in the provincial legislature, their size or membership; (3) the establishment of literacy in lieu of higher educational qualifications for women's franchise, or the entry of names of qualified women without application; (4) any other amendments as to qualifications of voters. The changes in head (3) may be made at any time, if a request is received from a province. Moreover, any of these matters may be varied by Order in Council at any time, but only after the views of the Government and legislatures affected have been ascertained. All Orders in Council must be laid in draft before Parliament and be approved by both Houses, save in emergency when the order may be issued, but will lapse unless so approved. Similarly drafts of instructions to the Governor-General and Governors require affirmation by both Houses.

14. *The Indian States*

Reference has been made above to the position of the Indian States in regard to the proposal of federation. Whether or not the majority of the States enter federation in due course, the relations of the States with the Crown must necessarily remain of great importance. The federal system indeed demands that the States should surrender sufficient of their autonomy to make the federation real. But what they surrender will, on the whole, be of comparatively little immediate importance to the States as compared with what they desire to retain, in the ordinary affairs of everyday life, complete autonomy to carry on the existing system of government in each, subject only to the paramount power of the Crown, and in return for acceptance of federation it is the desire of the States to secure from the Crown the limitation of that power by strict definition.

The distinction drawn between British India and India under the Interpretation Act, 1889, is that the former term means all territories governed by the King Emperor through the Governor-General of India or through any Governor or other officer subordinate to the Governor-General, while India includes any territories of any prince or chief under the suzerainty of His Majesty exercised through the Governor-General of India or through any Governor or other officer subordinate to the Governor-General. The new Government of India Act defines British India as meaning all territories for the time being comprised within the Governors' provinces and the Chief Commissioners' provinces, while India means British India together with all territories of any Indian ruler under the suzerainty of His Majesty, all territories under the suzerainty of such an Indian ruler, the tribal areas, and any other territories which His Majesty in Council may from time to time, after ascertaining the views of the federal Government and the federal legislature, declare to be part of India. The total area of the lands included in British India is, deducting Burma, 867,744 square miles, while the States account for 713,146 square miles, with a population of 81,310,845 as against 256,858,787. The number of States is given as 564, but the size varies enormously. The autonomy of the States differs greatly. Hyderabad, with over 14,000,000 people, enjoys full rights of civil and criminal jurisdiction, legislation, taxation, and coinage while in Kathiawar there are petty chiefs with no more than exemption from British Indian taxation and some nominal jurisdiction. But even from the greatest States is withheld the power to exercise jurisdiction over European British subjects and foreigners who are subject to the jurisdiction of the Residents or of British Indian courts, and jurisdiction is ceded over military stations and cantonments, civil stations, and railway lands.[1]

---

[1] On the limits of such jurisdiction see *Muhammad Yusuf-ud-din* v. *Queen Empress* (1897), L.R. 24 Ind. App. 137.

Much controversy has recently raged regarding the extent of British authority over the States. The position can only be understood in the light of history. The East India Company commenced existence as a feudatory of the Emperor not more than an equal of other feudatories. In its earlier days it was content to conclude treaties with other States on the basis of equality and alliance. As its power increased, it insisted on its allies adopting a definite state of subordination in external relations; they had to accept the control in these matters of the Company, to refrain from employing Europeans or Americans without the assent of the Company, and to afford the Company aid in its wars, either maintaining at their expense forces for this purpose or paying the Company to maintain such forces. The Company in turn was often willing to undertake non-intervention in internal issues. With the attainment by the Crown of paramount power in India on the extinction of the Mogul Empire, all the relations envisaged by the earlier treaties became out of harmony with the new status of affairs. But instead of denouncing the treaties the Crown adopted the only policy which permitted the continued existence of the States. Oudh had had to be annexed because the suzerain could not tolerate indefinitely utter misrule. In future the rulers would be secured by the operation of such a measure of intervention as would render suppression of the State unnecessary. Further, the States would be invited to contribute their aid to the advancement of India by conceding facilities for the construction of railways, military roads, telegraphs, etc., and by adopting social reforms, such as the abolition of widow-burning, infanticide, domestic slavery, and so forth. Had the treaties been rigidly adhered to, reforms must have been delayed, and the result was that by usage great inroads were made on State autonomy, accelerated after 1881 when Mysore was restored to native rule, after its administration had been completely reformed. The terms of restoration were regarded as the model which should regulate relations between the States and the Crown, and both persuasion and authority were employed to bring other States up to the Mysore standard. Objections were met by the argument of paramountcy, the right of the Crown, as representing the authority which maintained the whole system of the States, to determine when individual interests must yield to the welfare of the whole. Moreover, the States were indebted to the Crown for a vital concession; by *sanads* granted after the assumption of direct Crown authority, the Hindu States had been assured of the power to perpetuate their royal lines by adoption and the Muhammadan States were allowed to descend according to the Moslem law. The process by which the treaties ceased to be regarded as they read was not one of disregarding "scraps of paper"; it was the conventional working-out of the only system which could have preserved the States from annexation, such as befell Coorg under the old régime, when the Company felt precluded from intervention until it was justified in declaring war and extinguishing the dynasty.

It is a complete error to assimilate the position of the States to States of international law. That law was never adopted in India, and, though the Company in early days used the language of international law, the Indian princes neither knew nor cared for the system; they lived under a régime which recognised the theoretic primacy of the Mogul Emperor, which is now the effective sovereignty of the Crown. The issue was sharply insisted on by the Government of India in 1891 when the question arose of the murder of the Commissioner of Assam and certain of his retinue by rival claimants to the throne of the State of Manipur. If the relations of the State to the Crown were those of international law, clearly the persons responsible could not be deemed guilty of rebellion or murder; but they were held guilty and executed on that account, and the Indian Government publicly announced that the relations of the States to the Crown were not and never had been those of international law. By virtue of its paramount authority the Crown intervenes to remove unworthy rulers, as in the case of the Gaekwar of Baroda in 1875; more recently two rulers of Indore have been compelled to resign owing to accusations of complicity in murders in British India. In Kashmir unrest from 1931 to 1934 between the Hindu Rajah and his Muhammadan subjects led to British intervention and to the adoption of reforms, including the creation of a legislature partly elected, and in 1933 the Government of Alwar was placed under the control of a British officer and the ruler advised to leave for a time the State. Persistent absence is another ground for intervention.

Apart, however, from cases of gross misgovernment native institutions are not interfered with. Hence democratic government has made little way, and is regarded with profound scepticism in the States. As a rule the prince retains full authority to legislate and to tax; any distinction between his Civil List and the State revenue is a mere matter of his discretion; there are no constitutional securities for the life or property of the subject; there is no means of redress against acts of State officers; the courts are subject to the ruler's power of removal of any judge; in effect the rule of law is unknown in theory. Constitutional rule has been carried comparatively far in Mysore, where under pressure of events in the province of Madras a Legislative Council with a non-official elected majority has been created, with power to legislate, pass the budget, and move resolutions. Certain financial matters, the position of the ruling family, and relations with the Crown are excluded from its power, and the Executive is quite independent of it. More popular support apparently is given to a body more in accord with Indian tradition, the Representative Assembly which meets on the great holiday occasions to discuss finance, to hear Government policy explained, ask questions, and present petitions. In Travancore the same system prevails, but the Christian population objects strongly to the fact that the Nayar oligarchy commands, though barely a fifth of the population and with but 36 per cent of the voters, a majority in the Legislative Council. One desirable aspect of the campaign of M. Gandhi is that it has been proposed to abolish the law which penalises outcasts for distance pollution of those of caste. On the other hand, Hyderabad remains autocratic; the present Nizam revived on accession in 1911 the tradition of personal rule, which under his predecessor had been obscured through the skill of Sir Salar Jang, his great minister. Only after the war did he consent at British suggestion to establish an Executive Council of a President and six ministers, each in charge of one or more portfolios, while British officers have been employed in the Police and Revenue departments. The State has reorganised its forces, on modern lines, including a battery of modern field guns; its great wealth renders its prestige high in the Muhammadan world, and the heir-apparent is married to the daughter of the last Sultan of Turkey. The vast majority of the States are certainly not better administered than Hyderabad. Baroda is an exception: it has a Legislative Council, part elected, and local administration from the village *panchayat* has been steadily reconstructed; infant marriage has been discouraged and the education of the Untouchables promoted. But the Gaekwar is no more democratic than other princes; they believe in autocracy, and where the autocrats, especially ministers, are capable, their belief has much to justify it; the difficulty is that much misrule and injustice still occur. On the other hand, some States have improved considerably their courts, appointing British judges or officers with legal experience in British India. Finance has often been marred by grave scandals, some quite recent.

Since the taking-over of authority by the Crown, the duty of loyalty and allegiance have been insisted on. Successions are decided in case of dispute by the Governor-General, who has the right to assume guardianship of a minor ruler. Decorations, titles, and salutes are determined by the Crown, which also regulates the acceptance of foreign orders, and passports for travel are controlled by the Governor-General. Rulers have been expected to grant free of cost land for railway construction, and to cede jurisdiction, to accept the monopoly of telegraphs and telephones, and in part of postal services, and to acquiesce in control of the manufacture and sale of arms. Influence has been brought to bear to restrict State coinages, to secure the complete control of opium for the Government of India, to perfect the monopoly in salt, and to reduce to a minimum the privilege of levying customs duties on seaborne goods. During minorities administration has often been reformed and finance brought into a sound condition, only to be wasted when the young ruler is installed in power. "The sovereignty of the Crown is everywhere unchallenged; it has itself laid down the limitations of its own prerogative", was the view of Lord Curzon, and the policy of rendering the obligations of the States uniform was persistently pursued under his régime by the Political Department, which, largely recruited from the Indian Army and the Indian Civil Service, has done much to preserve the States from the disasters which their own weakness must have brought on them. Reaction against this system was natural, and it was greatly promoted by the tardy decision to abandon the policy long rigidly preserved of isolation of the princes. Lord Minto desired to secure their co-operation against the anarchic forces beginning to appear in India; their services in the war banished fear of their possible disloyalty, and the Montagu-Chelmsford scheme created the Chamber of Princes in which 109 princes are represented separately, while 126 choose 12 spokesmen. The Chamber has no executive functions, but is deliberative and consultative. The Governor-General is President; the Chamber elects its own Chancellor and Vice-Chancellor. Though the weight of the Chamber has been diminished by abstention on the part of some great States, such as Mysore, Travancore, Hyderabad, and Kashmir, it has served to strengthen common action by the princes to secure concessions.

The difficulties of the position of the States are patent.[1] Hereditary rule is always uncertain as a basis of effective government; princes educated in the Princes' Colleges or England have alike failed to show ability to rule, and the native plan of removal by insurrection is ruled out. To have democracy rising around them is inconsistent with the maintenance of autocracy; British intervention has, in 1932–3, been necessary to save Kashmir and Alwar from attacks from without. It is natural that politicians in British India should have demanded that responsible government should be established in India, and that the relations of the States with the Crown should be controlled by ministers; but the claim is clearly unjust and was definitely negatived by the Indian States Committee, 1928–9, though its defence of the paramount rights of the Crown proved unacceptable to the States. On the other hand, whether the States federate or not, there are certain plain requisites of their continuance; a reasonable Civil List; representative assemblies as advisory or consultative bodies and for passing legislation; a system of law based on modern principles; an impartial judiciary; a strong and efficient Civil Service with security of tenure; the subjection of the executive —except the ruler—to judicial control; and improvement of the armed forces by granting them adequate pay and recruiting officers from families with military traditions.[2] The policy of providing for Indian State forces—44,700—drilled on modern lines and properly equipped has become of increasing importance; such

[1] The India States (Protection) Act, 1934, seeks to protect them from agitation organised in British India and the influx of jathas, unarmed mobs of protest against State administration.

[2] Barton, *The Princes of India*, p. 319.

forces served with valuable results in the war of 1914–18.

Little progress has been made as regards settling difficulties between the States and the paramount power. The British Government has agreed to the principle that in case of misgovernment being charged against a ruler he should be entitled to ask for a commission of enquiry to ascertain the facts, and that courts of arbitration might be set up to decide disputes between two or more Indian States, or between an Indian State and the central or local government. But nothing has transpired in practice to show that much value attaches to such a procedure. Moreover, as already mentioned, Lord Reading pronounced definitely in 1926 that the Crown had sole right to decide any dispute as it thought fit, and derogation from that principle would involve risks.

Reference has been made to the judicial authority exercised in the States by the Crown. In some cases, such as those of the petty rulers of Kathiawar, the small Rajput States in the Himalayas, some Punjab States, and the feudatory States of Bihar, Orissa, and the Central Provinces, jurisdiction is shared with the ruler, the higher jurisdiction being exercised by a British officer, or, where it can be exercised by the State, sanction for capital sentences is required from the British officer.[1] In other cases during a time of difficulty jurisdiction may be assumed by British officers. In other cases jurisdiction is based on formal or practical assent by the ruler; the Resident exer-

---

[1] The jurisdiction is political, not judicial, and not subject to appeal to the Privy Council: *Hemchand Devchand* v. *Azam Sakarlal Chhotamlal*, [1906] A.C. 212.

cises jurisdiction over the Residency area, sometimes considerable, and those resident therein; he also exercises jurisdiction over European British subjects and foreigners, while Indian British subjects are normally left to be dealt with by the States. British military and civil stations are exempt from State jurisdiction, and for railway purposes ceded railway lands.

The British Government also has relations with States on the borders of India which are not Indian States. Nepal, which formerly was, under treaty relations dating from 1816, restricted in point of external sovereignty, was recognised by Treaty of 1923 as completely independent, externally as well as internally, and all restrictions on the employment of Europeans or Americans were withdrawn and Nepal was permitted to import munitions of war freely so long as she remains on friendly terms with the Crown. The British Resident was replaced by an Envoy, and in 1934 a Nepalese Legation was opened in London. The Government is hereditary monarchy, coupled with a hereditary Prime Minister and Commander-in-Chief; under Sir Chandra Shumsher's rule (1901–29) slavery was abolished, 60,000 slaves set free, and Kathmandu connected by telephone with India. But normally access to Nepal is closed, while India derives its splendid Gurkha forces, and many Gurkhas serve in the Assam, Burma, and Bengal police forces.

The position of the small State of Bhutan is less independent. Since 1863, when portions of its territory were annexed, it has been in receipt of a grant from India, fixed in 1910 at £6677 a year, while it has undertaken to be guided in external relations by

British advice, while remaining internally independent. A hereditary Maharajahship in 1907 replaced the former joint control by a spiritual and a temporal chief.

Afghanistan until 1919 was definitely recognised as falling within the British sphere of influence, Russia in 1907 having conceded this point. In May 1919 an attack was made on India which was repelled, but difficulties of transport and the undesirability of large expenditure during a period of internal unrest led to acceptance of Afghan overtures for peace, which was restored in the same year, Afghanistan being declared internationally independent. This position was repeated by Treaty of November 22, 1921, under which the external and internal independence of Afghanistan was recognised, the boundary adjusted, and arrangements made for the reception of a legation at London and of consular officers at Calcutta, Bombay, Karachi, and Delhi, while a British Envoy was stationed at Kabul, and Consuls at Kandahar and Jalalabad. Friendly terms have since been maintained; on Amanulla's expulsion Nadir Shah was recognised as king in 1929, and on his assassination his son Mohamed Zahir Shah in 1933.

The Indian States are not British territory, and the subjects of the rulers are therefore not natural-born British subjects. It has been held that they are capable of naturalisation under the legislation in force in British India. They are not bound by statutes referring to British subjects, but in order to secure their position when outside India they are ranked as British protected persons, and therefore in places where the Crown exercises extra-territorial jurisdiction they are

subject to the courts of the Crown.[1] The Indian legis- Chapter XI.
latures have no power to legislate for the States,
though the central legislature may legislate for certain
classes of persons in the States, and under federation
the federal legislature will legislate for federal subjects affecting the States. The Indian courts have no
jurisdiction over matters taking place in the States
in general, but they have criminal jurisdiction over
British subjects in respect of transactions in the
States under certain conditions, though such matters
may fall within the sphere of the court of the Resident.
The formal authority for British jurisdiction when
exercised is the Indian (Foreign Jurisdiction) Order
in Council, 1902,[2] passed under the Foreign Juris
diction Act, 1890, and confirmed in 1916.[3]

15. *Defence*

Indian defence has been consistently under the
supreme control of the Secretary of State for India,
and this condition will remain even under the new
constitution, pending such time as India may be able
to discharge the obligation of securing her own defence. In the India Office he has a Military Secretary,
a high officer of recent Indian experience who does
not, however, act as an Army Headquarters Staff but
performs secretarial functions on the same principle
as Secretaries in the Civil Departments. In India
the Governor-General has final responsibility to the

[1] Foreign Jurisdiction Act, 1890, s. 15.

[2] The Governor-General may legislate by order and delegate powers
necessary for the government of persons subject to British jurisdiction
in the States.

[3] 6 & 7 Geo. V. c. 37, s. 5; 25 & 26 Geo. V. c. 42, s. 294.

2 Q

Secretary of State. The Commander-in-Chief in India has regularly been a member of the Governor-General's Executive Council and of the Council of State since its inception. Under federation he will be a counsellor of the Governor-General and his representative in the legislature on army issues. He is responsible for army administration, the formulation and execution of policy, the efficient maintenance of the force, and the execution of operations based on India. He is also responsible for the air force and Indian navy,[1] which replaces the former Royal Indian Marine. He is aided by the Chief of the General Staff, the Adjutant-General, the Quartermaster - General, the Master-General of Ordnance, and the Air Officer Commanding. The Military Secretary at the India Office maintains liaison between Indian Headquarters and the War Office. These officers, with the Secretary of the Army Department and the Finance Adviser, Military Finance, Finance Department, make up the Military Council which advises the Commander-in-Chief, but without joint responsibility.

India is divided into four commands in which a General Officer is responsible for command, administration, training, general efficiency, and internal security arrangements. The Indian forces as sanctioned in 1934–5 include some 60,000 troops of the British Army of all arms; regular Indian forces much more numerous, some 155,000 of the active list, and 42,500

---

[1] Under the Indian Navy Discipline Act, 1934, the force is placed constitutionally on a basis analogous to that of Dominion forces; in emergency it may be placed at the disposal of the Admiralty. Provision is made for Indianisation—the 1935 ratio being two British to one Indian officer. The force is small, 5 sloops and minor vessels. It flies the white ensign.

reservists; the auxiliary force—36,000—of European British subjects first created in 1920, which is voluntarily recruited, and trained; and the Indian Territorial Force. This force—19,000 strong—is part of the scheme of Indianisation which is being applied as regards the regular forces to a whole division, including artillery. The Territorial Force opens opportunities to Indians who are not of hereditary martial profession,[1] and is to provide reinforcements for the regular army. There are provincial battalions, urban units, and University training corps; the principle is enlistment for six years with periodic training. Like the regular forces, the members may be called upon for service outside India in emergency.

There are certain important constitutional issues affecting the employment of Indian forces outside India. It is clearly proper that they should be used for that purpose where defence of Indian territory demands expeditions over the borders of India, and that India should defray the cost is proper. But obviously the use of the forces for Imperial purposes is open to more serious difficulty, for the Dominions are not compelled to give aid in war save at their discretion. It has always been the rule that the use of such forces outside India for non-Indian ends proper shall be brought to the notice of Parliament, the rule being that payment cannot be defrayed from Indian funds without the approval of Parliament. This requirement is continued in

---

[1] An essential difficulty in the way of Indian autonomy is presented by the fact that only a few races (Sikhs, Rajputs, etc.) provide recruits for the army. Indians were formerly admitted to the Military Colleges at Woolwich and Sandhurst and the Air College at Cranwell, to the Staff College at Camberley, and are now trained in the Indian Staff College. Since 1917 Indians have been eligible for the King's Commission.

the federal constitution in so far as the cost of Indian forces is to be borne by Indian funds only so far as they are used for Indian defence. It follows from this that in other cases the British Government must pay and must obtain Parliamentary sanction for such payment. But it is not proposed to limit the right of such employment if the Governor-General, with the approval or on the requisition of the British Government, deems action outside India in Imperial interest necessary. It must be admitted that the fact that so large a proportion of the British forces is tied up in India complicates the issue, and renders Dominion precedents hardly applicable. Further, the value of India as a school for British troops has been recognised since 1934 by the grant of an annual contribution of £1,500,000 each year from British funds to India as recognition of this service. India, of course, repays to the United Kingdom such proportion of the costs affecting the British troops supplied as may justly be attributed to their use for Indian service.

Forces from India have in fact been used in several emergencies, as well as on a wholesale scale in the Great War. Their use outside India has raised a constitutional problem of some interest which was eagerly canvassed during the European crisis (1877–8) when Indian troops were brought to Malta in view of the possibility of war with Turkey. It was contended that their employment without specific Parliamentary sanction was unconstitutional.[1] Clearly it would be so if they were introduced into the United Kingdom, but there seems no conclusive reason to hold that, if used without the Kingdom, their employment would not be

[1] Cf. Anson, *The Crown* (cf. Keith), ii. 205, 206.

proper. After all, due security for the safety of the liberties of the subject is afforded by the necessity of providing for their pay and maintenance.

It is clearly imperative that, while the Governor-General must be empowered to secure defence requirements by issuing orders to the federal and provincial Governments for facilities of moving and stationing troops, etc., there must be brought about as close co-operation with ministers as possible and the legislature must be induced to support defence with intelligent appreciation of the issues involved.[1] The Governor-General therefore must promote co-operation in these matters as far as is compatible with securing vital interests.

Unfortunately, as has constantly been shown, as at Karachi in April 1935, the use of British troops is imperative to suppress communal rioting, and to prevent it leading to internecine strife on a large scale, as during the Moplah rising in 1921, when large numbers of Hindus were murdered or forcibly converted by the Muhammadans. The difficulty thus presented to the grant of full control to ministers over forces for the maintenance of internal security is serious. The fact that British troops are especially valuable, because they are free of suspicion of communal sympathies, has rendered it impossible to act on the suggestion made by the Simon Commission Report that it might be possible to entrust external defence to Imperial forces while accelerating the possibility of responsible government in India by leaving internal defence to Indian forces primarily.

[1] The central legislature in April 1935 rejected the votes for the Army department.

16. *The Judicature and the Laws*

Reference has already been made to the changes in the Indian court system which will result from federation. In substance, apart from the creation of a Federal Court, the existing system will stand, under which criminal and civil jurisdiction are vested in the High Courts in the majority of the provinces, or the Judicial Commissioners of the Central Provinces, Coorg, Sind, the North-West Frontier Province, and British Baluchistan. Subject to their control, the more important criminal and civil causes are dealt with by sessions courts and magistrates and by district judges respectively, while minor cases are dealt with by justices of the peace, or village headmen, or in civil matters by small-debt courts. In tribal areas, such as British Baluchistan, local institutions such as the Council of Elders is employed. Appeal lies on defined conditions from the High Courts and Judicial Commissioners' Courts to the Privy Council which exercises a close control, and occasionally hears criminal appeals.[1]

While under the new régime the courts will remain without jurisdiction in revenue matters, they will apparently be able to issue the prerogative writs of mandamus or prohibition to ministers and counsellors, who are not to be exempt as under the Act of 1919 from the jurisdiction of the High Courts. The immunity of such officers from criminal jurisdiction of the courts will disappear, and there is no repetition of the old rule that an order in writing by the Governor-General in

---

[1] *Ras Behari Lal* v. *King Emperor* (1933), L.R. 60 Ind. App. 354; *Sheo Swarup* v. *King Emperor* (1934), 61 Ind. App. 398.

Council shall be deemed to justify any act, unless it affects a European British subject. Since legislation of 1923, unfair discrimination in favour of Europeans in regard to criminal trials has been abolished; the present system, which is safeguarded under the constitution, is based on securing impartial justice in all causes where racial feeling might affect the judgment of a jury.

The chief defects of the judicial system are due to the imperfect severance of judicial and executive functions, and to the close association of the magistrate with the police. But to remedy this state of affairs would be extremely costly, and much injustice might result as well as lack of efficiency in the control of crime.

The law administered in Indian courts is complex. The early charters did not contemplate anything more than enforcing English law, in respect of members or servants of the Company, in so far as this was permitted by local law. In 1661 the charter of Charles II. gave general power to judge according to English law; but territorial sovereignty proper was nominal outside Madras, and the first portion of Indian territory definitely subject to absolute British sovereignty was Bombay, acquired by grant from Portugal. There Portuguese law was in operation,[1] and not until 1672 was English law substituted for it as the law of the courts. Even so, of course, both in Madras and Bombay the natives were largely permitted to settle their own disputes according to their own civil law. The charters granted to Calcutta, Bombay, and Madras in 1726 and 1753 contemplated English law as the governing principle, but the latter set purported to exclude native

---

[1] Fawcett, *First Century of British Justice in India* (1934); Keith, *Indian Historical Quarterly*, xi. (1935), 57-69.

cases unless by agreement. The acquisition by the Company of the Diwani of Bengal, Bihar and Orissa, and its decision to exercise its authority by itself, led necessarily to the issue of regulations in 1772 by Hastings which recognise the principle that causes should be decided according to the personal law of the defendant. When the Supreme Court was created for Bengal by North's Regulating Act, 1773, it was to administer English law, but its jurisdiction was limited in extent, and, after grave difficulties had arisen from the obscurity of the Act, it was made clear in 1781 that, while the Supreme Court was to have full jurisdiction over all inhabitants of Calcutta, in all matters of inheritance and succession to lands and goods and in matters of contract and dealing between party and party, the decision must follow the personal law of the parties if they had the same law; otherwise the principle must be the law of the defendant. Like principles were laid down for the Supreme Courts erected at Bombay (1823) and Madras (1801), and for the courts of the Company as its territorial acquisitions expanded. They were maintained when, after the transfer of authority to the Crown, the Company's courts and the Supreme Courts were merged under the Indian High Courts Act, 1861, in the present High Courts. For Europeans therefore the law of India is in the main English law, much affected by statutory enactments; for non-Europeans there is the appropriate personal law, the two great systems being the Hindu and the Muhammadan law, but with local variations, while increasing weight has been attached of recent years to local usage[1] even where it differs from either of the two

[1] Cf. L. J. Robertson, *Journ. Comp. Leg.* iv. 218-28.

great systems of Hindu law or those of Muhammadan law. Among communities with special rules those of importance are the Parsis, the Jains, and Buddhists.

Criminal law for Europeans and residents in the Presidency towns was English law;[1] elsewhere the criminal law of the Muhammadan régime was applied with modifications in the way of humanity, until it was superseded by the Penal Code of 1860 which in general applies to all persons in India. Criminal procedure[2] and civil procedure codes have also been enacted, and some other branches of the law codified as in the case of the law of contract, but the codes usually save local customs or their conditions are restricted in scope to matters not dealt with in Hindu or Muhammadan law.

In the Indian States systems of Hindu and Muhammadan law subject to local custom prevail; in Hyderabad the rule still prevails that no murderer is sentenced to death unless the kin of the slain demands the penalty; happily even this practical immunity from the penalty has not rendered murder common in the State.

17. *British Burma*

It was recognised by the Simon Commission that in the interests of Burma with her predominatingly non-Indian population the link between that province and India should be severed. This view was shared by the British Government, but it met with some resistance

---

[1] How far statute law was introduced was disputed in connection with Nandkumar's condemnation under an Act of 1728 for forgery; apparently only statutes up to 1726 were really in force; Morley, *Digest of Cases in the Supreme Court*, Introd. pp. xi, xxiii.

[2] For the removal of racial discrimination in trials see *Parl. Pap.* Cmd. 1823.

in Burma, where it was desired to secure in lieu the right to enter the Indian federation, with the power at will to retire thence. The motive of this impossible claim was the view that greater freedom could be attained within the federation, and that, when this position was secured, Burma might secede and enjoy a wider authority than would be given to her as an independent Government. The view was plainly fallacious, and after discussion with two sessions of a Round Table Conference,[1] the British Government, with the support of the Joint Select Committee, decided on the separation of Burma and the grant of a constitution based on that of federal India. This means, of course, that the powers of the Governor must include those of the Governor-General and the Governor of a province.

The Governor, therefore, is given a Council of ten ministers, but he is to act at his discretion in respect of defence, ecclesiastical affairs, external relations, monetary policy, currency, and coinage, the Shan States and similar areas, and areas which are not British territory; he may be aided in these matters by three counsellors. His special responsibilities include those of the Governor-General so far as applicable to Burma, and he has the same powers as Governors of provinces in respect of the police and the prevention of crimes against the Government.

The legislature consists of a Senate sitting for seven years, and a House of Representatives sitting for five. The former has 36 members, half chosen by the Governor at his discretion, half elected by the lower house by proportional representation. The Lower House of 132

---

[1] *Parl. Pap.* Cmd. 4004. See *Joint Committee Report*, i. 389-408.

members is elective;[1] it represents non-communal con- stituencies, 91 in number; Karens, Indians, Anglo-Burmans, Europeans, commerce and industry, the University, Indian and non-Indian labour. Matters as to qualification of members, privileges, rules of procedure, and other questions are regulated as in India. The powers of the Senate are similar to those of a Legislative Council in India, and it has no voice in grants. The previous sanction of the Governor extends to the same matters as in the case of the Governor-General so far as applicable, but there is added immigration legislation. This is due to the desire to control action against Indians, whose presence in Burma is resented in some measure by the Burmese.

The Governor has power to apply Acts to the Shan States and similar areas subject to such modifications as he desires, and to make regulations for them. He has also power to make ordinances subject to confirmation by the legislature, and, in respect of matters of his own special responsibilities or the exercise of his individual judgment, he may issue ordinances or Acts as may be desirable. The powers of the Burmese legislature are subject to the same restrictions as those of the Indian legislatures, but unlike those of the provinces it can legislate for Burman subjects wherever they are. In regard to discrimination the restrictions imposed on legislation affect not merely British subjects domiciled in the United Kingdom but also subjects domiciled in British India.

Financial provisions follow those of the federation,

---

[1] 2,000,000 men and 700,000 women will be voters, over 23 per cent of the population; the number of women illustrates the difference between India and Burma.

save that the House of Representatives alone has authority to assent to grants, and audit is entrusted to an Auditor-General holding on judicial tenure. Home accounts may be audited by the Auditor of Indian Home Accounts. The Federated Shan States still retain a special fund, controlled at the discretion of the Governor, and the Crown in Council may determine payments to be made thence to Burmese revenues and *vice versa*. There is a Railway Board with similar functions to the Indian authority.

The High Court is secured in the same manner as the Indian High Courts, and the services are similarly safeguarded, while the Secretary of State is authorised to select officers for the Burma Civil Service (Class I.), the Burma Civil Medical Service, and the Burma Police (Class I.). A Burma Frontier Service corresponds to the political service in India and is under the Governor's control. There is a Burma Public Service Commission with similar duties to those in India.

In order to avoid undue disturbance in trade relations power is given to the Crown in Council to regulate the duties to be imposed on goods exported from or into Burma or India; maintenance of the *status quo* for three years is arranged. Financial relations have been determined by a Commission, and the Crown in Council may regulate the monetary system of Burma, and may regulate immigration in the first instance. For advice in Burmese matters the Secretary of State may have three advisers, on terms similar to those applicable to Indian government.

Most of Burma is British territory, but on the eastern boundary the Karenni States, 4000 square miles in area, are not British territory and there is a small enclave, the Assigned Tract of Namwan, in like condition. For these areas it will be necessary to continue to legislate under the procedure of the Foreign Jurisdiction Act. The other tribal areas for the most part will fall within the discretionary control of the Governor, but for the Salween district and some other lands he will only have a special responsibility to secure peace and good government. The military defence of Burma is essentially bound up with the policing of the areas excluded from the normal control of the legislature, but the absence of any immediate danger on the frontier renders the maintenance of large British forces needless and defence can be concerted with India.

The law of Burma differs from that in India in so far as Hindu law there has been modified by the principles of Buddhist religion, which is not based on caste distinctions, and by the racial characteristics of the Burmans.

As in India, provision is made for the suspension of the constitution in the event of a deadlock.

It rests with the King in Council to fix the date for the operation of the new constitution, and to alter, as in India, the composition of the legislature, the choice and qualifications of members, and the franchise.

CONCLUSION

THE events of the last ten years have seen a determined and successful effort to destroy the existing fabric of the Empire in order to assert the autonomy of the Dominions. The motive power has come from the three Dominions which in point of population are least British, if we restrict that term to cover English and Scottish. In 1931 Canadians of English race were reckoned at no more than 26·42 per cent of the population; the Scots were 12·97, the Irish 11·86, and the French 28·22, and in the ten years since 1931 the proportions had fallen in every case save the French. In the Irish Free State English and Scots form a negligible and declining minority, and in the Union of South Africa the racial predominance of the Dutch elements is unquestioned. These are the Dominions, moreover, where French, Irish, and Afrikaans compete with growing effect with English as a medium of everyday life. Canada, moreover, is naturally deeply affected by the political outlook of the great republic to the south, with which it is in the most intimate commercial, financial, and intellectual contact. The vital question of defence is simplified immensely for the Dominion by the existence of the Monroe Doctrine, which explains the refusal of the Dominion to make preparations for self-defence, and its complete lack of response to the suggestions of Australia in favour of Canadian co-operation in view of the risk of menace from the East, in special from Japan. On the other hand, the French-Canadian population is opposed to what might seem the natural policy of seeking inclusion in the United States; it fears that its language, its law, its religion, its culture, might fare as badly as have those of Louisiana. British elements in Canada value the British connection, and realise that, while within the Empire, Canada enjoys a more effective status than she would as an independent republic dwarfed by the United States. But even the British are unable to take interest in the affairs of Europe, sharing with the people of the United States an incapacity either to understand or to sympathise with the grave problems which the United Kingdom as part of the European system cannot evade.

In the Irish Free State hostility to the United Kingdom is the inevitable outcome of the long history of relations between England and Ireland. Unhappily for both countries, the existence of the Scots and English elements in Northern Ireland precludes the settlement on the lines of an Irish Republic eloquently urged by Mr de Valera in April 1935. Whether the United Kingdom would accept the project of a republic limited to the Irish Free State, it is impossible to say. The demand of the Free State for the reunion of the North precludes apparently an effective demand for republican status for the Free State area alone. The issue of defence adds further complication, though Mr de Valera has declared that a republican Government would guarantee to the United Kingdom complete security against any use of its territories or waters for purposes of hostile attacks.

In the Union the tradition of republicanism goes

back to the beginning of British connection with the
Cape. The hope that the generous treatment meted out
to the Boers after the South African war might reconcile them to the sovereignty of the Crown has never
been fulfilled, and the concessions made to Union
autonomy have left a republican opposition which is
rather likely to gain than to lose strength. Moreover,
the British population has clearly lost of late leadership and direction, with the passing out of politics of
its former chiefs, and in the United South African
Nationalist Party the principles of the Nationalists
have manifestly prevailed; the surrender of the British
elements has been complete, save for a tiny remnant,
now reorganised as the Dominion Party.

These three Dominions have successfully secured
the disappearance of all that was formal in Imperial
unity. The Union and the Free State have removed the
British Government from any intervention between
them and the King; the Canadian Government still
uses the Signet in the appointment of the Governor-
General and the Great Seal of the Realm in its treaty-
making, but otherwise it recognises the old bonds
of connection only in so far as its federal character
renders necessary, namely in the amendment of the
constitution and in the appeal to the Privy Council.
The Free State has abolished the appeal; in the Union
the power to abolish exists, and may soon be used.

No doubt, if the result of this plenitude of sovereign
power were the desire to create real bonds of union,
the situation would be gratifying. But, despite profuse
assurances that freedom is the necessary prelude to
co-operation, there has been vouchsafed no sign of
the latter. The Minister of Defence of the Union has

explained categorically that the Union cannot plan co-operation with the British Government in case of hostilities, as that might fetter its freedom to proclaim neutrality. Mr de Valera stressed in April 1935 the fact that he had not even been asked to participate in discussions of defence on the occasion of the King's Jubilee celebrations, which he felt bound to decline to attend. Nor is Canada prepared to adopt any arrangement with the United Kingdom which might fetter its right to refuse assistance in a British war. It is not denied that a British war would, under present circumstances, mean a war in defence of League of Nation ideals; but the Dominion regards the obligations imposed by the League as too onerous, and has endeavoured to have Article X. deprived of all substance.

All three Dominions have accepted the right to separate representation at foreign courts and have developed their distinct position in the League of Nations. In one field, however, they appreciate the advantages of co-operation, that of trade exchanges. They have come to realise that the British market has greater advantages than at one time appeared, and at Ottawa the unity of the Empire was revived to the extent that its units decided that they were entitled *inter se* to grant preferences to which foreign nations would have no claim despite the existence of most-favoured-nation clauses in treaties. Unfortunately, trade relations are apt to cause friction; the failure of Canada to afford better terms for British manufacturers, and Canadian demands which prevent the purchase of cheap lumber from Russia, afford reasons for doubting the permanent value of the Ottawa

2 R

accord of 1932, from the point of view of the United Kingdom. But trade advantages, coupled with sentiment and the real advantages of political connection with a great power, unquestionably suggest the maintenance of the connection between Canada and the Union and the United Kingdom, so long at least as the United Kingdom is not engaged in a great European conflict.

Australia and New Zealand have significantly shown little desire to accept the Statute of Westminster; it is noteworthy that in the Commonwealth it is the Labour Party, which has a strong republican and anti-British element connected with it, which has shown most enthusiasm for autonomy, and which insisted on selecting an Australian to be Governor-General. Neither Dominion appoints diplomatic representatives overseas; both are deeply concerned with the danger of troubles arising in the Pacific and desire to work in effective combination with the British Government to secure their position. Hence the contributions of New Zealand to the naval base at Singapore and the Australian determination to maintain an effective if small fleet unit whose vessels will be fit for exchange with British ships. Newfoundland in her distress found no help in Canada, and her loyalty to the British connection has been signally rewarded.

In the dependent Empire strong reasons tell in favour of the maintenance of unity. Britain has been generous to the West Indian Islands, which could not stand by themselves and would fare less well under United States control. In West and East Africa, despite the lamentable record of Kenya, British rule has been beneficial to the native races; it would be a misfortune if Northern Rhodesia were to fall under Union control, and even Southern Rhodesia would be a heavy loser by merger in a predominantly Afrikaans-speaking South Africa. The doctrine of trusteeship for native races is of far higher moral quality than that of domination and exploitation, however insidious may be the temptation to follow the latter. Ceylon can enjoy under British protection a degree of autonomy which would be denied to it otherwise. Mauritius, Hongkong, the Straits Settlements, and the Malay States are obviously gainers by British rule. The position of Gibraltar is determined by necessities of defence; in Malta there is the additional consideration that the vast mass of the population are not Italian by race, and that under the new British policy their language and culture are at last receiving due recognition.

India presents grave problems. Maintenance of effective British responsibility is inconsistent with political advance in Western style, and, without much consideration either of past history or of the present world position of democratic rule, the British Government is pledged to introduce British principles of self-government into India. This project, however, has been coupled with the idea of creating an Indian federation to include the Indian States which are governed by autocrats. It has seemed possible, by creating a federal legislature with disproportionate representation for the States, to secure a conservative central Government and legislature, thus minimising the risk of introducing responsible government in the provinces. The working of so complex and artificial a scheme must be awaited with interest. One

unfortunate feature of the movement for self-government has been the demand in India for complete independence with separation from the British Crown.
The demand has been asserted to be the logical concomitant of Dominion status as promised to India
in 1929 and 1935 as its ultimate goal. There are
obviously grave dangers in such an ideal for India,
which is hardly likely to be able to preserve its independence without British support. Unfortunately,
the difficulties which attend relations between India
and the Dominions, and which offer no possibility of
solution in the only acceptable sense of affording free
entry to Indian emigrants, render the presence of
India in the Empire difficult to maintain permanently.
On the other hand, the interests of the States point
to their insistence on membership of the Empire as the
essential condition of their own security.

It is interesting to note that Dominion status has
been regarded at times as a mode in which foreign
States might seek connection with the Empire, as in
the case of Egypt or even of Iceland.

It is significant that no progress has been made in
devising within the bounds of autonomy machinery
for closer co-operation. Even the logically necessary
step of creating a tribunal of permanent character to
deal with inter-Imperial disputes has failed to be
taken, and the efforts of the British Government
to encourage the residence in London of Dominion
ministers, members of their Cabinets, for more effective consultation, have met with no response of lasting
character; it is true that Mr Bruce thus represented
Australia in 1932–3, but, the immediate crisis over,
he reverted to the High Commissionership under the

normal tenure. Nor have projects for concurrent legislation been swift to materialise; neither British nationality nor merchant shipping has induced general action,
despite agreement in theory in 1930.

In one matter there is an enduring community of
interests among the units of the Empire. In the main
all accept the doctrine of the sovereignty of the law
and the necessity of ordered progress. There have been,
it is true, signs throughout the Empire of a diminished
regard for the sovereignty of Parliament. The opposition to Home Rule in Ireland from 1912 to 1914 set
an example of defiance of law which palliates the
Irish Rebellion, and helped British opinion to acquiesce in the surrender of 1921 by the British Government to *force majeure*. The General Strike of 1926, in
which the leaders of the Labour Party were implicated,
was a definite attempt to destroy government by
consent, and in every election since 1922 deliberate
efforts have been made to prevent discussion by
methods of violence. Canada has not been without
experience of resistance to law, since in 1917–18 conscription resulted in wholesale evasion, and in 1919
Winnipeg was for a time in the hands of mob rule. In
Australia and New Zealand Labour has organised
attacks on security of communications, the supply of
food and fuel, and the maintenance of the public
services; in 1923 the Commonwealth had under the
constitution to supply Victoria with military aid in
the crisis of a police strike. On the Rand in 1922 the
Union Government was confronted by an armed rebellion, and, though it put it down, it paid for its
firmness by defeat by a coalition between Labour and
the Nationalists in 1924. In India the reform scheme

has been opposed by boycott, by non-co-operation, and especially in Bengal by a most systematic terrorism. All these manifestations have so far been met and repelled by the good sense of Governments and people. But there is far too much evidence of a widespread failure to realise the fundamental importance of the rule of law, and the necessity that reforms should be effected by legal means.

INDEX

Abyssinia (Ethiopia), British jurisdiction in, 39, 494; spheres of influence, 496; Italian attack on, viii, ix

Act of Settlement, 1701, 263, 265

"Act of State", doctrine of, 245, 246

Act of Supremacy, 1559, of Elizabeth, 251

Act of Union with Ireland, 1800, 77; with Scotland, 1707, 77, 255, 256

Acts, passing of, 7, 323-5

Acts of Uniformity, 251

Addington, Rt. Hon. Henry, 274

Aden, government of, 474, 488, 489; defence of, 353, 489

Adherence to treaties, separate for parts of Empire, 132

Adjournment of Parliament, 312

Adjutant-General, in Army Council, 355; in India, 594

Administration, Parliamentary control of, 277, 278; in Dominions, 387, 408

Administration of Justice Act, 1920, 184

Administrative law, part of constitutional law, 4

Administrator, of provinces of Union of South Africa, 388, 432, 433; style of, 77

— of Norfolk Island, 430

— of Northern Territory of Australia, 429

— of South-West Africa, 518, 529, 530

Admiralty, Board of, 283, 284, 354, 355, 439, 441, 442

Admiralty jurisdiction, 446, 448; in Dominions, 448

Admiralty Offences (Colonial) Act, 1849, 446 n. 1, 448

Admission of Canadian cattle to British ports, 185, 186

Advisory Committee on Education in the Colonies, 193

Advisory judgments on constitutional issues, 59, 60, 368

Afghanistan, British relations with, 496, 592

African Liquor Control Committee, 193

Afrikaans, official language, 415, 530, 611

Agencies of international intercourse, 108-13

Agents-General, of Australian States, 81, 394; of Canadian Provinces, 83

Agra and Oudh, United Provinces of, India, 545, 562, 564

Agreements between Governments as distinct from treaties, 96, 165, 166

Agricultural Marketing Act, 1931, 297

Agricultural Merit, Order of, Quebec, 75 n. 1

Air Council, United Kingdom, 354, 355

Air Force, of United Kingdom, 353, 355; of Dominions, 437, 439, 441, 442, 443; of India, 594; prerogative as to, 14; under legislative control, 32; overseas, 36

Air Force Act, 353, 484 n. 2, 567, 571

Air Members, of Air Council, 355

Air navigation, regulation of, compels consideration of extra-territorial powers of Dominions, 39; rests with federation in Canada, 419; position as to, in Australia, 425; in India, 567

Air Navigation Convention, position of Dominions under, 106

Ajmer-Merwara, India, Chief Commissioner's Province, 566

Alabama episode, 135

Albania, admission to League of Nations, 103

Alberta, Canadian Province, 24, 385, 421, 422

Alderney, Channel Islands, government of, 20, 371

Alien, "Act of State" against an, 245, 246; owes local allegiance, 264

Alienage, disabilities of, 119; naturalisation, 117, 118, 119

Aliens Act, 1935, Irish Free State, 121

"The Story of the SHOP STEWARDS MOVEMENT in TWO WARDS"

Tales *False*

SUNDAY, APRIL 27th.

7.0.p.m.

CAXTON HALL, CHAPEL ST.

FULL DISCUSSION

The Speaker

is a well known engineer

who was a leader of the

London Shop Stewards in 1914

Organised by

MANCHESTER   LABOUR   MONTHLY   FORUM

12 Harbury Crescent, Wythenshawe.

THE END

Printed in Great Britain by R. & R. CLARK, LIMITED, *Edinburgh*

BY THE SAME AUTHOR

THE CONSTITUTIONAL LAW

OF THE

BRITISH DOMINIONS

8vo. 18s. net.

"The book adds yet another debt of gratitude to the long series already owed to the author by constitutional lawyers and by all students of the legal side of inter-Imperial relations. . . . Professor Keith also throws a great deal of new light on the Statute of Westminster."—*The Times*.

". . . wide learning, meticulous exactitude, and unflinching impartiality."—Professor ALFRED ZIMMERN (*Manchester Guardian*).

" The author, as usual, deals most thoroughly and most dispassionately with a delicate and complex subject, and besides explaining the precise effect of recent changes, as regards Great Britain, the Dominions and foreign nations, he gives his own views on doubtful points."—*The Spectator*.

"Professor Keith's survey is comprehensive. . . . Contains a valuable exposition of the constitutional law of the Dominions."— *The Scotsman*.

"Professor Keith has made a notable contribution to political and legal thought."—*Cambridge Review*.

MACMILLAN AND CO. LTD., LONDON

THE SOVEREIGNTY OF THE BRITISH DOMINIONS

8vo. 18*s. net.*

" Professor Berriedale Keith in this timely and well-balanced work aims at presenting a broad consideration of the growth of the sovereignty of the Dominions of the British Empire and the present extent and limitations of that sovereignty. . . . It is an extremely valuable work, and not least in the fact that it is written especially for the citizen to read, and not merely for the specialist to criticise."— *The Times.*

" This book is substantial proof of the rarely appreciated view that it takes a master of his subject to write a popular book about it. Professor Keith occupies an unchallengeable position as the highest living authority upon the constitutional problems of what Professor Zimmern has happily termed the 'Third British Empire.' It is not too much to say that this brilliant discussion surpasses even his own previous performances. It is a fundamental guide to the difficult and complex problems of which it treats."—Prof. HAROLD J. LASKI in *Time and Tide.*

" Professor Berriedale Keith's book faces the problems of sovereignty (to use a term which is not a term of art) in the Empire with a lucidity that brings the intricacies of those problems and the lines of solution into the intellectual horizon of the plain man who is not a lawyer nor a jurist but is intensely anxious that the British Empire, the greatest Commonwealth of Nations that has ever existed and the noblest guarantee for peace, should remain intact."—*The Times Literary Supplement.*

" Indispensable to those who wish to become acquainted with the tendencies at work to-day. It is not only marked by a wealth of learning, but is characterised by a moderation which might well serve as a model to other workers in the same field. . . . Should find a place upon the shelves of every public library in the Empire. —*The Saturday Review.*

" An invaluable book which can be read right through as a fascinating study in the extraordinarily elastic methods of British statesmanship, but which is also a work of reference."—*The Spectator.*

MACMILLAN AND CO. LTD., LONDON